Siege of the Spirits

Siege of the Spirits

Community and Polity in Bangkok

MICHAEL HERZFELD

The University of Chicago Press   Chicago and London

MICHAEL HERZFELD is the Ernest E. Monrad Professor of the Social Sciences in the Department of Anthropology at Harvard University and has taught at several other universities worldwide. He is the author of many books, most recently *The Body Impolitic* and *Evicted from Eternity*, both also published by the University of Chicago Press.

The University of Chicago Press, Chicago 60637
The University of Chicago Press, Ltd., London
© 2016 by The University of Chicago
All rights reserved. Published 2016.
Printed in the United States of America
25 24 23 22 21 20 19 18 17 16   1 2 3 4 5

ISBN-13: 978-0-226-33158-4 (cloth)
ISBN-13: 978-0-226-33161-4 (paper)
ISBN-13: 978-0-226-33175-1 (e-book)
DOI: 10.7208/chicago/9780226331751.001.0001

Library of Congress Cataloging-in-Publication Data
Herzfeld, Michael, 1947– author.
    Siege of the spirits: community and polity in Bangkok / Michael Herzfeld.
       pages ; cm
    Includes bibliographical references and index.
    "An ethnography of the community of Pom Mahakan in Bangkok which faces eviction in the name of urban renewal"—Publisher info.
    ISBN 978-0-226-33158-4 (cloth: alk. paper) —
ISBN 978-0-226-33161-4 (pbk.: alk. paper) —
ISBN 978-0-226-33175-1 (e-book) 1. Pom Mahakan (Bangkok, Thailand). 2. Historic districts—Thailand—Bangkok. 3. Urban beautification—Thailand—Bangkok. 4. City planning—Thailand—Bangkok. 5. Urban renewal—Thailand—Bangkok—Citizen participation. 6. City dwellers—Civil rights—Thailand—Bangkok. 7. Eviction—Thailand—Bangkok. I. Title.
HT178.T52B36 2016
307.3'41609593—dc223   2015023683

♾ This paper meets the requirements of ANSI/NISO Z39.48–1992 (Permanence of Paper).

for Prudhisan Jumbala
in enduring friendship

Contents

Preface ix

1. Claiming Culture 1
2. Community, City, and Polity 44
3. The State and the City 66
4. Law, Courtesy, and the Tactics of Temporality 90
5. Currents and Countercurrents 125
6. Time, Sound, and Rhythm 148
7. The Polity in Miniature 168
8. Building the Future of the Past 187

Notes 205   References 239   Index 255

Preface

This book is the result of many journeys—long hours in the air from Boston to Bangkok, a reaching back to friendships from my adolescent past, a discovery of the excitement of moving outside the safe spaces of long-familiar cultural contexts in Italy and Greece to a new world in Thailand, a translation of comparison from theory to lived experience, a deepening exploration of the lives of people whose struggle for dignity captured my imagination and engaged my deep affection.

At middle age, the greatest challenge was perhaps the learning of the notoriously difficult Thai language and the sense of jumping into the unknown without a parachute. But I was fortunate in my guides. At Harvard Mary Steedly assuaged my fears of entering an arena where others were so much more experienced by urging me to focus on topics I had already studied in southern Europe; my former student Saipin Suputtamongkol, now a colleague at Thammasat University, completed that injunction by suggesting the general framework of the Rattanakosin Island conservation project—an inspired idea, as it turned out after numerous false starts. My first Thai language teacher, Priyawat Kuanpol, cannot be held accountable for my errors—she tried, she surely tried!—but can take a great deal of credit for pushing me toward at least a measure of competence. And my assistants in the field, Nowwanij ("Nij") Siriphatiriwut and Viphaphan ("Kai") Siripakchai, kept an eye on things during my absences and industriously but often hilariously kept my spirits up and my frustration down. Irving Chan Johnson was among the first to engage me in real conversations in Thai—a true gift of friendship.

Others, too, lent invaluable assistance. Non Arkaraprasertkul helped by transcribing some of the more indecipherable materials and providing me with additional materials on architecture and planning issues. Claudio Sopranzetti and I engaged in mutual encouragement and critique over many years, first in Rome and then in Bangkok, and his involvement in a crucial stage of the present project also led him to his own research. Officials of the Bangkok Metropolitan Administration, the Crown Property Bureau, the Prajadhipok Museum, the Siam Society, and the National Research Council of Thailand all offered their assistance, whatever their views on what I was finding. Colleagues at Chulalongkorn, Prince of Songkla (Hat Yai), Chiang Mai, Thammasat and Ubonratchathani Universities, and elsewhere, gave my ideas a sounding board. Graeme Bristol—formerly of the King Mongkut Institute of Technology, now executive director of the Centre for Architecture and Human Rights (Bangkok and Victoria, B.C.), and a stalwart defender of the Pom Mahakan community—was a valiant companion along the road, as was Pthomrerk Ketudhat, an archaeologist turned activist whose defense of community rights and critiques of legal intransigence was a major inspiration. Then-executive director of COHRE Scott Leckie provided many helpful insights for our friends in the community and for me personally, while cinematographer-activist Fionn Skiotis, at that time also of COHRE, has been a tremendous interlocutor then and since.

For much of the fieldwork I was accompanied by my wife, Cornelia Mayer Herzfeld, whose always amazing capacity for garnering the affection of others even when she claimed (not entirely with justification!) that she could not speak their language cemented our collective engagement with the remarkable people of the Pom Mahakan community.

To two dear friends who did more than they ever knew to help me on this potentially rocky road, I can now only offer reminiscent salutes, but as much as I miss them, they live on as vibrant presences in my affections and those of many others. Yongyuth ("Khun Tao") Prachasilchai—friend and guide to so many anthropologists—took me through the twisting, confusing corridors of the Thai power maze and kept me safe and well informed, teasing and counseling me by turns, and introducing me to the world of Thai politics, journalism, and urban development. And the great anthropologist of Thailand, Stanley J. Tambiah, a colleague and mentor at Harvard (although he always joked that being my guru was too much of a responsibility!), first challenged me to justify jumping into such unknown waters and then, when he saw that I was determined in my madness, mitigated the insanity with sage advice and the warmest of support and affection.

For their invaluable critical comments on the manuscript of this book, I offer warm and grateful thanks to Non Arkaraprasertkul, Felicity Aulino, Naor Ben-Yehoyada, Graeme Bristol, Pandit Chanrochanakit, Namita Dharia, Erik Harms, Bronwyn Isaacs, Duncan McCargo, Federico Pérez, Pitch Pongsawat, Apiwat Ratanawaraha, Aranya Siriporn, Claudio Sopranzetti, Mary Steedly, Anand Vaidya, and Li Zhang. To Chu Jianfang (Nanjing University) I would like to express my respectful thanks for his helpful information about Dai Daikong (Dehong Tai) (Yunnan) social terminology, and more generally for his part in introducing me to this extension of the Tai language family and, with many others, to the pleasures of Chinese academia as well. I am indebted to Robert J. Bickner for some helpful clarifications of Thai syntax and semantics. Giovanni Zambotti, of Harvard University's Center for Geographic Analysis, worked patiently under my direction to produce a useful map. Chiara Kovarik was an able assistant at an early stage of organizing my materials for this book. At the University of Chicago Press, my wonderful friend and amiable intellectual sparring partner T. David Brent has kept my attention severely focused on this project despite all the distractions, edible and otherwise, with which he and others have mischievously tested my resolve; I also thank Ellen Kladky for her efficient and cheerful assistance, Dru Moorhouse for keeping a tolerant but effective editorial hand and eye on my manuscript, and Erin DeWitt for patiently guiding the proofs to completion.

On my very first visit to Thailand in 1997, I had the pleasure of meeting Paritta Chalermpow Koanantakool, formerly of Thammasat University and for several years the director of the Princess Maha Chakri Sirindhorn Anthropology Centre in Bangkok. Her theoretical acumen, pedagogical drive, and sometimes acerbic wit gave force and direction to her friendship and guidance at every turn. It was she who invited me back to Thailand to co-conduct a seminar with her students, one of whom, Saipin Suputtamongkol, already mentioned above, has shared my interests in both Thailand and Italy.

I was introduced to Paritta, and to so many others, by an individual who is one of my oldest friends in the world and was certainly my closest friend at school in England since I was about fourteen years old: Prudhisan Jumbala. He has advised, helped, and pleasantly distracted me during so much of the time I have spent in Thailand, and, respected and liked by the people of Pom Mahakan, has played a discreet but supportive role for them and for me alike during the conduct of this research.[1] To him, in the name of our enduring friendship, I dedicate this book.

Note on Transliteration and Naming

The transliteration of Thai is notoriously difficult and inconsistent; the rendition of street names, for example, can change from one corner to the next. I have adopted a somewhat idiosyncratic approach here, mainly attempting to minimize the differences that would arise between a British and an American reader trying to pronounce the Thai expressions given here (e.g., *bahn* instead of *barn*, *khaw* instead of *khor*), and I have avoided the use of *ua* for a sound that is close to the German "ö" (thus, *moeang* for the more conventional but misleading *muang*). I have decided not to distinguish between short and long vowels except for the *ah* (instead of *ar*) in such words as *bahn*, although duration is a phonemic feature of standard central Thai as are its five tones. An "h" after a "k," "p," or "t" indicates aspiration. My guiding principle here has been to maximize the plausibility of a non-Thai speaker's attempt to read Thai words off the page. No transliteration system can work perfectly, however, and I have respected Thai authors' and other individuals' preferred transliterations of their names, as well as the usual spelling of the currency (baht) and of some place-names, rather than force them into my preferred modality.

I have used pseudonyms for most residents in order to shield them from potential reaction by the authorities. The identities of the community president and of the masseur, however, have been rendered partly explicit in light of their public roles.

Siege of the Spirits

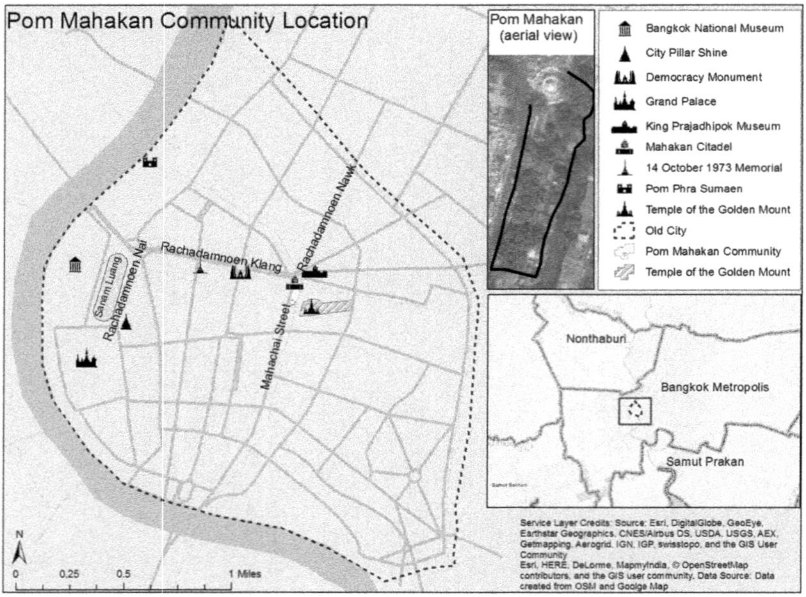

Pom Mahakan Community Location
Pom Mahakan (aerial view)
Bangkok National Museum
City Pillar Shine
Democracy Monument
Grand Palace
King Prajadhipok Museum
Mahakan Citadel
14 October 1973 Memorial
Pom Phra Sumaen
Temple of the Golden Mount
Old City
Pom Mahakan Community
Temple of the Golden Mount
Rachadamnoen Klang
Rachadamnoen Nai
Rachadamnoen Nawk
Sanam Luang
Mahachai Street
Nonthaburi
Bangkok Metropolis
Samut Prakan
N
0
0.25
0.5
1 Miles
Service Layer Credits: Source: Esri, DigitalGlobe, GeoEye, Earthstar Geographics, CNES/Airbus DS, USDA, USGS, AEX, Getmapping, Aerogrid, IGN, IGP, swisstopo, and the GIS User Community
Esri, HERE, DeLorme, MapmyIndia, © OpenStreetMap contributors, and the GIS user community. Data Source: Data created from OSM and Goolge Map

ONE

Claiming Culture

This is the story of a tiny community in the heart of a huge city—the community of Pom Mahakan, with its fewer than three hundred inhabitants, located among Bangkok's estimated population of slightly over 8.3 million registered inhabitants and in a nation-state of nearly eight times that number.[1] The community (and its claims to *being* a community are part of our story) lives beside the small whitewashed fortress for which it is named—a round citadel with crenellations and a pointed roof, with defensive cannons pointing outward, incongruously, over the honking traffic in the street. The citadel—originally one of fourteen emplacements in the defensive city wall built by Rama I (the first king of the presently reigning dynasty) in 1782–86[2]—is a dramatic focal point, one of the only two fortresses to survive the passage of time. Of the wall itself, a thick white stone construction with elegant crenellations, there are considerable stretches, one of which is directly connected to Pom Mahakan. These recall the original city plan now irrevocably shattered by the modern avenue, Rachadamnoen, that was cut through the wall without violating the sacred orientation of the older city plan, thereby extending royal authority over the newly mapped and clearly defined territorial nation-state.[3] The fortress was built in part to repel a feared French invasion; the subsequent construction of the avenue, by ironic contrast, was an attempt to create on Thai territory a modern ceremonial road that would rival the great city avenues of France. Their juxtaposition translates into urban and spatial terms the tension between enmity toward and emulation of the Western powers, a tension that also pits one way of

CHAPTER ONE

imagining the Thai polity against another and that plays a central role in the struggle of the people of Pom Mahakan to remain as the residents and guardians of this historically significant site.

On the other side of the inhabited area, a canal still used as a public transportation route by noisy longtail boats separates Pom Mahakan from a neighboring community, also mostly made up of ramshackle, partially wooden houses and attached to the imposing Temple of the Golden Mount. In quiet moments, the houses on the other side are reflected in the canal's murky water, through which occasional tangles of twigs, plastic, and paper swirl, leaving a tail of dirty foam redolent of detergent soap.[4] A few residents stake their fishing lines on the edge of the canal; poverty leaves poor choices even in the polluted waters that are all that is left of the old aquatic city. At other times, the sudden raucous rattle of longtail boat engines shatters the muggy calm of the day as boat operators call out and passengers, smartly dressed city folk and uniformed students and bureaucrats as well as casually clad tourists, hastily jump on board or clamber onto the narrow wooden landing stage.

Small Place, Large Issues

Pom Mahakan concentrates many dynamics in its small space: the tactical uses of history by poor residents and comfortably secure officials, the politics and ethics of eviction, concepts and consequences of attachment to place and past, the politics of culture across class and origins—all issues that lend themselves to comparison with the experiences of other poor communities around the world. The community seems to generate within its constricted location an intensity of experience that all the more brightly illuminates these larger processes.

The physical space is indeed spectacularly small. The dwelling places along the water are dwarfed by the looming golden stupa of the Temple of the Golden Mount (fig. 1). From high on the temple hill, only a few modest hints of human habitation break the leafy canopy that conceals the community,[5] so that its presence does not disturb the sacred place soaring above it—a deeply revered symbolic, religious, and architectural lodestar and (appropriately enough) a physically high point in a city where height is the determinant and expression of status. The community has squeezed itself into a narrow strip between the wall extending from the citadel along Mahachai Road and the relatively wide and still-used Ong Ang Canal, and its humble and mostly dilapidated houses cower under the luxuriant growth. Some of the trees are of considerable antiquity; a few sport the

1 The Temple of the Golden Mount looms over community festivities. Note the old wooden house in the foreground.

saffron cloth that indicates that they have been ordained as though they were monks. That practice spread from the north of the country in recent years, the visible sign of an environmentalism that, by laying a protective benediction on a community's flora against the march of industrial development, has also reinforced the collective housing rights of residents.

Sacredness is everywhere in the inhabited space. Most strikingly, it appears in the spirit shrines perched on platforms atop spindly pillars. These are arrestingly domestic ritual structures; one sports an umbrella to protect it from the elements, while clothes hangers with laundry dangle from another, and many of them are sporadically treated to bottled soft drinks and other small gifts of refreshment. The shrines remind the living that the spirits of the dead live on, demanding respect and inclusion, and that they must be protected from the sacrilegious disrespect of unfeeling bureaucrats willing to bulldoze them into oblivion. The homes of these spirits, no less than those of the today's residents, are under siege; the spirited living and the spirits of the long dead face the same wrecking ball.

It is a bureaucratic, mechanized modernity that threatens them; and that modernity is never far away. On the far side of the old wall, traffic races madly across the Phahn Fah Lilaht Bridge toward the phantasma-

CHAPTER ONE

goric postmodern city that is the commercial core of Bangkok, past huge hoardings with portraits of the royal family and a museum devoted to the life and reign of King Prajadhipok (Rama VII), the last of the absolute monarchs and an enigmatic figure embodying many of the contradictions that still characterize Thailand's political life. Near the first opening in the old wall, huge fireworks made in the community await customers. Inside the wall, the spirits of today guard the silence of the past. A narrow dirt path separates the thick, crenellated city wall from dilapidated wooden houses where occasionally one or two women preside over softly sizzling woks; a cat stretched indolently across the path sees absolutely no reason to make way for intrusive strangers. At one point the path debouches onto a neatly maintained square, used for meetings, over which a dignified older wooden house looms under the lambent aureole of the Golden Mount stupa shimmering in the sun and framed by the triangular monochrome flags strung across the square for Children's Day. In one corner, a community shrine hosts an ever-changing cohort of Buddha images and other sacred objects; opposite stands the austere community museum and archive, a small white building in a simplified but unmistakably Thai architectural style.

Why, as I have been asked by puzzled Thai colleagues, focus so much attention on so tiny a site and population? Part of the answer lies in the context of historic conservation in Thailand. In seeking a site that would help me gauge the effects of heritage management on local populations, I had been drawn to the Rattanakosin City (or Island) Project—a conservation scheme designed to celebrate the reigning dynasty and the fortified urban core, created by the dynasty's first king. It seemed to offer what I was seeking: a space designated as possessing national historical significance, in which groups of people with diverse ethnic and geographical origins and linked by politically and socially complex relations were confronted with a state-controlled historic conservation regime. Its 1982 launch, on the two hundredth anniversary of the city's foundation, officially framed the project in terms of a rigidly historicist and nationally homogeneous understanding of time.[6]

Within that larger setting, the story of the Pom Mahakan community is a story of a truly spirited resistance to overwhelming national and civic power; but it is also a story of extraordinary fealty to that power—the power monumentally represented by the grandiose ambitions of the Rattanakosin City Project. The tension between resistance and loyalty, moreover, while far from unusual in Thailand, appears here with a clarity that makes the case of Pom Mahakan exceptionally revealing of the country's cultural politics. Such tensions appear in many countries as what Kevin

O'Brien (1996) has dubbed "rightful resistance," a stance that operates respectfully toward constituted authority and generally avoids outright violence. In Thailand, those tensions reveal and reproduce substantial divergences between the bureaucratic, European-derived nation-state and an older, more fluid political idiom often encountered elsewhere in Southeast Asia as well.

The city authorities, operating in bureaucratic and legalistic terms, have repeatedly tried to evict the community in its entirety and to replace it with an expanse of lawn enclosed by stylized balustrades in gleaming white. Largely thwarted in this goal, which forms part of a larger plan to showcase the old city center as a monument to the greater glory of the monarchy and the nation, the authorities have mounted legal challenges to the community's legitimacy and right to remain on the site. Yet the Bangkok Metropolitan Administration (BMA) has also never completely annulled all official recognition of the community; most important, it recognizes internally elected community committee members as "the administrators of the communities whose task is to undertake community work and organize its activities throughout the year."[7] At the same time, the municipal authorities' spectacular neglect of the front area that they did succeed in taking over—it has become an embarrassing mess of cracked pathways among puddles and persistent litter—raises serious questions about their capacity to achieve more than the destruction of existing homes, in what Qin Shao has so aptly called "domicide," and their replacement by an aching void in the heart of the city.[8] So the future direction of municipal policy remains ambiguous, even murky—as murky as the stagnant water dotting the bedraggled lawn that is still the embarrassingly visible centerpiece of official conservation at Pom Mahakan.

Institutional and Political Background

Such half-baked results of municipal effort are far from rare. Perhaps that failure stems in part from the fact that the BMA is a comparatively recent part of the administrative machinery of state and has been constantly bedeviled by organizational and political difficulties. Created in its present form in 1973, in the same year that a student revolt at Thammasat University precipitated a short-lived experiment in democratic governance at the national level, it was headed after the first two and a half years by an elected governor representing the Democrat Party. This governor, however, clashed repeatedly with the military dictatorship that had brutally suppressed the democratic experiment in 1976, and was soon removed and replaced by new government-appointed officials. Since then, Thailand has continued to lurch between variable degrees of democracy and direct military rule.

It was not until late 1985, three years before one of Thailand's periodic returns from military dictatorship to parliamentary democracy, that an election for the governor's office was held again—this time by a former military man and devoutly ascetic Buddhist, Chamlong Srimuang, who was later to oppose the short military takeover of 1991–92 but then, in 2006, having played a prominent role in street protests against the five-year-old government of populist prime minister Thaksin Shinawatra, actively supported the military coup that overthrew Thaksin. Subsequent governors were also elected; one of them, Samak Sundaravej (2000–2004), a former president of the Rattanakosin City Project Committee and perhaps for that reason an implacable foe of the Pom Mahakan community, went on to become prime minister. In that role he was widely viewed as a "proxy" for Thaksin, who had been deposed in 2006 by a military junta that then permitted elections at the end of 2007. Samak's premiership, beginning late in January 2008, lasted only seven months, as he was then forced out of office—technically by the Constitutional Court, because he had illegally continued, while in office, to earn a separate salary as a television chef, but perhaps in political reality because the Yellow Shirt supporters, protesting his rule and the arrest of their hero Chamlong, had occupied Government House. After his successor, Thaksin's brother-in-law Somchai Wongsawat, took the reins of office, the Yellow Shirts occupied the government's temporary refuge at the old Don Muang airport and took over the main (Suvarnabhumi) airport, triggering a further series of reactions that led to army pressures on several parliamentary deputies to defect from the government and support a transfer of power to the Democrat Party under Abhisit Vejjajiva.

The term "democrat" clearly has variable implications in Thai; the name of the Democrat Party has shifted significance in the Thai political spectrum over its long life. This semantic instability may become more comprehensible as we see how the authoritarian side of Thai political life merges with an equally strong egalitarian impulse—a cornerstone of the argument of this book. In any conventional sense, for example, Samak, while clearly an ally of Thaksin's populist supporters, was no democrat. In 1976 he had been implicated in the massacre of students at Bangkok's Thammasat University during the military takeover of that year, and he continued a career of persecuting suspected leftists; moreover, when he became governor of Bangkok, his management style was harshly insensitive to the needs and aspirations of the urban poor. Like Thaksin—who has puzzled commentators because his welfare policies seemed to conflict with his huge commercial interests, and whose adherence to democratic principles did not prevent him from attacking NGOs and academics with ideas different from his own—Samak displayed a personal style that encapsulated extremes of populist-democratic and authoritarian elements, although his performance, predictably in terms of his ideological past, extended much more strongly to the latter. Such apparent self-contradictions in style and substance are crucial to understanding Thai politics, and form a recurrent theme in the story of Pom Mahakan.

Samak's successor as governor, Apirak Kosayodhin, who plays a very different role in the story of this book, represented the Democrat Party, of which he also became a vice president. Entering office with a campaign platform that included promises of radical institutional reform, he won a second term in 2008 but left office later that same year under the shadow of a scandal possibly created for him (although this is unverifiable) by backstabbing bureaucrats—many of whom evidently preferred the legalistic Samak's uncompromising leadership style. Apirak's successor, fellow Democrat Party member and minor royal Sukhumbhand Paribatra, was still at the helm at the time of writing, having won election to a second four-year term in 2013. The Democrat Party, meanwhile, operates under the shadow of accusations that its behavior over the previous several years had been anything other than appropriate to its name; the unelected Abhisit government had attacked the "Red Shirts" demonstrating on the streets and hung on to power until May 2011. Elections in that month brought Yingluck Shinawatra, Thaksin's sister, to power at the head of the political party (Pheu Thai, or "on behalf of the Thais") that had emerged from the ruins of Thaksin's Thai Rak Thai and its successor under Samak, the People's Power Party. But Yingluck's time in office was brief. Soon after a national election scheduled for February 2014 failed to reach completion, the Constitutional Court dismissed her for an alleged miscarriage of procedure; the street protests against her party's continuing rule, this time by the "Yellow Shirts"—who were bitterly opposed to the Shinwatra family and to their populist and welfarist policies, and who claimed to be acting in support of the monarchy—and the politicians' inability to resolve their differences and proceed to a complete national election provided the pretext for the military coup of 22 May 2014.[9]

Throughout all these political earthquakes, the BMA has remained relatively stable—perhaps excessively so, inasmuch as a bureaucratic fortress amid the roiling tides of political unpredictability, it often exhibits entrenched institutional reluctance to attempt new approaches to persistent problems. The BMA governor is answerable, at least in theory, to an elected

CHAPTER ONE

city council, and the practicalities of day-to-day administration are carried out by professional civil servants. These bureaucrats—who do not always take a benign view of the governors elected to command their services—are widely (and often correctly) viewed as intransigent conservatives. But their reluctance to innovate may not entirely be the result of ideological conservatism or endemic bureaucratic indolence. While the bureaucrats' tenure of office is largely guaranteed, the hierarchical nature of Thai society, which is especially visible in the meetings that take place in the vast city hall buildings, creates a nervous fear of innovative or creative action that often translates into defensive haughtiness in response to local communities' demands for recognition of their problems. That, sadly, is the BMA that the Pom Mahakan community knows best.

Activity and Activists

If the BMA seems immovable, so, too, does the resolve of the institutionally far more fragile Pom Mahakan community. At the time of writing, and after nearly a quarter-century of confrontation, it is still in place, an object of admiration for overseas visitors and a growing focus of attention for middle-class Bangkokians once accustomed to viewing it as a place of depraved criminality but now increasingly impressed by its confident self-management. The more intransigent elements in the BMA have unquestionably lost the propaganda war against it. Its future, although still uncertain, is increasingly linked to the politics of national heritage and has become the object of considerable sympathy on the part of the wider Bangkok public. What processes lie behind this remarkable transformation?

The answer is necessarily complex. It includes intelligent and organized leadership, strong support from academic and political figures, a central and symbolically important location that would make any brutal attack deeply embarrassing for the authorities, internal divisions within and between the various organs of state and municipality, a capacity for balancing between opposing political factions, and a series of national crises that at crucial moments have distracted the attention of the community's most implacable bureaucratic enemies. The community, moreover, has achieved an enviable visibility; its president has been an eloquent guest on television, activist accounts of its predicament are accessible on YouTube,[10] and student groups often visit Pom Mahakan to study community development. The residents' struggle has already been the subject of a book by political activist Thanaphon Watthanakun, as well as of an enormous range of newspaper and magazine articles, academic and NGO-directed analyses, and of two films (one a prizewinning production by the young filmmaker Apiwat Waengwatthaseema, the other a documentary produced for the international NGO Centre on Housing Rights and Evictions by Australian social activist Fionn Skiotis).[11]

Above all, however, the residents' remarkable staying power springs from their success in claiming the moral high ground by delicately calling official virtue into question. The *chao pom* (people of Pom [Mahakan]) delicately invoke the older model of the Thai polity represented by the original city wall. That model predates the present-day national state structure but continues to infuse the everyday activities of people at every level. Many of the city bureaucrats today seem wholly detached from the older substrate, a chimerical phantom that blends fleeting images of past glory with the comfort of intimate memories and familiar styles of interaction. The bureaucrats belong to a different world, a world of modernist planning, monumental architecture, and administrative legalism, a world that does not recognize a need to simmer pragmatic compromise in the warmth of social interaction or to parlay with the ghosts of bygone eras.

Other forces, however, have been more sympathetic. Almost throughout their struggle, the residents have been the focus of design projects by various groups interested in finding an alternative to eviction. Among the earliest projects, which were primarily designed to show that even such a limited space could sustain both a community and a public park, an especially notable attempt was designed by Canadian architect-planner Graeme Bristol's students from King Mongkut's Institute of Technology.[12] The exercise was designed shake the students, mostly middle-class Thais whose acquaintance with Pom Mahakan was their first real encounter with the human face of poverty, and whose education had been dominated by the usual Western-derived curricular models, out of their narrowly bourgeois vision of urban futures. The exercise was successful even if also somewhat utopian; it envisaged houses and a spatial organization that gave the residents a much more coherent spatial realization of their lifestyle than would have been the case with a collective move to high-rise apartments. Despite the students' inexperience, which certainly produced some ideas that would not have proved socially viable in the long run, their scheme opened up the possibility of a planning modality that was far from what the designers of the master plan had envisaged when they submitted their scheme for cabinet approval in late 2004.

In a meeting with a representative of the National Human Rights Commission, Bristol and his students discovered that alternatives to eviction were also a matter for lively interest on the part of those concerned with the brutalization of the poor. Although the project they developed was not adopted, its very existence was an important departure, one that gave the residents the confidence that foreign and middle-class support could provide and allowed them to dream. This experiment, moreover, was succeeded by numerous other student projects on and visits to the site, all of which helped to raise the consciousness of budding architects and social scientists about the intellectual and social qualities of which so-called slum dwellers were capable.[13]

More concretely, it led to political action, raising the visibility of Pom Mahakan and thereby protecting it from precipitate action by the BMA. Eventually, in a concerted effort, the Asian Coalition for Human Rights (ACHR) and the Community Organizations Development Institute (CODI) came together with Bristol's team in identifying Pom Mahakan as a prime target for rescue. They were soon joined by the Centre on Housing Rights and Evictions (COHRE), an international body that, by documenting particularly egregious evictions, helped to create more pressure on national and local governments. The COHRE documentary by Fionn Skiotis featured the community's precarious situation,[14] while subsequent publications gave Pom Mahakan a prominent place in COHRE's efforts to awaken the world's conscience to the plight of such communities.[15] On 18 April 2003, COHRE sent an urgent appeal to ESCAP (the United Nations' Economic and Social Commission for Asia and the Pacific, which is based in Bangkok in offices located very near Pom Mahakan), the two main English-language newspapers of Thailand (*Bangkok Post* and *The Nation*), various government and BMA officials, and the president of the National Human Rights Commission. The last of these had already been active in promoting the residents' cause. A subsequent report by UN-Habitat, the housing arm of the United Nations, may have been influential, and drew heavily on the work of COHRE (including the Skiotis film), the work of Graeme Bristol on the site, and my own writings.

But it was the Thai organizations that were especially active and effective. Among these, the Four Regions Slum Network played a consistently active part, particularly by sharing their experience of other struggles and providing connections and personnel to educate residents in the techniques of communal organization and activity.[16] The semi-governmental Thai Community Foundation lent expertise and further connections. NGO activity, despite its strong links to state agencies, has an impressive history of independent action in Thailand. It has a curiously dual set of origins also in the sense that while many of its leaders have come from well-educated and prosperous urban families, it invests deeply in the rural population. Perhaps this is not as paradoxical as it sounds; the bourgeois

Thais of leftist inclination who emerged from the student population of the 1970s, some of whom took refuge from military rule in the jungle, were heirs to a romantic view of the countryside.

Beginning as a social movement that sought to empower poor villagers (*chaobahn*, the term that residents often use of themselves) against unscrupulous governmental and industrial forces, these NGOs later came to encompass the poor slum dwellers of Bangkok. At times, moreover, they were able to influence government policy and to intervene in questions of environmental protection and the education of slum dwellers' children, although some of the NGOs—notably the Four Regions Slum Network—were adamant that they could only achieve their goals by maintaining total institutional independence from government bodies. By the time the Pom Mahakan situation started to receive public attention, the movement was neither purely rural nor, in its urban incarnation, as left-leaning as some of its rhetoric might have implied. With the rise to power of Thaksin Shinawatra, self-proclaimed champion of the poor of the northeast region (Isan), and given the tendency of NGOs to cast themselves as opponents of whatever political forces happened to be in power,[17] communities that could plausibly claim to be particularly loyal to the monarchy and to the established Buddhist religion were able to employ similar tactics and language even within the city.

NGOs were able to provide various forms of expertise to which poor communities would otherwise not have had access. This was important in part because it was the use of expert knowledge by the city bureaucrats that residents often particularly feared. Yet not all such encounters have been successful or amicable. Architects employed by the city hall were to be found lecturing local communities on the improvements they professed to be bringing to the local built environment. In most such cases, a few leaders invited the architects to explain their work; everyone listened respectfully, until the experts departed, at which point a hubbub of dispute would break out; direct confrontation was rare.[18] I attended such meetings in Tha Phra Jan's central alley (*soi*)—a space much frequented by tourists and students and faculty from nearby Thammasat University—and was struck by the relative silence of most of the residents during the formal proceedings, and, despite some angry mutterings after the visitors' departure, by their eventual resignation to a plan that in the end did not revive the local economy as perhaps some of them had hoped.

But Pom Mahakan was a very different matter. Most experts who appeared on the site or at activities organized by the community did so at the behest of the residents and their NGO allies. These visitors included several architects, one a minor member of the royal family, and an official of the Crown Property Bureau who turned out to be knowledgeable about the environmental aspects of the site. Others were social activists who specialized in various forms of communal self-help. Over the years, numerous academics and students came to the site as well, the students to study community self-help at firsthand, the professors more often to lend their expertise and contacts to the leadership. More recently, the Pom Mahakan leaders have claimed to know that they have sympathizers within both the Crown Property Bureau and the city administration. But while such internal differences in the different agencies, as also within the police and the army, can work to the community's advantage and also reflect the factionalized condition of much of the Thai polity today, the consensus is that most of the sympathizers are not "people with power" (*phu mi amnaht*). That situation may in fact be changing more rapidly in the Crown Property Bureau, which, while it does not own any of the Pom Mahakan land, has a vested interest in the site's future, since its status as a slum or a park can have a direct impact on the value of the surrounding real estate—much of which does in fact belong to the bureau.

The residents' perception of the split in the bureau is that some are only interested in questions of commercial value, while others are more concerned about social impact. That this may represent a difference of interests at a higher level is well understood but never openly discussed. To some extent, that particular problem is now fading, as the bureau appears to have divided its holdings into two distinct domains. One consists of highly valuable land that will continue to sustain the royal coffers. The other, made up of the areas slated for conservation, will be imbued with enhanced historical interest and populated in part by the descendants of the original inhabitants. That policy has already saved some shophouse communities; one of these, Tha Tian, was originally slated for demolition but has now instead become the object of a collaborative restoration project. In that sense, the bureau architect who so fearlessly placed his expertise at the disposal of Pom Mahakan may have been less atypical than I had supposed at the time; his attitude seems, in retrospect, to have anticipated the bureau's new and ostensibly more enlightened policies.

Despite the impressive alliances they have created and the diplomatic agility they have displayed in negotiating the shoals and shallows of the national polity, the residents of Pom Mahakan always made it very clear that they themselves were in charge of their own destiny. They were grateful for advice and support, but ultimately it was their capacity to manage their own affairs on a day-to-day basis that made their resistance to municipal authority feasible. Even internally, they saw offering advice as an act that should come with humility. Community president Thawatchai

Woramahakhun—Kop, "the Frog," as he is nicknamed—observed that he was "happy to have had the chance" to tell his fellow residents what they should do at moments of difficulty; that chance was a precious gift to him, not something he bestowed on others, and he expressed appropriate appreciation. As for my own role, I was often asked to stand up in meetings and offer advice of my own; it was not hard, in those circumstances, to say that the residents understood their predicament far better than I ever would, so that all I could offer was a set of connections and observations that I hoped might be of some help.

The residents were proud of their ability to reciprocate the services rendered to them. They would prepare lavish meals for monks who came to conduct rituals for the community or for visiting dignitaries and scholars. They also insisted on paying for the taxis that the merit-making lawyers and architects needed to take (since paying these kindly souls for their services would have been both beyond their means and a refusal of their virtuous motives). They needed no guidance in running the community savings fund once it was in motion. At the same time, they also displayed noteworthy skills and diligence in matters of self-management. They cleaned the pathways, set up notices enjoining cleanliness, and—even with no common language—guided foreign visitors who strayed onto the site (although here they were not averse to calling on my services). And in tiny acts of self-assertion they reproduced, over and over, their sense of dignified independence even in relation to those they regarded as stalwart friends.

Once I had returned for my second visit, the community knew I could be trusted to stay in touch. But still residents seemed to feel the urge to express their warm friendship. On another occasion when I was leaving the country, they organized a lavish banquet in my honor; it was laid out in the central square, and a number of residents joined in the feasting. Numerous dishes were provided by various households, and someone produced a bottle of foreign wine—an expensive luxury in a country where alcohol is heavily taxed. On another occasion, at New Year, a raucous group of men, already well lubricated with alcohol, called me over to sample some local liquor. They handed me a glass of rather viscous white liquid, which I drank; it was strong but not unpleasant. Then they produced a mauve version. Once I had downed that, with greater difficulty, they asked me which I had preferred. When I unhesitatingly said I preferred the first one, they cheered and laughed: I had passed the test of masculinity, as the mauve liquor was considered to be decidedly a women's drink. Here, perhaps, there was a little bit of the agonistic male power play that I have observed in southern European settings, although it was not clear that, had

I preferred the wrong liquor, I would have been openly mocked. Overall, I experienced that moment, as others when I shared food with residents, as one of affectionate conviviality.

Their formal governance is as impressive as their hospitality to their friends and supporters. From the start, despite the somewhat ritualistic forms that meetings often took, the leaders emphasized the importance of both collective and individual engagement. It was clear that in these meetings they had to display a secure mastery of procedure even while focusing on substantive—and urgent—practical matters. There has been a tendency, especially among foreign observers, to dismiss Thai meetings, which sometimes appear to be a national pastime, as purely ritualistic and ineffective.[19] The official models certainly exhibit a strong element of form for its own sake; I attended one daylong discussion of BMA planning, and it was clear that the entire event was carefully scripted, with panels of carefully selected experts and little substantive engagement from the public. As one disgruntled non-Thai observer noted, speaking specifically of the most recent five-year plan, such public hearings—which are technically required by law—are little more than an empty display of self-importance: "The public hearing is a total farce. They invite 500 people to come, and then they have a whole day of lectures, and it's a talking rather than a hearing!"

Even such heavily scripted events, however, do occasionally provide the setting for outbursts of anger against the authorities, who are thereby made aware of the need to act—though whether in self-defense or in proactive response to citizens' concerns depends very much on individual predilections and level in the bureaucratic hierarchy. Now that the municipality is also required by law to place its five-year plan on an accessible website, moreover, it is easier for others to intervene critically. When members of the Siam Society discovered that the plan only paid lip service to cultural heritage protection and offered no substantive descriptions of how such protection would be put into practice, they were able to lodge a serious complaint. The arrival of the Internet has already, it seems, begun to destabilize the capacity of those in power to shelter behind the symbolic authority of official pronouncements and, with the help of an increasingly supportive press, has opened up new ways of forcing the bureaucracy to listen. Meanwhile, the capacity of communities like Pom Mahakan to turn meetings to useful ends as well may eventually have some impact on the way in which official meetings are implemented. We should also not discount the importance, for a community regarded by some as uncouth, of being able to put on a fine performance of parliamentary decorum and sophistication. In that sense, the Pom Mahakan leadership is truly performing—in the transitive sense of performativity as a way of creating meaning and political action. Their mastery of official form, including royal and religious protocol, has been central to their success in mustering external support.

Socially effective movements almost always find it necessary to appeal to rules of order. Strongly motivated activists can place these rules in the hands of local social actors, encouraging them to take initiatives they might previously have feared to attempt, and that is the role—actively attacked by both sides of the Thai political divide—of many of the NGOs. A besetting obstacle to that kind of action lies in the apparently common Thai conviction that only a privileged few are entitled to lead, however deeply those who see themselves as followers may resent the leaders' policies. In the formal, municipal "talkings," to use my interlocutor's revealing term, there is little incentive for substantive disagreement or for bringing about some degree of change in policy. The goal of those gatherings is to confer recognition on those who support the official policies and to discourage more than a token modicum of open disagreement. That is not true, however, for local communities, where meetings are increasingly an arena for exploring real issues and tensions.

Although the community's meetings do exhibit some of the formalism of official events, then, they have increasingly diverged from the authoritarian Thai model. To some extent, this tendency has also been intensified by international pressures; the request for intervention by the United Nations Commission on Cultural, Economic, and Social Rights in Geneva, which I drafted, would have failed had it not been possible to provide assurances to the commission that the decision to send it was taken democratically and with full internal support. I was able to declare to a COHRE representative in Switzerland, who passed the my letter and the community's request on to the commission, that a videotaped record of the meeting to discuss this move existed and that "I was particularly struck by the fact that the person chairing the meeting, one of the signatories to the letter, made every effort to invite criticism and comment, but received unequivocal support for sending it. His insistence on making sure that he had full support for this action is further evidence of the community's adherence to democratic process and open discussion, a quality of which I have already collected an impressive wealth of evidence."

That said, it is true that the exhortations to a seemingly passive audience of residents—insistent demands that dissenters express their views, despite a recognized and pervasive disinclination to expose opinions in public—seemed highly formulaic. Were they also insincere? The ambiguity of their significance presumably had no interest for the commission's bureaucrats, whose interest was—again whether substantively or for the sake of appearances—in satisfying a requirement that intervention must be based on a democratically achieved consensus on the part of the requesters. (International bureaucracies are as dependent on performance as local agencies.) But it is certainly true that the residents had every opportunity to dissent from the request for the commission's letter of support, whether they were inclined to do so or not; not one of them, for example, tried to dissuade me privately from sending the letter, which would have been the obvious approach had they simply wished to avoid public confrontation with their leaders.

Brett Thiele, the senior legal officer of COHRE, wrote a further missive, dated 18 April 2003, that specifically mentioned Thailand's ratification of the commission's charter and other United Nations agreements and pointed out that the authorities were obliged to consider all other possible avenues before resorting to eviction. On 13 May 2003, the president of the commission, responding to these initiatives, wrote to request a pause to consider the residents' rights. This caused the BMA particularly acute embarrassment when it was revealed that the president's letter, like Thiele's, had been copied to King Bhumibol.

In fact, the consensus appears to have been genuine, and to have been crafted through a long process of collective self-education. The community operated with a "work committee" structure, coordinated by a group of three additional individuals and the community president, that had been set up when the community was still fully recognized by the BMA. Although formal recognition had been withdrawn in 1992, it was fortunate that the residents had maintained the committee structure, so the president and coordinators, signatories to the request, could declare, "The committees organize meetings for the entire community several times each week and encourage the full and open expression of their opinions by all residents." They added, "We have written with the understanding that we accept responsibility that this is done with the knowledge and consent of our fellow community members. With that authority vested in us, we are ready to fight the eviction and have already made preparations for doing so, but we would prefer to reach an acceptable solution in cooperation with the authorities."[20] That willingness to negotiate with the BMA was also matched by the community's determination, mentioned in my own letter, to engage the authorities in the Thammasat University conference that was already being organized to discuss the community's problems. That the BMA remained stonily unresponsive to such appeals—a common tactic being simply to hope that a nuisance of this kind will go away if it is ignored for long enough—did nothing to enhance its own standing in the case.

The rhetoric of democracy was, at least superficially, shared by the commission, the Thai polity, and the local community. But what it actually meant in terms of intentions and attitudes necessarily remains ambiguous, if only because the Thai proclivity for evasive inaction and indirect rhetorical forms, as well as the shifting political grounds of *prachahthipatai* (democracy), meshed perfectly with the equally ritualistic legalism of the international body. The community leaders must have known how unlikely it was that any resident would even want to speak out in open debate against sending such a letter. Perhaps the leaders genuinely hoped that someone would break with past patterns of passivity, as, in fact, began to happen at subsequent meetings. Today many community members, especially younger women, take active roles in such debates, and this intensified engagement may not have been the least of the leadership's achievements. But that development had not yet emerged to a significant degree. Still, no one could say that Thawatchai's exhortations to express dissent lacked passion or conviction.

In fact, there were already some precedents for the participatory and sometimes even contentious conduct of all discussions affecting the community's future, but those discussions usually had more to do with immediate, material issues that bore directly on the residents' economic interests. One serious dispute occurred over the question of whether and when to dismantle the barricades that had been set up in anticipation of the expected siege in 2003, and, although this was not the proximate cause of the major factional battle that occurred during the two decades of struggle, and indeed was conducted for the most part with exemplary openness to conflicting viewpoints, it did, at the very least, intensify the growing mutual distrust that eventually erupted in the definitive disaffection of one community elder and his family.

Discussions of whether to dismantle the barricades were obviously difficult: those who favored dismantling did finally prevail on the grounds that the community could hardly afford to sustain a permanent stance of lawlessness without also cutting themselves off from the few sources of income they possessed. Food hawkers, especially, would not be able to get their vending carts out onto the streets. But the opposing faction's fear of the authorities' potential for violent invasion was contagious and led to a heightened sense of impending doom until it became clear that the authorities, having failed to invade with physical force when the barricades were up, were not prepared to do so at a time when it might have been easier, evidently trusting in the power of the law to achieve their goals.

Questions of housing were less radically divisive. Individual family interests were certainly at stake, but these were more fragmented allegiances and would not lead to so central a division; rather, they generated discussions about how to organize the space so as to maximize everyone's access to resources. These themes, as we will see, were to resurface again when at last the residents finally dared to begin the risk-fraught labor of demolishing some of the more ramshackle houses and attempting to build sturdier structures in their place.

A Mysterious Capacity for Resistance

Even the impressive external support I have described does not dissolve the mystery of Pom Mahakan's ability to stand up to overwhelming pressure. Clearly something else is at work here: the effective public management of culture, heritage, and history. The rhetoric of the Pom Mahakan leadership is not solely a replication of NGO parlance, even though that idiom does surface frequently and usually to good effect. It is also a rhetoric that recalls the long history of facing the colonial powers waiting to pounce across the Siamese territorial doorstep, and it is a rhetoric that builds on the specific qualities of the Pom Mahakan community and its capacity to manage issues of cultural production and conservation.

I often wondered how these people managed to hang tough when my friends facing eviction in Rome, for example, able rhetoricians and politically well-connected though they were, could not impede the voracious gentrification of their old neighborhood. To be sure, there were other reasons for the Romans' relative inability to sustain their resistance for long: the acknowledged cultural difficulties of achieving collective and concerted action among neighbors, the sheer economic force of a real estate industry intoxicated with the idea of selling heritage to the wealthy, the unholy mix of church, money, and underworld arrayed against hapless residents. Moreover, they did not possess the ownership titles that protected the residents of the seaside community I had studied in Greece.[21]

But in Pom Mahakan most residents had no title either, and claims to the land, although they defended these in court, were never a promising means of defending their space. Their strategy was revealingly different. At one level it was quite simple: the agile management of a rhetoric of both cultural and civic identity, with its insistent if muted invocation of a political order antecedent to the modern nation-state, meant that attacks on the community could be represented as attacks on the traditional core of Thainess. Rome is the capital of a culturally fractured nation; even the rules of historic conservation itself vary regionally, and nothing in the Italian experience could generate such coercive concentricity in so tiny a space. In Thailand, a country that more closely resembles Greece in both its emphasis on cultural unity and its persistently troubled entanglements with European colonialism, such a focalization of nationalist ideology also draws, as Greek popular nationalism cannot, on a long-submerged political cosmology that stands in conceptual opposition to that of the modern nation-state.

That, rather than a familiar tale of slum dynamics, is the story of this book. Others have written extensively and insightfully on the political life of slum communities in Thailand, many of which have similarly been threatened with eviction.[22] But one might reasonably question the appropriateness of calling Pom Mahakan a slum (*chumchon ae ahd*[23]) at all. The community challenges such easy classifications. Indeed, I suggest, it is its repeated challenges to conventional wisdom that shed a particularly searching light on the politics of what we might call *cultural governance* and on the relationship between nation-state and local interests in Thailand. The dynamic that emerges also resonates with the larger geopolitical complexities of Thailand's relations with neighboring countries and with the dominant international powers.

A Microcosm of the Nation?

In this sense, the residents' strategy of identifying the local community with the entire nation, a strategy that in other countries might not have achieved such persuasive force, has exploited structural features peculiar to the Thai polity, within a political framework that firmly links the fate of Pom Mahakan to the official, royalist narrative of Thai culture. In this last respect, the community follows the pattern established during the massive protests that preceded the economic crisis of 1997, protests in which royal symbolism and local cultural displays from the poorest regions of the country merged in the potent display of mass solidarity known as the Assembly of the Poor. That movement had sought the sympathy of the rising middle classes precisely because, without that support and despite suspicions that middle-class supporters might be seeking ways of morally and even financially aggrandizing themselves through their activism, the protests could not achieve much impact.[24] But in reality middle-class support remained highly conditional and motivated. The establishment and middle-class-oriented Democrat Party became increasingly hostile to those protests.[25] Not coincidentally, 1997 was also the year in which the so-called People Constitution came into effect, but it was also at about the same time that the ongoing economic crisis lent urgency to the desire of the wealthy to invest in land—and to protect their investment. In this combustible atmosphere, which was coalescing at the time of my first arrival in Thailand, the sparks of cultural rhetoric and increasingly overt class conflict would soon trigger new explosions.

Pom Mahakan was then just beginning the trajectory that led to its partial identification in the public mind, if not so comprehensively from its own perspective, with the royalist Yellow Shirt demonstrators and with the Democrat Party.[26] At a time when facile journalism too often incorrectly assumed that poor communities would automatically side with the populist "Red Shirt" movement, this indigent community found a rhetorically compelling voice within a discourse more typical of Bangkok's newly confident bourgeoisie—a discourse largely derived from Western colonial models, filtered in turn by royal and religious institutions, but reshaped by the community to claim a significant stake in its own future. While undoubtedly most evictions that seek to remove poor residents to places distant from the city center are driven by the logic of capitalism,[27] and by a concomitant bourgeois horror of contemplating destitution close at hand, the people of Pom Mahakan are strategically reshaping and redeploying those attitudes for their own purposes.

In the process, however, they appeal to models of political relations that reach back to a time that significantly predates the emergence of the modern, consumerist middle class. Their tacking to and fro between the formal structures of the nation-state and the submerged practices associated with a very different kind of moral community reveals conceptual and practical strains that lie at the very heart of the political turmoil now afflicting the entire country. As Paritta Chalermpow Koanantakool has argued, even upwardly mobile middle-class Thais who emulate high-culture models may encase within their aspirational politics a capacity for seeing their cultural identity in terms far removed from the frame of official reference.[28] The residents of Pom Mahakan are engaged in something more complex than simple mimicry. Tossed in the tumultuous seas of class-based cultural conflict, they seek to define themselves as loyal citizens of the nation-state but also as people with a territory, a local identity, and a political goal that does not automatically concede moral authority either to the state bureaucracy or to any of the national political movements and parties.

The Pom Mahakan community is not so much a microcosm of the country as a whole as it is a social group whose claim to be that microcosm reveals much of the basis of today's political tensions in the country at large. Similar tensions exist elsewhere, notably in the Europe that supposedly originated the nation-state model as we know it. Ironically, however, given that the outward strategy of the community is to identify itself with the official model of Thainess, we find that the sources of tension are no less "Thai" than the omnipresent gilded tourist publicity images of an idealized and smiling "Land of Smiles"—smiles that in the lived reality of social interaction may express anything from harmony to irony and from warm friendship to resentful condescension.

Each story of the politics of eviction has unique features. A pattern of financially interested land investment in Thailand, however, has meant that economic motives feature largely in the debates around even those communities—of which Pom Mahakan is one—whose fate seems less tied to the immediacy of land speculation than it does to the representational strategies of state and monarchy. Despite the perceived significance of capitalist land speculation,[29] official plans for the land on which the residents live do not include sale to private owners; it is to be used solely, the local authorities have repeatedly insisted, as a municipal park—actually a large, mostly empty lawn—honoring the queen. Even occasional rumors that some concessions at Pom Mahakan would be leased to companies such as McDonald's have so far not been supported by any evidence, although that fear reflects a larger concern with the impact of commercial interests on city planning. Constructing an ornamental lawn would indeed be commercially insignificant compared with high-rise construction. Whatever its specific role, capitalist profiteering is not an exhaustive explanation of official heritage practices.[30]

But perceptions, grounded as they often are in the experience of class conflict and its attendant discontents, may be more persuasive than purely economic logic. Many are convinced that big capital is determining the future of the city and that "corruption" (*khorapchan*) too heavily influences the activities of local administrators.[31] Aware of these realities, residents have few options but to take such assumptions at face value and to deploy them strategically; they do at least have the advantage of credibility. Perhaps, too, it is a feeling of being on the wrong side of capital investment that leads residents to take a circumspect view of their long-term prospects even as they aspire to middle-class comforts and technology—an increasingly common desire among the nation's poor, as Claudio Sopranzetti has argued,[32] its frustration a cause of growing resentment and anger. Such aspirations do not simply mimic middle-class values; they strongly identify with the larger, vociferous movement for the rights of the poor and couch their protests in its symbolic idiom.

That idiom nevertheless reflects the middle-class values and practices of the core NGO tradition in Thailand: the use of royal portraiture, displays of traditional dance against a background of large-scale plans for the

CHAPTER ONE

renewal of their space, formal gatherings to emphasize their connections with the entire network of poor communities around the country, building and planting bees, and noisy but well orchestrated and spectacularly orderly public protests.[33] The attempt to arrive at an at least partial understanding of these apparent contradictions will take us right into the heart of Thai ideas about power and into the arenas in which political practices translate those ideas into policies and actions. In short, this tiny community offers an unusually clear view of the larger polity with which its leaders so assiduously identify their compact social world.

The facts of the case are not, for the most part, in serious dispute. Under the laws of eminent domain, the authorities had the right to evict the residents, especially after some residents accepted financial compensation for their removal, and to destroy whatever was left of their homes. The rationale behind this plan was closely linked to the long-standing goal of refurbishing the area as a public park as conceived under an overall conservation plan for the oldest part of the Thai capital—a plan that was also enshrined in a special law. The residents do not dispute that part of the official account; nor do they express any interest in breaking the law except in defense of what see as their legitimate interests. They say in self-exoneration that the plan to evict is grossly unfair; that the city bureaucrats took advantage of their gullibility and hopes for a better life, in violation of the spirit of constitutional as opposed to municipal law; and that they wish to serve the city and the nation by acting as the responsible guardians of a historic place to which they are tied by deep affect.

Their strategy and its vicissitudes form the core of this book. On the one hand, they sought to identify their community with the entire nation and its Buddhist heritage, so that any assault on their integrity could also be represented as an act of treason or sacrilege. As one man complained of state officials: "They never know that there is a historic community [on the site]" (*mai kheui sahp wah mi chumchon thahng prawatisaht*). By thus claiming the mantle of national history, residents neatly invert a scale of legitimacy of which the authorities, in their ignorance, have tried to place them on the lowest rung.

On the other hand, their identification with official narrative, and especially with the discourse of reverence for an increasingly controversial and beleaguered establishment, carried (and continues to carry) serious risks for their future. This predicament enhanced their acute sense of irony, which in turn often allowed them to negotiate with bureaucrats and politicians in ways that commanded respect. With exquisite gallows humor, a resident once remarked that the tense standoff between the community and the city authorities was particularly harmful in that it deprived the residents of tranquility, a value much touted by the authorities—and which, my interlocutor remarked, is what one seeks especially at the end of life.

The respect the residents were able to extract from grudging bureaucrats was always fleeting, evanescent, ironic. It was always also to some extent illusory—but it bought them time, and this, in a cosmology in which nothing is permanent, has delayed to an indefinite future the moment when—perhaps—they may be forced off the land they have so ferociously defended as their own.

My goal in telling this story is not to create a tale of heroes and villains. There are too many crosscutting ties among the various parties involved for the story to be that simple. Bureaucrats who appear lazy or hard-hearted entertain their own fears of the consequences of failure; residents sometimes cajole their neighbors mercilessly in order to achieve consensus on a course of action. Sometimes jocular or even intimate relations spring up between members of the opposed parties. We never really know what these connections are intended to achieve—whether they are forms of sociality for their own sake, whether there is some mutual exploitation, or again whether both sides simply want a respite from the unceasing demands of confrontation. At least in one case of physical attachment between a female resident and a male bureaucrat, it seems at least probable that each party was trying to extract information from the other. Even here, however, we can never do more than guess. And the indeterminacy of intention, which may shield quite destructive or self-serving motives, also muffles the emotion that certainly, at other moments and in the privacy of a conversation, may erupt as unmistakable fury.

Polarities and Complexities

At a time of deep polarization at the national level, moreover, the case of Pom Mahakan challenges easy assumptions about people's loyalties. Pom Mahakan, although a poor community with a considerable number of residents of Isan (northeastern Thai) origin, does not adhere en masse to the "red shirt" stereotype of angry Isan peasants turned proletariat (or at least does not do so to the exclusion of all other alternatives). Instead, it charts its own agile but risk-fraught course between various pairs of extremes that reflect and complicate the antinomies of national political life. What I have found perpetually fascinating about this community is thus a series of seeming paradoxes, and these are reproduced in the daily management of its affairs. It has a leadership whose ability to get itself democratically elected seems to be premised on the promise of both an authoritarian style and an ability to dragoon the entire community into collective action. We shall see that this tension, which reflects larger patterns of Thai political interaction and may be best expressed by the common conceit that everyone is *phi nawng* ("elder sibling-younger sibling") to each other, gives the leadership a great deal of flexibility, allowing it to command immediate compliance when urgent situations arise but to create an atmosphere of relaxed and friendly coexistence at easier times.

Many other seemingly opposed perspectives come together in Pom Mahakan. These include two religions and two major political factions. The residents are poor people with a strongly working-class identity who have found it expedient to embrace the values of a bourgeois city and the embrace of its dominant political party. Perhaps most interestingly of all, they display an adaptive capacity to resuscitate, in myriad subtle ways, the dynamics of a Siamese polity that predates and to some extent contradicts the Western-oriented bureaucratic philosophy and practices of a state to which it nevertheless repeatedly declares its undying fealty. To tell the story of such a place and its people is not to pretend to a new reading of Thai political culture, to be sure, but it offers a new perspective and one that refuses the simplistic polarities that so often dominate both social theory and Thai politics.

At the time that this book was nearing completion in 2014, the polarization between two nationally dominant factions, the Pheu Thai party and the "Red Shirts" on the one side and the Democrat Party and their "Yellow Shirt" allies on the other, had just collapsed into a military coup that—for all its leaders' protestations to the contrary—appeared to lend overwhelming support to the Yellow over the Red side. Yet the military claimed that they would not hold onto power for long, at least in a formal sense; perhaps the forces unleashed by the combination of left-wing populism and the creation of consumerist demand among the poor that many observers attribute to former prime minister Thaksin Shinawatra will indeed not allow the dissident voices to remain suppressed for long. The oscillation between binary poles does not itself favor a static binarism in political reality; rather, it creates a kaleidoscopic range of possibilities, none of which—attempts to stabilize them bureaucratically or by military force notwithstanding—can be denied in perpetuity.

This reading reflects a broader theoretical concern. Too often, anthropologists and others, in their haste to criticize the heavy hand of the state, have glorified the "informal" at the expense of the "formal." But this binary opposition cedes too much authority to the state itself, and—even if unintentionally—allows it to define what constitutes the formal norms and rules and what does not.[34] So-called informal communities—or what in Thailand are called *chumchon ae aht* (literally "crowded communities")[35]—survive in part by applying a host of explicit rules and regulations to forms of social activity. Around the world, we find such communities regulating the practices of theft, smuggling, revenge and so-called honor killings, gambling, prostitution, and urban resistance to a level that is entirely comparable with that of any official bureaucracy. Sometimes this is achieved through what Pierre Bourdieu calls "officializing strategies," but more often it deploys styles of governance that mock, parody, explicitly reject, or systematically ignore official forms.[36] What actually constitutes the boundary between the formal and the informal is performance, in the dual sense of performing functions and duties and of performing a role and achieving an effect.[37] Government rejects upstart local communities and denies them the mantle of formality, while taking refuge from critique behind a display of formalism that itself allows for a great deal of negotiation and simple muddling-through. But those communities often, as here, mount a sustained, stalwart response.

To describe such stances as performance does not necessarily mean that the social actors are insincere; indeed, the Thai self-deprecating mantra that "Thai people are not sincere" is itself a performance, a "disclaimer," that should not be read literally at all.[38] Even the well-known Thai concern with self-presentation, elevated to the political level in what Peter Jackson has so accurately pinpointed as "the regime of images," is not about insincerity or pretense so much as persuading a populace to accept the need to display conviction and loyalty.[39] These performances vary according to ability, personal style, and audience, but those that seem to achieve their goals most successfully, even in the hands of state officials, almost always involve creatively distorting normative roles—this itself being a significant challenge to the idea of state-defined formality.[40]

Engagement: The Story of Two Encounters

My own involvement with the community was richly serendipitous, and beautifully illustrates the compatibility of stylized but creative performance, the use of sometimes highly formalized images, and the emergence of deep emotion and attachment. A casual invitation by a local activist was the turning point. After a few months following my arrival in Bangkok, many people knew that there was an anthropologist in the area and that he was interested in community issues. In fact, I had come fully intending to spend roughly equal amounts of time in six of the many

CHAPTER ONE

small Rattanakosin communities of which more than twenty flank Rachadamnoen Avenue, the main thoroughfare linking the old Grand Palace to the modern city and a place that itself reflects many of the conflicts that have shaped the modern Thai polity.

Superficially, Pom Mahakan embraces the standard nationalist-monarchist historiography. It can still trot out a huge hand-painted portrait of the tuxedo-clad king to preside over major communal activities—especially when residents wish to draw a particularly strong distinction between the supposedly un-Thai lack of compassion on the part of the city bureaucrats and the positive institutional virtues represented by the figure of the benign and merciful king. On earlier occasions, especially when protests involved processions, portraits of both the king and the queen were borne aloft and in front, although such devices have faded with the growing preference for avoiding confrontation both internally and with the authorities.

Here, in fact, a delicate play of indirection and ambiguity is revealed with unusual clarity. It is by no means certain that changes in the deployment of royal portraits and symbols reflect an ideological shift. Neither in invoking royalty during the earlier protests, nor more recently in muting their once ostentatious monarchism, have the people of Pom Mahakan ever posed a challenge to the authority of royal charisma. On the contrary, they invoke it as the sole source of legitimacy that cannot legally be challenged by even the most imposing temporal power; and, rather like potential critics of the political status quo seeking refuge in the figure of King Prajadhipok, they can subsume under their generic royalism their principled resistance to a temporal power—the city bureaucracy—that they accuse of un-Thai attitudes. In so doing, they leave unsaid, but for that very reason unchallenged, the equation of Thainess with monarchy and especially with the reigning dynasty.

In the symbolic geography of the city, there is no doubt about the royal associations of the Pom Mahakan site, although a recent collaboration with the Prajadhipok Museum raises questions about the *kind* of monarchic association most favors the residents' interests. At the same time, one could argue that the Land Expropriation Act promulgated by King Prajadhipok in 1928 lies at the root of the problems of many communities, among which Pom Mahakan is but one small instance and the case of the population displaced by the proposed railway expansion a far more dramatic one involving massive public protests and fierce local resistance.[41] Such apparent contradictions abound, and are exemplified by the way in which Pom Mahakan has become famous for its resistance to the power of the municipality and the state. If the community can lay claim to a quintessential Thainess at all, that claim implicitly draws conviction precisely from its adroit management of the curious symbiosis of democratic and authoritarian values, or resistance and subservience, that characterizes so much of Thai political life.[42]

That symbiosis—or oscillation, a form it sometimes takes—may be characteristic of a wider geographical area, as observers have noted for a variety of cultural contexts ranging from upland tribal groups to city peripheries.[43] While it is sufficiently marked in Thailand to have attracted the attention of analysts of the bureaucratic system, it also appears to be more generally applicable to political life, and, in the confines of Pom Mahakan, it becomes sharply focused on the leaders' styles and actions and on the flexibility that they derive from it in their dealings with a bureaucracy that sometimes exhibits a similar dynamic.

It may thus help to explain the success of the Pom Mahakan residents at resisting the power of the state. An early observer of Thai bureaucracy remarked, "This peculiar combination of centralization and autonomy, which is as real as it is difficult to describe, is explained in part by a social system characterized by a high sense of rank reflected in automatic deference toward superiors, set in an atmosphere of much personal tolerance, or 'live and let live,' in which conduct is defined and discipline is focused essentially upon *personal* relationships rather than functional organization and accomplishment."[44] When I discovered how warmly and with what friendly language the Pom Mahakan residents sometimes engaged with bureaucrats whose only purpose in life at times appeared to be the immediate destruction of the community, I first thought that this combination of apparently irreconcilable attitudes was exceptional, or perhaps an unusually clear illustration of the stereotypical Thai penchant for elaborate courtesy and conflict avoidance. Later, however, it turned out to have considerable explanatory significance, but as a consequence, rather than a cause, of the political dynamics I was encountering.

None of this was clear to me when I first made the acquaintance of the Pom Mahakan community. I had reacted with some impatience when I was taken to see a small demonstration its residents were holding, not on their own site but in the visibly gentrified area surrounding the other surviving fortress in the old city wall, Pom Phra Sumaen. I did not know much about the community, and while I found the passion and intensity of the demonstration impressive, I did not sense much of a connection with the themes of my intended research. It seemed to me that what I was witnessing was merely another protest, among so many, of dispossessed residents. This was not without intrinsic interest; but it did not seem to be what I had come to study.

CHAPTER ONE

But a few months later, on my next visit, I discovered just how wrong I had been. A casual acquaintance who worked with one of the local NGOs told me that there was a demonstration at Pom Mahakan; would I be interested in accompanying him there and seeing the action? Somewhat grudgingly I conceded that I had little to lose by spending an hour or two at the site, and in any case my attempts to make substantive contact in the other areas I had chosen had meanwhile been frustrated at every turn—by my own clumsiness in Thai language and etiquette, by the fact that street merchants and others were really too busy to answer questions, by the fact that there seemed to be little overt local interest in the historical settings in which people were living and trading.

So I went along. My presence at this site was neither accidental nor, as matters turned out, of my own making. On the contrary, it was a humbling revelation of the extent to which an ethnographer's fortunes may depend on the agency of local people. The activists and the community leaders had figured out that if they could involve the anthropologist from Harvard, they would gain a useful resource. They were not seeking the kind of vertical patronage that might have allied them with influential scholars in the past, so much as creating a partnership in which they, not the visitors, were the prime movers. They must have been amused when I later advised them that they should use my association with that famous American university as a resource; but they were too polite, and perhaps also politically too adroit, to say so. This was one of several occasions when I experienced their ability to seize control of agency, whether in their political struggle or in small encounters with visitors representing hypothetically more powerful forces than themselves. At the time I first visited the community, I did not manage to foresee how neatly the residents and their allies had entangled me in their story. I also could not have anticipated the intense instruction they would give me in precisely the cultural areas in which my knowledge was weakest—the insights that every anthropologist seeks. They were generous and patient teachers; that was my reward, whether or not they saw it that way, for submitting with happy grace to an engagement that in fact drew me into a rich world of political and cultural activity.

When we arrived at the site, the protest was in full swing. In what I soon came to recognize as a well-established technique, a local leader and another NGO activist were conducting a stylized dialogue. Sitting at a table draped with a sheet bearing the slogan (all in red capital letters and in English) "Stop the War—Stop the Eviction," each offered short paeans to the historic importance of the site and to the residents' rights and virtues, to which the other responded with ritualistic bursts of the affirmative *chai . . . chai . . . chai!* ("true"). In a clearing next to the old citadel (*pom*) for which the site is named, more placards and posters and a set of plastic chairs—mostly, though sparsely, occupied by local people—defined the area of a protest that was not yet reaching the wide audience it was soon to acquire.

The stylized dialogue immediately caught my attention. The speakers were the male president of the community, Thawatchai, and a woman from one of the many poor people's alliances or networks that were the ideological offspring of the Assembly of the Poor.[45] The activist ran a community radio station, for which she later interviewed me, while Thawatchai was soon to show impressive rhetorical dexterity on television news broadcasts. Their dialogue exaggerated the rhythms of a normal Thai conversation, with its oral punctuation of particles *kha* (feminine) and *khrab* (masculine), and with the stylized turn taking (marked by pauses to allow each speaker to complete a phrase in comfort) that characterizes polite but informal speech.[46] Their performance partially resembled the speech-making that dominated most of the community's internal meetings, replete with the phraseology popularized by the NGOs that supported poor communities but also by government officials and academics. Using a formal rhetoric newly grown fashionable in vernacular public discourse,[47] they championed "a way of life" (*witthichiwit*) and "history" (*prawatisaht*) as strong reasons for preserving the community's habitat.

As soon as I heard these terms, I pricked up my ears—and since by then I had begun to film the protest, I also preserved for my own edification the embarrassing moment at which the activist began reading from my name card to show that the residents' cause was now getting international attention. What, she then politely but firmly demanded to know (making it hard to evade the question by handing me the microphone), was I going to do to help them? In very halting Thai (I was later told that it was actually quite difficult to understand), I explained that I was not prepared to promise anything—that I was not a politician; and I added, though this may have been the harder part to communicate, that I generally believed in the right to remain in one's own home but that I wanted to gather some data first before deciding how I felt about their specific case.

As matters turned out, although there was no way I could have predicted as much, this was by far the best response I could have given, since the residents felt that it was precisely the politicians and the bureaucrats who had brought them low—the bureaucrats by relentlessly pursuing the project of eviction, the politicians by appearing to take an interest whenever an impending election gave them a motive for doing so and then dropping them like an embarrassing garment as soon as the elections were over. I deliberately made no such promises. It may also be that my appeal to the possibility of mutual help—support in exchange for data—resonated with an already well-established rhetoric of reciprocity. "Helping each other think" (*chuai kan khid*) was a key element in community meetings.[48]

My involvement—which I have subsequently described under the rubric of "engaged anthropology"[49]—has been a source of great personal satisfaction and gratitude for me. I have learned a great deal about human dignity from people who for much of their lives have been treated with disdain and aversion by the majority of their fellow citizens, and I have watched with something approaching astonishment as they have worked successfully to stem and then to reverse that tide of contempt. But my involvement has also drawn some criticism, or at least puzzlement, in the context of informal conversations and formal presentations. Such reactions, sometimes from Thai scholars, apparently reflect the fact that while some of these scholars are deeply engaged in demanding social reform and in criticizing the Western paradigms that dominate public discourse, the positivistic language of much social-science discourse in Thailand is calibrated to a development paradigm that seeks large solutions and comprehensive redemption through the civilizing force of a Western-inspired and Western-imposed modernity.[50]

The residents professed interest in "self-development" (*kahn phatthanah tua eng*), admittedly itself a civilizational device redolent of the nineteenth-century Thai quest for Western-derived "civilization,"[51] as well, perhaps, as of current psychoanalytic fads. By contrast, these earnest scholarly and bureaucratic interlocutors operated with the equally derivative and considerably more colonial idiom of "development" (*kahn phatthanah*) *tout court*. I have been asked how I could possibly be objective in studying a community to which I ended up devoting so much involvement and passion. My answer, to which I hope this book will bear witness, was that involvement gave me a level of access that a deliberate stance of dispassionate distance would certainly have precluded. A further answer, which I rarely articulated in public discussions, would have been that this kind of objectivism is part of the conceptual armory—along with legal pedantry and official definitions of culture—against which the community was struggling. Above all, however, without a strong engagement with the community, I would have learned much less about its internal dynamics. Would fewer or poorer data mean greater objectivity?[52] On the same logic, whenever I was asked when I intended to interview my interlocutor, I answered that I did not wish to "interview" (*samphaht*) but simply "have a conversation" (*khui kan*)—an idiom suggesting the kind of reciprocity that was also part of the community's own style of describing its political actions.

At any rate, there was, it turned out, much to attract me to the community in terms of my original research interest in the local impact of historic conservation. Soon after my first visit, the residents held a tree ordination ritual to dedicate a fund they had created for the preservation of the fortress.[53] With the thudding beat of garland-festooned drums (which the residents had been testing for several days ahead of time) and with strong, rhythmic chanting, they circumambulated the fortress; this was followed by a formal dance display by residents clad in full ritual costume. An exhibit on the old wooden houses emphasized the historically deep articulation of the fortress with human settlement, while the tree ordination—an increasingly common practice among ecologically activist monks concerned to block the urban destruction of nature and originating in the northern part of the country—presaged in ritual fashion the expert claim I was later to hear to the effect that this tiny space was a precious niche for rare and highly localized plants and trees. The ritual activity invoked the shared substance of the trees and the "ancient" wooden houses to align self-traditionalizing culture with the forces of a sacralized nature—a Buddhist ritual that also appealed both to middle-class romanticism and to environmentalist sensibilities.

The intimacy that I eventually gained with the residents was certainly a precondition for any serious understanding of their internal dynamics. It was essential to gain the residents' trust; and the test was not long in coming. From the start it was clear that the people of Pom Mahakan were living under virtually unrelieved strain. They never knew when the authorities might decide to attack. A system of alarms and lookouts—six or seven for each given day of the week—had to be maintained at all times. The weekly roster, which did not spare even the community's highest officials, was unchanging, a modest monument in itself to the community's steadfast and unwavering determination. This was a war of attrition, and such a conflict is always psychologically draining. The authorities played cat and mouse with the community for months, indeed for years. At times they appeared to be ignoring all activity at the site; at others they sent official notices of impending deadlines with a formal demand that the residents leave within thirty days, or simply let it be known that they had reached the moment for decided—but unspecified—action. The impenetrability of their immediate intentions was the bureaucrats' strongest weapon in defense of their totally unambiguous long-term goal: to get the residents out of the space. But since their strategy failed to break the residents' resolve in the

CHAPTER ONE

early stages, it eventually only strengthened both their determination to resist and their ability to withstand the interminable psychological pressure.

The threat of sudden, drastic confrontation was always in the air, sustained by the common knowledge that lookouts on the old wall were constantly alert for trouble. One day in March 2003, word came that the city authorities had decided to mount a decisive and final attack on the morrow. Perhaps, after all, they were going to commit the direct violence that had so long been threatened but indefinitely deferred. Amid an atmosphere of suddenly peaking tension, the residents told me that if we wanted to see some action, my wife and I should arrive before dawn. Such confrontations rarely take place in broad daylight since too much that is illegal transpires and there is always a fear on the authorities' part that the media will denounce their tactics. The barricades, already assembled around the gates, were to go up at 4:00 a.m. But then again, one of our friends mused, perhaps we should not come, since there might be real danger—the authorities might send in a gang of toughs to burn down the wooden houses, and there might be fighting. Perhaps they had a good idea of how an anthropologist was likely to respond; they had already attracted the attention of a distinguished Thai anthropologist—Akin Rabibhadana—who specialized in the study of poor urban communities and who was certainly no opponent of engagement. In any case, our interest was irreversibly aroused.

So about a quarter of an hour before the appointed deadline, with the streets still bathed in the predawn gloom, my wife and I arrived—with not inconsiderable trepidation—at the high white wall of Bangkok's dynastic city below the round whiteness of the Mahakan citadel, where our friends were edgily preparing for a siege. Greeted with warm smiles (of relief? of complicity? of sensing the inability of an anthropologist to resist such a temptation?), we passed through the high front gate, already bristling with carefully ordered detritus that would soon provide a formidable barrier to unwanted invaders, past the pointed poles carefully placed against the inside of the wall ready to impale anyone foolhardy enough to try climbing over the top, and toward a scene of quiet, ordered, but tense activity.

Inside the walls, the most visible activity was conducted by a group of men who were preparing long nets to hurl across the canal, thereby preventing anyone from using a boat to attack the community from the relatively unguarded rear. Following some of the adolescent boys and one of the older men, I sneaked out through a back gate and along the road that leads up to the Temple of the Golden Mount, a resplendent tower of shimmering white and gold in daytime that at that hour was no more than a sketchy shadow in the inscrutable gloaming. Leaning over an elaborately decorated white balustrade fronting the canal, the boys tried to hurl their nets across the water, wedging the weighted further ends firmly on the other side. With some barely stifled shouting and a great deal of urgent whispering, punctuated by worried comments on the length of the ropes they had brought to secure the nets in place, they finally achieved their goal and, with nerves taut with anticipation (and some swaggering bravado from the adolescent boys), we trudged back under the yellow streetlights and into the besieged community, where more nets were being tested in case of later need.

As dawn came up and the damp heat of daytime drew a growing roar of traffic from the street, it became apparent that the anticipated attack was not materializing. At first cautiously, then with a growing sense of confidence, a small group of younger women, some with babies, ranged themselves on the sidewalk in front of the main entrance. This is a time-honored technique among communities resisting eviction; the assumption is that even the most vicious street thugs would hesitate to strike women and children in broad daylight, especially in such a tourist-frequented and temple-studded area. The talk among the women became more animated. They smiled warmly at us, clearly delighted that we had provided moral support at a time of fear; my wife was sitting with them. By midmorning it was clear that no violence would happen that day.

Why no attack? The residents were not expecting the police to conduct the raid; I was often assured that they were not afraid of the police, with whom they had cooperated in shutting down the drug dealers' activities within the community and with whom they sometimes cooperated on an individual basis in activities that were distinctly less legal—for example, sharing a bribe as a reward for standing in for a prisoner who wanted to get out at night to tend to his business. Indeed, when BMA officials appear, one resident told me, the police look away and pretend not to know the inhabitants. The residents play along: "We must also take care of their [i.e., the police's] rights." It is obviously not in the residents' interests to get these complicit police sympathizers in trouble. Such collusion is less usefully treated as corruption than as moral solidarity between poor residents and poorly paid officers. In another district, a newsagent friend once confided to me that the local police would comment on alleged infractions by local shopkeepers and then accept a small gift of money "under the table" (*tai to*) as the price of not prosecuting—an interaction that my interlocutor did not see as a form of extortion.[54] Such descriptions, far from representing the police as extortionate predators, suggest instead a rela-

CHAPTER ONE

tively amiable social symbiosis—at least when both parties see a genuine advantage in it.

The residents were more afraid of the army. That fear later materialized, when soldiers occupied the front area and demolished some houses. On the day of the threatened attack, however, the army was not involved. The residents might also have feared the motorcycle taxi drivers, who are sometimes held to cooperate with the authorities when violence offers an easy solution to intractable confrontations; but since one of their leaders belonged to this profession, with its well-organized if legally rather shadowy solidarities,[55] there seems to have been no risk on that front. On this occasion, their real fear was directed at the underworld toughs who reputedly would do the bidding of the authorities by setting fire to vulnerable wooden structures and driving the distraught inhabitants away from their collapsing homes.

But those goons did not materialize.[56] Perhaps it was the prospect of confronting the calm array of women at the entrance. Possibly, too, the authorities had gotten wind of our presence. I was filming the action; the residents were clearly pleased that we had come and perhaps thought that our presence might have deterred the authorities. But it is equally possible that the bureaucrats never intended to provoke a violent confrontation and hoped that panic alone would do their work for them. Or perhaps they had simply decided that the risks outweighed the possible advantages of an attack, especially as the residents' preparations had hardly been conducted in secret and might themselves have served as an effective deterrent. Because Pom Mahakan is in the heart of the old city and thus part of a major tourist attraction as well as of the symbolic and historic core of the city, violence at the site would never pass unnoticed. We will probably never know why nothing happened. But it was a nothing that seemed to give new life to the community's determination to stand firm.

Initially, the city authorities had successfully—if untruthfully—painted the community as a haven of drug addicts and wife beaters. On one occasion early in my research, when I called the then city clerk from the community itself to express my concern over what was happening, she—having initially encouraged my research on the Rattanakosin Island communities and offered her assistance—reacted with horror. That place, she said, was full of bad people—prostitutes, drug addicts, and other nefarious types. The professor, said she in what seemed unequivocally tones of command rather than advice, should not go there. It is certainly true that she herself assiduously avoided entering the area even though she was spotted going down to the boat stop nearby. Perhaps she believed what she was saying, but, as one of the residents pointed out, she had no way of knowing the truth of the situation because she never visited the community.

Despite such calumnies, there was a gradual improvement in the community's reputation. This partly arose from events such as the first two of the academic conferences, which were held at Thammasat University (on 31 May 2003) and at Chulalongkorn University (on 25 August 2003), and from a concomitant, and significant, shift in the content of media reportage; at one point the community had successfully taken a newspaper to court for slander, but, by the time I appeared on the scene, matters had already improved enormously.[57] The general change in attitude was reflected over time in the fact that taxi and *tuk-tuk* drivers,[58] who professed never to have heard of Pom Mahakan when I first started going there, eventually often found the name more recognizable than that of the nearby and historically significant Phahn Fah Lilaht Bridge.[59] By 2014 a taxi driver assured me that the Pom Mahakan leaders were successful in resisting the municipal authorities because they were *khemkhaeng* (tough, resilient) and because they were all *phi nawng* (older and younger siblings) to one another—a revealing quotation of a common vocabulary that has come to seem particularly associated with Pom Mahakan. The effect of the academic conferences is hard to gauge; while the fact that major universities were implicated in these efforts will have spoken to middle-class sensibilities, at least one foreign activist was offended by what he saw as a "college lecture" without—in the invitation that was initially distributed—any recognition of the residents' participation. That, to be sure, was something of a misunderstanding, since residents played very active roles on the panels and from the floor at these events, but it illustrates some of the perspectival conflicts that any middle-class involvement could evince.

Local academic activists were also involved in the conferences, and they played a part in coaching the residents. One of them, for example, drew up a list of key themes he thought the parties should address at the Thammasat gathering. This, I suggest, was not because he thought the residents incapable of formulating their objections and responses; several of them had already proved to be remarkably articulate, and he was consistently respectful of these capacities and indeed saw them as a reason for supporting the community. Rather, a concerted effort required focusing on a few key themes. These, enunciated in a document distributed in a community meeting ahead of the conference, included the international ramifications of the Pom Mahakan case and the interest of foreign academics in learning from it; an assessment of the probable impact of the development plan on the community; the community's recommendations for improving the plans for the refurbishment of the space; and the need for a creative, nonviolent solution in the long term. Other topics included the history of the community and a consideration of its need for living space, as well as a rejection of the idea that the residents were squatters at all. And the residents were also exhorted to consider how best to organize themselves for their own salvation. While none of these were particularly original points, focusing attention on them ensured—as the event demonstrated—a lively sequence and a productive engagement with the larger public.

While some local friends insist that I had played a key role in reversing the community's invisibility and ensuring its survival over the decade of my involvement, I prefer to think of this engagement as being the product of the inhabitants' and others' intentional agency acting on my initially rather unaware curiosity.[60] But the residents were generous in their interpretation of my involvement. On the day of my departure from my major period of field research (6 September 2003), they organized a lengthy farewell ceremony at which Thawatchai formally explained that my involvement "meant that we began to know that in the future of Pom Mahakan we need people who come to help; he came to look after (*du lae*) us . . . and we began to know ourselves better. . . . We had the feeling that this professor was no longer the high professor from now on. . . . He ate food with us . . . . Now he is a friend; he's an important fellow (*phu yai*); and now the brothers and sisters of Pom [Mahakan] feel that he's a member (*samahchik*) of the Pom Mahakan community." After the presentation of amulets to ensure my safety as I traveled away, there was the inevitable photo session; I was flanked by Thawatchai's wife and mother, and many other residents joined the group—all people whose even-tempered embrace of my inquisitive presence reflected patience, stoicism, and playful humor. Then Thawatchai turned toward me and suddenly flung his arms around me—something that he could hardly have done with a Thai professor, and that brought me into the realm of those intimates to whom, formal address notwithstanding, he could express open, warm affection.

Embodied Ambiguities

Humor and friendship are important resources for a community under siege; and at Pom Mahakan both are in plentiful supply. Even (or perhaps especially) when a friendship is close, the teasing that ambiguity makes possible is never far away. Conversely, however, formality can frame affect in a way that intensifies its impact. Thawatchai still greets me formally as *thahn ajahn*, honored professor,[61] and his *wai* is respectful, if not as deep as the one he reserves for the elderly retired palace policeman, a garrulous enthusiast whose collections of clocks, stamps, postcards, and assorted memorabilia and documents have made him a valuable resource (if a somewhat obsessive hobbyist) for establishing historical details about Pom Mahakan. This man grew up in the community—the last, perhaps, of the royal bureaucrats whose homes had constituted the original settlement, although some of his own kin and fellow residents in the neighboring community where he now lives, people who also view Pom Mahakan as a squatter settlement, dispute his royal connections. The president of Pom Mahakan cannot afford to be swayed by such backbiting. By indexing a living link to the royal past through exquisite bodily attention to protocol, he reminds the world that Pom Mahakan has a distinguished history.[62]

Thawatchai's engagements with me, by contrast, are redolent of the ambiguities and oscillations that are a central theme of this book. When we have not met for several months, or as I am about to depart, he often embraces me again. He also sometimes calls me *"my uncle"*—the English words suggesting that our relationship may not be strictly grounded in Thai protocol. Even this, however, is ambiguous. *Lung*, patrilateral uncle, is an honorific prefix and term of address for a respected senior member of the community. But Thawatchai never uses the Thai kinship term for me, so that his choice of the English term marks the conceptual space in which he is free to make the equally un-Thai gesture of hugging me. In this way, he negotiates the balance between showing his co-residents and outsiders that he is respectful of the foreign professor while also showing me an affection matured in the our joint efforts. His use of the formal address mode simultaneously indexes what is supposed to be a thoroughly Thai idiom of hierarchy, placing me in a position where I have no choice but to adopt the same code of formal courtesy. It simultaneously evokes the historically unequal relations between Thailand and the colonial powers that have sustained the idiom of hierarchy all along.[63]

Thawatchai clearly relies on his own status as community president to legitimate his open display of affection. Other residents are a little more circumspect, although Maew—also a member of the leadership group until marital misadventures led him away from hearth and home—often indulged in a similarly warm embrace. But he generally made a point of being less formal than Thawatchai with me. Maew, a smiling, energetic man with slightly graying curly hair and a dramatic voice that alternated between gentle mockery and firm resolve, had extensive experience of networking with poor communities in the north. An eloquent manager of relations with the bureaucracy at times of crisis, he was never afraid to cor-

CHAPTER ONE

rect my Thai speech or to inspect my handwriting and spelling. Sometimes he would ironically imitate something another resident or I had said, usually to make a point about the unfairness of the residents' situation—not, it seemed, as an example of the Thai way of checking intended meaning by polite repetition, but as a submersion of hierarchy in the pointed pleasures of banter.

Time and Culture: Embodiments of Experience

Time is more than an abstract historical sequence. It is a domain of shared experience, in which multiple temporal idioms, from the rhythms and disruptions of habitual bodily movement to the disciplined march of official historiography, shape people's entailment in the flow of events. The residents both experience and manipulate time, pace, and rhythm—all aspects of what we collectively call temporality—in relation both to their understandings of a complex and contested past and to the day-to-day management and defense of the tiny space in which they live and from which they live in constant fear of violent expulsion.

That minuscule space is, they aver, a microcosm of Thai culture. At various times and in varying combinations, Pom Mahakan has hosted Thai kickboxing, "ancient style massage" (*nuat paen borahn*, the traditional and nonsexual form), the production of terra-cotta models of *rusi* (Buddhist ascetics), the raising and training of fighting cocks, and the manufacture of fireworks and of bird cages (fig. 2). Although the man who makes the cages is a Muslim, and is following his father in the craft, this is not a southern practice but is representative, so his wife (who was raised as a Buddhist) told me, of the style of Petburi in the central plains. One family formerly ran a gold-extraction furnace; they would buy the slag from the many goldsmiths concentrated in the Bangkok Chinatown (Yaowarat), manually extract the minute traces of gold, and then resell the now purified gold to the goldsmiths at a profit. Because the laborious extraction process was insufficiently lucrative and too productive of noxious and potentially dangerous fumes for the goldsmiths to be willing to undertake it for themselves in their more densely populated part of town, the enterprise disappeared when the army removed the front area (about twelve hundred square meters in size) from community control, leaving under the community's control insufficient open space for such a polluting activity.

One household produces an astringent liquid smelling salt, very popular in Bangkok, that is dabbed on the nostrils to provide temporary relief from the persistent atmospheric pollution. In addition, many of the

2   A bird cage hangs in the shade of the old wall.

inhabitants produce and sell on the streets a variety of foods, ranging from northeastern delicacies to fish maw soup and several kinds of noodles. These hawkers form the largest professional group, and their cooking skills are also greatly in demand when any major event (such as several iterations of the annual Children's Day) is staged in the community space. One woman makes Western-style cookies for sale; these may not contribute to the claims to Thai culture, but they are an attractive and relatively easy source of minor income, and do actually fit the current taste of many middle-class Bangkokians.

The kickboxing and massage experts have both now passed away, taking with them attributions of high professional status that were also useful in countering the implication that Pom Mahakan was a lair of uncouth villains. The kickboxing master was prominent in all the public rituals of the community, and, although his eventual disaffection from the leadership of which he had once been an active member led to some deep hostility between his family and the majority for several years, by now the gentle waters of conciliation have swept such memories into a distant, dusty corner of a complex internal history. For his part, the masseur, dignified Uncle Phim, who had been known in his early life as something of a hoodlum and thief (and whose wife-to-be had made it a condition of their marriage

CHAPTER ONE

that he abandon his life of petty crime), had become an expert masseur and a man of extraordinary gentleness by the time I knew him; he was the only person I could ever imagine allowing to massage my eyeballs, and people came to him from quite distant parts of the city, or had him visit them, to have their bodies pummeled and stretched into more relaxed postures for what, even by local standards, were absurdly small sums of money. Uncle Phim could also always be induced to demonstrate his art on distinguished visitors, some of whom were palpably surprised at finding such remarkable skill in so small and poor a community. He would talk to them in a soft, almost droning voice, occasionally checking to make sure they could stand the pain, his craggy face serene in the gloaming in the space under the magnificent old traditional Thai stilt-supported house that was his home, his hooded, elderly eyes occasionally darting toward the pet bird that hopped nonchalantly around the mattress on which his customers relaxed.

With the exception now of the kickboxing and the massage, the activities discussed here are all highly visible, as are the artistic skills encouraged in the children as they draw and paint to express their deep attachment to their community. Indeed, the leaders make a point of showing the evidence of all these skills to visitors, foreign and Thai. Such skills constitute a recognizable symbolic resource in asserting the legitimacy of the community's claims to quintessential, multigenerational Thainess in a place of peaceful, law-abiding, and creative citizens.

Admittedly, the residents' enthusiastic embrace of the official discourse of Thai culture sometimes too easily leads to self-reification, from frequent reiterations that the community has a distinctively Thai "way of life" (*witthichiwit*) to the architectural institutionalization of collective wisdom and experience as a "pavilion of the community's local knowledge" (*sahlah phumpanyah chumchon*). This invocation of a distinctively local wisdom is an increasingly common feature of communities resisting official authority or simply trying to establish visibility on the map of Thai culture.[64] Such reifications produce an air of artificial or even enforced consensus that occasionally seems to challenge even the most relativistic versions of anthropological forbearance. Yet we should be careful not to assume that such apparent emulation of official models of cultural form represents passive complaisance in official interpretations, or that those who adopt those models necessarily surrender their agency and with it some imagined quality of authenticity. On the contrary, as Yujie Zhu has argued for China, exactly the opposite may be happening, with imitation masking a process of reverse co-optation.[65] The only way to find out whether this is in fact happening is through long-term ethnography and ongoing contact.

Perhaps a more immediate problem lies in the capacity of such reifications of culture to render the community more "legible" to the state,[66] and thus easier to attack. Thawatchai, as one of the most vocal and effective architects of the community's cultural program, put it in these terms: "Our problem in the past is that Pom Mahakan was intangible (*man mai mi tua ton*, literally 'it has no body'—that is, in the here and now). So it never got anyone coming to conserve, take care (*du lae*) [of it], or be responsible [for its condition]." Now the situation is changing: "Now, no matter what happens in the future, Pom Mahakan is genuinely tangible. No matter whether it's the case of which people in Pom or of the state in any sense, that state has never been active in this way. I think we now have a problem and that problem is that [now] it [the community] is tangible." He said it was a problem for the residents and for the state functionaries in equal measure, and a matter for fear, because now every person's attitudes and beliefs would be identifiable. In using the language of tangibility and intangibility, Thawatchai was, with what appears to have been unintentional irony, evoking the international jargon of heritage, but in an unexpected way: by acknowledging the dangers attendant upon materializing the culture and presence of the community, he also made it clear that this process represented a potential trap, since the increasingly clear image of this community not only equipped it with a realistic defense against those who denied its legitimacy but also made it an easier target.

The community's claim to a concentric relation with the nation evokes the ethnographer's characteristic task of drawing from a small case study some deeper knowledge of the larger national, religious, ethnic, or other entity in which it is embedded. Such knowledge cannot be gained through the most massive deployment of direct interviews and surveys. While today the focus on small and especially isolated communities is no longer the methodological and topical requisite it once was, small urban enclaves can be especially illuminating, and research in such places does not preclude following through with connections outside the community limits. My comparison of community and discipline is thus not fortuitous; it springs from my frequent sense that the residents of Pom Mahakan, much like anthropologists trying to see the "big picture," were intent on representing their community as a small-scale map of the national entity.

But there is a difference. The anthropologist tries to extrapolate from the small spaces certain features that can then, with luck, be traced across a larger map and through parallel subsets within that space. The residents of Pom Mahakan were engaged in a work of actively *constructing* themselves as a tangible reproduction of national culture—of performing their claims to representative authenticity. A small space in which people quite literally know each other well, warts and all, can also focus the imagining of the larger entities of which it is part. The residents of the community I describe here are engaged in precisely such an ongoing work of creative imagination, identifying their humble dwellings huddled between the wall and the canal with the quintessence of Thainess.

Their success in establishing that identification is but one strand in a complex political story. Their capacity for managing time corresponds to remarkable success in getting others to reimagine their space with them. That time-space expansion, to invert a widely celebrated formula for understanding the postmodern condition,[67] rests, in turn, on a series of strategic choices that have enabled the residents of Pom Mahakan to resist overwhelming odds for over two decades. It is the articulation of these several elements that have enabled such a minute entity—a population that numbers around three hundred souls (including many relatively recent migrants), distributed among seventy-seven houses or ninety-two family units (mostly nuclear families or couples)[68]—to defy the bureaucracies of city and state for so long.

Pom Mahakan is in no sense typical of "slum communities" in Thailand, simply because there is no such thing as a typical slum community.[69] Nor is it useful to describe it as typically Thai, despite its intense, frequent evocation of stylized images of Thai culture. Anthropologists are often taxed with choosing atypical or marginal social groups to study, but that charge presupposes that typicality is what interests them. Rather, it is a particular group's capacity for reinventing itself in relation to larger entities such as city and nation that helps us understand the cultural politics involved. In that respect, the residents' reimagining of Pom Mahakan as a microcosm of Thailand is of enormous significance. By examining claims of national belonging through the eyes and ears of a community that is trying to establish its legitimacy within the larger polity, we can more easily perceive how that encompassing nation also constructs itself.

The idea of the community as microcosm is a strategic conceit. It is also a familiar one for Thais, who have encountered miniaturization as a technique of nationalist expression in the form of the so-called Ancient City park. This is a privately founded reproduction of the country's religious and royal monuments, a wealthy eccentric's genuflection to nationalist sentiment, displayed on a miniature ground map with disputed border zones shown as securely within Thailand.[70] The Ancient City park gives expression to the metonymic relationship between the local and the global that is widely shared in the whole country. The residents of Pom Mahakan exploit this relationship to the full to establish a sense of the concentricity of their tiny enclave with the large nation-state in which they also live, but, unlike the contraction of a national territory with live-size monumental replicas into the small space of the Ancient City park, they portray their own much smaller space as a pure refraction of the national essence. Doing so is arguably their best hope for survival as a community and is therefore an ineluctable and nonnegotiable necessity. They are, they say, a miniaturized version of the polity as a whole. But the question we must now answer reveals the source of much of the ambiguity surrounding the community's status: what kind of polity is it?

TWO

Community, City, and Polity

The stand taken by the residents of Pom Mahakan throws the very nature of the Thai polity into sharp relief. That polity is a far more complex entity than a simple definition in terms of territoriality and national culture would suggest. Even the layout of the Ancient City (*moeang borahn*), entirely straightforward in its territorial irredentism, obscures an underlying uncertainty, hidden by the translation of *moeang* as "city." The *moeang* is the kind of polity evoked in the park's signage as Siam rather than as Thailand. The Ancient City is thus both a model of the self-idealizing territorial nation-state (*prathaet*) and a miniature version of the encompassing cultural and conceptual community that both undergirds and contradicts the logic of the centralized nation-state. Pom Mahakan inhabits both polities, the *moeang* and the *prathaet*, simultaneously but selectively. The play of difference between these two models is crucial to understanding the community's ability to chart a course through political upheavals at every level.

Two Models of the Polity

Thailand oscillates between its historical antecedent as a "pulsating galactic polity" and its modern incarnation as a clearly demarcated territorial nation-state[1]—much as all Thai political life oscillates between extremes of authoritarian and egalitarian discourse.[2] The older model, the *moeang*,

COMMUNITY, CITY, AND POLITY

was reproduced at multiple levels from the local to the national. It signifies a place where, whatever their differences, people regard themselves as sharing in a sense of community—where, in the Thai idiom, they are *phi nawng kan* ("older and younger siblings to each other"). It may indeed be a city—hence, presumably, the extension of the name to modern urban spaces—but this is predicated on the idea that the city is a civilizational center. The underlying model is a more modest extension of kinship idiom to a communal existence that transcends all hierarchical differences. In that sense, it corresponds precisely to what Evans-Pritchard recognized as "moral community," a term that also nicely describes Tambiah's Siamese pulsating galactic polity. In northern Thailand, where the people (*khon moeang*) and local language (*kham moeang*) implicitly claim a sense of cultural superiority in relation to ethnic minorities, the term also conveys the sense of "urbanity" that also underlies such notions as the Italian *civiltà*—the knowledge of how to behave as fellow citizens of a moral community at once culturally urban and morally urbane.[3]

Replacing the *moeang* in the Siamese official imagination was the bureaucratic "country" (*prathaet*) designed on the Western European model. The adoption of well-defined geographical frontiers and a complex, pyramidal bureaucracy was the primary condition for the agreement of the closest colonial powers, Britain and France, to desist from invading Siamese territory—a perfect illustration of David Harvey's observation that capitalism forces radical restructuring of space and time on populations that may deeply resent and resist such changes.[4] And indeed, as in any Western country, what anthropologists would recognize as the segmentary arrangement of the polity remains perpetually ready to call the authority of the bureaucratic structure into question.[5] That the formal Thai polity exhibits many of the features that the Western powers profess to decry—corruption, inefficiency, and waste—has simply provided those powers with a stick with which to beat the Thai state whenever it seemed to be stepping beyond the limits of the highly circumscribed independence these colonial powers were prepared to grant it.

Thais use both terms in speaking of their homeland. While they are loyal to the idealized, institutional state called *prathaet thai*, especially when it is under foreign fire, the more informal *moeang thai* conveys affect and sociability. From long residence overseas, for example, they return to the *moeang*, not the *prathaet*. This verbal distinction preserves a trace of the older polity, which rests on the principle of segmentation whereby the demarcation of lines of conflict and cooperation, instead of being determined only by bureaucratic structures and territorial integrity, is relative to the social relations at stake at any given moment. But the

CHAPTER TWO

moeang structure is more than a series of nesting boxes, as James Taylor has noted; its smallest unit may reproduce the moral authority of both the encompassing polity and the royal, mandala-based central city.[6] Indeed, it reproduces as a polity the moral cartography of a range of social entities, made mutually analogous by their possession of shared spiritual characteristics, from the individual person to the entire nation and beyond.[7] While anthropologists have traditionally treated segmentary and bureaucratic states as contrasted forms, in reality even the most rigidly centralized state may conceal or even facilitate thoroughly segmentary perceptions and processes in everyday life. In Thailand, these represent a substrate of ideas that no amount of sometimes heavy-handed Westernization has suppressed—in part, perhaps, because the prototypical *moeang*, the capital city, is a royal space in its own right.

In European countries, overt political segmentation is typically seen as a failure of bureaucratic control even though the essence of European identity admits of an almost infinite number of sublevels of national and regional identity.[8] In Thailand, by contrast, while the bureaucracy is largely modeled on the European nation-state and the bureaucrats (who in consequence generally portray themselves as representative of the state's modernization) may resist segmentary tendencies with all their might, officials are still citizens who, as such, share a common culture and language with the vast majority of those over whom they exercise their authority.

They thus still implicitly understand the polity in terms of the ancient segmentary model, which rests on a venerated Buddhist cosmology that it ostensibly shares with the official nation-state. Yet the older idioms of mapping national and urban space, which either reproduced the cosmological order or responded to it in the context of pragmatic concerns about warfare and trade,[9] are completely absent from modern planning documents; and official legalism makes no space for relativistic models of allegiance. This is one of many unresolved tensions in Thai society today—unresolved, in part, because it is often difficult to discuss the paradoxical dependence of the strongly nationalistic ideology on externally derived models of identity and its concealment of older modes of moral solidarity.

While such evasiveness may seem to favor the formal institutions of state in the short run, as proponents of the draconian laws against *lèse-majesté* must logically believe, the story of Pom Mahakan shows that it also stymies the state's efforts at total control. To be sure, the formal administrative model of governance (*kahnpokkhrong*), enshrined in the institution of an Administrative Court that repeatedly turned down Pom Mahakan's appeals for legal recognition of its rights, wins formal battle after formal battle. But communities like Pom Mahakan continue to persevere and even to win a considerable amount of public support for their opposition to official dictates.

This happens because the people of Pom Mahakan have preserved something of this older substrate in their social organization; the essence of the *moeang* was its reproducibility even at relatively minute levels of social aggregation. We should nevertheless not succumb to the romantic lore of fragments and survivals that such an account would imply. Rather, the logic of concentricity resurfaces as a result of the residents' self-conscious efforts to portray themselves as a microcosm of the country as a whole—efforts that have been remarkably successful at least as a rhetorical and political strategy in gaining support from the more liberal elements of the bourgeoisie, although they have also partly tended to pull the community into the orbit of those elements and away from that of those who would seem more natural bedfellows, the poor communities that are widely assumed to have been the most committed supporters of the "red" faction of the politically polarized country.

The residents' strategy has largely been to reinforce the reciprocal identification of community and nation, with the latter rather vaguely defined so that in practice it does not become too closely identified with either of the currently dominant factions. Attacks on the community— which is itself very clearly defined by a precisely demarcated if contested territoriality—thereby become attacks on the entire nation and on its transcendent and today highly fragile unity. In the same logic, the community, in a move that is consistent both with the principles of segmentation and with the NGOs' insistence that all poor communities should work together to achieve their common desire for a dignified life and particularly their goal of achieving land reform at the national level, effaces itself as a "small body" (*tua lek*) within the larger struggle of Thailand's poor. As Thawatchai remarked, Pom Mahakan's struggle is never solely about Pom Mahakan. Indeed, the housing issue that lies at the heart of its refusal to move is shared in some form with approximately two-thirds of the poor people of the entire Bangkok administrative area.[10]

The persistence of the segmentary *moeang* helps to explain how the strong tension between two national self-stereotypes, egalitarian and authoritarian respectively, can be sustained over so many decades. That tension inheres in one of the most common expressions used for self-description at every level: *phi nawng*, literally meaning "elder siblings [and] younger siblings." The phrase is so common that knowledgeable readers may be tempted to dismiss my emphasis on it as overkill. But it is precisely the ubiquity of the usage, which sometimes seems to mean little more than a friendly "hey, everyone," that makes it the ideal expression of the

CHAPTER TWO

tension between the two extremes of political attitude. Siblings are the closest members of the same generation and the same family; but age—which, in Thailand, is a serious component of hierarchy—separates them from each other.[11]

The expression *phi nawng*, a friendly commonplace that recognizes but does not emphasize hierarchical difference, thus falls easily from the lips of every politician seeking votes or whipping up the crowds, or simply thanking the people of the politician's constituency for their trust and support.[12] Thus, for example, did the Yellow Shirt demagogue Suthep Thaugsuban, a former deputy prime minister who had been held responsible for the fatal shooting of Red Shirt demonstrators while in office, address the crowds during the 2013 "shut down Bangkok" movement—a movement that aimed to paralyze the government of then prime minister Yingluck Shinawatra and eventually precipitated the following year's coup d'état. The term *phi nawng* encapsulates the tension between egalitarianism and hierarchy, and thereby characterizes and reveals the flexible polity of the *moeang*. For the *moeang* is not merely the urban center, although the emergence of that specific meaning presumably enhanced the tension between communal and hierarchical models of belonging and fuels the ire of middle-class Bangkokians resentful of the recent influx of politically active country folk.[13] It demarcates the entire conceptual space—the moral community, as I have called it—within which Thai political life unfolds.

The terminology that I have been discussing here appears to be deeply rooted in the history and language of the region. In the wider Tai-speaking world, even in communities geographically and historically far removed from the modern Thai state, these two pairs of terms appear to reinforce each other's defining properties. Among Tai speakers of Yunnan Province in China, for example, the term *bī: luàng* (older siblings, younger siblings) "in its broader sense . . . often refers to all villagers who have good relationships. It is, however, not used to refer to people who have good relationships but live outside the village although it is used to refer to real relatives living outside the village." Moreover, just as in Thailand, it is used with a reciprocal particle (*gan*, Thai *kan*) to mean membership of a shared community.

The flexible meanings of the Yunnanese Tai *měng* similarly incorporate the concentric sense that we also find in the etymologically cognate Thai *moeang* (including the locution *měngtai* for "Thailand" itself). In the Thai *moeang* the territorial implications that we find in the way in which the Yunnanese Tai employ the *měng* concept are associated with a powerful sense of solidarity, in which the concentricity of various political entities serve as metonymic representations of a transcendent identity that the state has latterly reified as "Thainess" (*khwahm pen thai*). That condition often seems to represent a highly Western understanding of national identity and even Western cultural or technical knowledge, and it exemplifies the effects of the Western cultural control over Thailand and other ostensibly independent countries that I have called "crypto-colonialism."[14] The Yunnanese Tai example, which occurs outside the crypto-colonial framework of the Thai state, helps us to discern ordinary people's more flexible understanding of the polity and the kinship model that underlies the way in which it is conceived.

In the sense thus made possible by a segmentary perspective, the "refracted" term *"phi nawng Pom"*—the siblings of Pom [Mahakan]—falls easily from the lips of community leaders; this is, as it were, the inner circle of fictive siblings. Occasionally a community elder might not even know the formal name of a member of the leadership group; the common practice of using short (usually monosyllabic) nicknames suffices within a family, even when there is a dispute, and the rhetoric that the community is all one "family" (*khrawpkhrua*) has become a regular refrain. The details of actual kinship beyond the household unit, moreover, seemed to be a relatively unimportant consideration in the conduct of community business. *Khrawpkhrua* (family) literally means "those who gather around the cooking hearth." It was given material expression by the many women who prepared and cooked food in the open spaces on the lanes around the central square, some for domestic consumption, many for sale on the streets, and all, at times, for communal events. While food is often shared informally, I take the force of the metaphor to derive less from explicit links with food preparation and domesticity than from an ethic of reciprocal affect and support.

The metaphor of family was convenient for several reasons. Internally, it helped to explain away the factional disputes and personal quarrels that erupted from time to time; such things happen in families too. It also provided a blanket explanation for the extent to which an individual household's problems might become a topic of discussion in a meeting of the whole community—a far from rare occurrence, and one that helped to solidify the community's resolve. Perhaps most convenient of all, it was consistent with the royalist leanings of the community. Meetings were often overshadowed by the huge hand-painted portrait of the king. As Felicity Aulino points out,[15] the ideological position that the king is the father of his people helps to remove any sense of incongruity in the involvement of others in personal and familial issues. Indeed, the fact that the community president might sometimes also be viewed as a virtual "father" (*phaw*) does not contravene the king's authority, especially given the royalist sympathies of both the president and the majority of the residents.

CHAPTER TWO

To the contrary, it evidences the segmentary properties of the local *moeang* by suggesting that the president's role is idealized as homologous with, but in no sense a challenge to, that of the monarch.[16] This logic makes it particularly difficult for the authorities to attack: it means that they cannot impugn the community's national and royalist credentials without also placing their own in doubt, a view that is further enhanced by the residents' claims that the spirit shrines fronting many of the houses (fig. 3) no longer simply honor and appease the spirits of deceased residents alone but have become the shrines of all the Thai people.

With this familial model, all other levels of the polity are morally and demographically concentric. The cyclostyled program of a meeting of Pom Mahakan and several other communities to discuss the strategies of emphasizing their role in the national culture laid out a clear goal: "It is to raise up [our] professions and the local knowledge of Pom Mahakan and of various [other] communities; it is to stage a meeting (*waethi*[17]) to exchange experiences and present our thoughts; it is to build up our connections and our being the *phi nawng* of poor people throughout the country."[18] The community is in this sense concentric with the larger polity in the bureaucratic sense as well; actions against it can be represented as attacks on the very essence of Thai culture. While its detractors point out that some residents are reasonably comfortable in economic terms and therefore undeserving of support, a degree of diversity—both cultural and economic—reinforces the community's image as a microcosm of the nation. To some extent, indeed, most Thai communities regarded as "slums" exhibit the same internal diversity as the nation in its entirety: "A community is a small model of social structure at large. There exist several groups of people according to their status. In slums, there are the rich amid the poor; there are the poorest of the poor."[19] But that is also a good description of the smallest unit, the family household.

Argument is encouraged, not always successfully, within the community. Exhortations to canvass a wide range of opinion were, despite the formulaic air with which they were delivered, neither purely ritualistic nor unique to this one community, although there were occasional grumblings from those who felt that the power brokers had everything their own way so that those outside the charmed circle "could not speak." Overall, however, the openness professed by the leadership did not seem to be mere rhetoric. Thawatchai, for example, insisted that I should meet with his severest critic, a man who consistently opposed every move the president made and eventually sought to reach a deal with the authorities, and demanded that I pay respectful attention to both sides of their dispute. He also expressed approval of my visiting with the bureaucrats who were leading the attack on

3   Appeasing the spirits' thirst

his community—and this from a man who was as adamant in his denunciations of injustices done to the community as he was of fellow residents who undermined the collective effort from within. The lawyer president of a nearby middle-class community similarly urged me to visit his predecessor and sworn nemesis at the latter's pig-stomach specialty restaurant, so that I would not take a one-sided view of their ongoing conflict.

Such openness is rare in the ethnographic literature on Thai slums. Most authors give greater emphasis to the prevalence of petty factionalism and self-interested power games.[20] Pom Mahakan has certainly not escaped some degree of factionalism despite its small size. A willingness to entertain dialogue with opposing interests, however, seems, at least in some of the Rattanakosin communities, to be an important dimension of the self-presentation of leadership. It lends a pragmatic cast to the pattern of oscillation between authoritarian and egalitarian models of governance, and explains the intense interest locals take in remaining connected with both major factions even while declaring their allegiance to one or the other. Thawatchai, an uncompromising royalist, took particular pride in the fact that supporters of the Red and Yellow Shirts, both represented in the community, never allowed their political differences to undermine the solidarity of Pom Mahakan. Taking sides, so the reasoning suggests, not only should be on an informed basis, but should always encompass the possibility of engaging with alternative viewpoints even though, for much of the time, that engagement remained largely at the level of hypothetical futures.

This openness contrasts dramatically with the frequent official refusals to treat with community members, as it does with the polarization that has increasingly poisoned Thai political life since before the 2006 coup against former prime minister Thaksin Shinawatra. Compromise was a professed goal of the residents, although their oft-reiterated mantra that "the community does not surrender" (*chumchon mai yawm*) established clear limits to that willingness. For the most part, municipal officials found themselves cast in a contrastive role as people who would not compromise at all—because they did not think they had to, and because, in particular, they thought that time was on their side and that the residents would eventually become weary of the struggle.

State Culture, Community Culture: Strategies of Reification

Despite their flexible vision of the polity and of the world of activism alike, the Pom Mahakan leaders also make use of the reified and stratified concepts of culture and society that characterize the bureaucratic nation-state. This is a strategic choice born of necessity; as they negotiate with "the administrative side" (*fai kahnpokkhrong*), a term that suggestively bridges the historical gap between the galactic polity and its more elaborately bureaucratic successor, they can appeal to powerful images that give them, as so many other communities, the appearance of being one version of a larger, transcendent model of social cohesion. By trying to preserve their physical space as a microcosm of Thai culture in general, they manage both to be loyal to the larger entity and, as Harvey's comments on space and time would lead us to expect, to push back at the centralized bureaucratic and commercial forces that want such challenges irrevocably cleansed from the capital.

The most visible signs of the residents' perspective are the omnipresent spirit shrines. A "big shrine" stands for the entire community; in the past, it was venerated on special days such as birthdays and was supposed to bring residents luck in their search for employment and happiness. No less than the huge shrines now erected in front of many of Bangkok's most phantasmagoric department stores and business towers, it imitated the grander architecture of famous temples, though it did so in terms necessarily dictated by the use of very humble materials and tiny financial and spatial resources. By the same (visually) segmentary logic, many of the shrines that the residents have erected next to their homes follow the same design principles, although some bear the evidence of particular ancestries (for example, traces of Chinese artistry). While shrines are usually erected to the spirits of particular ancestors (*bahnphaphurut*), the collective shrine indexes the most inclusive level of communal ancestry in the segmentary logic of the *moeang*.[21]

The same logic allows the residents to make use of the fact that the spirits commemorated in the individual house shrines are not, for the most part, those of their own ancestors, but rather of a past population that includes the original royal bureaucrats who first settled here; the shrines thus belong, they say, to all Thais. This perspective, enhanced as it is by such links to the royal foundation of the city, has enormous consequences for the residents' historical claims. Whereas the bureaucrats deride the residents as mostly not descended from the earlier inhabitants, the residents present themselves as guardians of a historically deep spiritual and national trust indexed and symbolized by the shrines. In the residents' logic, the fact that most of the spirits are not those of their own ancestors amplifies their claim to represent something greater than their tiny present-day community. Kinship morphs into domicile, which thereby becomes the moral basis of a territorial claim—a metonymic claim to sov-

CHAPTER TWO

ereignty, analogous to that of the nation itself. The community does, as we have seen, maintain a fictive claim on kinship as a "family" (*khrawpkhrua*). In Thai, however, this is a spatial and commensal entity rather than one conceived purely in terms of descent. The dominant image is thus, again, that of a small-scale model of the imagined nation.

A similarly metonymical thinking infuses the display of many other "traditional" cultural forms within a space already demarcated as part of the historic core of old Bangkok: a locally made, terra-cotta representation of a bearded ascetic's face, gilded and gaudy, hung on a sacred tree; ornamental wooden lamp holders decorating the corners of the community's meeting area in the cramped main square; wooden finials on a small house designated as the community museum in what an observer might construe as a parody of the nearby National Museum. Every respectful *wai*, a greeting made by pressing the hands pressed together at a height that marks the relative status of those exchanging the gesture, every careful introjection of formal modes of address and polite sentence endings, is a localized, personalized reproduction of this same Thainess, a reminder of the shared moral universe of all good citizens, in which—just as in the *phi nawng* relationship—hierarchical differences are encapsulated and acknowledged but do not contradict the transcendent commonality.[22] The armory of cultural artifacts and practices thus emergent in every waking moment of the residents is remarkably useful in promoting the idea that Pom Mahakan is a miniature model of the entire polity.

In that sense, the community has adopted the same logic as the Ancient City park (and of so many other, similar projects in other countries),[23] and has done so not only in terms of monumental buildings but also in the daily practices of living people. In a community like Pom Mahakan, however, such miniaturization and focalization do not only promote the encompassing national ideology. They also turn that ideology on its head by claiming to represent it in a peculiarly intense, concentrated, and pure form, so that any threat to these materializations of national craft and good manners becomes a disloyal and sacrilegious attack on the entire polity.[24]

In claiming its right to survive in situ, Pom Mahakan is thus able to make a constant appeal to the discourse of national heritage—not so much to the idea of heritage as such (the Thai term *moradok* has never held great appeal except as a policy term[25]) as to the idea of participating in a larger vision of the past, or history (*prawatisaht*), materialized as culture (*watthanatham*).[26] While the state appropriates culture for its own homogenizing and domesticating purposes, the people of Pom Mahakan have shown themselves to be remarkably skilled at re-adapting that national strategy for their own purposes. Moreover, they do so in ways that link images of Thai tradition and culture to a substrate of Thai political thought that contradicts the homogenizing, rationalizing logic of the nation-state and its purified version of Thai Buddhism as rejecting the veneration of spirits.

From the official perspective, the presence of the spirit shrines, which can be represented as materializing an ancient Thai tradition, has nothing to do with the religion that is a basic component of official Thai identity. From the perspective of the residents, however, it is the exterior manifestation of a collective identity that morally trumps the Western-inspired bureaucracy's notion of Thainess. In this sense, the residents have been able to reap some advantage from their unquestionably Thai ethnicity and from their command of the central Thai dialect that is also the official language of the state. Whereas official policy in Surin province has removed minority Khmer-speakers' performances of a musical genre from communion with the performers' ancestral spirits and reframed it as a folkloric production, as Alexandra Denes has shown, the people of Pom Mahakan reappropriate the official discourse of history and culture to represent the threatened destruction of their spirit shrines as an assault on the very essence of Thai culture.[27] Michael Rhum has argued in a related vein that the worship of spirits in northern Thailand conceals a reaction against central Thai hegemony; given that northerners see themselves as "people of the *moeang*," their implicit opposition to central Thai culture parallels that of Pom Mahakan to the centralized bureaucracy, albeit with the addition of a geographical and historical base of differentiation. In all three cases, the spirits are the repository of something that does not sit easily with the modernist, Western-patterned *prathaet*.

The Thai distinction between heritage and history should not suggest that in Thailand they are respectively representative of political factions at war with each other, as E. Valentine Daniel has persuasively claimed for the ethnic conflict in Sri Lanka.[28] Rather, it speaks to the greater flexibility of the local term for history than that used for heritage. *Prawatisaht*, history, is a word that—despite the resonance of its Sanskrit etymology—can be applied as much to local as to national history and that can consequently serve both the official and unifying narratives of the state and the segmentary logic of dissident communities like Pom Mahakan. While "local history" can also become a tool of exclusionary politics,[29] that same flexibility means that it can also be turned to the service of cultural diversity and of generosity toward outsiders without sacrificing any claims to national or religious exceptionalism. As we shall see, that claim—essentially, a noblesse oblige logic according to which being Thai demands tolerance toward cultural and religious others—is an important, flexible, and highly effective component of the strategy of self-representation on the part of the leaders of Pom Mahakan.

History thus conceptualized, then, is the fulcrum of the rhetoric in terms of which Pom Mahakan has chosen to make its pitch for recognition and survival. The community's claims to legitimacy rest not on bureaucratic recognition, which was withdrawn at the beginning of the present struggle, but on its aggressively proclaimed self-identification as a "historic community." The fact that almost none of the present residents are descended from the original inhabitants of the site does not devalue their claim as it might in a country where bloodlines were given greater emphasis. Rather, it is their assiduous cultivation of their identification with the site and its original residents that has made the label convincing to many Thais. Their strategy latches effortless onto the official ideology that motivates historic conservation at the level of the state in Thailand and in most other countries. The very concept of a historic center or historic city, like the idea of tradition, only became possible with the adoption of the largely Western-derived model of a linear progression toward modernity; historic monuments, too, are modern markers of reimagined pasts located, through a strategic space-time conversion, in strategic physical spaces.[30]

The model of conservation that animates the Rattanakosin City project exemplifies that pattern. If realized, it would virtually eliminate whole communities that do not fit the officially sanctioned ethnic Thai model. As Napong Rugkhapan has argued, for example, a substantial area inhabited mostly by people of Chinese origin and lying well beyond the confines of Rama I's wall was effectively locked out of consideration as historically significant.[31] By contrast, Pom Mahakan's claim on historic status, in response to its summary dismissal by many of the municipal bureaucrats, reproduces and embodies Thailand's modernist pursuit of monumentality in key respects, and its rhetoric often echoes the ethnic nationalism of the state.

Strategies for Claiming the Past

Other communities might be able to point to much more specific, kinship-based ties with the original inhabitants of the Rattanakosin area, but such claims do not in fact guarantee success. Appeals to a more generic history are in fact fairly common, and may well be more effective because they place a lien on the entire polity. At a seminar to discuss the social impact of changes in traffic regulation in Bangkok, convened in 2002 by the BMA and the United Nations Economic and Social Commission for Asia and the Pacific (ESCAP), for example, the representative of the Prawanrangsri community, which sits athwart Rachadamnoen Avenue not far from Pom Mahakan, declared that his community had come into being at the time of the original foundation of the Rattanakosin city area, and noted that it was "very important for us to conserve the buildings which of course have certain historic backgrounds and meanings for our community. And the community should lead the Thai ways of life—that is, our community should be a real lesson area for the Thais to reflect [on] the Thai ways of living." "Transnational companies," which would disrupt that lifestyle, were not, he emphasized, necessary for the local development of tourism.[32] No attempt to solve the community's problems would work if it did not emanate from the community itself, he added, because those who felt they had not been consulted would inevitably object to any decisions taken.[33]

This is the rhetoric we also meet in Pom Mahakan: the appeal to local culture, history, and way of life; the importance of community participation in any wider decision making; and above all the image of the community as a "lesson" (*bot rian*) in the virtues of the true Thai lifestyle—an image that was to become central to the community's self-projection when, for a brief while in 2004–5, it looked as though the BMA was changing its policy and would actually hail Pom Mahakan as a "place for exchanging knowledge about community history and culture."[34]

But Pom Mahakan has one special advantage: its location. It is spatially focalized on the single, dramatic presence of the citadel and situated on the tourist path to a canal docking station for longtail passenger boats and beside the access road to the Temple of the Golden Mount.[35] That richly symbolic setting made it easier for the public to visualize the community, enabling it to capitalize all the more effectively on both history and culture. The Pom Mahakan residents, like those of many communities fighting for survival, actualize culture in the present as "a local way of life" (*witthichiwit thong thin*).

Using this terminology, community rhetoric merges easily with the increasingly popular discourse of "cultural rights."[36] In one of their more polemical statements, issued in the April of 2003, the community leaders emphasized that the location of Pom Mahakan among so many palaces and temples meant that "the history of Rattanakosin also refers to the history of the people who have continually sustained life, generation after generation, in this very old place"—and added the inducement that this would be important for tourism. This was a clever move inasmuch as it capitalized precisely on the authorities' spectacular disregard for both

CHAPTER TWO

people and their vernacular culture, as many local observers have pointed out,[37] in favor of royal and religious monuments; it made the monuments themselves a reason to support the community's survival. Even in writing to the police to express their dismay at the prospect of being evicted in March 2003, the community leaders argued that the possession of a local way of life and of "local knowledge" demonstrated that they had a right to remain in place and that they were not squatters. The crafts and other traditional professions in the community "are coupled and connected with the community the whole time," they said, so that eviction would disrupt a peaceful settlement—and they were then also quick to remind the police that they had also enjoyed a close collaboration with the force's representatives in suppressing the use of drugs within the community.

When I first started working with the community in early 2003, its residents had already been embattled for eleven years, and their leaders were superbly practiced in the rhetoric of culture and history. They were also well practiced in the arts of negotiation, but the authorities essentially refused to accept that there was anything to negotiate and, as a result, each side was soon calling the other "obdurate." While the authorities saw them as "invading" (*bukruk*) a space intended as a shared recreational area for all Thais, they reciprocated with the accusation that, by muscling in on their community, the authorities were the true invaders.[38] Such reciprocations of the terminology of insult fit the residents' segmentary view of the polity and so gave the residents a rhetorical advantage in their struggle against bureaucrats whose favorite strategy was recourse to a literalistic invocation of the rule of law.

When the residents hurled the insults back at the authorities—often through meetings loudly projected onto the streets outside their community through the use of inefficient but extremely loud amplification—they were therefore acting in an idiom that was perfectly understandable to the larger Thai public. There is nothing "un-Thai" about such behavior except, perhaps, the open way in which it expresses anger. But if the official image of Thailand as "the land of smiles" does not stereotypically accommodate direct expressions of ire, such outbursts are again perfectly recognizable to the vast majority of Thais, whose experience of dealing with the official state has a painful history and who in reality are as able to express their anger in public as any other nation—as the fierce exchanges between the two main factions in the street demonstrations since 2009 have very dramatically demonstrated.[39]

On the surface, then, the claims that the "people of Pom" make to authentic Thainess appear largely consonant with the official ideology, even in the context of their political opposition to state and municipal power.

The reality, however, is more complex, and the basis of that complexity rests in the complementary opposition between the two very different models of political power, the segmentary and the centralized. Authority may today be vested in the country-as-nation-state (*prathaet*), as the panoply of coins, stamps, official pronouncements, and billboards proclaims over and over; but the intractably chimerical *moeang* provides ordinary people with the comforts of a familiar polity and the political adaptability of everyday techniques of survival. The symbol of Bangkok's municipal authority is the figure of the god Rama riding his elephant and thereby raised royally above subjects for whom height symbolizes power[40]; but when its bureaucrats, who are frequently accused of lofty high-handedness redolent of the old aristocracy and its claims to cosmologically ordained superiority, threaten to destroy local communities and their sacred objects and trees, ordinary people reject the bureaucrats' right to such attitudes and instead charge them with rejecting the fundamentally Thai and Buddhist virtues of compassion and respect. Such misdemeanors are not uniquely the prerogative of municipal bureaucrats, although they have certainly been guilty of their fair share; even modernizing monastics have been known to commit the same offenses.[41] But the city authorities, as guardians of the main symbols of royal power, often appear to transgress the terms of their responsibilities.

Citizens—and here the people of Pom Mahakan are no exception—make an explicit distinction between the institution and its staffers, much as they do between the institution of monarchy (here the appeal is implicitly to pre-*prathaet* forms of order combining power with renunciation) and those who invoke its authority for their own less noble ends.[42] Ordinary people do not necessarily expect bureaucrats to behave with honesty and kindness, and they have certainly seen a remarkable parade of venal politicians over the years. But Buddhist morality, even when (according to purists) it is misstated, provides a critical resource for asserting what are assumed to be traditional values. Western geopolitics demanded that Thailand become a *prathaet*, a nation-state, and internal politics sealed the compact. In everyday practice, however, few Thais abandon the familiar perspective of the *moeang*, with its intimations of the impermanence of power and wealth as well as of the relativity of political allegiance.

The word *moeang* is, as we have seen, sometimes translated as "city"; other terms, such as *nakhawn* (Malay *negara*, from Sanskrit *nagara*), seem to have been more explicitly tied to the idea of a powerful city, and live on in numerous place names.[43] Today, urban regeneration is often presented in the rhetoric of the "livable city," and activists speak and write of "urban development." The search for livable conditions was especially prominent as the theme of a huge NGO event, Big Bang Bangkok, which allegedly was attended by one thousand people. The event gave me my first opportunity to meet Apirak Kosayodhin, who, elected as Bangkok governor in August 2004, came to play an important role in the drama of Pom Mahakan that forms the central theme of this book.[44]

Even such relatively benign-sounding renditions of urban regeneration as the search for a "livable city" have a slightly ambiguous flavor for those who live at its symbolic core, since in the older image of the polity the dynastic center, although a space of intense ritual activity and monumental commemoration, was not necessarily, at least for those reasons, a radically different kind of place to live—more sacred, yes, but without the conceptual and physical barriers that modernist planners prefer to erect between places of worship and the messy commercial effluents of everyday life. Older photographic and other evidence shows such ongoing integration beyond any shadow of doubt. The new policies appeared to promise an abolition of social life in the name of making the city more livable, a misguided and self-contradictory idea that in Bangkok seems to have taken off in the aftermath of the popularly acclaimed restoration of the other surviving fort from the old city's original defensive walls, Pom Phra Sumaen, in 1999.[45] While that restoration, which also involved the forcible removal of some homeless people, opened up a vista of the Chao Phraya River and furnished a pleasant park for general use, official plans for Pom Mahakan, while perhaps a prelude to framing the Temple of the Golden Mount in a more dramatic isolation, would sacrifice a vibrant community to some abstract notion of the common good and permanently sever the social ties that currently still connect it to the several temples in its environs—ties that have not always lacked friction, to be sure, given that one of the temples once owned part of the community space and continues to exert some resistance to the residents' goals.

In contrast to the small communities that have always benefited to some extent from their proximity to Rachadamnoen Avenue, the much larger, peripheral slums were in far greater need of being made "livable." There, indeed, the situation is sometimes nothing short of desperate, and attempts to improve living conditions may, as long as they do not simply lead to gentrification or the destruction of entire quarters, offer some relief. At the core of the old city, however, the bureaucrats' rationale has less to do with alleviating distress than with satisfying the imperatives of a system of classifying functions and keeping them clearly demarcated on the ground—a classic aspect of modernism.[46] These projects have usually been addressed not to the improvement of living conditions (which is what the rhetoric of the livable city implies to residents) but to the spatial cleansing of a previously—and, to the bureaucratic sensibility, chaotically—mixed-use area. In short, the bureaucrats wanted to relocate slum dwellers away from the monumental center and send them either to apartments or to places "outside the city"—both solutions that the BMA bureaucrats have tried at different times to inflict on the residents of Pom Mahakan[47]—so that access to the monumental architecture could be undisturbed by the inconvenient presence of humanity.

For their part, the residents, who have a wily capacity to deflect official rhetoric into the channels of their own ambitions, can, quite reasonably, make the word *moeang* sound more as though it would more appropriately be translated as "polity,"[48] although in most cases the meaning was appropriately vague since, as I have just noted, the capital city is supposed to be the innermost core of a set of conceptually concentric entities, all of which are called by that name.

In the older idiom of Siamese (and more generally southeast Asian) urban life, the city was itself modeled on a cosmological image, that of the mandala, its center being the supposedly phallic "city pillar" that symbolized the generativity of the realm; encompassing territories were imagined as expansions of this basic schema. The city pillar was the point about which the polity expanded and, in times of retrenchment, contracted; the *moeang*, or moral community, transcended considerations of mere scale or of the fixed levels at which bureaucrats today operate the Western-derived model of the *prathaet*. Ironically, because *moeang* also means "city," it can be used to evoke an *absence* of communal solidarity, as when someone complains that in the city, "There's nobody who's willing to do work cooperatively!" Events at Pom Mahakan, however, repeatedly belie that pessimistic assessment.

At the level of practical politics, that logic allows residents to identify their collective cause with the national interest. During a confrontation with municipal officials, one man remarked, "Our problem was born of the *moeang*. It should be a livable *moeang* that can develop the homeland (*bahnmoeang*, literally the house/village *moeang*), so that our descendants will have land to live on in the future. So I ask now, right here, 'Are we Thai people or not? Are we Thai people or not? Are we brothers and sisters (*phi nawng*) Thai people or not *khrab*?'"

The language of this miniature speech, with its dramatically repetitive rhetoric, is intense with political implication. The nation is a "household" (*bahn*)—a home of villagers, *chaobahn*, as the residents call themselves; the *bahn*, as Marc Askew has noted in a very different context, is as sus-

CHAPTER TWO

ceptible of losing face as the individual because the individual's actions reflect on the group at every level of segmentation.[49] In this logic, too, a nation's territorial rights can be retroactively recast as those of a local group; they belong to a "homeland" (*bahnmoeang*) defined by the fictive kinship of siblinghood that also expresses the internal merging of hierarchy and equality (since age is a determinant of status but siblinghood also implies a transcendent equality of affect and value). Much of the political agility of the Pom Mahakan community lies in its leaders' capacity to move seamlessly between *moeang* and *prathaet*, as well as between these two key levels of the *moeang* model, utilizing language that glosses over the historical and practical differences between these conceptual poles of Thai political experience. Moreover, unlike the Lao-speaking villagers from the northeast who added the polite central Thai particle *khrab* to their Lao (Isan) speech during the negotiations that the Assembly of the Poor achieved with government officials in 1997,[50] the Pom Mahakan leaders, as residents of Bangkok, spoke the central Thai that is the official language of government and law. Their deft use of such linguistic markers and other attributes of formal politeness—the markers of "face"—reinforced their demand to be understood as equals and as fellow Thais, rather than as uncouth upstarts.

The distinction between the encompassing national *moeang* and the local community is productively evanescent, a conceptual Cheshire cat that fades in and out as it becomes more or less useful but never quite goes away—an ironic quality that is, indeed, a key element in its usefulness. At the same time, the distinction between the *moeang* and *prathaet* models is at least implicitly present at all times, and is sometimes rendered verbally palpable, in all the disputes between community leaders and the representatives of state and municipal power. The residents present themselves as the guardians of those spirits whose shrines they preserve and protect—in contrast to the bureaucrats, whose sacrilegious intention of destroying the shrines casts doubt on their right to be considered true members of the spiritual community of the Thai *moeang*. The lurking difference between the bureaucratic and the segmentary, often expressed in the rhetorical use of the term *moeang* as the ultimate form of shared identity, also plays out in the residents' management of history, which in turn is realized through a metonymic collapsing of the national territory into the tiny space of the community.

This play on scale operates at multiple levels of social and cultural identification. When the residents held their tree ordination ritual to raise funds for conservation, they were, in effect, snatching the initiative back from the national bureaucracy—a bureaucracy that, while it represents the *prathaet* in precisely such matters as historic conservation, cannot reject the encompassing *moeang* of which it worships the symbolic center, but that has suddenly been transposed onto the concentrated spatiality of Pom Mahakan. And that space is truly minuscule.

Those who view Pom Mahakan as a slum are, in Thai official parlance, focusing on its "crowded" (*ae ad*) condition. But foreign visitors do not see the dirt, desperation, and drugs that are normally associated with slums in Thailand and elsewhere. They see battered but beautiful wooden houses crammed with every kind of usable material, stoves cooking outside. They see a middle-aged woman dozing in her deckchair, as she has done for decades, across a spotlessly clean pathway, as nonchalant as the cats that share her narrow berth, her family busy around her producing food for sale on the street throughout the day. They see elegant old latticed windows and doorways dignified with faded varnish, some sporting Chinese lanterns and paper amulets in red and gold, others portraits of the Thai king. If they enter one of the houses, they find a lovingly preserved antique Chinese cupboard with multiple folding doors. They see a carefully maintained children's playground beside a huge and elegantly lettered notice asking for people to keep the place clean and tidy; they observe families eating quietly in their homes, sleeping on mattresses laid on the floor, or watching television. Occasionally they might encounter a group of residents enthusiastically twirling Hula Hoops—Nok, a young woman who had just recovered from a stroke; a tough youth with his bare chest covered with tattoos; Bun, the quiet community treasurer; and Nit, the friendly laundrywoman—all laughing cheerfully as they watch each other's highly variable success with the hoops while some of the children perform with verve. The visitors might exchange nods with sage old Auntie Mae as she sits watchfully on the pathway beside the old stone wall, nodding as she laconically engages her neighbors and passersby in desultory conversation, occasionally cooking some item in front of her house; she is a respected elder, but part of her standing, it turns out, stems from the fact that she is a faithful follower of the leadership group and adamant that those who are already in leadership positions have demonstrated their capacity and appetite and should stay on the job. They would meet the young woman who sits on a corner near Auntie Mae's watch post, hoping to sell some small food item to the occasional visitor and watching over the small children playing on the pathway.

These women are the guardians and promoters of the community's care for the shared, cramped space that defines its daily life. Everywhere the

CHAPTER TWO

visitors see evidence of the importance residents attach to keeping their minute houses as free of litter as the pathways. They may even be briefly surprised to note a separate area for smokers, who are asked to go down to the canal about two meters away from the nearest building rather than risk a conflagration among the wooden houses. In short, where the authorities see a disorderly disruption of their too-tidy plans for a monument they propose to depopulate entirely, sympathetic visitors instead see a strong sense of order, intensified as under a magnifying lens by the crowding that so offends the official eye. Under the stress of poverty, these shabby but dignified houses display remarkably few untidy or unswept patches, much as the community exhibits few moments of truly disruptive discord in the face of relentless official pressure.

Spatial arrangements are the accumulated expression of temporal patterns of aggregation as well as a response to the inflexible perimeter of wall and canal. The residents' adaptability is especially evident in the ways in which they represent many different kinds of time. Not only do they record the moments of struggle with photographic displays that have gradually spread over the walls of all but the most hidden crannies, but they demonstrate a flexible capacity to relate these locally important events to the linear historicism of the bureaucracy. The sequence of reigns by the kings of the present dynasty, used to date the "ancient houses," has provided one especially striking way of playing official discourse against its bureaucratic bearers; it anchors the action, rhetoric, and politics of community mobilization to a national narrative.

But that is just one dimension of the residents' skillful management of temporality. A wide range of bodily movements and gestures, and the rhythms of cooking, play, and fanning on hot and humid afternoons, both tranquillize and syncopate the relentless march of historical time, bending it to the needs and emergencies of every passing moment. Another dimension appears in the refashioning of origins, a piquant theme in Thai culture and one powerfully associated with the ancestral spirits whose shrines are now claimed as a collective heritage.[51] These spirits of long-dead inhabitants are as much under siege as the spirited living. The ancestors of the earlier inhabitants merge with those of the current residents, whose moral responsibility it is to care for their shrines. In response to the BMA's projects for removing the community, the residents objected on the grounds that their proposed new location would be "far distant from their original place where they have lived." Their "call," repeated in various forms at frequent intervals, was "to live on their original land (*khaw yu nai thi din doem*[52])"—a view that was contested by the BMA, which in 2009 specifically insisted, on strictly legal grounds, that the space was "land belonging to the BMA." The community's rhetoric recalls the formal term for "aboriginal" or "native" (*dang doem*), but it does not entail the exoticism of that label. Rather, it is a claim to having put down territorial roots as a community, the dissolution of which would cause enormous distress to the living and tear the spirits from the soil.

THREE

The State and the City

The Thai state is a complex amalgam of monarchy, faltering experiments in parliamentary democracy, a decidedly old-fashioned and (so some would claim) feudal bureaucracy, and a fractious and high-handed military. Police, army, central government, municipal administration, and political parties and movements pursue sometimes conflicting interests and engage in internal factional struggles even as they severally claim to represent the nation's interests. The multiplicity of sources of political authority enables the residents of Pom Mahakan to seek alliances with one powerful actor, such as the police, even as another acts against them—for example, the army when it removed the community's original public area and destroyed some of the houses to make way for the empty lawn that Kai, the chubby, cheerful displaced young wife of a Muslim resident and active leader of one of the five subsections of Pom Mahakan, described, with knowing irony, as "nature."

One State, Many Forces

Not only do different state institutions pull in different directions, but each is internally factionalized in ways that some see as reflecting splits within the cosmologically ordained power structure. The army and the police, which in 2014 came close to clashing with each other, represent two such fractured institutions; former prime minister Thaksin was a police officer, so that the police were assumed to be close to his sister's government at the time of the opposing Yellow

Shirt movement to "shut down Bangkok"; the army was thought likely to oppose police support for the government. Such associations, imaginary or real, feed conspiracy theorists' fantasies. Evidence, however, is lacking at best; for example, the police, who were relatively well-disposed to Pom Mahakan, do not appear to have had any influence over the Thaksin government's attitude to the community, which it clearly saw as a nuisance.

It is often claimed that even the palace, the highest symbolic authority, can do little to interfere in the actions of other governmental institutions—that indeed, under the rules of a constitutional monarchy, it cannot afford to do so. Critics, however, complain that this is an argument of convenience; it invokes the constitution, or the deaf ear of powerful bureaucrats, as a reason for nonintervention. Privately, members of the palace community may feel, as one sympathetic observer complained in 2003 when I sought some background on the Pom Mahakan case, that removing local communities can create dangerously deserted spaces in the name of protecting monuments. But sympathy does not, or, if one takes the palace's view, cannot lead to direct action.

The same observer was quite caustic about the partial destruction by the BMA of a famous market (Pahk Khlong Talahd), an act intended to impress the city's beauty on visitors to an Asia-Pacific Economic Cooperation (APEC) forum on 6 October 2003 by clearing away obstructions to a view of one of the city's most famous temples. This perspective echoes the criticism of planners' equally narrow vision in Pom Mahakan, where replacing a living presence with an empty park would allow drug dealers free play.[1] Thaksin's government also wanted to turn the Pahk Khlong market site into a national showcase for its vaunted "one district, one product" policy. His own Ministry of Culture was initially opposed to such destruction, but his views prevailed and the Ministry of the Interior later tried to evict many of its stallholders to make way for the proposed exhibition space.

A constant difficulty is that of persuading an order-obsessed bureaucracy that some forms of disorder are socially benign, and specifically, as the social critic Suchit Wongthes so nicely expressed it in a newspaper headline, that "a genuine Bangkok must have people, not just spirits, ghosts, and angels!"[2] It is the living who give presence to those spirits and ghosts in the "City of Angels" (*Krunghthaep*, the Thai name for Bangkok), as the Pom Mahakan community has always understood. Against the rigidity of bureaucratic administration, the living must struggle to secure social justice. The fractured official polity, moreover, must contend with its own forms of disorder. The overlapping and often competing areas of administrative power, inconsistencies in the legal frameworks, and the special interests to which each fragment of each institution is beholden all provide justifications for both inaction and arbitrary interventions. Sudden changes in political leadership, in particular, can produce equally sudden reevaluations of what it is expedient to destroy or preserve.

By examining a community that has dealt separately and in ingeniously varied ways with this complex morass, I have sought a doorway to the encompassing intimacies of the nation-state—which is not to say that the local community is simply a scale model of the nation-state, especially as its emphasis on the *moeang* that preceded the modern state changes the rules and meanings of scale. Few if any of the communities studied by anthropologists can be called "typical" of their encompassing national polities, but their peculiar circumstances often allow us to tease out aspects of those larger entities that are not so easily discerned in the everyday formalities of bureaucratic structure or electoral politics.

Beauty and the Bangkok Beast

Frequently emphasized in the rhetoric of the planners' pursuit of urban renewal is the uncritically universalizing concept of "beauty" (*khwahm suai ngahm*). A plan commissioned by the authorities claims, along with what have become commonplace statements about the importance of the site for the "history, archeology, art, and architecture of Rattanakosin City over a period of more than 200 years . . . so as to preserve the historic appearance and the connections and linkage between the past and the society of today," that its goal is to contribute to the beauty of the larger area of which it is part. These planners, whose proposal had won the first prize in the competition for tenders, proposed to achieve this noble aim by opening up a space with a broad, open view that would permit visitors to appreciate the important monuments of the area and would support tourism-related activities.[3] History, culture, tourism, society: these are all components of the language used by both sides to the conflict. But their respective usages reflect radically different understandings of what kinds of society and space are expected to emerge, and thus also of what kind of history and heritage would claim the visible mantle of Thai culture at the very core of old Bangkok. They also reflect mutually antithetical understandings of inside and outside: for the residents, it is the authorities who seek to invade their space, whereas a 1995 planning document—even though it mentions the presence of a living community—shows that for the authorities Pom Mahakan represents the exterior edge of a much larger cityscape, a structural vantage point rather than a human presence, from which visitors should be given the broadest possible panorama of old Bangkok.

Such an obviously subjective and culture-specific criterion as urban beauty deserves careful analysis in every context in which it occurs. Beautification is a mantra for modernist planners worldwide, but their conception of it has a specific, narrow history, mostly in Western schools of architecture and planning. It has a long history in Bangkok; early in the twentieth century the central street of the old royal city, Rachadamnoen Avenue, was conceived as both commercially and aesthetically a source of modernization in the European mode, shaded by trees that perhaps also anticipate attempts to render Bangkok's unyielding cement more hospitable and healthy.[4] Idealizing intentions notwithstanding, however, the effects of this kind of planning almost always fall hard on the poor, whose own ideas of beauty may not coincide with those of the affluent, Western-oriented classes from which the planners themselves are drawn.[5] The planners operate a vague concept of common good, curiously defined in terms of temples and palaces and the profit-making goals of tourism. While they do also argue for recreational space for a hard-pressed city, forcible and inadequately compensated eviction adds an intolerable burden of irony to such invocations of social welfare and development. It is precisely this hijacking of social ideals that Neil Smith excoriated in his demand that "urban renewal" be relabeled as "gentrification"—that is, as a forcible takeover by the privileged classes.[6]

Urban beautification thus reflects a class-based aesthetic, in Thailand as elsewhere. Just as middle-class Thais emphasize personal appearance as a mark of good character and background, with women in particular often parading recognizably Thai silks, they also expect their city to be attractive in a way that captures both some sense of Thainess and a Western-derived standard of aesthetic satisfaction and modernity. But the aggressive tough with tattoos over most of his upper body and a riot of amulets hanging from the neck—a common sight in poor communities—represents a vision of Thai masculinity that contrasts startlingly with the soft femininity more often paraded in the fashion magazines and at socialites' gatherings. The precariousness of slum dwellers' lives leads to the accentuation of aspects of Thainess very different from those of the rich and powerful, whose architectural tastes are also more directed toward an international aesthetic standard. Such differences both confirm and complicate the "regime of images" model by suggesting, perhaps, more of a "battle of images," in which appearances are important to all concerned, but in which all equally claim to represent the quintessence of Thai culture. Neverthe-

CHAPTER THREE

less, the planners' intention of building "a highly impressive pavilion" certainly belongs to the official aesthetic regime that Jackson describes.[7]

Given the history of Bangkok as the center of the self-modernizing Siamese polity, it is not surprising that the Thainess in question often appears to be shaped by Western models of national identity—a persistent tension in the country's cultural politics to the present day.[8] To most middle-class Thais, and therefore to the majority of the BMA officials, the very idea of a slum is anathema—something to be hidden from critical foreign eyes at all costs, and to be cleared away as efficiently as possible. That many slum dwellers have in fact resisted clearance and eviction with lasting success speaks volumes about both their determination and the internal divisions of the bureaucracy.[9]

The middle-class desire for an aesthetic redolent of a Western style of modernity is superficially shared by the residents of Pom Mahakan, as it is to some extent by all slum dwellers who see in improved appearances a chance to upgrade their social status in the city at large.[10] In that respect, they do not differ greatly from the Saigonese described by Erik Harms, who reports that even those displaced by the Vietnamese state's massive construction projects see no contradiction in praising the new amenities even as they lament their catastrophic impact on their own social life.[11] But they part company from both their Vietnamese counterparts and the official vision of beautification by refusing to see anything attractive in a space stripped of its human population and the daily life that goes with it. While their desire for modernity often seemed entirely bourgeois in origin—they envisaged future homes with comfortable Western-style furnishings—and their ideas of Thai architectural style displayed a high degree of conformism, they rejected any notion of urban beautification that was purely monumental and uninhabited by ordinary people. In short, they rejected the core principle of the beautification the planners wished to engineer. This, in turn, has led some residents to challenge the aesthetic itself. During one confrontation with city officials, the term *suai ngahm*, the usual term for "beautiful" in official discourse about urban regeneration, became the object of a fierce challenge by a feisty widow who was not prepared to acquiesce in the municipal bureaucracy's self-ascribed role as the arbiter of urban taste.

Despite its grounding in a city form that follows the pre-*prathaet* logic of the *moeang*,[12] the Rattanakosin Island Project is uncompromisingly an expression of the aspirations of the self-consciously modernizing, Western-influenced, crypto-colonial nation-state—a state, in other words, that pays for its nominally independent status (and for the creative subversion of Western models that this status sometimes permits in practice) by displaying adherence to colonially generated models of national identity.[13] One could even see the adoption and subsequent revision of the original mandala-like ground-plan as a deliberate act of conversion or assimilation, designed to suppress the fissile tendencies of the *moeang* concept whether these appeared as forms of local separatism or as the basis of demands for democratic rights and greater popular participation. Yet the logic of the nation-state is always and inevitably also segmentary, because it must incorporate the fruits of conquest and of cultural disparity even when the outward rhetoric is deeply nationalistic. Those who have argued for the restoration of the national name "Siam," for example, suggesting that it is not as ethnically exclusionary as "Thailand," perhaps overlook the implications that this reversion would have for the reconstitution of an imperial system in which minorities—and weaker groups more generally—were subjugated to centralized power in a system of vassalage.[14] The power of the ethnic majority remains untouched.

Thus it is with the organization of the city. It, too, expresses the bounded identity of the modern nation rather than the shifting allegiances of an earlier era. The Rattanakosin City Project is the seal that a cultural bureaucracy has placed on the oldest part of a city that, in its more modern districts, expresses modernity in more obvious form. Above all, it is a project designed to enhance and sustain the image of the monarchy, the historic link between models of essential Thainess and the desire to emulate the powerful colonial countries. Wandering along the congested sidewalks of Rachadamnoen Avenue, dodging lottery sellers' stalls and rogue motorbikes, one inevitably bears away from among the memories of such minor inconveniences a lingering impression of billboard overkill even further enhanced by rather temporary-looking mythical beasts in gold and other gaudy colors and by frequently changed portraits of the royal family down the central section. This sense is today further anchored by a museum dedicated entirely to the "Rattanakosin era"—the time that began even before this part of the city became the dynamic center of the emergent *prathaet* that was eventually nationalized as "Thailand."

The project emerged from a campaign launched by the military dictator Sarit Thanarat (prime minister, 1957–63) to refurbish the standing of the monarchy, weakened at that time by the internal dissension and disengagement that followed the abdication of Rama VII Prajadhipok, and to deploy its appeal in support of the prevailing Cold War ideology of unyielding anticommunism. Sarit's faction among the military—much like many of their colleagues in other states such as Greece, Iran, and Nepal—saw the institution of monarchy as a symbolic bulwark against the threat of communism, and excoriated communism as "un-Thai."[15]

CHAPTER THREE

Although Sarit's revival of Rama VI Vajiravudh's slogan—"Nation, Religion, King"—might have suggested a more "nativist" and thus ostensibly less Western-inflected ideology than Phibul's, as some have argued,[16] the staging of stylized Siamese-inflected ceremonies and the building of commemorative monuments served Western-directed interests very effectively. Foreign influence disguised as native tradition is symptomatic of the particular dynamics that place Thailand, along with the other countries just mentioned, firmly among the "crypto-colonial" nation-states, and it fits easily with the Thai state's ongoing and thoroughly modernist practice of establishing certain sites as historic monuments and cities.[17] It was not so much that Sarit's ideology was less foreign-inflected as that the inflection was structural rather than iconic. Thailand's proudly upheld national culture has long been subject to models and constraints dictated, sometimes in subtle ways, by European colonial powers as a condition of immunity from invasion. This is not to say that Thais did not invent any part of their culture—that would obviously be a ridiculous claim—but, rather, that cultural idioms were framed and reified in accordance with a model of culture-as-property that had taken form in Europe in the late eighteenth century.[18] The National Museum in Bangkok is a tribute, architecturally and in terms of its content, to that vision. It is a vision that also inflects self-conscious nationalism in everyday life; the forms of many of the spirit shrines at Pom Mahakan and of the Pavilion of the Community's Local Knowledge reproduce these visual stereotypes in humbler, simplified renditions, while other versions—in shop-fronts in Suvarnabhumi Airport, for example—project the same message of cultural homogeneity and tradition for foreign consumption.[19]

In thus creating a national culture, especially one with claims to modernity, the genesis of a new urbanity was clearly central. Capital cities are often constructed with a deliberate intention of focalizing the symbolic representation of national identity. In Bangkok, Western architects and planners have powerfully influenced both the monumental aesthetic and the larger design of the modern city and its incorporation of historical elements, thereby also shaping the ways in which "Thainess" is apprehended and inhabited by the population at large. The very notion of monumentality as a fixed site of memory is a Western conceit, as Françoise Choay has argued,[20] and its prevalence in the thinking of the Bangkok (and national Thai) authorities—as well as of their critics—is a fair indication of how the politics of design in Thailand continues to reflect a derivative conception of national identity. In considering possible parallels between European and Thai modalities of cultural management, Bangkok's premier historic conservation zone thus promises a window onto the ways in which the national imagination has been directed—one might almost say straitjacketed—through architecture and planning, and perhaps most of all through the monumental emphasis both of new building and of historic conservation and reconstruction.

A Geography of Political Ambiguity

In its most recent iteration, the refurbishing of Rattanakosin City formed a key part of the master plan of 2004. Of this plan, one Thai expert had this to say: "The master plan represents not only the latest attempt of Thai authorities to commodify monuments, sites and their settings in Rattanakosin precinct into [a] prime tourist attraction, but also the crisis of heritage conservation in Thailand."[21] It is not that the commentator in question objected to the creation of a glorious monument to Thai culture; to the contrary, the question is whether such a monstrously dehumanized plan represented that culture at all. One would not have to be a critic of the monarchy, it seems, to feel that something was deeply wrong with a plan that so clearly reflected both Western influence and commercial interests while ruthlessly removing the local people whose way of life gave the area its distinctive character. Such critiques anticipate and echo the complaints of the present-day residents themselves.

The project to refurbish Rattanakosin Island, as it is sometimes called because for some time it was encircled by canals, has indeed long been controversial. This is partly because, in their zeal to burnish the architectural image of a monarchic state at once supremely Thai and yet also thoroughly modern in a Western sense, the planners either ignored or sought to destroy the vernacular architecture that still existed in rich profusion and because they eventually hoped to expel most of the living population as well. Their authority, moreover, was vested in institutional structures that were exceedingly hard to defy; the royal committee appointed to oversee the plan was subsequently expanded, in two further stages, to become in its most recent version a body responsible for the preservation of "old towns" (*moeang kao*) throughout the entire kingdom. Like the archaeological services of countries like Greece and Israel, but with an independence of the Fine Arts Department that stemmed from its privileged position in the projection of the monarchy, the committee became a virtual state-within-a-state.[22]

More recently, however, it has collapsed into a surprising irrelevance, perhaps because it was too confident of being able to maintain its supremacy through a policy of silence and avoidance, and perhaps because,

CHAPTER THREE

as Nut Nonthasuti has observed, only one (extremely powerful) member remained in place while the rest of the committee's composition has been in a constant state of flux.[23] Today, according to one well-informed observer, it "refuses to meet with anybody" and in fact it is not clear that it ever now meets as a committee even on its own. If the achievement of a lofty distance was its goal, it clearly overplayed its hand; whereas it could have been a power in the land, today it has relatively little practical authority at all. Its approach, insofar as it has ever articulated one, lags considerably behind that of the Crown Property Bureau in terms of at least making a display of sensitivity to the well-being of the local population, and the continuing inaccessibility of its membership makes its decisions virtually immune to realistic debate or action on the part of that population. Its record of inaction, which has been striking even in a country where the avoidance of conflict is a familiar dimension of political struggle, led one knowledgeable commentator, an expatriate representative of a venerable scholarly institution located in Bangkok, to describe it to me as "disgraced." It has satisfied neither knowledgeable specialists in historic conservation nor social activists concerned about the possible destruction of social life in the area, and, despite the royal affiliations of its members and its genesis as a promoter of the royal image, now finds itself morally and pragmatically outflanked by the body most concerned with the practical management of royally owned real estate, the Crown Property Bureau.

The bureau, meanwhile, although alleged by some observers to be internally divided between opposing factions, appears overall to have progressively embraced the idea of historic conservation as a resource for inhabitants as well as landowners, developing projects through which residents can be temporarily housed elsewhere during the refurbishment of their homes and then permitted to return in exchange for guarantees that they will care for the property in exchange for the right to continue living there—exactly the arrangement that the Pom Mahakan community would like to achieve. Such projects have already advanced substantially in respect of the Chinese-style shophouses in the immediate vicinity of the Grand Palace, enhancing the area's attractiveness for foreign visitors through both the refurbished architecture and the services conveniently provided by many of the shops and restaurants. Not all residents are enchanted by the new versions of their houses, feeling that the comfortable sense of living in a well-worn space has somehow evaporated with the new elegance. Most, however, seem happy to have found a way to reconcile urban beautification with the option of staying in their old haunts under affordable conditions and with the prospect of enhanced revenues from tourism.[24] And it has at least spared them the destruction of their old homes to make way for the rampant construction that so often attends tourist development in Thailand, not to speak of the destruction of community life—a danger to which the people of Pom Mahakan are especially alert.[25]

The reconciliation between advocates of a more aggressive building policy and those who instead preferred to maintain the local population in improved circumstances reflects the emerging realization, already much further advanced in many other countries, that "historic houses" can enhance the value of the real estate on which they stand.[26] Such policies also help to maintain a population loyal to the political establishment in the vicinity of the Grand Palace—not an inconsiderable advantage, given the recent history of street demonstrations and other forms of unrest. Some problems persist and require adjustments; in particular, although local residents have been brought into a process of active participation, the rental increases have already proved too steep for some, and the result has been gentrification in the classic sense.[27] That said, the broad outline of the new policy offers a compromise that can be fine-tuned to slow or even reverse such demographic upheavals. Some elements within the BMA are gradually beginning to warm up to the policy, doubtless encouraged by the positive media publicity the Crown Property Bureau's initiatives have garnered. But the more die-hard BMA bureaucrats are reluctant to concede an inch.[28]

The central axis of Rattanakosin Island, Rachadamnoen Avenue, marks the substantive start to the transformation of the royal mandala-city into a European-style national capital—away from the *moeang* and toward the *prathaet*, away from moral concentricities and toward top-down surveillance. Its initial extent, known as Inner Rachadamnoen (*Rachadamnoen Nai*), connects the City Pillar, the old Grand Palace, and the sacred royal ground (Sanam Luang) with the rest of the city via Central and Outer Rachadamnoen Avenues (*Rachadamnoen Klang* and *Nawk*). The reorientation thus initiated occluded the sacred design in favor of the burgeoning modernity of the fast-growing capital—a modernity that, as Henry Delcore has astutely noted, is conceptually at ease with the idea that the city is the focus of royal power while overlaying the symbolism of that power, or imbuing it, with its own distinctive appurtenances of wealth and prestige.[29] Yet officialdom never quite gets away from the old imagery; government officials still pay their respects to the City Pillar, the regenerative core of the *moeang*, when they are about to initiate projects of national importance.

Today Rachadamnoen Avenue is also in many ways the prime point of display for all the paradoxes that the crypto-colonial condition engenders.

CHAPTER THREE

Intended as a grandiose celebration of monarchy from the start (its name means "The King's Walk" or "The King's Progress"[30]), it attracted a host of contrarian ideological constructions of varying degrees of prominence and permanence. Moreover, virtually every state authority has seen the avenue, rather than the City Pillar, as the center of the new political universe. If the City Pillar was the heart of the *moeang*, a term that appears in its Thai name (*lakh moeang*, which we could very roughly and circuitously translate as "the city's most basic principle and symbol"), Rachadamnoen Avenue soon became the core of the new *prathaet*.

That process was materialized in planning decisions. The partial dismantling of the walls and the removal of most of its citadels during the reigns of Rama V and Rama VI signaled a major reorientation that was both spatial and political, not only because the citadels no longer served a useful purpose[31] but also because the polity modeled by the capital city was itself changing. The close association of the Pom Mahakan community with one of the two remaining citadels perhaps helps to explain their success in, at least implicitly, invoking the *moeang* model as it battles with the authority of the newer polity. But traces of a more accommodating order also remain elsewhere along Rachadamnoen Avenue. If today the street is home to the state lottery, for example, the hordes of lottery sellers with their stalls right opposite the official headquarters precisely emblematize the Thai capacity for accommodating activities of which the moral leadership supposedly disapproves. We should not be surprised, then, to find that the avenue also accommodates widely divergent political presences.

In 1932, Rachadamnoen Avenue was widened to make space for the so-called Democracy Monument; some years later the military dictator, Marshal Phibul, confirmed (or, rather, expropriated) the original designation by Rama V of the now-enlarged street as the "Champs-Élysées of Asia," which had meanwhile been enhanced by the Democracy Monument as its nearest approximation to the Arc de Triomphe. The destruction of entire neighborhoods to make way for these grandiose dreams occasioned considerable resentment then, and anticipates much of what I will be describing here in more recent times. Indeed, the theme of re-creating the Champs-Élysées in Bangkok has resurfaced repeatedly under governments of supposedly very different character in the years since I began doing exploratory fieldwork in Bangkok in 2002. Georges-Eugène Haussmann's Parisian original was intended as a means of militarily controlling a restive populace—a history that was partly repeated in Mussolini's remodeling of central Rome, and that has had many imitators since.[32] Although the removal of the main campus of Thammasat University to a site far outside the Rattanakosin area (and indeed outside Bangkok itself) is officially justified as a necessary concession to expanding numbers and resources, the suspicion remains rife that it was at least partly inspired by the desire to remove the traditionally most activist student body from its historic location as a durable symbol of resistance to authoritarian rule.

For the military and political establishment, Rachadamnoen Avenue is thus the central axis of official control over the historic core of the city. It also marks the erasure of the old mandala-based city plan and the concept of the polity that it had enshrined: the Pom Mahakan citadel, a remnant of that older plan and polity, does not so much rise above the avenue as hold the awkward pose of a wounded but prestigious prisoner deprived of the trappings of a vanished glory, the sidewalk that separates it from the streaming traffic an obstacle course of huge steps that emphasize its dissociation from the modern city. For many Thais, moreover, the historical transformation brought about by the avenue's creation is overlain by a contemporary paradox that also perpetuates its attendant tensions: the avenue's significance is both a symbol of royal magnificence and a locus of protest. Here, perhaps more than anywhere else, hierarchy and egalitarianism are brought into a tense spatial fusion. There is surely a historical irony, for example, in the 2009 spectacle of an avenue so unambiguously designated as royal filled with red-shirted demonstrators calling, not, to be sure, for the abolition of the monarchy, but for the dismissal and punishment of politicians who have been among its most ardent supporters.

We should not forget, however, that even some of the most vehement critics of the establishment tended, until the popular protests that followed the fall of Thaksin put a virtual end to the practice, to demonstrate under the banner of their professed loyalty to the throne. The use of royal portraits in demonstrations, including those by the residents of Pom Mahakan, underscores a key difference between Thai political dynamics and those of, for example, the Western European nation-states. While most protests in Europe take place under party-political emblems and flags, all sides to any Thai dispute were likely to display royal portraits until quite recently, and were still actively doing so at the beginning of my fieldwork. It was certainly the strategy of the Assembly of the Poor, for which it apparently served as a way of seeking middle-class support by associating democratic social activism with the conservative values of nationalism and monarchy.[33] This has changed, perhaps irrevocably, with the Red Shirt protests; the change may signal a deeper disaffection than people dare to express verbally, and possibly also suggests a new middle-class wariness about becoming too closely identified with a monarchy whose future is sometimes quietly debated despite—or perhaps because of—the fiercely defensive and often unscrupulously exploited law against *lèse-majesté*.

CHAPTER THREE

The organization of Rachadamnoen Avenue also articulates spatially the key paradox of Thai political dynamics. Despite official plans to ensure its primary function as "a road that communicates the continuity of the history of the Chakri dynasty," a phrase that perhaps unconsciously suggests a parallel between the "king's walk" and the twin notion of cultural progress and physical progression implied by the verb *damnoen*, it remains visibly—to the chagrin of the establishment planners—a politically contested space.[34] Along the final stretch (Rachadamnoen Nai) lies the royal holy ground of Sanam Luang, part of the original, mandala-based city plan that reflected both the old segmentary polity and the symbolic center of the bureaucratic nation-state. Not far up Rachadamnoen Klang, across from the national lottery office and to one side, is a relatively modest monument erected to honor the victims of the democratic uprising of 14 October 1973. In the form of a stupa, its construction was initially the object of strenuous objections from the military; today it is not only a place of pilgrimage but the site of a cluster of small bookstores and very clearly a fixture in the political and urban landscape. Even this monument is ambiguous: although it represents the push for democracy, it also symbolizes the role of the king in forcing the leaders of both the military and the civilian factions of the time into exile, thereby clearing the way for a brief experiment in democratic governance, and its use of the Buddhist stupa form provided a protective cloak of legitimacy associated with the institutions of royalty.

Further up the street, in which much of the royal portraiture already mentioned seems to emphasize the bourgeois inclinations of the dynasty (such as the king's famous enjoyment of his favorite hobby, photography), the optimistically named Democracy Monument celebrates the military and bureaucratic coup that forced King Prajadhipok (Rama VII) to accept the imposition of a constitutional monarchy on 24 June 1932. Plans to substitute Prajadhipok's statue for the central segment of the monument have never materialized, perhaps because the military have themselves been ambivalent and divided about the proper role of the monarchy.[35] But at the upper end of that stretch, right next to Pom Mahakan, stands a museum dedicated to the life of that same King Prajadhipok, a building often overshadowed today by the vast portraits of the reigning royal family. This king was an ambivalent figure even in his own time; because he *was* a king, invoking his authority is a relatively safe haven for those who do not entirely sympathize with the military and bureaucratic vision of royalty today, and his abdication letter, invoking what the king saw as Thailand's destiny of becoming a democracy under a constitutional monarch, even afforded a sympathetic context and symbol for the students who rose in revolt against military rule in 1973.[36]

The paradoxes do not stop there. One of his most fervent living admirers (and a passionately democratic royal family member at that) has been a strong supporter of the rights of the Pom Mahakan community to resist a law of eminent domain enacted by King Prajadhipok himself. It was also King Prajadhipok who, while he abdicated because the military were no longer prepared to accept his absolute rule, had also insisted that royal legitimacy grew from the respect he showed for the people.[37] His latter-day admirer recalled this sentiment in 2013 in a private message to the incumbent BMA governor, a cousin descended in the same degree from Rama V, when that worthy seemed to be on the verge of ordering the Pom Mahakan community's eviction yet again—apparently, it later transpired, because the Ombudsman's Office had been pressuring him into doing so.

Was Prajadhipok an unsuccessful despot or a compassionate and caring monarch? The ambiguity of his historical legacy is yet another instance of the Thai polity's capacity for encompassing what seem to be extremes of hierarchy and egalitarianism (as well as uncertainty about the role of the military in both promoting and constraining the power of the throne, an issue that has resurfaced strongly after the 2014 coup). It is mirrored in the political face of Pom Mahakan, a community that appears to be fiercely egalitarian and fiercely royalist at one and the same time. Once again, we see here the maintenance of mutually reinforcing contradictions in accommodations that in many other political systems would be treated as unsustainable. In the Thai monarchy, they were often combined: "The monarch was of course the people's leader in battle; but he was also in peace-time their father whose advice was sought and expected in all matters . . . [and who] was . . . accessible to his people" but who "was also liable to be blamed by his filial subjects on occasions of national as well as personal calamities."[38] The presence of Prajadhipok in this story is hardly accidental; in many ways, his conflicted personality and ambiguous ideological role offer a model for understanding the community's equally conflicted balancing act. Architecturally, Rachadamnoen Avenue itself dramatically displays these contradictory dispositions.

The King Prajadhipok Museum stands right on the corner of Rachadamnoen Avenue where it splits from another major road, Lahn Luang; it is a modest building, originally designed by a Swiss architect and completed in 1906 for a Western-style clothing store during the reign of Rama V Chulalongkorn. It was subsequently used as a construction materials store and then as the headquarters of the national Public Works bureaucracy.

CHAPTER THREE

Ceded for use as a museum in 2001, the building is physically overshadowed by the Thai Airways International office tower, but the highly polished marble floor in front of the building and the neoclassical design of the facade frame a small space of calm amid the swirling traffic. That space was respected even during the noisy 2013 demonstrations by royalists demanding the downfall of Yingluck Shinawatra's government.

Close by, Pom Mahakan is another space of surprising tranquility. From most points within the community, the imposing golden stupa of the Temple of the Golden Mount seems to hang ethereally over the residents' lives. To the residents, the temple and the citadel itself are not simply marks on a map or historically interesting monuments. They delineate both the physical outer edges and the affective inner core of their collective being.

The architectural arrangements of Rachadamnoen Avenue are thus spatial, political, and personal, and they express both the intense association of Thailand both with its monarchy and with the possibilities and limits of political dissent. They are regarded as deeply and irrevocably Thai and, at the same time, strongly redolent of foreign influences, from the larger ecumene of Buddhist spatial cosmology to the strong impact of the colonial powers that once bordered Thailand and that still influence its political, cultural, and economic trajectory.

Subversive Respect

Such intersecting and overlapping architectonic introversions of paradox provide a framework for understanding the idiom of the Pom Mahakan community's struggle for survival and political legitimacy. That struggle can be characterized as an enduring strategy of subversive respect for central authority. At every stage in their struggle, the residents reiterate their deep attachment to the rule of law and to the institutions of monarchy and the Buddhist faith, but at the same time express their condemnation of their foes as traitors to the fundamental principles that they are supposed to sustain. One is never entirely sure whether and to what extent declarations of loyalty to the institutions of state can be read as potentially ironic, but such ambiguity neatly fits the Thai self-stereotype as a people much given to indirection.

More specifically, the constant harping on the failure of officials to live up to their high moral responsibilities is thus understood locally as being as stereotypically Thai as the ambiguous urban landscape that animates the residents' affective attachment to place. In terms of the segmentary logic of the *moeang*, moreover, it depends upon, and repeatedly reproduces, the community self-image as a "small body" within the entire polity—an important conceit when it comes to engaging the alliance of other communities with equally serious problems and an equally difficult relationship with official power. As such, this small, embattled community implicitly reflects the most intimate level of segmentary fission within the *moeang*, while explicitly it represents itself as a perfect reflection of the total nation (*prathaet*).

The double vision of Thai national identity lends particular force to the often-repeated declaration that "we are Thai people" (*rao pen khon thai*)—a perhaps unconscious echo of one of the leaders of the Assembly of the Poor,[39] and an unimpeachable declaration of loyalty to the nation. Their invocation of Thainess is not without its problematic side. By constantly harping on it, they risk framing themselves in conceptual opposition, not only to foreigners but also to the minorities of the border areas still denied full citizenship in the Thai state. At the same time, they challenge the right of haughty bureaucrats to deprive the residents of the right to live on the land of their collective choice. By decrying what they claim is the officials' un-Buddhist lack of compassion, they seem to accept the hegemonic implications of the Thai NGO culture, with its aura of a charity that reinforces dependency.[40]

The risks of sliding into dependency are far from imaginary, as residents are well aware, and spring from their tactic of aligning themselves with official and establishment interpretations of national culture. But they do have means of resisting the temptations of aligning themselves with the formal discourse and institutions of the state. By at once making a clear distinction between the state as an institution and its bureaucratic representatives on the one hand, and by representing themselves as virtual villagers on the other, they invoke a romantic ideal of rural and moral purity amid the polluting chaos of the city and its corrupt politics—while *also* invoking the equally idealized image of the Thai *moeang*, the symbolic urban core of what it means to say that they "are Thai people."[41] As both romantic villagers and upholders of ancient tradition, they aspire to reconstitute themselves as a "living museum"—a term that, significantly, is almost always rendered in English.

There has been some public support for the living museum model, especially from cultural crusader Suchit Wongthes. This public intellectual castigated the BMA for its narrow perspective and for its failure to realize that "Bangkok is not an 'island,' so it is also not 'Rattanakosin Island'; Bangkok is a great *city* (*moeang*) that has history as the successor of Sri Ayutthaya [the previous capital] and Thonburi [the original settlement on the far side of the river]; so Bangkok is a *historic city* that has both life

CHAPTER THREE

and spirit on both sides of the River Chao Phraya." Suchit argued that Pom Mahakan was an ideal site for a living museum, especially as it would attract the attention of tourists. Furthermore, the site would become part of a set of museums devoted specifically to Bangkok and showcasing aspects of Bangkok history and life.[42]

At first sight there might seem to be a contradiction between Suchit's enthusiasm for the idea of the city as symbolic center and the adulation of the rural that we find in the energetic traditionalism of the residents. Both they and their middle-class admirers have mined one of the oldest of European ideological conceits: the role of the poor, honest, traditional, and above all morally pure representative of the country in its double sense of nation and rural space.[43] The contradiction, however, is illusory. Another of the Pom Mahakan community's most ardent supporters used the occurrence of spirit shrines in combination with sacred trees—in a caption to a photograph showing one of the shrines leaning lopsidedly against a venerable trunk, a battered trace of corrugated iron roofing indicating the presence of someone's home well ensconced in the ensemble—to suggest "the inseparability of nature, belief, and way of life that one would not look for in a public park [such as the authorities envisage constructing on the site]."[44] Some of the shrines are old and picturesquely dilapidated, while the trees betray great age in their gnarled trunks and spreading roots. This evocative image—at once visual and conceptual—of a religious bond with nature at the heart of the polity clearly appeals to romantic middle-class sensibilities in crypto-colonial Thailand as much as it ever did in Victorian Europe.

The apparent contradiction between city life and rural style thus disappears when we consider what the idea of the city meant to the Siamese before the advent of Western influence—a notion that Suchit's usage retains. For him, the term *moeang* clearly does mean both "moral community" (as in the *moeang Phut*, meaning the Buddhist nation of the ethnic Thais) and "city"—but a city that represents not (at least primarily) the postmodern phantasmagoria of consumerist Bangkok today but the symbolic core of royal authority, transferred in succession from earlier reigns and sites. In this sense, it is well represented by northern Thais, who use it to denote people defined by their assumption of urban habits in contrast to the overwhelmingly rural non-Thai minority peoples.[45] The *moeang* is a moral community that in Bangkok is most fully represented by such urban villagers as the people of Pom Mahakan.

In another of several articles he penned to address the Pom Mahakan situation, Suchit makes his understanding of the *moeang* even clearer. Comparing the district (Phra Nakhawn) with its exact analog in the previous Siamese capital, Ayutthaya (complete with a dominant temple stupa rising above the fortified wall), and pointing out that both districts sported commoner dwellings on the outside of the city wall (in the case of Bangkok the earliest settlers were probably, he suggests, Khmer, Cham, Lao, and Mon people), he argues that since the other Bangkok fortress (Pom Phra Sumaen) has been stripped of any living community, Pom Mahakan should continue its historic mission of maintaining an older style of Siamese living culture. He allows that the changes at Pom Phra Sumaen have given the city an enjoyable place of recreation, and he also concedes that the western side of Pom Mahakan was probably never settled by commoners because it faced two of the most important royal palaces. Nonetheless, he argues, Pom Mahakan offers a unique opportunity to preserve a way of life that represents continuity between the old and new capitals—between, as it were, two instantiations of the *moeang*. It would be hard to imagine a clearer discovery in the modern confusion of Bangkok of its relationship with its segmentary predecessor, and implicitly also of the similar relationship between the now-vanished Pom Phra Sumaen community and the living one in Pom Mahakan.

Suchit does not need to mention Tambiah's adoption of the thesis that southeast Asian cities were typically modeled after the mandala. The idea would have been implicit for most of his readers. It is certainly strengthened, however, by the easy parallelism he draws between Ayutthaya and Bangkok and by the way he evokes the model of an infinitely reproducible city plan.[46] Indeed, the relationship between the Rattanakosin city plan and that of Ayutthaya materializes as urban space the logic of the *moeang* as an infinitely reproducible moral community.

Suchit's defense of Pom Mahakan is thus also, and not always implicitly, a critique of the bureaucratic state and its management of history. Significantly, he warmly welcomes the prospect that the local museums now envisaged for Bangkok, and potentially exemplified by Pom Mahakan, would go far beyond the narrow extent of the national-level Fine Arts Department's vision. For him, as for the community, the answers do not lie in Western-derived bureaucratic management, but in a lifestyle defined as quintessentially Thai. If this attracts Western tourists, so much the better; but that is a secondary (although economically valuable) effect of rediscovering a lost way of being that embodies the most fundamental of Thai cultural values.

In these and similar formulations, the romantic Western vision of an unsullied and exotic nature and the Siamese adulation of royal moral authority over the *moeang* converge in an easy symbiosis. In that comfortably hybrid discourse, the "city" (*moeang*) is not opposed to nature; it partakes of it, and, when that metonymy collapses, so too does the old Siamese order, ravaged by the forces of uncontrolled consumerism. Such ideas are popular in Thailand; the king's promotion of his ideal "sufficiency economy" is another iteration of the same basic rejection of excess and endorsement of a harmonious coexistence with the forces of nature.[47]

The Pom Mahakan leaders are fully aware of the purchase that such ideas have on the romantically inclined bourgeois imagination. They therefore constantly harp on their role in conserving "tradition" (*praphaeni*).[48] Against official attacks on their legitimacy, they are able to deploy an unnerving combination of this peasant image with a sophistication, acquired perforce during two decades and more of fighting for survival, in the management of the rhetoric of the *moeang*. They are in this sense an urban equivalent of the people of Laos, who have similarly exploited the Thai proclivity to see Laos as an older version of Thailand as a way of attracting the newly wealthy Thai tourist trade and to satisfy the demand for Lao silks.[49] The fact that many of the residents originated in the Lao-speaking northeast of the country perhaps adds a slight further sense of romantic exoticism to the community's image, although their presence is not an unusual feature in the demographic profile of the capital.

Royal Associations

It is perhaps worth pointing out that neither the plans for replacing the community with a park nor their own alternatives constitute examples of gentrification in the strict sense. While that concept has had a long history and has not always been applied with much precision, it always implies that the refurbishment of an old and dilapidated district entails the removal of a working-class population and its replacement by people of a wealthier class.[50] The authorities do not have the slightest wish to replace the community with other residents; indeed, their entire attitude, an echo of an older attitude more commonly associated with formal museums, is that people should not be living on a historic site at all. The residents, for their part, are not interested in refurbishing the site for the benefit of wealthier people who could afford to pay higher prices for the privilege of living there.

If gentrification is to be involved in any useful sense, one could perhaps speak of "self-gentrification," a phenomenon I have observed in a small town in Greece where the residents, economically poor but legally the owners of the houses in which they lived, after initially resisting the bureaucratic control of the historic conservation authorities, discovered that the resulting complex of elegant Renaissance dwellings had become a major tourist attraction. It was consequently making them relatively prosperous even as the country as a whole was heading into a major economic and social crisis that has resulted in massive unemployment and persistent social unrest.[51] The residents of Pom Mahakan speak of "self-development," which is a term that allows them to calibrate their experience to the dominant developmentalist ideology without forcing them to surrender to its dictates.[52] Whatever we choose to call the phenomenon they represent, however, they have undeniably adapted to their own purposes the aesthetics and social values of the bourgeoisie and the state it governs.

The residents' ability to deploy the bourgeois self-image of the Thai nation-state is also a clear mark of the persistence of Thailand's crypto-colonial relations with the rest of the world. Above all, however, it is a strategy that both serves their goals and, in the sense that perhaps they genuinely have little to lose by hanging tough, has some basis in experienced reality, especially as it has never prevented them from simultaneously exploiting the language of poor people's human rights. Their position is precisely that even though they are poor, they are true Thais and, as such, entitled to as much respect and consideration as their wealthier fellow citizens.

In one confrontation with city officials, a community leader intoned, "[We are] ready to demonstrate the energy of poor people. For that reason, it's pure energy. It's energy that has nothing to conceal." "Energy" (*phalang*) is a common term of the rhetoric of NGOs working to help poor communities. Although the word might more idiomatically be translated as "power," when used of ordinary people it sometimes stands in conceptual contrast to the "power" (*amnaht* or *paowoe*, the latter a rendition of the English word) of bureaucrats and politicians—the kind of power that does, in the popular view, have a great deal to conceal. Politicians seeking to present themselves as democratic and engaged, and thus as different from the old guard, have therefore also exploited the term *phalang*; for example, one of the candidates in the 2004 governorship election, Wutipong Phriebjariyawat, titled his campaign booklet "A Strategy for the BMA: Weaving the Energy of the People."[53] But such political maneuvers followed rather than led the NGO movement. In the well-established view of the Four Regions Slum Network,[54] for example, it was essential "to have the energy of the masses (*muan chon*) and political culture of ordinary people (*prachahchon*) involved in building negotiating power."[55] Shades, these, of the Assembly of the Poor—the massive mobilization of the 1990s—with its slogan announcing the "collective energy of the poor (*ruam phalang khon*

CHAPTER THREE

jon),"[56] a slogan that the network maintained on its own letterhead. This stance is reinforced by the claim, implicit in the statement that community power has "nothing to conceal," that only those with pretensions to power would be corrupt enough to avoid addressing the key issues directly.

This stance is in itself a direct and explicit challenge to aristocratic models of Thainess, with its aversion to direct speech—something on which the Pom Mahakan leaders openly pride themselves, and that they also practice in their public pronouncements and actions. This stance recalls the similar mode of entrenchment and negotiating from strength by so-called nail households in China, where compensation is similarly inadequate and the desire to remain in place equally powerful.[57] There is, of course, considerable risk in cultivating uncouthness, and so they balance it with impressive displays of political horse sense as well as compassion for those unfortunate enough not to share in the deep Thainess that they enjoy. Their assumption of a moral right to remain on such a symbolically important site is a physical, spatial claim on an identity that by definition, as they explicitly argue, also requires them to treat non-Thais and non-Buddhists with respect and affection.

Both sides to the conflict, the people of Pom Mahakan and the bureaucrats of the Bangkok municipal government, exhibit deep respect for the institutions of royalty. In practical terms they have virtually no alternatives, although their ways of displaying that devotion, and the purposes for which they do so, are significantly different. In that sense, the institution of monarchy is itself "refracted" through the conflict, acquiring different lineaments on each side but providing a shared discourse that both permits communication and, at the same time, blocks any leaning toward outright disaffection.[58] The settlement at Pom Mahakan, although technically outside the walls of the royal city, was born of royal initiative. Unlike much of the increasingly disaffected urban proletariat,[59] the residents do not forget their royal connections. Rama III Jessadabodindra (1824–51), whose nocturnally illuminated and magnificently enthroned statue—displacing, significantly, a popular theater[60]—adorns the temple complex across the road from the community, gave title to an area of about 7,500 square meters to two royal functionaries. Their settlement, which gradually began to attract other state bureaucrats and functionaries of a newly established royal temple, is generally taken to signal the beginnings of the present-day community. The middle third of the land was eventually turned over to the Rachanatdaram Temple, a glittering, gilded complex of impressively well-preserved buildings and tidy open spaces where Rama III's statue directly faces Rachadamnoen Avenue and sits at right angles to the old wall and the community. In the time of Rama V a few more houses were constructed, and from that base the community began to grow. The functionaries who lived on the site were responsible for keeping the temple in good shape, for gold smelting (perhaps a direct forerunner of the gold-smelting operation that until recently was still running on the site?), and for providing music for ritual events. Thus, by the beginning of the twentieth century, these bureaucrats had shaped the community, in the vicinity of which, moreover, artisans and merchants had plied their trades at least since the time of Rama II. Pom Mahakan was part of a vibrant, living city, its people a variegated community with deepening ties to the place.

In 1949, however, a different version of history caught up with the community. In that year, the Fine Arts Department declared the entire space to be an "ancient site" (*borahn sathahn*), a designation that recognized the historical significance of the buildings but did not acknowledge the role of the inhabitants in conserving the antiquities or keeping them in use. The designation thus effectively handed the site over to the planners of the Rattanakosin City Project, a venture in which the BMA was charged with the key executive role. In the 1990s, in preparation for turning the entire site to a new use as envisaged in the project, the BMA expropriated those segments of the land that were still in private hands, so that the temple and the BMA were now the sole proprietors. People continued to live on the whole area until the front part, which up to that point had served as the main gateway into the community, was cleared of houses and, in 2004, forcibly taken over by the BMA using army personnel to enforce their wishes.[61]

Royalty has continued to have an active association with the site, but is a conflicted association; the BMA is intent on executing a plan to honor Queen Sirikit, consort to the present king, by creating a recreational park that would bear her name, but the site's past history as a settlement of court functionaries strengthens the hand of those who argue that it should remain a site of residence. The residents know well that the real threat comes less from the various master plans that have formally mandated their removal than from the fact that the park intended to replace their homes is to be dedicated to the queen. As Lisa Kim Davis has argued, major events provide an incentive for mass evictions as cities are reorganized to celebrate those events and to perpetuate their memory.[62] When Governor Samak Sundaravej attempted to squelch the community by burying the garden it had created in place of a park by dumping truckloads of garbage on the newly planted areas, he was exploiting a moment of heightened international visibility just such as Davis's analysis would predict—the APEC meeting of world economic ministers in Bangkok. But

CHAPTER THREE

he miscalculated. The final, awful destruction of the garden only strengthened the residents' resolve to remain on the rest of their land.[63]

Their resistance drew sustenance from the fact that a more important event was part of a recurrent calendrical set, the conclusion of the queen's sixth twelve-year cycle in the Thai Buddhist birthday system. By celebrating such a cosmic event with exuberantly noisy displays of locally made fireworks, the residents effectively inoculated themselves against any suspicion of disloyalty to the crown and instead visibly identified one of their local specialties with a demonstration of their fealty, a stone's throw from the enormous portraits of the king and queen lined up along the central core of Rachadamnoen Avenue. Far from caving in to pressures to quit the site because it was to be used to honor royalty, as has happened elsewhere,[64] the residents of Pom Mahakan showed that they could perform that function in their own distinctive way.

Royal interest in Pom Mahakan has been demonstrated in part through the intermittent engagement of the neighboring Prajadhipok Museum with the community's desire to remain as a living museum. While such interest has been discreet, it has resulted on at least one occasion in direct contact between a member of the royal family and the community's leadership. The authorities cannot easily attack the legitimacy of these connections without serious imperiling their own good standing, so they largely ignore them and instead invoke their own highly visible commitment to celebrating the institutions of monarchy in their shaping of the cityscape. By rejecting the residents' carefully constructed garden as well as the spirit shrines and sacred trees and declaring such local marks of territorial control as irrelevant to their own grand schemes, they allowed themselves, ironically, to be drawn into the segmentary logic of the *moeang*. In that logic, the destruction of an enemy's sacred objects is a defense of one's own. By refusing to take the community's veneration of religion and monarchy seriously, they were not so much—at least in their own view—committing acts of sacrilege as they were posing a counterclaim backed by superior force and all the trappings of officialdom.

What had begun as a rationalization of the landscape under King Rama IV Mongkut, with the attendant destruction of sacred trees as unbefitting a modern religious place, now, in the residents' hands, became instead an attack on that very notion of a unified Thai culture that it had been the king's intention to promote. The BMA saw its actions as a logical extension of the modernist and developmentalist paradigm begun in the nineteenth century. To the residents, however, those actions were an affront against their community, and one that they could also represent as an affront against the Thai people and against the very institution that they were ostensibly intended to celebrate.

The residents' wily posture effectively paralyzed the more rigid mechanisms of the modernist bureaucracy. Their defiance of those mechanisms demonstrates the lingering, often concealed, but ultimately potent impact of a submerged political substrate on bureaucratic governance in the present. The spirits in those shrines, once the ancestors of particular households and families, took on the lineaments of a collective national ancestorship redolent of that earlier polity. The segmentary properties of the spirits and their shrines, not unlike those of holy images in some Christian societies, could be reversed to suggest an inclusive sense of divine protection that extended to the very edges of the nation.[65] In the next chapter, we will follow some of the events through which the residents reactivated the structure of the segmentary polity and so frustrated the mechanisms of its modernist successor, the constitutional state.

FOUR

Law, Courtesy, and the Tactics of Temporality

To understand the real effects of the tension between the opposing models of the polity, we must focus on the day-to-day details of the residents' management of their ongoing struggle with the representatives of the city bureaucracy. Here, the details of their rhetorical tactics, and especially of their handling of concepts of culture and history, become vitally important to understanding how they were able to stave off disaster for so many years. Above all, they have shown themselves to be adept at managing the implicit—at suggesting, through indirect hints in some cases and through explicit claims in others, the concentricity and convergence of their interests with the essence of Thainess. Their vision, moreover, is not confined to the abstractions of identity. Albeit in a very different modality from that of the Ancient City park, it represents their tiny space as a microcosm of the national territory, their struggle as a small-scale replay of the national struggle for sovereignty.

Contests over land ownership are thus central to their struggle. Legally, the entire currently inhabited area now belongs to the BMA. Unable to mount a successful legal challenge to that apparently ineluctable fact, the residents have chosen instead to stake a moral claim grounded in the segmentary logic of the *moeang* and in claims to represent the quintessence of Thai culture. While, at the time of writing, this has not resulted in a conclusive victory for the residents either, not only has it worked as a successful delaying tactic, but it has also engaged the sympathies of a wider Thai audience and thereby increased the long-term grounds for hope. The residents have made creative use of the Thai code of manners and have adroitly deployed aspects of the legal system, with all of its apparent rigidity, to gain tactical and moral advantage over the long haul.

Face and Friction

Part of the authorities' difficulty lies in the fact that different elements in the power structure have held different views on how to manage the situation. Like the residents themselves, moreover, they have generally regarded direct violence as a last resort. On 24 March, 2003, my wife and I arrived at the site with visiting colleagues Akhil Gupta and Purnima Mankekar in tow, to find a lively discussion with uniformed city officials in full swing. The officials had come to demand the dismantling of the placards and banners protesting the eviction that had sprouted all over the front area (the part then used for meetings) and along the wall on the public street side. These banners declared the residents' intention of staying put, but in the form of making claims about the site rather than through the direct threat of action: "For 200 years this place has had more than ten ancient wooden houses and big trees; now the BMA comes to evict and remove."

But the discussion was less acrimonious than one might have expected. For the moment, the most senior officer appeared to be principally concerned with the immediate goal of "making [the place] look good" (*hai du di*)—a frequent concern animating the "beautification" of the city as well as the protection of personal reputations (which for the officials, at least, might have been a concern of material implications). In the end, a compromise was reached; the residents were allowed for the time being to keep the placards and banners in place in their public space, while they moved quickly, under the officials' watchful eyes but also with the full involvement of the community leaders, to remove them from the street-side walls. The community president told the officials not to worry (thereby showing some empathy with the officials' own potential vulnerability), the officials thanked him courteously, and both sides expatiated on the virtues of cooperation.

Nevertheless, it was clear that the residents felt the desire for cooperation was in fact one-sided. When they remonstrated that they had attempted to work with the district officials, the BMA and army officers largely ignored them. Moreover, as one community leader pointed out, without the visible signage on the walls the residents' plight would never have been noticed by the larger population of Bangkok. By emphasizing the need to reduce tension, the residents were not so much surrendering to the demands of the city government as they were playing for time in a discourse that oscillated ingeniously between self-pity and recognition that the officials could easily find themselves in an awkward situation themselves if they failed to produce any action.

In allowing the officials not to lose face, moreover, the residents yielded not one iota of moral ground. The officials argued that the placards and banners should be removed because they were not "beautiful." Thawatchai, the community president, rose to the challenge, pointing out that some of the signage had been made by people from other communities: "Their message is a request that their opinion be exhibited." Here the logic of being "just a small body" within the polity plays out to the residents' advantage: the implication was that the authorities should not suppress a message that transcends the local and expresses a national desire. All the officials' spokesman could do in response was rather helplessly appeal to the residents' compassion for his own personal worries about being perceived as ineffective. He was able to get the residents to compromise, but, to achieve that outcome, he had to appeal to his personal situation—which the residents certainly must have understood as the harsh reality that lower bureaucrats perpetually faced in the hierarchical system in which they worked—rather than to the incontestable authority of the state, itself the source of his fear. In so risking a serious loss of face, he clearly conceded a moral victory to the residents, whose almost offhand management of the interaction proved more adaptable and at the same time less vulnerable than the officials' bureaucratic invocation of rules and norms.

One of the BMA officials tried to reverse the damage by demanding to know why the residents could not engage in the argument "with tranquility," to which Maew, a community leader distinguished equally for his political intransigence and for his quiet speaking manner, remarked that when he had requested a similarly peaceful engagement the city officials had ignored his request—so why should he offer them a tranquil discussion now? Faced with this reversal of his use of such an ideologically and morally laden term—a tactic at which many of the residents are masterly—one of the officials laughed uneasily, suddenly willing to question what he had just been insisting on—namely, that such matters of style were really important.

At this point, Thawatchai returned to the fray and reminded his already somewhat humiliated interlocutors that he had enjoyed a cordial collaboration with borough (*khet*) officials in the past and saw no reason to discontinue the practice. In effect he was offering them a choice: work with us, or expect us to create major headaches for you, since we have allies within your system and at multiple levels of inclusiveness—the segmentary *moeang* again, now shown to be lurking within the formal bureaucracy of the city. Moreover, he made it clear who was in charge locally: first making a semi-humorous gesture pointing to his eye and wondering aloud whether the placards were giving the visitors an eye abscess, he then immediately announced that in any case the whole affair was "not a big deal" (*mai pen rai*) as he had "already organized" (*prasahn laew*) the work of clearing up the external wall. After retreating frequently into a conversation on his mobile phone, he then smilingly gave a series of perfunctory and thus barely respectful *wai* greeting gestures to all the officials and, without waiting for a response, bustled off to organize the partial cleanup. His jerky, rapidly distributed *wai*, reminiscent of a teacher giving sweets to a group of children, contrasted strongly with his respectful obeisance to the elderly former palace policeman and with his affectionate softening of the same greeting toward me. In thus modifying the embodied model of hierarchical relations, he demonstrated the agency and mastery of practice through which egalitarian impulses reshape the inculcated cringe of respect—a cringe that even foreigners, perhaps unconsciously, often absorb.[1]

Clearly, so level a playing field was uncomfortable ground for bureaucrats accustomed to giving orders but not to recognizing the authority of local leaders operating outside the BMA's formal structures. Thawatchai's performance was pitch-perfect. He did rather perfunctorily beg the officials' pardon, so that no one could accuse him of not showing at least formal respect; it was then their turn to say that it was "no big deal" but, in a final twist, to add that the residents had to clear up the mess as it would not be suitable for municipal civil servants to do so—a desperate grasp at the shreds of an already badly reduced dignity. Having watched the community president clean up garbage, water flowers, and make decorations for the community meeting space, I have seen that he—although a staunch royalist—does not tolerate or reproduce the bureaucratic habit, which the Red Shirts have repeatedly pilloried,[2] of treating ordinary people as "commoners" (*phrai*) from whom they are entitled to abject respect.

By taking the moral high ground, the community leaders were able to turn the tables on the city officials. The officials' revenge, to be sure, was not long in coming, but it was not they who performed the closing scene of the act. Some ten months later, the army moved in and destroyed two rows of houses and the community's meeting space, placards and all, and so made way for the first installment of the disastrous lawn that had been key to the original plan. Here again, however, while the authorities no doubt hoped that such a violent irruption into the residents' lives would bring about immediate collapse, the residents instead regrouped and prepared to defend the remaining space to the bitter end.

An Archaeological Aesthetic?

Even before the two rows of houses were demolished, another military intervention had triggered a considerable scare. Army officers arrived to inspect the site, taking measurements under the watchful eye of a delegation from the Fine Arts Department. This understandably terrified some of the residents, who saw the army as a more ruthless and hostile force than the police, and who wondered what all the measuring they were doing really portended—whether the soldiers were actually spying out the land in anticipation of a sudden, violent invasion. A group of journalists also showed up, perhaps expecting dramatic developments. But little of any serious import happened on this occasion. One woman, an officer of the Fine Arts Department, at one point declared herself to be quite sympathetic to the residents' desire to become the guardians of the historic site; her view echoes the strong criticism of the BMA's policy by her office the previous year, to the effect that archaeologically it made more sense to perpetuate a well-populated space that would give a sense of the traders who in the early nineteenth century had probably crowded in on this same piece of land.[3]

She expressed a good deal of frustration that no one really knew what was going to happen to the site. For her, the most interesting outcome of the inspection would have been the possibility of "excavating in order to find scholarly evidence," perhaps some pottery or other materials that would show what the life of the site's earlier inhabitants had been like. As she announced, "This is a matter of the basic principles of historic conservation everywhere!" Her irritation at not knowing what was going to happen or when it would happen (and consequently, one may surmise, at realizing that the scientific goals of her department were being treated as a secondary concern by the other officials) was palpable; but the Fine Arts Department has little or no legal authority to impose its own policies, and there was nothing she could do to advance its interests. At the same time, her open frustration must also have contributed to the uncertainty that was gnawing at both the community and, because of the residents' refusal to back down from their demand to take responsibility for the site, the BMA. Thus, while it perhaps undermined both principals' determination to reach a resolution, it also reinforced their capacity to use time as a weapon against each other.

The most senior army official, who announced that he was from the army's development office (an ominous status for the residents), pointed out that the BMA "had not yet reached a resolution about who was going to do what." In other words, the appearance of this official delegation did not presage immediate eviction. Although he spoke in a friendly way, the term "development" (*phatthanah*) does not necessarily imply social welfare; indeed, the residents themselves had begun to articulate a public critique of the suffering to be expected from "the development [practices] of state functionaries."[4] The army officer's appearance therefore looked suspiciously like part of a longer-term process of wearing the community's resistance down by incremental degrees.

Indeed, he hinted at the possibility that some construction might be envisaged, remarking that his office could be involved in any kind of arrangement, but he emphasized that for the moment his job was simply to inspect the situation. Beyond admitting that the BMA was involved in the operation, the military personnel said very little about what they intended to do, limiting themselves to vague hints that they were involved in development work at the state level. Their presence seemed above all to presage the end of real dialogue with the BMA, leading one academic activist to declare himself disappointed because the chance for conversation had evaporated. Yet one of the military officials emphasized the importance of continuing to talk: "We must have a conversation with several parties." While the BMA officials did not really seem interested in dialogue as such, and used the trappings of polite discussion to reinforce their position, all parties realized that "conversation" was preferable to confrontation, and all used their commitment to this principle as a delaying tactic in hopes that the others would eventually let their guard down.

For the leading Fine Arts Department official, prevarication also made practical sense. Experienced in dealing with the disastrous impact of rapid development on the preservation of archaeological remains, she remarked (in a homily that could easily have been addressed to any group of archaeology students), "We could excavate, or we could leave it in its original state. For collecting materials from underground is a form of historic conservation. Equally, bringing them up [out of the ground] is an act of destruction![5] So we do very well know—surely you've thought about this?—that this business of bringing up [artifacts from the ground], come sun, come wind, that's the whole plan. . . . It's the normal situation of all kinds of ancient material. We know it's here; we've studied [the terrain]

CHAPTER FOUR

and know it's right here. That's already happened. One part of it's about destruction, because we fear the sun and the wind. . . . I'm not talking about just one thing. We've got to collect every kind of object in order to be able to say whether we should bring it up, whether we should collect it or not so we can put it in the museum, to be preserved from then on. It's all meticulous work. We can't answer back when we don't know anything." Such matters required calm deliberation, she remarked. Her stance, insofar as anyone really paid attention to it, suggested that the decision-making process was even more unpredictable and sluggish than it had been before.

The pause in operations that followed these encounters was transitory; the front area was taken over by a detachment of the army corps a few months later, on 15 January 2004, allegedly to facilitate access to the original jetty area of the Phahn Fah Bridge longtail boat stop, and two rows of houses were then demolished.[6] But for the moment both principals—the community and the BMA—enjoyed a brief respite. Curiously, given all the talk about preserving the historic site, the delay did not visibly advance the Fine Arts Department's interests one iota. In any case, even had excavation been an immediate possibility, that did not automatically mean that it would be necessary to demolish the majority of the residents' houses; the Fine Arts official certainly seemed to think that such measures were unnecessary and perhaps even wrongheaded. While both of the principal parties looked to the Fine Arts officials as a potential source of legitimation for their respective positions, all three colluded in their shared prevarication.

Time, in short, was in plentiful supply. This was partly a result of the circumstances, but partly also an aspect of the residents' ability to take a cosmologically long-term view. In a community where one man, the eloquent Maew, could without embarrassment ask Uncle Phim, whose body was visibly shrinking from cancer, "Are you afraid of dying?" and was given the serene affirmation, "I'm not afraid of dying," the authorities repeatedly failed to create either panic or fatalistic resignation. The resignation was there—but to the march of mortality, not to an inevitable victory of the equally mortal bureaucrats. During one confrontation between the residents and BMA officials, an elderly woman commented with wicked irony on the current plan to evict and redesign the space, "If it's twenty years off, it doesn't matter, I'll be dead already. So go ahead and have everyone gradually help each other think and act"—blissfully ignoring the fact that the bureaucrats had come to tell the residents that they and their houses had no long-term future at all on the site.

I will return below to the issue of time and the opposing forces that pit the legalistic chronology of calendric time against rhythms and tempi—in other words, against creative, playful, and manipulative disruptions of a time that can be measured in formal terms. Calendric time has become so much a part of our own common sense that it would be useful, first, to examine the ways in which the uses of law sometimes disrupt its attachment to that taken-for-granted temporality that buttresses the letter of the law but crumbles in the breach of its spirit.[7]

Eminent Domain or Immanent Belonging?

First, however, we must see what resources the law brings to these conflicts, and what objections the residents raised. Beneath all the legalisms that we are about to examine, the two sides differ on one simple issue: the community claims a collective identity as heirs to the long history of settlement on the site, while the BMA disaggregates that sense of collective identity into a set of individual histories that represent much weaker, or even nonexistent, legal claims to the land. The BMA also invokes the compensation many residents have accepted under the rules of eminent domain to argue that this fact alone makes them squatters.

As we have already seen, the original settlement occurred through an act of royal dispensation. Gradually, however, even while title still remained in the hands of many of the original families, most of the other relatively privileged families moved away to more comfortable or modern quarters, and a steadily increasing proportion of those who replaced them were either renters or casual new residents without title. This had not generated much concern until the moment at which, in 1959, the government decreed that the site was to be included in the overall refurbishing of Rattanakosin Island, not as an architectural monument—vernacular architecture had no place in the official scheme—but as a public park. The entire complex of houses was to be swept away. At that juncture, the question of title suddenly acquired paramount importance. But what kind of title was involved—a legal document or a moral claim?

As a bureaucratic institution representing a subdivision of the nation-state, the BMA based its arguments on a paper trail and on the absence of documentation on the community's side. The community, by contrast, appealed to concepts of collective cultural inheritance as well as to the evidence that they had already demonstrated their attachment to, and care for, an important site that also happened to be of great national historical importance. The official focus on the letter of the law sometimes gave the residents a huge moral advantage, since they, rather than the officials, seemed to care more about what the site meant for the people of Bangkok and indeed of Thailand.

CHAPTER FOUR

The residents also proved to be tough negotiators. Despite official attempts to reach what the BMA presented as a negotiated settlement with the residents, the owners of 21 plots (slightly under a third of the total) saw the BMA's position as intransigent and refused to yield. Still nothing much happened until 1978, when a more determined attempt was made to move matters forward, using a master plan that made Pom Mahakan integral to the government's plan of restoring the whole area as a special historical zone, with Pom Mahakan specifically designated as a place for the "people" (*prachahchon*) to use for leisure and relaxation.[8] In this formula, characteristically, respect for royalty and the ideals of public benefit are fused in both rhetoric and policy.[9] To achieve the stated goal, the BMA exercised eminent domain and demanded that the residents accept compulsory expropriation with some compensation to enable them to relocate (*waen khoen*).

Although some did accept money under this deal, the terms were ungenerous at best. The residents would only receive a quarter of the assessed amount in the first instance; they would receive the remaining 75 percent only after their homes had been demolished. A document I was able to see at the site recalled that the entire community was threatened with deportation by truck if they did not accept those terms within three days. The residents, although reluctant to flout the law, remained deeply unhappy about the prospect of moving away from what they had become used to calling their place of origin. Various alternative sites were mooted, but none offered much satisfaction; one involved high-rise buildings that would have disrupted the social interactions to which residents had become accustomed, while another would have removed them to Minburi, about thirty-five kilometers outside the city, where not only the infrastructure would have meant little schooling or medical support but where the new arrivals—most of them street vendors—would have had difficulty establishing a clientele and might have had difficulty coming to terms with the local toughs who allegedly controlled the commercial street activity. So although many of the residents initially accepted the bad deal and received the first installment of the payment, and although most of these residents were prepared to accept the additional 75 percent in anticipation of rebuilding their community in Minburi, in the end, after inspecting the proposed site in 1997 and seeing its deficiencies for themselves, they offered to return the original payment and collectively decided to resist. A BMA official told me that the authorities had hoped to help the entire group build a "permanent" community in their new setting exactly "as they were before" and were prepared to help in any way they could. But, at least at the time, the people of Pom Mahakan were unconvinced; they preferred to keep their existing houses intact instead of chasing what they increasingly suspected was a mirage.

The BMA had already exerted more or less continual, incremental doses of pressure—as, for example, when, with only a few days' notice, they announced that on 9 July 2001 they would remove all buildings, equipment, and other movable property associated with the raising and selling of animals as part of the eminent domain agreement that would lead to the creation of a public park, and ordered the residents to take their personal property away. The residents, now legally outlaws and squatters, coalesced around an emergent stance of civil disobedience.

The peremptory language of the official notice seemed to offer no alternative options, no possibility of compromise. The intention to "clean up and refurbish" the space had by then already become a mantra of official intransigence,[10] signifying, through the rhetoric of visual purity with its components of beautification and order, the undeflectable intention to proceed to the removal of all forms of habitation from a space designated as a public park. The threat is quite explicit in the notice served on the community: "We therefore request of all proprietors and users of such built installations to remove their property, effects, and accessories from the said area in order to assist in the convenience of the functionaries who will be carrying out the work, and we further inform you that any interference with the work of the functionaries of the BMA will result in prosecution according to law, which may lead to punishment by imprisonment not in excess of one month or a fine not in excess of 6,000 baht, or a combination of confinement and a fine." Some nine months later, a meeting in the prime minister's office resulted in a statement that reiterated the same determination to remove all traces of habitation from the site.

These incremental pressures resulted in minor disturbances of community life and in increasing the sense of fear, but the only effect they had on the will of most residents was to solidify their resolve not to move. Despite repeated legal attempts to proceed to the eviction of the entire community and the destruction of all the houses, and despite the payment of the first round of compensation, most residents decided to hang tough. But they did not give up on legal approaches; indeed, they have been meticulous about adhering to legal requirements in all other respects, attempting to portray the BMA by contrast as the offender against both constitutional law and the laws of Buddhist morality.

Meanwhile, they began mounting protests. The first time I encountered the community, a group of residents was demonstrating for their cause in an area—Banglamphu—in which middle-class activists had already chalked up significant achievements in their effort to bring various improvements to their residential area. The next time I encountered the people of Pom Mahakan, by contrast, it was to be at the protest on their own territory—the protest I described in the first chapter. By then, they had begun to build their identity as tough defenders of their right to live on the land where they had put down roots, and were fighting in the media and through all available administrative and legal channels.

In that spirit, the residents showed both resilience and legal acumen. Told again on 24 January 2003 that they would "urgently" have to leave within one month so that the important work of cleaning up and refurbishing the site could begin immediately,[11] they fought back and gained another month's stay; in March, the BMA again announced—and again with the usual thirty-day advance notice—that the eviction would proceed on 22 April. A National Human Rights Commission intervention on the community's behalf was referred to the prime minister's office in the March of 2003, but Thaksin's attitude to those representing human rights in Thailand was notoriously cavalier and the governor of that time, Samak Sundaravej, was to become his ideological successor in the prime minister's office.

The residents, undeterred by the powerful alliance ranged against them, promptly sued the BMA and Governor Samak in the Central Administrative Court. Because of the complexity of the case, which involved many different potential owners and renters, on 17 March the court asked both sides to provide additional documentation, with the stipulation that nothing would be accepted after a further seven days. The court then did initially issue a stay of eviction at the last moment, on 21 April. The BMA, as skilled as the residents at playing a waiting game, had apparently already quietly once again postponed the eviction date. The day after the stay of eviction was announced, the BMA also applied very public pressure. The deputy city clerk sternly assured the press that no further delays would be tolerated, and announced that the planners of the Department of Works had already done their work on Phase One—the reconstruction of the front area—with a budget of some ten million baht already earmarked for the work, while funds for Phase Two—demolishing the remaining houses and extending the park to the rest of the site—were to be sought for the following year.[12]

The residents had taken their own countermeasures against eviction. These measures were symbolic, but they were also potently political in the sense I have been describing throughout this book. Invoking cosmology to reframe the legal temporality of the deadline, they invited some monks to make merit offerings to the site's ancestral spirits—a move that once again symbolically fused the local with the spiritual ecumene.[13] There was no contradiction between this symbolic move and the legal perspective of the community, which responded to the legalism of the bureaucrats with a vague invocation of "the constitution"; it was not always clear whether the then-current "People Constitution" of 1997 was explicitly intended, but of all Thailand's many constitutions the 1997 charter probably offered the most useful conceptual resources. Given the generically assumed constitutional guarantee of the right to housing, the BMA would have to prove that it could offer a viable alternative before it could evict. This did not mean, to be sure, that even a decent offer would by now have resulted in a willing departure by the residents; the majority seemed determined to stay. But they would in any case have preferred legality to a fight to the bitter end; it would have been more consistent with their principle of representing their cause as just in every sense.

In the event, the optimistic view that constitutional rights and the historical arguments put forward by expert witnesses would prevail over formal legal arrangements proved illusory and short-lived. On 30 June 2004, the Administrative Court made its ruling. Maew, on the way to the court, held forth about local society's capacity to resolve its differences with the "state's side" (*pak rat*), arguing that the residents would be happy to negotiate with the state but that its functionaries simply would not engage with them; the residents therefore had no alternative but to stand firm. At the court, after what seemed to be an entirely formal procedure that I was able to attend, the court found against all the plaintiffs, individually on the grounds that none of the owners could produce written documentation to support their claims to ownership, and collectively because the process of eminent domain had already been approved and financial compensation accepted. While the 1928 act, especially as modified under the Expropriation Act of 1987 and the Constitution of 1997, does require that fair compensation be paid to those who are displaced by the exercise of eminent domain, the judges were evidently less interested in criteria of fairness that would recognize social as well as financial hardship than they were in enforcing a legally correct (or at least literal) interpretation. In particular, they upheld the principle that the rules of eminent domain did not permit the construction of a public park that contained any kind of residence. In this way they used a legal nicety to discredit the idea, one of the key elements of the residents' vision, that Pom Mahakan could become a "living museum." The outlook seemed dire.

Law and Land Sharing

Law remains a central issue. In one document circulated among its supporters and dated 4 October 2004, the Four Regions Slum Network declared that in the approximately two thousand slum communities in Thailand the largest and most urgent problem was that of secure housing, surpassing in significance even the lack of economic and educational opportunity for slum dwellers and their offspring, and that the BMA policy of invoking the laws of eminent domain to raze entire communities with the goal of enabling street widening, sewage improvement, and other enhancements, especially in the absence of any kind of cooperation or negotiation with those most directly affected, simply created an increasing homeless population while violating constitutional rights. The network's support for Pom Mahakan was thus entirely consistent—consistent, that is, with its larger goal of exposing the real-life effects of a *lack* of consistency in the legal system.

Similar clashes of principle occur all the time in Thai legal proceedings, and, as the Four Regions Slum Network keeps pointing out, they almost always work against the interests of poor claimants. They favor the authorities both because civil servants are able to impose their own interpretations in specific situations and because new laws do not necessarily supersede older ones. Thus, for example, recent constitutions have recognized the right to "dignity" and by extension to a living space, and in 2010 the central government promulgated a Regulation on Community Land Deeds that "allows a community to live on a particular piece of public land under the condition that the community looks after such land and does not expand the occupied areas."[14] Because a deed so constructed would ascribe ownership to a collectivity rather than to any individuals, this device ought to offer a solution to situations such as that of Pom Mahakan. But, as the legal scholar Khemthong Tongsakulrungruang has pointed out, as a government edict this law cannot supersede others enacted in parliament or by royal decree, and a cynic might argue that the government of the time was deliberately creating a smokescreen in order to disguise the various kinds of land grab that have been more typical of disaster situations in Thailand, or at least as a way of ducking responsibility for failing to reverse the sweeping tide of expropriation.[15]

Activists' response to such legalism is to argue that it is the law that needs fixing, not the intransigence of people who understandably do not wish to be uprooted. In their view, the issue is not that of how to force communities into submission, but how to rewrite the law so that it treats the poor with dignity and ceases to clash with the constitutional concerns that animate much of the critique by human rights activists. The Regulation on Community Land Deeds seems to be a case in point. If it was a genuine attempt to address the poor communities' grievances, it has not offered much hope.

It is easy to see why this is the case. There were already too many precedents that demonstrated how the formal letter of the expropriation and compensation laws, perhaps reinforced in the background by the political pressures of administrators desirous of enhancing their credentials by bringing the royal park into being, would always trump more generic concerns under the present system. One pertinent example, some six years before the regulation was promulgated, is the Pom Mahakan community's defeat at the Administrative Court, a naked demonstration of its vulnerability. The residents' disappointment was certainly palpable, but they claimed to be unsurprised. Their lawyers—one a professional lawyer performing the task as a merit-making equivalent of pro bono work, the other the younger brother of a community leader—immediately set to work to explore the potential for appeal, although this attempt, too, proved unsuccessful. The leaders intensified their public relations efforts, laying particular emphasis on their cultural rhetoric as a defense against the refusal by literal-minded judges to consider their moral claims on the space.

Technically, however, the BMA is on firm ground as long as it stays within the strict interpretation of the specific laws of eminent domain and the creation of the Rattanakosin City Project. The courts are extremely formal in their interpretations, and their judgments tend to focus on specific issues that can be resolved in relation to such particular forms of regulation. The activist Somsook Boonyabancha, in a letter of 12 March 2003, suggested that a government budget intended to relieve the housing needs of the poor should be deployed in an economically efficient move to solve the residents' difficulties by adopting the land-sharing scheme. The scheme hardly made exorbitant demands; it would have left over two-thirds of the land area for the park. But on 10 June 2003 the BMA, in the person of Governor Samak, bluntly rejected Pom Mahakan's request to discuss a land-sharing plan on the grounds that the budget already approved by the government for the year had allocated funds for the conversion of the space into a public park.[16] In this way, a budget, which is supposed to be an estimate, became instead a command, superseding another budget that had not specifically been earmarked for the Pom Mahakan case.

On that same June day, the National Human Rights Commission, which (as Somsook had already mentioned in her missive) was supposed to deliberate on the situation before any action could proceed, sent a stern letter to the prime minister's office, pointing out that one of its functions was to recommend adaptations of existing law. That intervention was no more effective on the surface than its previous attempt to help the community; it may nevertheless have served a minatory purpose and thereby

CHAPTER FOUR

contributed to the continuing stalemate. The BMA ignored the commission's protest and continued to maintain its own familiar position of legalistic rigidity. Samak may well have feared the risk of precedent, since the land-sharing model—with its implications that slum communities are operating from a position of moral generosity—would have opened up a swath of disputes to the same mode of resolution, especially as the Four Regions Slum Network, which was advising Pom Mahakan, had made this a central plank of its citywide operations (notably in the notorious harborside slums of Khlong Thoey). The network was especially concerned to amend the law so that the newly constructed homes of the slum dwellers could be retrospectively legalized. This a common device in some other countries, notably Italy; in Thailand, the usual way of talking about it (*kae kodmai*, "fix the law") clearly recognizes that the law is—at least morally and perhaps also logically—deficient and in need of remedial intervention.[17]

Struggles Over Legitimacy

The bureaucrats' attempts to delegitimize the Pom Mahakan community took a number of forms. The city clerk's injunction to me to avoid the community was an instructive instance; she had initially encouraged me to pursue my research on the uses of history in the Rattanakosin Island area, but that I should be positively interested in Pom Mahakan, a community she was trying hard to discredit, was too bitter a pill for her to swallow. For their part, the residents were indignant that she so easily slandered a community she had never troubled to visit; they saw her avoidance as willful ignorance reinforced by pure snobbery.

The systematic denial of legitimacy, with its legal basis in the original decision to evict the residents, took several forms. Some in the BMA administration worried that the gradual demographic expansion of the community would make its constricted dwelling space untenable in a relatively short time, while there was also no guarantee, if the authorities accepted the residents' desire to remain as guardians of the historic site, that the next generation would honor the agreement, or that a collective contract could be enforced in perpetuity. Others—though not all—took the view that Pom Mahakan could not be counted as a real community because it had not emerged according to what one in particular saw as the only genuine genesis for a true Thai community: as a single profession, as in the case of villages and neighborhoods of begging-bowl or paper umbrella makers.

That they were cooks specializing in various delicacies—one of the signs they put up in imitation of official heritage signage celebrated the production of fish maw soup—cut no ice with the bureaucratic die-hards, who may have known that residents of at least one neighboring area shared this narrow understanding of community. Perishables evidently did not count—or, as one official put it, they did not represent productive activity. For that official, such activity is simply a matter of individual household economics, not of community culture. The observation that "traditional commerce is the major characteristic of the local people's culture which forms the identity and unique nature of the place,"[18] a reiteration in scholarly terms of the language of cultural rights, matches the residents' strategy of cultural self-assertion, but it ran counter to the official's understanding of what could legitimately be claimed as a collective cultural identity.

The official, in fact, made a very telling observation about the relationship between culture and commodities. I had responded that his view of Thai community production was like the government's OTOP ("one tambon [district], one product") policy of organizing the entire country around the local manufacture of typical Thai goods, with each community's sole specialty contributing to the totalizing image of Thai culture. I fully expected a reprimand for my cheekiness. To my surprise, however, the bureaucrat beamed his approval. His refusal to recognize food preparation as a basis of community identity, however, was perhaps further from the government's attitude than he realized; it was around this time that Thailand began an energetic campaign to promote Thai food overseas, and also to encourage food vendors to identify with official criteria of aesthetic as well as culinary taste by using vending carts—soon rejected as inefficient by their intended users—sporting stereotypically Thai architectural ornament. It is interesting that nearly a decade later, during intercommunity Children's Day celebrations at Pom Phra Sumaen, a Pom Mahakan resident was selling the locally produced liquid smelling astringent under the label of "OTOP"—a clever reappropriation of government policy (fig. 4).

Given that the battle over Pom Mahakan is at one level an argument about culture and its role in the self-definition of Thainess, it is interesting that the municipal functionary took a culturalist rather than a legalistic view of the definition of community. In part, this may have been possible because a besetting problem of the legal status of communities in Thailand is that there is no formal legal definition of the term *chumchon*. There is clearly a general acceptance at the official level that such entities do exist, hence the term "community police" and the name of the Thai Community Foundation (*Munithi Chumchon Thai*). Pom Mahakan—like

CHAPTER FOUR

4 Selling relief from the pollution, OTOP-style

many other residential groupings all over the country—happily accepts this reification of a vaguely understood concept in its own promotion of "the community's local knowledge." Yet the word *chumchon* appears to be a relatively recent coinage dating back to the Cold War, and its current popularity—especially in conjunction with the concept of "culture" (*wattanattham*)—has been closely associated with a royalist and bourgeois vision of romanticized poverty, and especially with the king's promotion of "sufficiency economy."[19] For many Bangkok people, by extension, it signifies a slum, with intimations of a heroic struggle to survive. It also has a broader meaning, as appears in the Thai title of the *Cultural Heritage Atlas of Rattanakosin* (*Phaenthi Chumchon Krung Rattanakosin*).[20] But precisely because of these politically laden associations, the term is not universally popular. Its strongest source of popular legitimacy appears to be the active engagement of academics and NGOs in promoting ideals of community solidarity; for these observers, there is no contradiction in recognizing that a community can come into existence through forms of activism that gather together poor people struggling to fend for themselves and finding solace and advancement in collective action.[21]

The official, to be sure, raised some practical issues as well, arguing—and here he was in accord with at least one of his seniors—that in order to allow a community to take hold in such a place, one would need much more information about the conditions under which they would live there, and especially how many of them would do so. But he then demurred that this was not really the main issue. For him, it had to do with the origins of the people themselves. As he said, "But the problem I'm thinking about is this: in the event that we let them live there . . . if they have a way of life, if they have a community identity, if it turns out that they really have a way of life and they are a genuine community," it will be for the BMA to establish whether those people "have lived here for real, [whether they have lived here] a long time or not"—in other words, if they had "a descent line [there] for a genuinely long time," then he would "agree that they had the right to live there." But if they were "other people," people from other areas of the country, they should not be included. And this argument takes us right back to the question of whether they can be considered a true community. Add to this, he said, the fact that there was one faction—albeit essentially consisting of a single family—that disagreed with the leadership, and the situation must be deemed untenable.

Moreover, he argued, those who followed the leadership only did so because, given that Thawatchai was one of the few with real title to his land, they were afraid that if they did not support him and hang together as a group, he would end up in possession of his home while they would all be forced to leave. Most of all, he argued, even if a social problem would be solved by allowing the residents to remain, as long as this was illegal "the problem could not be solved," especially as—so he claimed—the wider society would not tolerate an exception being made for this one community when it had violated the terms under which many of its members had already received compensation. Such is the bureaucratic adherence

CHAPTER FOUR

to the letter of the law, even though this man also admitted that a bureaucrat could in fact contemplate making such an exception were it not for the social disapproval that would result; the BMA could only do so if the central government took the responsibility—"it depends on the central government." This goes against the activists' view that it was instead the law, not the specific problem, that had to be "solved." Like every good bureaucrat, the official was afraid of any precedent that contravened existing policy and sought protection in an appeal to the authority of the national government. The fear of precedent provided an easy justification: if the residents of Pom Mahakan could go on living on the site, squatters "everywhere would feel they could live there in the same way." But perhaps, although he did not say so, he may also have been afraid that if he conceded too much to the community, he too might fall victim to the harsh realities of bureaucratic hierarchy. Fear is a strong motivator of bureaucratic actions, as we also saw in the confrontation over the protest signage on the old wall. The official who talked to me about the community's overall future was clearly relieved that I wanted to hear his side of the story, which he partly laid out for me in the privacy of his car while driving me home from his office through the interminable Bangkok traffic jams; he seemed to be especially concerned to set an impossibly high bar for letting residents defy existing regulations and court decisions.

Whether the functionary's more political observations about community dynamics were justifiable or not, it is interesting to hear him invoke the same culturalist rhetoric that has been community president Thawatchai's central argument and a strong element in that of the community's NGO and political supporters, but to deploy it, by contrast, against the idea that the people of Pom Mahakan constituted a genuine community. It is clear that, for both sides, the arenas of "way of life," "culture," "community," and "history" are the crucial spaces in which the battle for recognition is fought.

For Pom Mahakan, which has chosen to yoke itself—however ironically—to the vision of national culture promulgated by the royal establishment, securing recognition as a *chumchon* in the larger public arena—the BMA officially does not recognize it in law although they do so for most practical purposes including the provision of electricity and water, as well as the disposal of garbage collected by the residents—has been a vital element in its self-presentation to the wider Bangkok audience. Its rhetoric appeals to the romantic image of rural life; "we are a family" (*khrawpkhrua*), the residents declaim, invoking a vague sense of shared kinship and household identity. In rural northern Thailand, where the term *chumchon* is undeniably a recent arrival, the anthropologist Anan

Ganjanapan has noted that it appears to replace *bahn*, a word that elsewhere simply means "house" or "home." The implication that a community in the heart of Bangkok can be seen as a cluster of kin living together thus evokes an image of idealized rural Thai life that serves as an antidote to the alienation and anomie of modern urban life.[22] Thus, denying the reality of the residents' claim to share a way of life strikes at the very heart of their moral claims on the right to remain on the site.

Behind the idealized facade of family harmony, there is also the lived reality of family tension. The evidence of occasional dissension within—such as that mentioned by the BMA official—is unsurprising. An architect who has worked closely with the people of Pom Mahakan, for example, admitted that there were sometimes difficulties in getting them to agree on a common course of action but he conceded that this was a normal dynamic and one that over time might well be overcome. In some ways, the tightly bounded and carefully organized social space of Pom Mahakan throws any disagreement—the disaffection of one family following the removal of its head from community office, the disinclination of other members to join in the necessarily wearisome effort of maintaining the cleanliness of a vegetation-rich urban space day in day out and for years on end, the endemic reluctance of most inhabitants to take administrative responsibility, and the persistent if low-level grumblings about the self-enrichment of those who run the community's community savings fund—into sometimes embarrassingly sharp relief. Yet the bureaucrats, in the long term and despite the attempts some of them have made to exploit any stirring of internal dissension, have failed to break the overall cohesion that Pom Mahakan enjoys. Perhaps, indeed, their unyielding refusal to grant the residents long-term legitimacy has galvanized the residents, animated as they are by a segmentary understanding of political relations, into a greater unity than they would otherwise have been able to muster. Even the occasional departure of a few families with enough resources to back their unwillingness to live with the perpetual tension of being under siege has not terminally weakened the collective will. The longer the residents remain under threat, the greater the feeling of being a true community—and, in consequence, the greater the residents' appeal to a bourgeoisie that had previously looked on them with disdain.

This could constitute a problem for Pom Mahakan in the very near future. The popularity of the term *chumchon* is now suffering from attrition because of the bourgeois and crypto-colonial ideology that originally generated and sustained it. Many activists in fact prefer the English word "community" (although this may be more an index of their own bourgeois and academic leanings than of a critical stance toward the term's history),

CHAPTER FOUR

while others argue that there is no such thing as a community at all. One skeptic, a wealthy but dilettantish planner who knew the Pom Mahakan situation well, conceded that it constituted a rare exception, since it had developed a more decidedly communitarian ethos than any of the more middle-class areas that surrounded it; his explanation invoked the residents' poverty and the fact that they had more to lose than to gain from disunity. But even the evidence that it had coalesced into an entity capable of collective action was not a sufficient or acceptable basis for according it legitimacy in the eyes of those who, like my BMA interlocutor, refused to accord it that status of a community. Indeed, it was precisely that capacity that had rendered it a real thorn in the side of the bureaucracy and a dangerous precedent setter in the city's ongoing attempt to impose some degree of order on its notorious chaos.

In public discourse, the language of community increasingly smacks of bureaucratic jargon, largely because its legitimacy has come to depend on such a shift. In the same way, the older understanding of *moeang* shifts to its more territorial and bounded sense of "city," in a way that is not unlike the shift in Italy from a socially grounded notion of being "civil" (*civile*) to the precision of "civic" (*civico*) action and rhetoric.[23] A statement written for a meeting held by a group of social activists, *Witthyalai kahn chadkahn kahn sangkhom*, in collaboration with the Pom Mahakan community on 24 March 2005 illustrates the shift well:

Chumchon is the model of a place that has constructed meaning, opportunities, rights, and functions for the people who live in the *chumchon*.[24] Caretaking and organizing the community is a process that must arise from people coming together to collaborate, because an urban space (*phoenthi moeang*) can build the presence (*tua ton*, literally "tangibility") and meaning of the people who support it. For this reason the lives of the people in an urban community (*chumchon moeang*) are not merely about the meaning of the physical place but have to do with the presence of the people, of their experiences and memories that underlie the history of the older generations that have inhabited the community.

This statement reveals how repetition and circularity embed the process of reification in a discourse that, while it is clearly intended to challenge official actions, partakes of some of the same logic that animates official statements. Willy-nilly, it seems, the activists collude with officialdom in concealing the flexible implications of term *moeang*, reducing it, quite explicitly in the original statement, to a translation of the English word "urban." And yet it is hard to see how the activists could have done otherwise.

The Western models that animate their thinking are first cousins to the bureaucratic logic of the authorities; but in that kinship perhaps there lies some possibility of communication.

To be fair, not all BMA bureaucrats refused to acknowledge that Pom Mahakan could be considered a community simply because it was too diverse in its origins. One high-ranking official openly scoffed at such a narrowly culturalist idea. But here, too, we see an important element in the overall dynamic. The low-level but insistent hum of internal dissension within the BMA—which is replicated in many of the other structural institutions involved—also suggests why the hostility of particular officials has so far not translated into decisive physical action. At least two officials told me, on separate occasions, that the real issue was one of overcrowding—a socially much more compassionate explanation of their attitude, although again almost certainly a mask for the legal demands of the Rattanakosin Island Project. Their position, however, is scarcely more persuasive than the culturalist argument. It is true that the population of Pom Mahakan has expanded slightly, but it is equally true that many of the residents have moved away over time, making exact census taking quite difficult. Younger people do not stay in the community if their education secures them a better wage and the living conditions that it brings.

Even though the BMA bureaucrats did not always agree among themselves about whether or on what terms Pom Mahakan had a moral right to consider itself a true community, however, most of them were apparently united in their view that the eviction should go forward without delay. Their implacable attitude only served to reinforce the residents' unity. It focused the residents' attention on the need for coordinated action and constant vigilance, and, while it is not clear that the bureaucrats themselves all desired an immediate end to the conflict, the intransigent face that they presented in public provided the residents with a perfect foil. In a country where bureaucratic hauteur is frequent, and is sometimes understood as a survival of the bad old habits of feudalism, the lines were clear.

A Meeting on Site

On one rare occasion, a team from the Department of Public Works agreed to come for a discussion with the residents. Despite some initial excitement at the prospect of a direct discussion, it quickly became clear, after that meeting, that nothing concrete had been achieved. Residents complained that the encounter had not facilitated a conversation; the bureaucrats had simply come to give orders. Nevertheless, to the many outside observers who were present, it did not look like a resounding success for the bureaucrats either.

The observers themselves were clearly a source of irritation to the bureaucrats, no doubt as the inhabitants had intended. The meeting impressively displayed the community's capacity for networking far and wide. It was attended by several outsiders—several Thai and foreign academics (including me), Graeme Bristol (the Canadian activist, architect, and planner who had drafted his students into designing the first major plan for the community), Apiwat Saengpattasima (the young filmmaker who produced the punningly titled documentary *Behide the Wall*), the community's pro bono lawyer, the architect from the Crown Property Bureau, and a fiery woman activist from the Four Regions Slum Network—all of whom had been invited to observe, perhaps in the hope that their presence would shame the bureaucrats into acting more compassionately. Moreover, most of us spoke up to express support for the community.[25] Early in the proceedings, the archaeologist and activist Pthomrerk Kedudhat, in a characteristically brief but pointed speech, admitted, with a sorrowful smile and in a voice of sweet reason, that he did not know the then recently elected governor (Samak Sundarawej) and so did not know what his policy was to be; nonetheless, he said, the governor really should come and see the site for himself and discuss matters with the residents. Moreover, he insisted, wagging a professorial finger at the bureaucrats, no matter how long it took, the conversation had to take place on an individual basis with every one of those who would be affected. This was a key theme in the response of the community and its friends.

A dreadful politeness, like a cloud of cheap scent, seemed to fill the tense space around the bureaucrats, whose white shirts and neckties and stiff demeanor emphasized their detachment from the poverty-stricken but socially vibrant life around them and the conceptual as well as ideological distance that separated them from the residents and their supporters. The formal speech and, at times, noticeably strained smiles of both sides did serve a useful purpose, by preventing the proceedings from deteriorating into a shouting match, although the conventions only thinly masked the mutual anger and contempt. Perfunctory applause followed every short speech, even those of the visiting officials.

Nevertheless, the meeting was not simply a ritualistic exchange of veiled hostilities. To the contrary, it was—as later events were to make clear—something of a turning point; it very clearly demonstrated that the residents would not accept a decision handed down from on high but would fight in the courts and on the site itself. They demanded the right to discuss their predicament directly with Governor Samak, and they wanted each and every resident's concerns to be addressed.

Their supporters, too, almost all had something critical to say about the current stance of the BMA in more general terms. Pthomrerk, for example, admonished the governor that if he wished to take over the whole of the Rattanakosin area, he would have to take care of forty communities all at once. Filmmaker Apiwat, a young man with a long-standing interest in urban aesthetics and social problems who also felt that the BMA had effectively excluded architects from taking any part in its plans for the site,[26] gently dismissed the "beautification project" for its total absence of living people. During these presentations, the visiting bureaucrats listened impassively, occasionally conferring among themselves, but refused to be drawn into a serious discussion of the residents' complaints. When their most senior member, a bespectacled, gray-haired official of the Department of Public Works, finally rose to speak, he did produce a pad on which he had jotted some notes during the previous speeches; but this, too, seemed more of a theatrical prop, designed to demonstrate both concern and precision.

Predictably, he spoke about the necessity of following procedure and of engaging in a calm and considered discussion. At that point, a resident—the brother of a lawyer who had worked with the pro bono lawyer to argue the community's interests in court—interrupted him. This is a relatively rare occurrence in Thai meetings, but he carried it off by a respectful use of tone and posture. Although still speaking with a rueful smile, he firmly indicated that the residents were prepared to act independently of whatever procedure the BMA had in mind. The officials could hardly attack his intervention, which must have been unsettling for them, without belying their claims to being reasonable negotiators.

In general, the residents were all restrained, eloquent, and concise in their complaints. One elderly woman, Thawatchai's mother, was especially articulate in addressing the residents' strongly felt need to talk directly with the governor. She also spoke passionately about the consequences of unemployment attendant on living virtually under siege, and of not knowing where they would go if they were evicted. She proclaimed the community's solidarity in ringing terms that were also a defiant challenge to the bureaucrats to meet the residents on their own terms: "We live in the *moeang*, right? We talk to each other. We have conversations. We can do the whole thing." At a later point in the meeting, she firmly told the bureaucrats that she was prepared to fight to the end, "because this is my birthplace and the *moeang* where I sleep. I was born here; I must die here." Unimpressed by the senior bureaucrat's entreaty to converse quietly and gradually and "to help each other think this through" (*chuai kan khid*)—this phrase is one that officialdom shared with the NGO culture in which the residents are increasingly enfolded—she insisted that if the whole project was going to take another two decades, she would be dead before anything actually happened.

A few years later she did indeed pass away, the community still firmly entrenched on its disputed territory but also still under constant siege. In death, at least, her truculent defense of the link between lifetime and birthplace had won her and her fellow residents a victory of sorts. The bureaucrat's retort was grounded in the official discourse of the nation-state: "If we are the owners of the country (*prathaet*), we know that this place belongs to the *prathaet*. It's a public place. We have lived together for twenty years . . . thirty years . . . fifty years! So we all know already that this place is a public place. We must therefore come to help each other find the way to expand, the way to solve the problem, to help each other think and act." The defense of the *prathaet* offered the municipal bureaucracy a less slithery frame of reference than the *moeang* despite the ironic circumstance that the logic of identification (here, of the city with the nation-state) remained, as much as for the residents, the segmentary *moeang*. But the same logic required the usual invocation of collaboration, of doing things together. In Thawatchai's mother's death, at least, the senior official was cheated of the tactical advantage he had clearly hoped to achieve for the official world he represented.

The community's agility in deflecting bureaucratic power is not just a matter of knowing how to operate seamlessly between conceptual levels of identity, important though that factor is. It is also a matter of concerted political action—action that serves a delaying purpose rather than the achievement of final goals. The residents' patience comes in part from their awareness of a larger solidarity. The segmentary model is more than a formal relic of past social and political organization. Its implicit or virtual structure thrives on the realization that within the national polity there are many other local communities in equally dire straits, almost all of which are forever ready to enter into strategic alliances with each other at many levels of mobilization. That realization, which also infuses the many political demonstrations on left and right that have at times paralyzed the streets of Bangkok since the fall of Thaksin, both nurtures and is sustained by a remarkable practical capacity for networking—a capacity that, at the national level, has also had important consequences for the nation's politicians and even, perhaps especially, for the palace.[27] Some of the community leaders have had extensive experience, often through opportunities created by NGOs and resting on a tradition that reached its

LAW, COURTESY, AND THE TACTICS OF TEMPORALITY

clamorous apogee in the Assembly of the Poor's work in the 1990s,[28] to work with other poor communities around the country. Such cooperation rests on a deeply respected principle of reciprocity.

They have also attracted considerable support from the academic community in Thailand and abroad. Perhaps the first scholar to take up the cudgels on their behalf was Akin Rabibhadana, the Thai activist and anthropologist who had already pioneered ethnographic research on slum communities. He agreed to join a group of "friends of Pom Mahakan" that, in 2003, aimed to discourage the authorities from any precipitate action.[29] But the most important outside support without question comes from an impressive array of similarly disadvantaged communities and networks within Thailand. Their involvement is made palpable by frequent visits; delegations from up-country as well as from within Bangkok and also from other Asian countries are hosted at Pom Mahakan and participate in highly visible (and audible!) meetings.

When, early in my association with the community, I first joked that the residents really owed the BMA gratitude for forcing them to defend their shared interests, the response was an appreciative chuckle. With the passage of time, the joke became received wisdom, useful as a way of explaining to outsiders why the residents were so willing to defy the legally constituted authorities—and, as I have already noted, why they had increasingly been identifiable as a genuine community. There was, it seems clear in retrospect, some considerable truth to my jest. In part, this was because the residents always insisted on showing up en masse to any confrontation of significance with the authorities, who preferred to operate on a divide-and-conquer strategy that the residents easily learned to identify and to resist.

A Meeting in the Lair of the Foe

On one such occasion, two days before the destruction of the front area by the army corps detachment, I accompanied some forty members of the community to the Public Works Department (*Krom Yothah*) of the BMA. Two days still earlier, on 12 January, they had successfully resisted the administration's attempt to begin work on clearing up the space. Now their demands were simple but strategic.[30] They requested to "live as renters on their original land" (*khaw chao yu thi din doem*), a phrase that emphasized their moral claim to the place. They also requested that the BMA not destroy the "public garden" that the residents had erected in honor of the queen—a challenge, especially in these days of excessive use of the draco-

115

nian Thai *lèse-majesté* laws, that the BMA simply ignored on the grounds that what the residents had constructed did not qualify as a park.

In very polite language, they asked whether the BMA really needed to encircle the area with a wall, given that the presence of such a confining structure could have a direct effect on the residents' way of life. With a specific request that the residents be allowed the perform the tasks currently assigned to the military, they suggested that they themselves be entrusted with the care of the land belonging to the BMA—a subtle assertion of their insistence on the legality of their demands. They also indicated that the BMA plan was incompatible with the local environment, and that, especially if the BMA did not deign to answer their demands directly, the authorities nevertheless would not bring any heavy motorized equipment into the space of Pom Mahakan. These demands all were cleverly framed, implicitly but unambiguously, so as to put the maximum moral and even legal pressure on the authorities by hinting that the BMA was being disrespectful of the royal family, of the natural environment, and of the historic site whose name the residents collectively bore.

After an initial conversation with a secretary, the group of residents settled down to await developments in an open-air space in the department's very capacious building. They were initially told that the officials they wanted to see would not receive all of them together, but, in accordance with the usual bureaucratic strategy, were willing to treat with the residents' chosen representatives. Had the residents consented to this stipulation, they feared, the officials would have hoped to create new factional disputes among them. So they refused to accept this condition and settled in for a long wait, prepared to sit out whatever delaying tactics the officials decided to employ.

Maew, with his considerable experience of mobilization in similar situations in the north of the country, took on the task of rallying the residents and making sure that they did not yield on the key tactical issue. "What did we come here to do?" he demanded, dramatically but in a calm voice, contesting the authorities' divide-and-conquer tactic head-on. "This is what we will say. . . . They [the residents] will go into that meeting room in their entirety. None of us has a representative; each of us is a resident. There's no one who is a leader; everyone wants to know, wants to see, and wants to hear. If they insist on seeing representatives, we should not go in [to a meeting]; if we do go in, that means that we are going for the purpose of informing ourselves." It was "absolutely forbidden," he went on, to treat with the officials on the individual basis that the latter were demanding.

In invoking the notion that such a move was "forbidden," as much as when he insisted there were "no leaders" even as he acted in that capacity, he underscored the combination of ambiguity and balance that we also see in the invocation of "elder and younger siblings" reiterated several times in the list of demands and constituting the single signature at its end (*phi nawng Pom Mahakan*). His was an authoritative voice, even an authoritarian one, but he spoke in the name of the collectivity, and the collectivity was there to reinforce what he enunciated. In a community where people often disclaimed responsibility by calling themselves "followers" (*phu tahm*) as opposed to "leaders," the statement that there were no leaders, made by a man who was clearly viewed as one of those who commanded the authority of leadership, did not ring hollow.

In the flexible, segmentary view of the world as a *moeang*, strong men could serve as both representatives and leaders; their leadership was always contingent on their command of the rhetorical trope of equality.[31] But it was not just a trope. The insistence that all should go in to the meeting together grew from an awareness that it was only by committing their followers to the confrontation with officialdom that the leaders could ensure their continuing solidarity in the face of the seemingly endless war of attrition. In this way, moreover, no one could claim that deals had been struck behind their backs, favoring some residents over others. Despite the remarkable solidarity the community has shown over time, such sources of tension as the suspicions of larceny that sometimes attach to the managers of its community savings fund show that it is only prudent to face the enemy as a collectivity.

In the end, the Pom Mahakan residents achieved their immediate goal. The officials, conceding a battle in order to win the war, eventually, and with evident reluctance, agreed to meet with them all, and everyone crowded into the meeting room. No one objected to the fact that both Apiwat and I were filming the encounter. Perhaps the officials thought that they would more effectively convey their policy if it was recorded in this way, but it seems more likely that they simply did not wish to antagonize the residents even more, especially as an unseemly row would also then potentially have been recorded for posterity. It was these officials in particular who, on another occasion, took considerable pains to explain to me why the residents' demands were unsustainable.

Clearly, moreover, the residents' refusal to accede to the officials' demand that they appoint representatives to speak for them was something of a milestone in the process of consolidating their identity as a community. The meeting that they eventually held, while it did nothing to persuade the officials to change their stance (even had those officials been empowered to do so), achieved a more immediate goal: establishing beyond reasonable doubt that they were capable of collective, unified action as a

CHAPTER FOUR

community—especially in reaction to the obduracy of the bureaucrats. The officials had overplayed their hand. Expecting a quick capitulation, they were instead forced into what for them was a dangerous precedent they would have preferred to avoid.

A Dissenting Voice

Ironically, it was the most vociferous opponent of dismantling the barricades who subsequently became the most embittered internal critic of the community's resistance. This man had originally been a tireless advocate of community concerns. Interviewed at length by filmmakers and journalists, and prepared at every turn to denounce the authorities' lack of the compassion of the true Buddhist, he was always a leading presence in any major happenings—notably the consecration ritual that the residents mounted in early 2003 to raise funds for the conservation of the eighteenth-century citadel.

His pride of place, however, soon turned to sour humiliation. Inclined to present himself as the community's leading spokesperson but unwilling to cooperate with other leaders and disgruntled by their refusal to grant him the key public role to which he felt his seniority entitled him, at some point he contacted some of the municipal bureaucrats on his own account. Even when he was opposing the reopening of the main gate against the food vendors' wishes, his disaffection had, it was later to become clear, already begun to fester. He was known to be extremely sensitive to real or imagined disrespect; and he was suspected of encouraging the authorities to speed the removal of one of the oldest houses, the owner of which was willing to reassemble it in another location. If he had still managed to hold onto some shreds of respect up to that point, especially as a rather vocal representative of the community in any encounter with NGOs or other important visitors, from then on he was seen, as one of the gentler residents put it, as "pitiable." "Some people," remarked this commentator, "if they don't get respect, are just not satisfied." And this man ended up getting very little—indeed, he lived out his last years in offended isolation from his fellow residents, greeting visitors from the outside who virtually had to step over his family and his several cats by one of the entrances in the old wall, and always willing to declaim his contempt for his erstwhile comrades-in-arms.

He also wrote a long letter to the BMA, presenting himself as the victim of his own honesty and casting his plight as that of a figure out of traditional epic poetry—Norasingha, the honest steersman, who had preferred to be decapitated rather than lie to his king. The community leaders, he complained, had departed from the original land-sharing plan, which he had supported, and had instead engaged the wider public and various NGOs and networks in a much more ambitious and illegal plan to take over the whole inhabited area. Many of the residents, he complained, had accepted the compensation originally paid out by the municipal authorities, only to creep back and reoccupy their houses, while others had simply used up the money they had accepted and were now unable to move because of their fecklessness. In language that was both richly poetic and yet also reflective of a relatively poor command of written Thai, this disgruntled representative of an older generation portrayed himself as alone in his noble honesty.

There can be little doubt about the sincerity of his feelings, whatever their original cause. I frequently heard his complaints, which redirected his earlier bitterness at the BMA to the community leaders who had displaced and isolated him. His central argument remained an insistence on the legal point that those who had accepted money had no right to continue to live on the site, as "the place belongs to the BMA." He went on, "I've not taken any money from the BMA, but I can't live there," and he argued that the residents were obliged to follow the administration's plan for development no matter what it portended. He himself, he claimed, was living "in his original place" (*thi din doem*) but had received no compensation. Why should these power-hungry freeloaders fare any better? "Professor," he told me, "you don't have real enough information . . . These people are breaking the law!" Moreover, asked whether the BMA could not simply decide to let the residents stay, he replied that this was not a decision the BMA could make; only the government could do that. He did acknowledge that wherever he ended up being forced to go and live, he would be unable to earn a living—a key theme in his enemies' justification of their insistence on staying on the site. Perhaps that mattered little to him; he was already elderly, and died a scant few years later. His enemies—whom he had named in his letter to the BMA—had meanwhile firmly consolidated their control.

Perhaps his greatest error lay in confusing seniority with power. During community meetings, I often observed the oldest members of the community being seated in a way that raised them physically above the younger people sitting cross-legged on the ground, or wandering in the background with a smile of tolerant acceptance. The kickboxer, however, despite his strategically useful skill as a repository of Thai tradition, clearly wanted a more central role. During my early acquaintance with the community, he was always ready to declaim the iniquities of the city administration; to take the lead in any ritual or demonstration; and to edge into any newsworthy picture of visiting dignitaries. Once disaffected, however, he did not fall silent, but deployed the same complaints against his fellow residents, and especially against the elected leaders.

His discontent, dressed in appeals to distant history in a rhetoric he shared with the leaders, barely disturbed the community consensus. The kickboxer's personal tragedy was that his aggressively self-serving style alienated him from those who were giving material expression to the dream of which he had at first been such a fervent exponent. In the war of attrition with the authorities, this lone man's voice of discontent faded to miserable irrelevance as the two sides grimly prepared for battles ahead.

Resilience and Retrenchment

The garden, the pride and joy of the residents, was violently destroyed before it could be completed. Four days after the military had begun their pressure, the residents stopped resisting, but, as one newspaper article put it, responded with "tears and sadness." The same article quotes City Clerk Nathanon Thavisin: "I want to make the community understand that it's about national development (*patthanah prathaet*), and developing the place so as to make it beautiful, which means refurbishing the place so as to make it compatible with Rattanakosin Island; and that the BMA has been moving forward on this for a long time already through the payment of compensation according to the law."[32] This official had for years never lost an opportunity to speak disparagingly of the Pom Mahakan community, and her diatribes represented a larger system of bourgeois and bureaucratic values. National policy, beauty, law: these components of the official mantra were no less yielding than the residents' claims on history and legitimacy. And the BMA, too, insisted that its version of the park was being constructed to honor Her Majesty the Queen's seventy-second birthday—the auspicious completion of the sixth twelve-year cycle of her life.

In the rhetorical contest over legitimacy and its royal underpinning, it was not always clear who had the upper hand in the eyes of the larger Bangkok population. Perhaps the most remarkable aspect of Pom Mahakan's long resistance has been its adroit handling of a rhetoric it shares with the state. The community has counted on its self-projection as exemplifying the Thai polity as a whole, steadily increasing its staying power simply through the consistency of its response to the equally consistent—and unyielding—opposition of the BMA bureaucrats. The residents' insistence that "the community will not yield" (*chumchon mai yawm*)—which, perhaps not coincidentally, resonates with Thammasat University activists' slogan, "We won't move away" (*mai yai*)[33]—has intensified with the time its delaying tactics have bought it. This in turn has brought about a gradual change in its status, paralleled by the shift in its reputation in the larger city environment, and further enhanced by Governor Apirak's ultimately unsuccessful but well-publicized and well-received attempt to support its rebuilding project. Once characterized by BMA officials as "obdurate" (*doe*), they were more recently, as we have seen, lauded by Apirak as "resilient" (*khemkhaeng*); the difference between these terms speaks less to changes in the style or content of the community's actions than to differences in perspective between the permanent civil servants (*khah rachakahn prajam*) who saw them as an utter pest and the one senior politician who openly supported them—and who, by so doing, saw them as useful allies in his self-projection as a caring and socially responsible civic leader.[34] Apirak was encouraged in his course of action by the leadership of his party, of which he was soon to become a vice president, presumably because it was important for a party increasingly seen as representing bourgeois interests to show active and visible interest in the poor. In this regard the central location of Pom Mahakan doubtless also played a role.

Other forces were stirring as well. Somsook Boonyabancha, a well-known housing rights activist and leader of the Community Organizations Development Institute, a fighter who often preferred to operate in the background while acquiring a powerful reputation for getting problems addressed, had suggested Pom Mahakan to Graeme Bristol, who was looking for an appropriate case to have his students at the King Mongkut Institute of Technology work on a specific community design. The group, having been at work for some two months at the end of 2002, was at the site on a dramatic day early in the new year when the residents had just learned they had thirty days to vacate their homes and were watching a television broadcast about this grim demand; a month later the group had completed its report, with the key recommendation that the park incorporate community housing.[35]

In June 2003 Somsook announced a plan to work with the Thai Community Foundation and others to promote the residents' architect-designed land-sharing plan, which, according to the press, she "expected the governor (Samak) to support"—no doubt a deliberately optimistic provocation, given Samak's notorious intransigence.[36] In the event, Samak ignored the appeal, with the excuse that he had read the report prepared on the basis of the various submissions by the interested parties and submitted for his consideration by the Ministry of the Interior—a classic tactic of bureaucratic evasion, especially given that he was close to the government of the time.[37]

A group of at least ten soldiers then entered the community space, panicking the residents into expecting the worst.[38] Their fears appear to have been precisely what the cat-and-mouse operation aimed to achieve. By the time I arrived on site, the soldiers were bantering quite easily with the residents, and they claimed that their role was simply to conduct a survey, but it became clear that as a form of intimidation their presence was, if not exactly successful in getting the residents to leave, at least an added and considerable source of anxiety. They appeared to be nosing around the grounds in anticipation of action at some future but unspecified date. In fact, the military and municipal authorities were legally required to await the official legal verdict, which arrived, with uncompromising finality, on 21 August 2004.

"Administrative Court judges squelch Pom Prakhan [sic] community's dreams," one headline screamed that day.[39] Worse, the residents were given just eight additional days of respite before the BMA could begin work preparing the landscaping in time for the queen's birthday early in the following year; and their pleas for alternative housing were dismissed by the BMA on the grounds, now enunciated with the harsh hauteur of the law, that the residents were now all considered to be squatters and that completion of the park in the queen's honor took priority over any other considerations. The court struck down most (88 out of 104) of the householders' claims individually on the grounds of the absence of written (as opposed to oral) evidence that their homes belonged to them as a result of a completed transaction—this, in a culture where such contracts were, during the relevant period, relatively rare, and in which, the community's pro bono lawyer argued, there was in fact no legal basis for requiring anything more than a verbal agreement. For the 16 householders who were still considered legal landholders because they could produce written proof of ownership, but who had received three-quarters of their allocated compensation under the eminent domain expropriation, the BMA had followed procedure by depositing the remaining one-quarter of the compensation in the government's Housing Bank, thereby securing the right to proceed with the demolitions after sixty days. Such procedural care appeared to bolster the administrators' case. The lawyer, however, had also argued that the verdict could be challenged on the grounds that the BMA governor's mandate to expropriate land had actually expired in 1966, while the Four Regions Slum Network was later to suggest that the BMA could not invoke its right to evict and demolish because the decree in question was the work of a dictatorship and therefore had no continuing validity.[40]

The BMA, however, could easily make the counterargument to the effect that the original act of expropriation had occurred many years before the expiry of its mandate to expropriate land,[41] while the validity or otherwise of edicts issued under various regimes is notoriously subject to the subsequent vagaries and policies of whatever government happens to be in power; neither Thaksin nor his opponents would necessarily have wished to deprive themselves of an entire category of arbitrary laws in order to serve some abstract notion of justice. To make matters worse, the impending APEC summit scheduled for 6 October of the same year had triggered a beautification campaign in Bangkok—not the first of its kind, and, as before, intended to hide what the authorities considered eyesores (slums and their protests) from the critical eyes of the distinguished visitors. Any community harboring alleged squatters from up-country would receive no sympathy from Governor Samak, who declared that he would pack all such individuals off to a specially constructed camp in the far north of the country since no one in Bangkok had any excuse for being homeless![42] Pom Mahakan was once again in the firing line, and this time as part of a much larger target than before.

Once again, the two sides had reached an impasse. The alternative housing that had already been offered to some residents was in places that lacked water and electricity, and those elderly souls who were now forced at the end of their lives to face the trauma of relocation remained adamant that this was an unacceptable resolution. The BMA, ever adept at playing the bureaucratic waiting game, would do nothing before 29 August because its officers required final clarification of the court's decision. The residents, meanwhile, had decided that they would not resist the actual demolition of their houses, but would refuse to quit the site, thereby creating a much larger embarrassment for the authorities as they would be able to expel the residents only through the use of force—a humiliatingly public, brutal display of failure to achieve a peaceful resolution. They had anticipated the court's final decision and were prepared for the demolition of their houses, Thawatchai informed the press, but they would then request tents so they could continue living on their site because Pom Mahakan "is the original place of the roots (*khoe rahk haeng dang doem*) of a community that has lived together for longer than 150 years."[43]

In all these confrontations, the residents showed themselves to be especially adept at managing the conventions of formal courtesy. This allowed them to claim an aura of respectability that the BMA had long tried to

CHAPTER FOUR

deny them. Perhaps even more important, they commanded social and political forces that were only just beginning to make themselves felt. As we will see in the next chapter, a fortunate convergence of these developments with a change in the leadership of the BMA allowed for a radical shift in the grounds of the conflict—not a definitive one, to be sure, but certainly a dramatic change in the fortunes of Pom Mahakan.

FIVE

Currents and Countercurrents

Forces for change were gradually building up a head of steam, in turn generating new tactics of intransigence in some quarters of the bureaucracy and renewed determination to resist on the part of the community. In particular, the strong academic interest in Pom Mahakan was contributing to the creation of a "current" (*krasae*)—in other words, a wave of public support, fanned by increasingly sympathetic media. The residents certainly hoped that their construction of the front-area garden might reinforce that support and demonstrate their capacity for self-management and for what one newspaper report called a "handcrafted" solution to the question of how to have a green space in combination with residential quarters.[1] In addition, on 25 August 2003, residents and academics joined forces to hold a second conference, with a focus on the rights of the Pom Mahakan community in the context of nongovernmental tourism policy, at the country's premier academic institution, Chulalongkorn University; among the participants were two minor members of the royal family, numerous academics, and active residents of the community, as well as a former deputy governor of Bangkok.[2]

Then, on 29 August 2003, came the official final announcement of the final verdict of the Central Administrative Court, a package of bureaucratically wrapped doom that appeared to spell the end of any hope of further reprieve.[3] Yet still the formal decisions did not translate into action; the residents continued to mobilize their multiple sources of support, and the BMA hesitated. About half a year later, however, Samak delivered a particularly insulting blow: he sent in the army to destroy the residents' carefully constructed public garden (which had been built over several days in mid-late July) by dumping truckloads of garbage—taken from the cleanup that had been carried out in anticipation of the October APEC meeting—on top of the remains. Even then, the community did not yield. They appealed to the Supreme Administrative Court, without success, but at least with the benefit of staving off final disaster for a while more.

A Change of Guard, a Change of Heart

That delay saved the community from imminent dissolution. In the meantime, the final months of Samak's governorship were a time of vigilance and organization. What no one could have predicted was that the election of his successor, Apirak Kosayodhin, on 29 August 2004, would dramatically change the situation. Apirak's election was unexpected in part because Prime Minister Thaksin had thrown his Thai Rak Thai party's considerable weight behind a well-known children's and women's rights activist (and social development and security minister in the subsequent government of Thaksin's sister Yingluck), Paveena Hongsakul. Paveena, who had resigned from the Chart Pattana party ostensibly in order to run as an independent candidate and who was initially opposed by one faction of the Thai Rak Thai party,[4] was clearly the front-runner in this contest, but she made at least two tactical mistakes: she apparently took her eventual success for granted, failing to show up at a major meeting of most of the twenty-two candidates at Thammasat University on 26 August 2003; and she paraded herself dressed as a market woman with her panniers on the streets of Bangkok—a device that was so patently ill-suited to a bourgeois politician that it totally backfired and made her look ridiculous. While her closeness to the Thai Rak Thai government of Thaksin might have offered some advantages, residents thought, her failure either to show up at the general meeting or to visit the Pom Mahakan site itself did not augur well for their future. Meanwhile, Apirak, whose speaking style was as quietly serious as his personal manner was charismatic, and whose background as a student activist turned successful entrepreneur and business leader appealed to the socially aware but commercially active middle class, engaged a wide range of communities in conversations about their future, and, as events were to show, became progressively more interested in Pom Mahakan itself.

The Thammasat meeting was unquestionably a watershed in this evolution. Apirak found himself seated on the platform directly next to former governor Bhichit Rattakul. Present with them were several other candidates, including Chalerm Yubamrung, a former police officer whose sons were acquitted on charges related to a much-discussed murder,[5] and who was later to be deputy prime minister in the Yingluck government, and the even more colorful Chuwit Kamolvisit, a massage parlor operator who parlayed his notoriety into a political career as a member of parliament and leader of a small but vocal party, and who was at something of a disadvantage in this debate because he was still awaiting trial on a charge of having forcibly demolished houses in an area that he controlled for his nighttime operations.[6] Chuwit tried to secure the gay vote by advocating for the creation of a "homosexual zone."[7] Apirak, clearly well prepared and level voiced despite having his right thumb in a bandage, was especially direct and matter-of-fact in fielding questions. He was also well prepared to confront the issue of the disadvantaged citizens of Bangkok even though a recent poll had shown that, whereas 32.55 percent of respondents considered the notorious traffic problem to be paramount (Apirak in fact addressed this in his first term as governor, extending the Skytrain and attempting some other measures albeit with rather limited success), only 7.55 percent put slums at the top of their list—a finding that may explain why, less than three weeks before the elections, not one of the candidates had visited the worst and largest of the slums, Khlong Thoey.[8] But at Thammasat University, located within the Rattanakosin Island area, the specific issue of "historic" but poor communities carried greater resonance, and he responded effectively to the challenge.

A self-styled "representative [*phu thaen*] from the Pom Mahakan community"—none other than Thawatchai—stood up to question Apirak on how he would handle the fate of twenty-five "old communities (*chumchon kao kae*)" that were facing eviction or other difficulties, and especially how he would help them develop as tourist attractions.[9] This was a clever question but also a very convenient one for Apirak, since it spoke to both of the candidate's key interests: entrepreneurship and social reform. Apirak's reply, broadly optimistic in general import, was couched in a delicate balance of official discourse, NGO-speak, and the jargon of official policy. Above all, he said, he would invite the representatives of the communities to participate in conversations articulated through the creation of participatory councils, paying attention not only to tourist development but also, and especially, to the sites' historical significance and questions of physical appearance and landscape. He called on community leaders to join him in looking at each community "in respect of

CHAPTER FIVE

the way of life (*witthichiwit*), in respect of spiritual life, in respect of history (*prawatisaht*), in respect of the background to the way of life (*khwahm pen mah khong witthichiwit*)." But he conjoined these themes familiar from the community leadership's discourse with a call for attention to "urban development of the city" (*kahn pattana moeang*), "landscape" (*phumitat*), and "beauty" (*khwahm suay gnahm*)—all terms of official policy.[10]

The encompassing idiom of his reply thus did not depart significantly from the official script of cleaning up the city. The commitment to a developmental vision was later to get him into some trouble as, not long after his election, he challenged Bangkok's ubiquitous hawkers to accept a more disciplined use of public space—an issue to which he alluded in this election meeting as well, insisting that there would be a decent (*riap roi*) way to permit food vendors to operate in designated spaces while allowing pedestrians to walk easily through the streets.[11] Such language reflected more his bourgeois constituency's preoccupation with "looking good," although he was careful to show concern for the hawkers' interests as well. But his emphasis on talking with community representatives as a matter of policy and his open acknowledgment that the threat of eviction was a key problem for these communities both sounded like a breath of fresh air. His stated view that communities could and should be involved in historic conservation in plotting a future trajectory for the Rattanakosin area and his declared intention to make that engagement a central part of his policy represented a novel recognition of precisely what Pom Mahakan had been striving to achieve. His stance also displayed a revealing contrast with the policies of his predecessor—policies that had been both occluded and facilitated by the latter's refusal to treat with the community at all. On one occasion, we were able to espy Samak in a ceremony in the temple complex on the other side of the main road; he showed absolutely no interest in crossing over to visit the community that by now had evidently become as much an archenemy in his eyes as he had in the eyes of the residents.

Apirak declared that he would invite representatives of all the Rattanakosin area historic communities to discuss what to do, arguing that for him "conservation" was not merely a matter of ancient monuments alone but also of conserving history, and, in consequence, of a way of life together with the "older and younger siblings" of the community as well. That statement, in which he rearranged the familiar terms of official and NGO discourse to offer a more participatory vision of the future, represented a significant shift of attitude and presumably won over significant numbers of voters on election day.

And indeed, three days after that lengthy public meeting at Thammasat, riding a sudden wave of enthusiasm, Apirak was elected with a strong mandate and a clear majority (he won 40 percent of the total votes, against runner-up Paveena's 16 percent). As the vote count came in (I was able to follow some of the process inside the cavernous City Hall), the soon-to-retire city clerk, a stalwart of the civil service administration that was trying to evict the Pom Mahakan community, stolidly announced a result with which she could hardly have been comfortable. Having been openly hostile to the idea of my studying the Pom Mahakan community, she suddenly proved very affable and allowed me to watch the vote counting—perhaps because she had already anticipated the change at the top.

In the early days of his governorship, there was an air of excitement as Apirak began the delicate task of reshaping the BMA from within—a task that he also, rather daringly, enunciated in his postelection manifesto.[12] He airily told me soon after his election that the bureaucrats would be happy with his reform program and that they wanted a better system. Events were to shed considerable doubt on that assessment. Not only was there little evident change in the bureaucracy's handling of public relations, but Apirak soon became embroiled in an unsavory story about the sale of Austrian buses to the BMA, an affair on which he (it seems) innocently signed off and thereby fell into a trap apparently created, whether out of vindictiveness or because his predecessor himself hoped to make a profit while still in office, by Samak. Some of the bureaucrats within the system must have connived to present him with the documents for signing. Apirak had the good sense to withdraw quickly, accepting his own personal responsibility for having failed to inspect the documents with sufficient care and arguing that his resignation would serve as an example to other Thai politicians. He thus cleverly reversed an attack on his own reputation by representing himself as unusually clean, and in 2010 was formally cleared of all charges of corruption on the grounds that he had only done what he had found himself contractually obliged to do. One can only speculate the exact role the disaffected bureaucrats had played in helping to engineer the original charges against him, while also defeating the project that Apirak and the Pom Mahakan leaders had created. They cannot have been displeased by his discomfiture.

But I am jumping ahead, although this preview of the sequence of events after Apirak's election will help to make sense of the sequence of events that led him, after a year in office, to enter the Pom Mahakan fray more directly. At that point, the bus scandal was still a mere blip on the horizon, and the governor was riding high in public esteem. The task Apirak now faced was that of maintaining the idea of a symbolic Thai center while respecting the rights of those who lived in it. His postelection manifesto was suitably vague and not a little nationalistic in tone, retaining the lan-

CHAPTER FIVE

guage of "beauty" and linking it to the goal of turning Bangkok into a city of the arts and culture; he aimed to "build a mechanism of knowledge, understanding, and awareness that would make the people and the youth look to the quality of art, culture, and indigenous local knowledge, in order to generate pride in the characteristics of Thainess (*khwahm pen thai*)."[13] This language is typical of Thai political discourse; it promises value to all comers but makes no specific proposals. Apirak did in fact invest considerable energy during his time in office, as he has continued to do, in promoting the idea of Bangkok as a center of artistic activity. But the specific commitment to take care of the poor residents of historic communities does not appear in this document.

On the other hand, nor does the grand vision thus articulated explicitly clash with the promises he had made, especially in response to Thawatchai's question, during the election campaign. Perhaps inspired by those promises, vocal commentators, especially those with an interest in maintaining the old center as a living part of the city, kept up the pressure; there was no contradiction, they suggested, between refurbishing the old city and allowing the residents to remain. Just a day before he took office, the planner Karin Klinkajorn, for example, challenged him to "revive Krung Rattanakosin to reflect 'its grand spiritual heritage, which is unmatched anywhere else in this world' so that he would be recorded as the city's greatest governor in history."[14] As the same writer remarked in a subsequent article, "Some overall heritage conservation policy might be necessary. However, without a deep understanding of local realities and a real public participatory process, it will impose destructive values of[,] and be administered from[,] the top down administration. . . . A high level of public participation in heritage conservation is needed as well." Local communities, in this view, should be active players in the conservation regime—that was itself, as Karin remarks, struggling to overcome the modernist heritage of the 1950s, when old buildings, trees, and canals were considered to be antithetical to the march of civilizational progress. Such attitudes are still widespread in Asia and elsewhere, and the enfolding of conservation practices in regimes of "development" and "progress" remains highly problematic.[15]

Despite all the initial vagueness, hints in the election campaign that change was in the wind meant that Apirak would be also judged differently from many previous governors. The language of "participation," which itself (as we have seen) is a staple of the democratic jargon of the NGOs, was not necessarily a guarantee of positive action. But even at the start Apirak had seemed to be bringing something new to the table. Like his questioner's brief speech, Apirak's very concise remarks, delivered in a rapid-fire, well-paced, and non-histrionic display of confident expertise—in contrast to the theatrical performances of some of his rivals—elicited a round of warm applause and, to general amusement, a huge bouquet of flowers. While his insistence that he would be the representative of all Bangkok people, no matter how poor, was not a novel political platform in itself, the careful detail of his responses (so much in contrast to the generic rhetoric of the postelection manifesto) and his direct, enumerative manner (he used his hands to disaggregate his otherwise rather generic proposals into what then looked more like a series of specific points) gave the impression that he would consult much more widely than his rivals. In promising that he would introduce "new rules, a new life," he at least implicitly seemed to suggest that he might be willing to tackle the more intransigent uses of the law by the entrenched bureaucracy he was about to inherit.

Apirak's 2004 victory had occurred exactly one year, to the day, from the Administrative Court's 29 August decision against the community. With the municipal administration now in the hands of this unexpectedly triumphant politician who had offered reassuring insights into the policies he intended to adopt toward historic communities, activist Somsook must have realized that the chances of changing the course of events had improved as never before. But it was another year before events took a significantly different turn. Despite both the promises and the challenges, many within the community retained a wait-and-see attitude well into the first year and more of Apirak's tenure of office. And they waited. Over that year, the mood in Pom Mahakan gradually became more somber, as nothing further happened to convince the residents that they were safer than before despite all the election promises of consultation. And so the residents decided to organize a demonstration in front of the imposing city hall.

Early in August 2005, a day or two before the residents staged their demonstration in front of the imposing BMA building, Somsook had very bluntly—as I was later told—informed Apirak that he was morally obliged to save the Pom Mahakan community. Somsook, who rarely minced her words, is on record as describing eviction as "a form of violence that will simply lead to more violence."[16] In the meantime I had met a wealthy entrepreneur—culturally a Thai, the blond son of Finnish Methodist ministers, a hard-drinking, expansive bon vivant who was inclined with British-inflected irreverence to refer to the Rattanakosin (Royal) Hotel in the heart of the project zone as "Ratters"—who had actively bankrolled much of the election campaigning of the Democrat Party, to which Apirak belonged. This man had expressed an interest in helping the community because he thought that doing so would be good press for the party, and arranged for me to meet on 4 August with the party leader and a group of associates including a party-political appointee in the BMA structure. The meeting took place in the Democrat Party headquarters. The senior politician, later to become prime minister, entered the room with a small entourage of party officers. He was clearly intrigued by the political advantages that supporting the cause of Pom Mahakan might offer a party that had been upstaged in matters of social policy by the populist Thai Rak Thai then still in power at the national level; but he had some residual concerns. Speaking by choice in impeccable upper-class English, he quizzed me about what opposition Apirak might encounter if he supported the community's claims. I replied that I thought that such opposition would come from three sources: the government, then in the hands of Thaksin's Thai Rak Thai party; one disaffected family within the community; and some of the civil servants. This last observation elicited a knowing smile from the BMA official, who was wearing the administration's insignia, but who was perhaps supposed to watch out for the Democrat Party's interests (and guard the new governor's back) within the ranks of the city hall bureaucracy. The meeting concluded with an assurance that the party would be interested in considering the suggestion that it should lend its support to the Pom Mahakan cause.

That such a decision was quickly made at a very high level within the party represented a turning point in the community's status in the larger political universe, although this was not immediately obvious, and although the community leaders were at pains to emphasize that their loyalty was always to their own collective interests and not to a particular political party. While not all observers seemed persuaded by the leaders' stance of party-political neutrality, it became an important rhetorical and political resource when, a few years later, the furious street demonstrations by the Red Shirt movement prompted a violent response under the aegis of the Democrat Party government. The community leaders were able to persuade the demonstrators not to invade their space but to respect the fact that the community residents, too, were poor people fighting for their rights. It is worth noting in passing that the community has, even since the eruption of street violence in 2009 and thereafter, experienced very little of the intense internal political factionalism that has riven Thai national politics, and that its capacity for compromise has served it well, both in protecting its space from the incursions of demonstrators and—in contrast to the country at large—in demonstrating its adherence to highly valued ideals of non-confrontation.

The third factor that evidently played a role in Apirak's decision to explore the option of supporting the community's project was the demonstration by a group of Pom Mahakan residents armed with loudhailers and banners in front of the Town Hall the day after my meeting with the party leadership. That morning I was supposed to go to Thammasat University to speak to a seminar about my field research. Before I left home, however, participant observation took over from academic life. Thawatchai called my cell phone: we are about to demonstrate in front of the city hall, he said, and I want you to come. I phoned Claudio Sopranzetti, and he and a friend joined me in the square in front of the municipal headquarters, where Thawatchai, backed by an orderly phalanx of perhaps fifteen residents, was haranguing the facade of the building through amplifiers erected on the back of a parked pickup truck. I feverishly began filming, hoping I could get enough interesting footage before my speaking obligation dragged me away. It was already an unrelentingly hot summer morning under a cloudless sky, and the Pom Mahakan demonstrators were mopping their faces. There were a few city policemen standing around in uniform, gazing with stoic bemusement at the small but clearly well-organized demonstration, a tiny group of people making a loud but disciplined noise in one small corner of the recreational and ceremonial plaza facing the huge city hall building.

An Unexpected Visit

It was now almost exactly a year since Apirak had won the election. With no clear sign of progress in resolving the residents' plight, there were reports of deep disappointment in Apirak's apparent failure to keep his election promise.[17] While he had responded to pressure from COHRE by writing in a letter that Pom Mahakan could "serve as an example for other ancient communities," his slightly defensive-sounding statement that the BMA "always respects the housing rights of our residents," while perhaps more sincerely intended than past experience of the BMA as an institution would have led anyone to expect, was not, given that history, the stuff of which reassurance is made.[18]

The demonstrating residents' mood was consequently truculent but also, in keeping with the usual style of Thai demonstrations, respectful of key conventions and institutions.[19] They, like Somsook, must have realized that they now faced their best chance in years of reversing the tide. In front of the truck from which Thawatchai was barking out his fiery speech, a few residents held up a pair of handsomely inscribed white cloth banners; fine lettering is a common sight in protests and failure to

CHAPTER FIVE

provide it would be seen as a mark of the protesters' lack of civilized values. One of the banners proclaimed, "Communities are a social, cultural, and economic asset. A governor is the Thai person who should be preserving (*anurak*) and refurbishing (*feuan fu*) them"—language that is more commonly used for the preservation of material objects, especially antiquities. Between the banners two of the demonstrators also held a wooden-framed printed portrait of the king, at a younger age and resplendent in a military uniform, symbol of their commitment to the official polity in its purest form, and, next to it, another of the queen.

Thawatchai, flanked by several other residents and wearing a T-shirt sporting the logo of the government's "Secure Housing" (*bahn mankhong*) program, was getting into his stride. His face strained with effort and dripping with rivulets of sweat that he would occasionally impatiently wipe off or sweep hastily from his upper lip, his voice growing hoarse and his neck strained with the visible physical effort of his impassioned rhetoric. He was meanwhile apostrophizing the invisible governor, complaining that his people had nowhere to "nourish their lives" (*bamrung chiwit*). Recalling Apirak's electioneering promises to respect the rights of people living in historic communities, he affirmed the Pom Mahakan residents' reciprocal commitment to the maintenance of their site.

A key theme of his lengthy but surprisingly unrepetitive speech, which was richly illustrated with factual details, was the claim that the people of Pom Mahakan were capable of participating in urban development. This theme had been prominent in the academic conferences held at Thammasat and Chulalongkorn Universities in 2003; now, Thawatchai laid it out in the context of the new governor's mandate. He reminded Apirak that a predecessor in city hall, Bhichit Rattakul (who had also been a candidate in the 2004 election but was completely upstaged by the younger and more charismatic Apirak), had already stated explicitly that the community could, in fact, coexist with a public park.

We can, declared Thawatchai, echoing some of the language of self-sufficiency his friend Tao had used at the Chulalongkorn conference, participate in such a development on our current site "for the benefit of society" (*peua prayot khong sangkhom*)—a smart move, given that one of the arguments the BMA bureaucrats had often used against the community was that a small group of people should not be allowed to deprive the larger public of a common good.[20] He then went on to detail the site's historical importance, especially mentioning its foundation by royal bureaucrats and its symbolic prominence where *likae*—a distinctively Thai mode of musical performance—was first performed in Bangkok. What we want, he said, is to take part in the collective vision of Thailand. So if the plan is to create a public park, "we do not reject that"—another allusion to the practicability of combining park and community. As for the tourists, he thundered, they represented a chance to show the world that ordinary people in such communities were part and parcel of the Thai territory. And he went on to develop a familiar theme: "The older and younger siblings (*phi nawng*) are not squatters (literally 'invaders,' *bukruk*)." Documents, he pointed out, showed that since ancient times houses and gardens had existed on the site, but that coexistence now faced extinction. Disarmingly admitting to the earlier compensation agreement and noting that "perhaps the people [of Pom] are not the original inhabitants," he nevertheless demanded of the BMA to take advantage of the occasion by working with the residents.

After several minutes more of the same argument, he declaimed, "We need the legitimacy you, Mr. Governor, can bestow." He also briefly mentioned other candidates who had contested the gubernatorial election. But then, briefly, he dropped his declamatory tone, and in a gentler voice full of entreaty, said, "You must go and see [for yourself]"—potentially the most fateful and effective sentence of his long harangue. (The formal particle, *khrab*, with which he ended the phrase implied, not intimacy certainly, but a more sociable mode of talking directly to the governor as a possibly compassionate individual rather than to an anonymous building and the political forces it represented.)

Having offered some more reflections on the historic and present situations of the community, his voice growing still more strained but rarely decreasing in volume, his eyes constantly attentive to the almost empty plaza (he broke off briefly to *wai* a passing official he recognized at one point), he turned to the municipal election of a year earlier. He reminded the governor that, before some of the most prominent of the other candidates, he had pledged to pursue a new policy of consultation with the historic but poor communities of the city.

After a while, Nok, a young woman who was to become the leader of one of the five internal zones of the community until she succumbed to a premature stroke, took the president's place. Also a passionate and fluent speaker, though not as experienced as Thawatchai (and therefore occasionally a little more hesitant in finding her words), she touched on many of the same themes, especially that of the community's desire to participate in a collaborative approach to development with the BMA. Her speech was more openly emotional and directly personal, but she also reminded Apirak of the documentation that would demonstrate the

CHAPTER FIVE

community's willingness to cooperate. She provided both a contrast and a strong backup for the president's long speech while he went off to address a news conference.

Eventually, with reluctance, I had to leave the demonstration and rush to the seminar; apologizing for my late arrival there, I commented that at least those present now knew that they were hearing about the most current situation in my field site. But my claim, it turned out, was in fact not quite true, because the three sources of pressure—the activist's harangue, the demonstration, and my meeting with the party leadership—had, unbeknownst to me, been building to an unexpectedly immediate effect. The precise causality is unclear, but at least one well-informed Thai academic and activist thought that the combination of these three nearly simultaneous interventions had triggered the surprising development about to unfold.

That evening, while I was being driven to a dinner hosted by the seminar organizer, I received urgent calls from archaeologist-activist Pthomrerk Ketudhat and from Thawatchai, both asking me to go quickly back to Pom Mahakan as Governor Apirak was about to appear there. My colleague turned the car around and we made a hasty return to Pom Mahakan. Excusing myself from the dinner (a move to which my host, herself a noted political activist, graciously assented), I went directly back to the community to position myself for the event. Sopranzetti, who first dashed to my hotel to pick up some additional videotapes for me, sped back with the help of a motorcycle taxi to join me just before Apirak arrived. It was, he tells me, his first experience of the mobility that was to become the topic of his doctoral dissertation and would, ironically given the Democrat Party's role in the events of that evening, lead him, through the motorcycle taxi drivers, to the heart of the opposition Red Shirt movement that many of them supported.

Previously, only one governor, Bhichit Rattakul, had shown any inclination to treat with the residents, but he had done so in the municipal offices, and in the end he had not granted the residents anything more substantial than an early deferral of eviction. (His deputy, architecture professor Banasophit, had suggested at the Chulalongkorn University conference in August 2003 that redirecting funds budgeted for community development so that they could be used for the community's own plan would not be illegal; as she also pointed out, the actual park construction need not be very expensive.[21])

Another key Democrat Party politician, Khunying Kalaya Sophonpanich, following a long conversation that two local activists and I had with her about urban issues in Bangkok, visited the community on a fact-finding mission. Her experience, and especially the warm reception she received, may have fed party interest in the residents' plight. Like others before and after her, she emphasized the importance of conversation and of looking around the community. Despite her aristocratic status and elegant dress, she sat on the hastily prepared mat laid down for the meeting as soon as the community knew of her arrival and engaged the residents in an animated discussion of their plight. Although she exuded goodwill, however, her visit generated no immediate results. The earlier fact-finding tour by the then president of the Bangkok City Council had created a positive impression, but he, too, was careful to make it clear, during the press conference he held at the end of the visit, that the legal questions had to be disentangled before anything could be done to help the community.

At least these politicians earned the residents' polite respect. But not all politicians' visits to the community achieve unqualified acclaim. In 2008, during a subsequent election for the governorship of Bangkok, a candidate who had quarreled with the Democrat Party leadership and in his pique launched an independent campaign decided to visit the community. This time, the reception was far from uniformly friendly. Although Thawatchai, irritated by what seemed to be the politician's proclivity for changing his mind about the rendezvous to suit his own convenience, did not show up, many of the other community leaders—but few other residents—sat around the meeting mat. The politician, affable and well-spoken, talked about his interest in dialogue with the residents, but did not seem to be able to capture their attention. In part this was because he seemed unable to articulate a clear policy; his vague expressions of goodwill sounded decidedly lame. Maew, a leading member of the community and an activist with strong links to local activists in the north of the country, later remarked that with such politicians mutual trust was simply not possible (*choea kan mai dai*). It is not clear whether the residents' marked lack of enthusiasm sprang particularly from their annoyance at the politician's high-handed management of the appointment, because his smooth and rather unctuous style did not sit well with people who were looking for active commitment, or because these very savvy denizens of Bangkok sensed that his chances of election were minimal. His visit, in any case, made no lasting impression, especially against the vivid backdrop of Apirak's visit and the remarkable events it triggered; that was an event that set the bar very high. Let us return to that sequence.

Apirak's first visit was truly a sensation and an event of a completely different magnitude from those earlier attempts of his party colleagues. When I arrived, I found the community in a state of high excitement. The small children of the community had been hastily marshaled in the space

CHAPTER FIVE

where Apirak was expected to meet with the community en masse, in front of the huge portrait of the king, and instructed that "the children and grandchildren of the Citadel show their respect to Mr. Governor"; they were shown how to *wai* in unison while chorusing the greeting *sawatdi khrab/kha* in very carefully enunciated tones. The adults looked on with indulgent amusement, but it was clear that they themselves were no less excited.

When Apirak finally arrived, his entourage contained some of the same bureaucrats who had been organizing the eviction of the community. They did not look particularly comfortable at finding themselves in a supporting role for a venture that seemed likely to go against all their efforts. The governor, solemn but friendly, offered a respectful *wai* to the assembled elders of the community, who were seated in rows facing him with Thawatchai off to one side. Thawatchai, speaking with a microphone to make sure that the event was totally audible to the community (as also to the journalists who were following the governor and perhaps also to any passersby on the other side of the old wall), immediately launched into his favorite theme of the community's ability, as citizens of the city, to join hands with the BMA in a development plan that would combine a public park with living quarters for the residents.

Then he conducted Apirak on a brief tour, visiting points of interest including the area where fighting cocks were being raised. Throughout, he addressed the governor through the microphone, emphasizing that the community had demonstrated its ability to solve its own problems (and therefore, he implied, would be a reliable partner for the BMA in any future collaboration). Apirak mostly nodded, looked around, and asked an occasional, quiet question. The tour took in the old house that was intended to serve as a community museum before it was removed from the site; Thawatchai continued his speech with a detailed historical explanation of what they were seeing. Despite the oppressive nighttime August heat, Apirak, a slim and youngish-looking man who at that point looked a great deal cooler than the community president, gamely ducked into narrow doorways, ignoring the asphyxiating press of journalists and residents, and then returned to a discussion with the community elders about their plight and their hopes that he was now bringing a wind of change. The politely attentive governor in white shirt and tie and the sternly stentorian community president sporting a T-shirt and chunky amulets around his neck presented a revealing contrast, both nevertheless unequivocally laying claim to moral authority by means of their respective management of sound, posture, and dress.

While this momentous event did have a slightly staged quality both as a result of the use of microphones and because the children had been so hastily rehearsed in greeting the governor, the exceptional nature of Apirak's visit lay in the contrast he displayed with the deliberate indifference of most previous governors and their staffers. His mien was that of a politician who aimed to be different. Not only did he decline to use the microphone for most of his visit but, at the end of his tour, listening to the community elders and discussing their problems with them, he showed becoming humility by sitting on a low seat.

One elderly woman who had led the residents in confronting the BMA bureaucrats on an earlier occasion, and had been especially eloquent on her fears of ending up homeless, was so moved that she suddenly and passionately exclaimed, "Today I feel very happy"—an unusual declaration of warmth toward anyone representing the BMA, and one in which she was joined, almost as if in a chorus, by another woman of slightly less advanced age sitting beside her. It seems likely from that confident echo that the first woman had been wonderingly saying the same thing over and over already to her friend. And she went on to express particular amazement that she was now actually talking with a governor of Bangkok about the problem of housing—something that only a day earlier had seemed an improbable dream.

At the end Apirak accepted the microphone for a very brief, unrehearsed speech; having been handed a set of documents compiled by the community youths and by visiting students, and having been told of the activity of visiting academics (including Pthomrerk and myself), he explained that he would now need time to digest all the information but that in any case he looked forward to continuing the exchange of ideas. Throughout this more authoritative phase, he retained the same serious but approachable manner. Finally, it seemed, hope had come to Pom Mahakan.

Apirak did not leave matters long in limbo. Half a year later, on 7 December 2005, he returned to attend a press conference at Pom Mahakan, where he signed, together with the community president and the rector of Silpakorn (Fine Arts) University, a contractual agreement to recognize Pom Mahakan as "a community of ancient wooden houses." The community's publicity organization announced, in a happy Thai echo of the original English-language slogan that had greeted me on my first visit to Pom Mahakan, "The war is over . . . the eviction is over (*yut songkhrahm . . . yut lai roea*)." This, then, was the background to that electric press conference at the site at which the three parties signed a formal agreement to put the new plan into motion.

The intention of the land-sharing formula was to rebuild the majority of the houses considered to be of slum quality, while integrating both these and the seven old houses deemed historically noteworthy into an overall plan for a public park. There was no disagreement about the need for "development" and "fixing" of the site's material aspects. The residents were both to continue living on approximately one-fifth of the site, in exchange for which they would be partners in the restoration and maintenance of the entire space. While reserving one *rai* (sixteen hundred square meters) of the site for residential purposes,[22] the inhabitants specifically asked to take additional responsibility for the security of the one additional *rai* of uninhabited land, currently free of houses or habitations of any sort (this was the area cleared by the army in 2003). This was a place where itinerant vendors sometimes came to rest or sleep through the night; it was often full of their paraphernalia, including Buddha statues and other religious objects, not to speak of the rubbish left from their nocturnal sojourns, and in consequence was at risk of becoming a dangerous place. In drawing attention to this situation, they were, at least implicitly, recalling the concern that an empty park could revert to use by drug addicts and pushers. Certainly the authorities cannot have much liked the UN-Habitat description of their handiwork on the lawn area: "Despite all the warnings and pleas, the area has been transformed into the type of place that few people, whether Thai or tourist, would care to visit."[23] Because the BMA could not provide adequate supervision but was preventing the residents from having access to it, it had fallen into serious disrepair, the "manicured lawn" of the UN-Habitat report having become sodden with puddles and often covered with stray garbage, while the "concrete pathways" that crossed it were cracked and dilapidated.

The spirit of the new agreement, which was in line both with Apirak's electoral campaign declarations and the urging of the UN-Habitat report, was based on a sharing of responsibilities and tasks. The details were still to be worked out at the time of the press conference, but this kind of sharing of both the land and the responsibility for its upkeep was also exactly the solution for which the residents had been fighting, and they were wildly enthusiastic. All the doubts and misgivings about Apirak's motives that some had expressed were finally laid to rest, although the rhetoric of the occasion also raised questions about "the rights of the poor within the city" in a discourse that, in retrospect, seems strikingly consonant with, and anticipatory of, the intensifying global and revolutionary language of the "right to the city."[24]

That it was genuinely Apirak's goal to promote this plan, there can indeed be little doubt. It was also a cost-efficient plan, built on the expectation that the residents would not change their lifestyle and would therefore be satisfied with only a slight adjustment to their modest financial situation, that sat well with Apirak's embrace of the king's "sufficiency economy."[25] It seemed, quite simply, the logical as well as the ideologically appropriate course of action. The bureaucrats and Apirak's personal political woes, however, decreed that matters would not be quite so simple.

The plan had actually been gestating for some time. In the October immediately following Apirak's visit to Pom Mahakan, a Silpakorn University architect, Chatri Prakitnonthakarn, was called in for consultation, and the new plan was hatched. Chatri, as someone who has also made something of a splash by criticizing designs for the new Thai parliament building as unnecessarily nationalistic and therefore irrelevant to the vernacular traditions and democratic needs of the people of Thailand,[26] was in this sense a particularly appropriate person for the new vision of Pom Mahakan. He had long been interested in the old vernacular architecture of Bangkok and, as he told me in an interview, he had first visited Pom Mahakan in search of materials for an essay in 2003,[27] at about the same time as I was initiating my own fieldwork there. At some point, he received a fax—he says he does not remember where it came from—telling him that then-governor Samak was preparing to evict and destroy the community in order to build a public park. He decided to pay a visit to the community. "I went to see for myself. I went to find out how the residents were fighting. I didn't know anyone. And then I went to meet the community leaders, and then they showed me around." He then wrote his findings up in the journal *Silapa Wattanatham* ("Art [and] Culture"); as an architect, he said, he had gone to see the situation because he was interested in really old wooden houses and "community atmosphere." Wooden houses were something of which "these days there's not much left."

His article was provocatively titled "Pom Mahakan: To Conserve or Destroy History?" He discovered, as he recounts in the article, that the decision to go ahead with evicting the community and razing the houses had gone to the highest government level: it had been confirmed in a meeting at the prime minister's office the year before (on 14 April 2002). The residents had reacted by continuing to offer the compromise of a land-sharing agreement, but their overtures were again rebuffed because the site was part of the Rattanakosin Island project. Although the authorities appeared to be immovable, the article eventually triggered the first significant change of policy and attitude.

In the October following Apirak's initial election, Chatri received a phone call: Apirak had read Chatri's article and invited him to come for a consultation with some of his staff; he thought that something along the lines Chatri was recommending would be "one [possible] alternative" to allow the residents to continue to live there under decent (*nayu*, livable)

CHAPTER FIVE

conditions while also permitting the BMA to create a more attractive environment. "Mr. Apirak made an appointment with me to go for a chat about how, if I were to go and clean up, develop, and preserve the community, I would set about it." As a result of that conversation, Chatri was authorized to begin the necessary on-site research, which he conducted with a team of students from his university, assessing available materials and residents' needs and priorities.

The result was a plan to preserve "the Pom Mahakan community of ancient houses outside the Phra Nakhawn Wall," detailed in an impressive book of background history, data, and plans. The volume was still formally clad (through its title) in the rhetoric of "conservation and development" (*kahn anurak lae phatthanah*). But here the more literal meaning of *anurak* (conservation) emerges, especially in conjunction with the idea of community: the word is derived from a root meaning "to take care of something or someone" and, at a further remove, "to love." This suggests the affective and caretaking relationship with heritage that some Western theorists have also associated with conservation and with anxieties about future conditions—a linkage that still has weak echoes at best for many Thais, for whom "care" is a pragmatic rather than an affective concern.[28] Archaeologist and activist Pthomrerk's stinging criticism of the authorities' "failure to understand the meaning of the word *anurak*," and indeed of history itself,[29] similarly recuperates the sense of human engagement from a term that bureaucrats were more inclined to treat as a purely technical concept. The report subtly shifts the meaning of conservation in that same direction.

Recognizing the conservation of the historically important site as the fundamental principle to be respected, the report's principal author (clearly Chatri) thus also—in contrast to Pthomrerk's more direct fulminations—employed a tactically artful avoidance of confrontation with royal power by attributing "good intentions" to the Rattanakosin Island committee. In that vein, he offered "the inferior important point" that the august body in question had been ignoring the historical complexity of a highly diverse city. "Driving people out of the *moeang*," he suggested, would deprive Bangkok of its living history by failing to recognize that people were a "significant component" of that history. Note that here the term *moeang* could mean either the city at large or Pom Mahakan in particular; this term plays havoc with modernist planners' literal-minded assumptions about scale. Moreover, the author continues, official historic conservation creates "a green place with the remains of buildings, but it is an urban space that lacks life," and the historical representation of Thai culture should not be restricted to the reign of Rama V alone in the idiom (*krawp naewthang*, "conceptual framework") of the BMA master plan and the Rattanakosin Island Committee; "the city (*moeang*) is a complex of many eras and various things that have occurred to give their entire meaning to history and urbanity (*khwahm pen moeang*, literally 'the essence of being a *moeang*')." Ordinary people ("small people," *khon lek khon noi*), he argues, are also producers of art and culture. While this language perhaps outwardly reflects an older discourse of patronage (and patronizing attitudes) toward the "lesser orders," as the terminology suggests and as the respectful jockeying for authority with the once-powerful committee still required, none of the community's academic and professional supporters today can claim to be directing the leaders' actions, and the author of the article is well aware that the community does not easily supplicate for the condescending pity of the rich and famous.

That change is consistent with a much larger and more radical shift in the structure of cultural authority. The author's strongest fire is reserved for the "Western" values of the architects and planners who had created the problem in the first place,[30] and here we see that his position is in fact more or less convergent with Pthomrerk's in essence, if not in rhetorical style; Chatri's role was less that of a gadfly critic than that of a tactful insider participant in the process of planning reform. While the idea of appealing to an encompassing Thai aesthetic was clearly intended to resonate with the nationalistic ideals of the Bangkok bourgeoisie, the more direct critique of the crypto-colonial paradox—that Thainess is often created in the idiom of Western national identities—suggests that Pom Mahakan could provide a setting for a new approach in which those foreign models no longer predominated. That, however, as the author daringly (but still respectfully) remarked, meant that long-suppressed working-class practices and values would at long last be recognized as culturally significant.

The research conducted on the site represents a careful division of labor. There were four groups. The first was assigned the task of poring over all available documents. The second was charged with developing a sense of cooperation among all the parties, residents and professionals (including those of the BMA)—an interesting recognition of the difficulty that such a project entails; its duties included convening meetings to discuss the limits imposed and the possibilities enabled by existing laws.

The third group was a field research team tasked with establishing the various parties' attitudes toward refurbishment, conservation, and landscaping the total setting, while also conducting field research recording the residents' way of life.[31] Much of the field research was done in public sessions and using questionnaires to establish basic demographics and information about house ownership and livelihood. While in general questionnaires do not yield much information of a culturally intimate kind (and the students who applied them seem not to have paid much attention to the gossip that broke out at the end of the interviews), the information thus collected provides a solid base for the practical actions that Chatri and his team intended to pursue. Against these plans, however, it was equally important to anticipate the possible legal consequences of those actions, especially with regard to the more distant future; this was the responsibility of the fourth research group, which canvassed the views of prominent legal advisers including the then vice rector of Thammasat University.[32] The legal team had its work cut out for it because, as was painfully apparent, different levels of the law—for example, various versions of the national constitution, the laws regarding eminent domain, municipal regulations, and special edicts authorizing the Rattanakosin Island Committee to make key decisions—were often in conflict with each other.

The report appears under the joint aegis of the BMA and Silpakorn University; the mere fact that such sentiments could be voiced out of city hall indicates a genuine conceptual shift at the very top. Almost as soon as the report appeared, however, matters once again started to unravel. The bureaucrats insisted on performing a legal examination that they clearly hoped would lead to a cancelation of the plan, as in the end it did—officially, at least. But perhaps more important, the ever-ebullient Chatri, who had warm social relations with many of the residents, encountered a practical problem in the community itself: not a few residents, especially those who had no tradition of urban living and had come from various rural areas during the years of accelerating rural-to-urban flight in the 1960s and 1970s,[33] seemed rather lukewarm toward the cultural project that he had developed. As a result, Chatri, in conjunction with the community leadership, found himself engaged in a process that bordered on cultural proselytization, trying to convince the relative newcomers that investing in "history" and "culture" was a necessity if they wished to remain in their homes. It was also important to train all the adult residents in being able to guide visitors, and especially tourists, around the site; he implied, but did not say, that this aspect would be important for the community's economic survival.

Given that people were being evicted all over the city, he pointed out, the most important thing was to get the residents to understand that their best assets were the history and way of life that their community exhibited; that, and only that, would constitute a basis for making an exception to the widespread pattern of eviction. Moreover, the residents' insistence on regarding the situation as a matter of rights was clearly irksome to the bureaucrats, who, Chatri felt, might have been more willing to compromise in practice if the whole matter could be handled with greater delicacy and less confrontational tactics requiring an open surrender by the BMA. Legally, the BMA remains the sole owner of the site, and that is an ineluctable fact that the residents would do well to take seriously. Because Pom Mahakan is situated in a densely symbolic area and one that attracts many tourists, its cultural aspects were the only resource the residents could effectively deploy. Clearly a process of self-education was required—one that would, once again, insert the residents of Pom Mahakan in a cultural frame that reflected the self-exoticizing and self-reifying crypto-colonial ideology rather than the life experiences of the residents themselves, but that might perhaps have enabled them to continue with their daily practices under the guise of acting like quintessential Thais.

None of this, however, provided protection against the bureaucrats' legal maneuvering. They persuaded the Administrative Court that a park was by definition incompatible with private residences, and this put an end to the plan Apirak and Chatri had developed only a few months after it had been announced. Thawatchai remarked that it was important, in the wake of defeat, for Apirak to "think anew, do anew (*khid mai . . . tham mai*"—an ironic slogan to apply to a Democrat Party leader, given that it was a rallying cry of the opposing Thai Rak Thai party of Thaksin Shinawatra.

Despite having seen a vision of a possible solution thwarted by the bureaucrats and the court, the leaders continued to argue for dialogue. Thawatchai was characteristically eloquent: "It's like this: we'd make a presentation to request to live in our original place (*nai thi doem*), right, professor? The issue would just be, *OK* [this word was in English], it's like we are asking to live there, in our original place, right? In what way will we live there? Because there's one point, which is that the BMA has never lived with me! What that means is, how will we live, we'll have to think this through together, right? So my calculation is that the state, which is really close to Mr. Apirak, should open up the opportunity to have the ordinary people think together with them. That, *OK*, the ordinary people live right here, what's the way they live together? Because—here's one point—I see, I observe, that Mr. Governor wants to see . . . what a resilient (*khemkhaeng*) community is like." In short, was there a way—which Apirak in fact much later hinted to me might be possible—to allow the residents to remain on the site, not as legally entitled inhabitants but through a special arrangement that recognized their skills and abilities?

Thawatchai thought that to achieve such a goal would require a serious attempt to get the BMA to join communities—not necessarily Pom Mahakan in the first instance—in appealing to the state for its support for a radical change in the methods and style of civic administration. From this point on, the leadership, at least, was more confident of its ability to set a good example. One of them told a graduate student, "If the officials will just let us live in our original place (*thi doem*), we won't have to transfer our rights to outsiders, but we'll be happy to cooperate with them in looking after (*du lae*) the place; we can save money for the budget, and conserve (*anurak*) the culture . . . One of the work committee members pointed out that just as in the past inside the community we have elections for the committees that take care of keeping the place clean and caring for the various public utilities and we collaborate with the district office and the metropolitan police station . . . for example, to keep the fortress wall and the canalside street clean, trim the trees, campaign against drugs, practice our professions, have the community children do sports in collaboration with the nearby communities."[34] It was this persistent attention to clean living and self-governance, always with a respectful bow to those official entities that accepted such collaboration, that the leadership steadfastly maintained as the basis for community survival, and that so impressed the new governor.

To the extent that this change of attitude at the top might actually bring about a real change in administrative practice, Pom Mahakan had to remain in a state of constant vigilance lest its denizens relax and so fail to demonstrate the community's continuing viability. "The residents (*phi nawng*) see the various activities. No matter what we've already done, we have to get the residents to do more. Work. . . . You said correctly that it's a beginning. But we can't let people think, 'This is a successful job completed!'" That warning was sadly prescient. The plan articulated by Chatri was thwarted, and once again the community faced the corrosive force of uncertainty.

In the face of such continuing frustration, sustaining the collective commitment and motivation has proved to be perhaps the leadership's hardest task. There have been factional squabbles galore; while at least one student writing about this community told me he was advised to avoid discussing these in his thesis lest the BMA take advantage of the dissension, my own sense is that the BMA is very well informed about such matters, but that even the die-hard foes of the community fully understand that the leaders handle squabbles with great skill, so that dissension has not really undermined the collective will to any lasting extent. A thoughtful member of the leadership group observed that the community was "not *perfect* [he used the English word], not 100 percent," but such realism does not obscure the fact that Pom Mahakan has managed to hang together remarkably well and for a remarkably long time.

Grinding poverty, to be sure, has reduced the available temptations that might lead some individuals to go their own ways. Indeed, prosperity, although desirable, may be as much of a problem as the burden of poverty—"it's something to fear," as I was told. The example of the nearby middle-class areas that have failed to create a sense of solidarity in opposition to official interference is a constant warning. One well-educated activist from the Golden Mount community that overlooks Pom Mahakan told me that their leadership is secretive, so that the residents never know what is happening; that one of the community leaders is especially touchy but also fearful of serious action; and that women do not speak at community meetings because they feel disrespected. Although the residents have a long history of working in a single trade, lumber preparation, and although they were scarcely more willing than Pom Mahakan to surrender to the BMA's pressure tactics, each of the Golden Mount community's households tends to focus on its own interests rather than seeking to reinforce a collective will. All this—which can certainly be matched in other middle-class areas such as Phraeng Phuthorn—contrasts strongly with Pom Mahakan.

Perhaps the most remarkable aspect of Pom Mahakan at that moment was its control of discourse and procedure. That control, which had already been steadily developed over more than a decade of struggle, gave it the palpable ability to act more like an arm of government than many of the more middle-class areas. The orderly organization of the community committee, with its clearly defined functions and its onstage flexibility as well as its subcommittee of five "zone heads," provided a strong institutional template for the more elaborate organization required by the sudden new situation. Added to the community committee was now a "board" superstructure that had six community representatives (the first being the community president), three "scholar-experts" (including the archaeologist Pthomrerk Kedudhat and the architect Chatri Prakitnonthakarn), representatives of three networks and four NGOs, and three representatives from the BMA.

Ultimately, however, the Chatri plan failed because the BMA bureaucrats, as we have seen, adamantly insisted that a public park and private residences were mutually incompatible. Meanwhile, Apirak's political difficulties resulting from the Austrian bus scandal led him to resign. His successor as governor, Sukhumbhand, was a man of very different temper and inclinations, and the residents found themselves, once again, engaged in a war of psychological attrition.

SIX

Time, Sound, and Rhythm

Wars of attrition translate the individual experience of waiting into a time marked primarily by social intensity, balancing dependable communal solidarity against unpredictable hostility lurking outside and stretching endurance to the breaking point.[1] The tauter the tension, the more impact every unexpected maneuver achieves. In these respects, the Pom Mahakan community is striking both in its investment in official history and in its deployment of disruptive tactics, so that the tensions that proliferate throughout the Thai body politic come into especially clear focus there. The daily experience of time and space both shapes and responds to the social and political tensions of Thai life, and the economically, territorially, and politically straitened circumstances of Pom Mahakan sharpen the tensions and bring them into high relief.

Pacing Events

No less than kinship and reciprocity, time and space often appear to be rigidly structured, but turn out instead to be flexible and malleable—subject, in short, to the social poetics whereby style is negotiated and modified in everyday interaction. The committee's management of pace offers an especially rich illustration. The members must adjust their speed and rhythm—what Pierre Bourdieu calls the management of *tempo*[2]—to the city administration's sometimes unpredictable use of formal timing. The subtle management of time at community gatherings tweaks the solemn march as well as the insidious prevarications of officialdom.

Foreigners are often struck by the degree to which Thais appear to accept quite passively the twists and turns of political fortune, but also, paradoxically, by their enthusiastic engagement in street protests and political factionalism. In reality these are not mutually antithetical habits; nor do they represent a variant of the stereotypical fantasy of "oriental fatalism." Thais live in a politically volatile environment. They often sound like modern Romans attributing to their sufferings under papal rule their currently sardonic attitudes to authority and their refusal to be pushed into anxiety; they express themselves through a host of expressive forms that subvert the stern punctilio of officialdom.[3] In that view of the world, it makes more sense to assume and prepare for the worst and enjoy the social immediacy of the present while also resigning oneself to the attrition of waiting for unpredictable but probably unpleasant or at least unsatisfactory outcomes.[4] This is a Thai modal narrative, the official history of the Siamese kingdom's long, tactical prevarication in dealing with the colonial powers that sought to erode its territory and perhaps one day to invade it. Long-term interest accrues to the skilled tactician, whether a maverick community president or a canny king.

Prevarication is a skill, and it is one shared by all the players in the story I am telling here. In Thai, as in English, it is called "buying time" (*seua waelah*). Consider the letter I wrote Sukhumbhand to protest his renewal of the eviction threat and to offer help in promoting his predecessor's alternative strategy. I am morally certain that the letter was not diverted by self-interested bureaucrats because it was sent to him privately both by a mutual friend and by a Democrat Party insider and government minister who was well-disposed to the residents. Sukhumbhand did not reply; but the threatened move against the community did not materialize, and on 25 July 2013 his office sent an invitation formally addressed to the "president of the Pom Mahakan community" (*prathahn chumchon Pom Mahakan*) to attend a ceremonial dinner at which the governor was to present awards to various communities for their sporting and cultural activities and, as the English-language dinner invitation said, "to celebrate Bangkok as the world's best city." It is unclear whether the puzzlement this invitation provoked reflects the governor's unofficial decision to favor the residents by doing nothing (as at least one of his predecessors and several other commentators have thought) or a devious extension of the bureaucrats' psychological warfare against them.

Even under the perpetually hostile Samak, the BMA had punctiliously acknowledged the community's communications, but this was no mark of friendly intentions. Versions of one such letter, dated from the point at which serious record keeping in the community seems to have begun (February–March 2003), carry meticulous notations acknowledging receipt and indicating the relevant clerk's telephone number; another version shows the stamp of the Ministry of the Interior, to which the letter had also been sent. Many of these letters, one of which was sent to the relatively sympathetic president of the city council, Samart Malulim, are also dated and carry telephone numbers. These minor details of bureaucratic procedure are interesting both for the awareness they demonstrate of the need to keep a "paper trail" and in the light of what did or did not happen thereafter. There is no record of further municipal or national government action. Despite Samart's seemingly friendly fact-finding visit, the BMA governor was apparently still prepared to play with the residents' nerves. The ministry officials presumably preferred to treat the case as an internal matter for city hall.

Samak, whose interests lay in pushing ahead with the Rattanakosin Island plan, thus ignored the residents' polite entreaty to arrange a meeting before the projected eviction date of 24 February 2003—a meeting that, they argued, would avert the threatened violence and destruction. As the community's letter stated, there was no guarantee of security for people or goods, and there was a genuine threat of violence on the part of those carrying out the eviction. That the threatened attack never took place brought some relief, but it left some very frayed nerves in its wake as well. It is hard to believe that such was not the intention. It was hardly in the BMA's interests to use violence in the midst of all the temples and tourists; far better, clearly, to wear the residents down, and to create an atmosphere of tension and fear. But the residents, it turned out, were equally adept at the waiting game.

They could also anticipate the bureaucrats' moves in some ways. Non-acknowledgment of communications as well as an acknowledgment that does not result in a substantive answer are two effective ways through which officials can safely create uncertainty. While the inscrutability of officially directed events might appear to favor attrition, however, it also seems to strengthen the residents' frequently reiterated resolve not to yield. There are numerous additional devices through which a lack of clarity about intentions, or at least a refusal to declare them specifically, can serve the interests of any of the parties. When the bureaucrats took Apirak to court and so succeeded in wrecking his plan on purely legalistic grounds, he announced that while he could not now permit the rebuilding, he was nevertheless not going to expel the residents. This was a classically inexplicit move that, apparently on purpose, favored the residents.

TIME, SOUND, AND RHYTHM

Moreover, time bought is publicity gained. As the tense negotiations and confrontations have continued to feature in the news, the residents have succeeded in attaining a visibility that might otherwise have eluded them. It is one of their strongest weapons in their campaign to remain on the site.

Agility in playing with time—syncopating events according to their own preferred rhythms—is thus a crucial means of recasting those events to the community's own advantage.[5] Many of the seemingly last-ditch stands launched by the residents were explicitly understood to be tactical ways of "buying time"—and the residents also understood this technique to be something the authorities also used against them.

In the same sense, Apirak's refusal to evict them was also a proactive move that bought the residents time. Such temporalities reproduce, in instantaneous interactions, cosmological concepts of temporality, refracting the latter through the exigencies of particular moments of struggle; the undulations of Tambiah's "pulsating galactic polity"—the segmentary properties of the *moeang*—reappear in a cat-and-mouse game in which the authorities do not always emerge as the cat. This is not to say that the bureaucrats lack such temporizing skills. To the contrary, they utilize them to the full—or, at least, reluctantly recognizing that they are up against equally skilled opponents, they try to do so.

Waiting Each Other Out

A senior member of the BMA's Department of Public Works exemplified this quality. Although he never wavered in his long-term goal of enforcing the BMA's authority and removing all the houses from the Pom Mahakan site, he blandly declared that his sole purpose in coming to discuss plans with the residents was to ensure to maintain its "orderliness" (*khwahm riap roi*)—a revealing term inasmuch as it is mostly commonly used to suggest a certain type of bourgeois respectability exemplified, as the art historian Maurizio Peleggi has demonstrated, by the monarchy's adoption of Western middle-class habits and aesthetics, and redolent with fascist notions of order.[6] By repeatedly emphasizing the advantages of calm conversation and a cooperative attitude, he tried to disguise his temporizing as well as the harshness of the underlying message of inevitable eviction by suggesting that everything could be resolved by discussion over time. The residents were not fooled; they explicitly rejected his approach as one that did not in fact admit of any real discussion at all.

From the bureaucrats' perspective, waiting was simply the prerogative of those who wrote the national master-narrative: resistance would ultimately prove futile since the law was intransigent and unambiguous (another important technique being precisely the denial of legal ambiguity) and represented a trust vested in the royal state (*rachakahn*) by a series of wise monarchs. They clearly felt secure in this attitude, and their serene sense of entitlement was the clearest mark of the feudalism with which more radical activists frequently charged them. The residents were living an economically hand-to-mouth existence exacerbated by the need to be constantly alert to danger while the bureaucrats (*kha rachakahn*, literally "the servants of the royal state," and thus invested with its formal legitimacy) were salaried, possessed of at least nominal power (*amnat*), and able to sit out any conflict.

What the bureaucrats did not expect, however, was that the community leaders could garner respect as "tough" or "resilient" (*khemkhaeng*) and were prepared to suffer for their cause[7]—a quality that the bureaucrats regarded as mere foot-dragging and obstructionism, but that Apirak saw as a guarantee that they would not let him down if, as eventually happened, he went out on a limb on the community's behalf. These leaders would, over time, prove considerably more skilled than the bureaucrats at manipulating social time, and could, in addition, effectively invoke Buddhist values to bring opprobrium on the heads of their enemies—in this case by accusing the bureaucrats of lacking true Buddhist compassion for the sufferings of others. No fatalists they, they used their karmic condition as a community oppressed to push back, hard and long, at the intransigence of official power; and, in so doing, they also appeared to offer a model of resilience to other communities suffering a similar plight.[8]

Passivity in the face of suffering is often assumed to be a characteristic of Buddhist societies. Those in power might well find it convenient to encourage such an attitude, much as the Catholic Church in Rome lauds poverty as a refining discipline of the soul in those who face eviction at the hands of the church's local representatives. As in Rome, however, the sufferers themselves are far from passive. In the same way, Chinese evictees in Shanghai, by petitioning the authorities, ignore Buddhist and Confucian canons cynically used by the socialist regime to enjoin submission to the will of fate and secular power alike.[9] In all these cases, residents are ready to wait; but their waiting is not the endless waiting of the resigned. Schemes to render the poor content with their lot, or with "sufficiency" in the currently regnant discourse of anti-consumerist developmentalism in Thailand, do not necessarily achieve the complaisance they seek.

Waiting can thus serve exhibit agency as much as it may reflect bureaucratic oppression and client resignation. Like boredom,[10] of which it often takes on key aspects, it can serve as both an instrument of control—Thai citizens are accustomed to official prevarications that are often deliberate in both senses of the word—and a temporal space in which to regroup and resist. The Pom Mahakan residents have one advantage on their side. Those who are out of work have all the time in the world to wait out bureaucrats, and the community as a whole has no more pressing concern than to hang tough in all its negotiations with the representatives of municipal power.

At another level, the importance of mastering time is equally clear from the way in which the community leaders have adopted the language of historical conservation and cultural resource management. Houses that are no more than two hundred years old, but that represent styles associated with phases of official history, are classified as *borahn* (ancient)—some bear proud placards proclaiming them to be "ancient houses" (*bahn borahn*)—and are attributed to particular reigns (*rachakahn*; cf. Hindi *raj*) of the present royal dynasty; a visitor will be told, for example, that such-and-such a house dates to "the Third Reign" while another is from "the Fifth Reign"—an effective device for calibrating local identity with the state's reading of history.[11] The use of the word *borahn* similarly represents an attempt to claim a deep link with antiquity. When I first visited Pom Mahakan early in 2003, there were eight houses considered to be deserving of that epithet. One of these was designated as a community museum and funds were raised to restore it to its former glory, but it was removed at the behest of a dissident community member before much could be done. One of the most astonishing aspects of this financially poor community's campaign for recognition is the extent to which it has been prepared to go in order to associate to itself resources that are contested by other actors; the residents had similarly held a ritual to initiate fund-raising for the restoration of the citadel itself but, after the front area was sequestered by the army and covered with a grass lawn, their further access to it was cut off by a metal fence—the latter a cause for considerable concern, as it seemed to presage the tightening of the noose around the community.[12]

Today, while there is still much talk about its historical significance, the majority of the community's efforts are directed to more immediately human ends, notably, through the operation of the community savings fund, the pooling of sufficient funds to support the building of new homes (fig. 5). The community savings fund has three explicit goals, of which the first is to help residents deal with housing problems; it was relatively easy to translate this purpose into using a significant outlay to enable the actual construction of new homes when that became possible, albeit with considerable risk of immediate demolition.[13] The other goals are to help residents avoid the exorbitant interest rates of loan sharks, and to assist

CHAPTER SIX

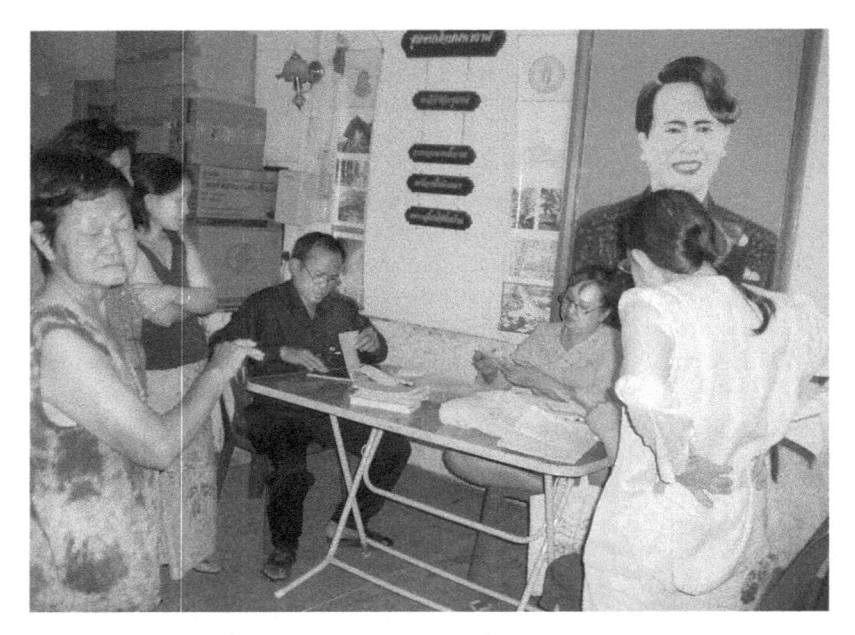

5 Keeping accounts—the community savings system in action

them in creating and maintaining their professional livelihoods.[14] Members of at least six months' standing can take out emergency loans of up to 3,000 baht, but cannot do so again until they have repaid the previous amount at a monthly interest rate of 3 percent (of which the communal fund receives 1.5 percent while the other 1.5 percent is paid out in dividends to the membership).

The relevance of rotating credit to the tempi of competitive waiting lies in the fact that the fund reduces the level of uncertainty within the membership. Residents know that they can always rely on emergency support; meanwhile, the few who have dared to build new houses could do so with the security of knowing that they could finish quickly, before the authorities were able to intervene—once a house is complete, a demolition order is harder, at least in theory, for the authorities to secure. The regularity of payments provides a soothing counterpoint to the suddenness of the emergencies against which the fund provides protection, but it also enables the community, at moments of its members' choosing, to disrupt the authorities' vision by enabling members to create a less precarious habitat and therefore, perhaps, to construct a more secure future on the site.

Broad Temporalities: Adjusting to Antiquity

Despite the shift of emphasis in the community's fundraising from historic conservation to the management of current problems, the label of "ancient" continues to carry enormous significance. It is the one device through which attention can be diverted, albeit often with difficulty, to vernacular architecture, some of it fairly modestly proportioned, amid the glittering gold and the silvered mirror slivers decorating the surrounding temples. Vernacular architecture is a hard sell in Thailand, to be sure; while some wealthy Bangkok people have begun to construct traditionalizing huts on their land, much like the *yurt* that one sees in Central Asian backyards, very few of these are actually used as residences; their function is more that of gazebos or places for entertaining guests.[15] But for the community the presence of "ancient houses" amid the more slum-like constructions is one of the few material resources they can deploy in support of their goals, especially as they can be attributed to particular periods in the dynastic chain.

Such self-historicizing maneuvers are often opportunistic and fictional. A Thai film company wanted to produce a historical documentary about musicians of the Fifth Reign at the site, justifying their activity as "building up and conserving Thai culture,"[16] thereby partaking of the language that the community was using to justify its continuing existence but also—subversively—fitting the community's story to the Rattanakosin City Project Committee's specific goal of reconstructing the Fifth Reign on the site. To achieve its goals, the film company requested permission to make some physical changes to the landscape, including the removal of a shrine. But this was all in the interests of a historical performance that served the community's self-projection perfectly, and it also recognized the community's virtual ownership of the space—the one area that has subsequently been removed from its control and turned into a lawn.

The residents responded with alacrity to the company's subsequent request that they participate as extras, girding themselves with the clothing of that era and flooding the space under the bossy command of the film director and his associates. Such activities, factually ill informed or imaginary though they may sometimes appear to be, helped to reify the community's historical status against the insistent claims of the municipal bureaucrats' insistence that the residents were squatters who shared no common origin and no historical connection with the site. Their claim, later strengthened by the association of the space with the first Bangkok

CHAPTER SIX

performances of the traditional *likae* dance drama genre, is not simply as a community, but, once again, as a metonym or microcosm of the entire Thai polity.[17]

In the case of the film, they took advantage of a rare opportunity to play out a social drama. During the days of filming, any visitor who chanced on the site would see almost all the residents dressed in period costume, their hair arranged in the topknots of that period that for many Thais paradoxically represents both the apogee of quintessential Thainess as well as the decisive turn to the West. Their enthusiasm matched the seriousness with which they also, at other times, staged traditional dance displays and collective rituals.

Clothing the body in period costume affirms a link with the past no less effectively than posting heritage signs with explanatory texts, as the authorities have increasingly begun to do, and, in the case of the filming, it allowed the residents to connect their bodies rhetorically with an era critically associated with the emergence of the modernizing Siamese state. In the same way, claiming antiquity for the houses they now inhabit affirms a collective lien on the past, as opposed to the more dubious and contestable claims the residents sometimes make to individual rights of possession.

The discourse of antiquity is an effective weapon. It has a long history of its own in Thailand. Rationalization, Westernization, Buddhist reform of a "protestant" kind, and the first attempt to create a sense of an ancestral national culture all converge in the stern figure of Rama IV Mongkut. Here we see in emergent form the concern with archaeology as a validation of presentist identity that also achieves noteworthy emphasis in other cryptocolonial settings such as Greece and Iran. Pursued still further by Mongkut's successors, this invocation of a single cultural identity traceable to specific points of origin has been the cornerstone of conservation policy in Thailand ever since, and nowhere more so than in the Rattanakosin City Project.[18] In the hands of the various committees and officials whose task it was to promote the project, designation as a place of antiquarian significance became a key instrument of cultural policy. Pom Mahakan, officially declared a *borahn sathahn* ("ancient place") in 1949, was an obvious and early target for listing.

The bureaucratic idiom of cultural antiquity proved to be a double-edged sword. The seemingly straightforward designation of the site as "ancient," quickly adopted by the residents to describe vernacular architecture as we have seen, also served to link the physical presence of the houses and of the entire site to that of the people living there. Antiquity, it seems, can also be refracted through a rebellious social order. In one tense meeting between BMA officials and residents, the leader of the BMA team tried to argue that his task was simply to facilitate a process of historic conservation (*kahn anurak borahn sathahn*, literally "to preserve ancient places"). The community president's ever feisty mother, a woman who could combine artful debate with an argumentative voice and an imposing presence, retorted in disgust, "So then you don't think that ancient people live here at all? If there are ancient places, there are ancient people living there!" The bureaucrat tried, rather ineffectually, to respond with a lecture on the rules of historic conservation. But she had captured, as many of her fellow residents did on various occasions, a more potent use of the term "ancient" that merged archaeology with a living population and with the spirits still inhabiting the shrines. Her considerable age reinforced her semantic ploy, and her status as a third-generation resident and as an articulate defender of community rights gave her views unquestionable authority. Her speech, brief though it was, clearly dented the official's ability to maintain his cool, his repeated exhortations to work through their differences calmly and slowly fraying noticeably as the argument continued.

Small Temporalities: Gesture, Tempo, and Sound

The tightly enclosed area of Pom Mahakan lends intense focus to the residents' historical discourse, including their use of parodic signage. But the deliberate pursuit of antiquity is also reinforced by far less obvious forms of temporality. The tiny gestures that animate everyday life serve to create a sense of belonging precisely because they are predictable, endlessly repetitive, and utterly ordinary. Rhythms of daily action, compressed within the tiny space of Pom Mahakan, take on a powerful significance, especially when contrasted with the unceasing roar of traffic on the other side of the high wall that bounds most of the site.

During the heat of the day, a powerful contrast that is both spatial and auditory separates the community from the raucous modern city. As visitors slip off the noisy roadway running alongside the old wall, balancing on the narrow, uneven strip of sidewalk and dodging electricity poles and the firework sale display at the entrance to the park, passing wobbly *tuk-tuk* three-wheelers and overcrowded buses before ducking into the narrow path on the inside, they experience a sudden but soothing quiet. It is broken only by the inconsequential muttering of a television set, which is largely ignored by one woman whose uncomfortable relationship with other community members isolates her near that entrance. She is usually

CHAPTER SIX

to be found dozing in her favorite spot or chatting with family members while several cats snooze heedlessly on the ground around her. A quick laugh, a child's playful cry, the tinkle of a fruit vendor's bell, the rustle of an occasional breeze in the trees—these light, clear sounds seem to bury the rushing traffic outside, its frenetic screeching and squeaking muffled by the thick eighteenth-century stone wall of the old city. That wall is half a meter thick; an architecturally muscular embodiment of permanence, it insulates the community from the clattering transience of the chaos without. The tranquility on the community's side of the wall defies the discomforts of modernity, bringing relief to deafened ears and fume-stuffed nostrils.

Technically, it is the community that lies outside the wall, or crouches behind it; but as one passes into the quiet narrow lane on the community's side of the wall, it is the city that becomes extraneous. The residents' perspective reverses the official, historically established order of the city, transforming its apparent spatial clarity into an arena of contest. While the city authorities regard the community as a disposable nuisance, the residents' entire struggle is invested in demonstrating that their looking-glass perspective encapsulates a microcosm of Bangkok and even of Thai national life. Pom Mahakan is more than a peaceful urban village; it is also a place of sometimes surprising gentility and respect. Soft speech and a quiet demeanor are signs of good breeding and high-class aspirations in Thailand; the community's peaceful rhythms reproduce these desirable traits as a collective virtue, belying the brawling reputation that some would like to attribute to the residents. As Apiwat Saengpattasima's punning film title *Behide the Wall* declares,[19] the community hides, enfolded in sleepy quiet on the "other" side of the wall; but looking out from that refuge, it is the city that appears to be somewhere "out there," a menacing, noisy, bureaucratic, but also deeply familiar force perpetually threatening to engulf and destroy the community. Tranquility is a gentle but, for daily purposes, effective and enduring defense.

Toward evening, however, the dreamy rhythms of the day are sharply interrupted by the sudden crackle of amplified static and then by the president's strident voice, formally but insistently demanding that the residents gather for a meeting, organize for a safety drill, or present their contributions to those now managing the community savings fund at a table in the main square. His diction is formal, punctuated with the usual masculine polite particle *khrab* (which one does not ordinarily use in intimate discourse) and framed in unmistakably institutional phrases. His voice, intense with political urgency even in relatively casual conversation, leaves little doubt that all residents are expected to do their duty.

Its timbre seems markedly at odds with the elaborately polite formality of his language: harsh, clipped, and amplified to a tinny but inescapably stentorian echo, his orders—for so they appear to be—are the audible sign of both his paternal authority and his political passion.

Soon the residents foregather. In particularly hot and oppressive weather, the women's fanning motions, a sign and creator of harmony, refashion the turgid air as a shared and welcome breeze. From time to time, the quiet in the square is split by another amplified eruption from the president as he crouches before the microphone inside the community museum, frowning with the intensity and urgency of the need to convey his message to all, and sometimes with the difficulty of dealing with uncooperative equipment that intermittently disintegrates into a loud crackle.

Sound and movement: both emphasize the durability but also the syncopated synergy of social relationships within, in contrast to the aggressive anomie of the streets on the other side of the wall. This is the space that the residents are prepared to defend against invasion—a community of shared interests and harmonious living. Yet all is not peaceful. The president's imperious harshness, the irritating static noises from the monstrously inefficient PA system, the occasional eruption of angry altercation and anxious, urgent questioning during the frequent and endless meetings that often occupy the evening hours—these are all signs that the community is not living in an idyll. Even the recent appearance of small but well-constructed new houses cannot disguise the persistent poverty and misery or the unrelenting tension of living under siege.

The use of microphones and loudspeakers, while a new technology, is not incompatible with Thai notions of soft speech as part of good manners (*marayaht*). Indeed, it introduces an honorific system of its own. Those who control the soundscape have a power that links them with both the academic and media worlds and with the chaotic but powerful city beyond, through conventional verbal expressions that signal their comfort with the language of NGOs and academia. And the use of loudspeakers that reach both the members of the community and passersby on the other side of the perimeter wall affirms the status of the community as a microcosm of the nation's political life, with democratic participation and stentorian leadership vying with each other as its organizing principles at both the national and the local levels.[20]

A humble demeanor and soft speech may be marks of genuine deference, but they can also index a self-confident moral authority. Similarly, declining to use a microphone may also be a sign of power. While the community leaders' use of amplification dramatized their reputation as "resilient" (*khemkhaeng*), Apirak's refusal of the microphone when he addressed the community elders was an effective invocation of the soft speech that marks consideration for others—a diction that renounces violence and celebrates good breeding.[21] It elicited a polite and relatively soft set of responses from his audience, which included the president's mother—and she was quite capable of loudly haranguing her foes, as the BMA bureaucrats had discovered to their acute discomfort.

These sonar dynamics are best understood in the larger context of the Thai verbal soundscape. For urban Thais, at least, the ostentatiously quiet speech that bespeaks high status is not the barrier to communication in noisy spaces that it would be in the English-speaking world. First, Thais are, as a rule, extraordinarily careful respecters of turn taking, so that interruption is rare and pauses at the end of each utterance are usual. Second, and arguably more important, the tonality of the Thai language reduces dependence on consonants and allows speakers to communicate *under* a general level of noise rather than having to *overcome* it (as we would say in English). Residents rarely seemed to experience the slightest difficulty in chatting sotto voce while their leaders' most stentorian exhortations blared forth from the amplifiers. Just as some Thai conference-goers seem to think nothing of using a mobile phone during a talk, people in their everyday conversations seem undisturbed by loud music, traffic, or the occasional altercation.

Thus, amplification, which is also prominent in community meetings, seems to bother no one, and is not necessarily at odds with ideals of politeness (*marayaht*), especially when what is amplified is rendered polite by the use of appropriate particles, formal registers, and honorific forms of address. Indeed, in such circumstances, it is the insistent if formulaic evocation of politeness, rather than the sound itself, that is amplified. Whereas to some foreign observers the intimations of harangue might seem threatening, and whereas the repetitive firing of polite phrases such as *na khrab* can sound like a verbal fusillade or a parade-ground bark, to Thais these are simply the accoutrements of leadership, reminders that those who are elected as leaders exercise their authority through an idiom of mutual but unequal respect.

There is nevertheless also no doubt that the use of amplification sets the leadership apart from other members and gives them crowd control as well as an air of authority. And the amplification can be deafeningly noisy, especially against a backdrop of a quiet rendered more palpable, first by the occasional tinkle of a fruit vendor's bell or the shouts of children playing in the tiny square that has become the community's symbolic and administrative center, and then also, increasingly, by the intimations of a less controlled and even greater and more continuous racket—

the roar and rumble of traffic, the blare of horns and car radios—on the other side of the wall. On certain occasions, too, some leaders would use loudhailers outside the community—for example, to marshal residents for almsgiving to monks on a religious holiday, when curious passersby might be impressed by the community's visible (and audible!) capacity for self-governance. (There are other uses for amplification: a woman in the Muslim community of Ban Khrua used it to shame drug dealers circling that community on the outside by directly accusing them over a similar but more massive public address system.[22]) The same holds true for the regular calls to attend meetings; these are fully as audible on the outside as the sermons of monks trumpeted from the electronic systems of certain temples, and they effectively advertise the community's democratic engagement and conformity to the ideals of Thai fictive siblinghood.

In this way, the use of amplification both imposes hierarchy and also creates the equal access that guarantees—or at least promises—democracy. These ambiguities match the uncertain meanings that ordinary politeness often carries. Thai manners are remarkably well equipped to convey both irony and ambivalence; their very conformity makes them susceptible to delicate, nuanced play in context, as when a deferential *wai* becomes an act of possible sarcasm, through an exaggerated raising of the hands to an absurdly high level, between two social actors whose relative status is implicitly challenged by the ostensibly lower-ranked partner.[23] Similarly, loudspeaker announcements that implicitly project the authority of certain recognizable voices also thereby assert the presence of functioning democracy and mutual respect; as long as "followers" insist on voting for the same "leaders" on the grounds that their respective standing reflects innate differences between the two groups, however, it is clear that some people will always have the right to amplify their voices even as they proclaim their desire to escape from the burdens of power, and that others are always silent if watchful witnesses because that is their ascribed—and, significantly, self-ascribed—role.[24]

A few individuals, almost all women, occupy a middle ground. During meetings, when the leaders take turns at using the loudhailers to exhort the crowds to "help each other think," these women—who are either married to leaders or are in charge of one or another of the community's five subsections—comment on the ongoing stream of rhetoric. From time to time, one of them shouts out a more or less facetious answer to one of the rhetorical questions, but much of the time is spent joking "under" the blare of the amplified voices, and most residents only respond when a leader demands, "Isn't that so?" (*chai mai*)[25]—and then only with a chorus, abrupt and laconic (and often still reluctant and hesitant), of a single

CHAPTER SIX

exclamatory "True!" (*chai*). Sometimes Thawatchai throws even more aggressive rhetorical questions at his audience, notably "*Shua mai*" (Are you sure [that you understand what needs to be done]?). The use of an English word—another such phrase is "*Khlia mai*" (Is that clear?)—perhaps sounds more authoritative; no one would ever dare admit, under such public questioning, to being unsure or unclear.

Thus, the sonar instruments of collective action and democracy actually establish lines of authority that reassert stereotypically Thai ideals, including some that subtly appeal to the prestige of English speech. In this society, one cannot be a democratic leader without powerful self-assertion. Doubtless, as Thawatchai frequently suggests, such apparent inevitability is indeed an exhausting burden for the leadership. It takes a physical toll; he himself is frequently hoarse from the constant speeches and interviews he gives. And there are few avenues of escape—not because of any inherent Thai fatalism, but because habits of rule and submission are repeatedly enjoined and inculcated in an enormous array of social settings, and because it would take an enormous effort of will (and a great leap in the dark) to countermand them in a conscious and effective manner. Modernity has intensified, not reduced, such constraints; electronic amplification has enhanced more than decibels. It has lent the trappings of technological modernity to the perpetuation of hierarchy, but it has also democratized discussion, bringing all within hearing range into its embrace.

Agency and Leadership

Both here and in the Phraeng Phuthawn community, local leaders told me to speak to their opponents, both communal and official—something that would have been well-nigh unimaginable in some of the southern European communities in which I have worked. These were proactive demonstrations of strength and confidence, creating a space for the agency that residents often asserted. I saw that agency repeatedly asserted in tiny incidents, of which two will serve to make the point.

In the first, the residents had decided to set up a series of signs that would direct visitors to the museum spaces they had created. I suggested that, if we did some of the signs in (at least) English, this would attract tourists, and we could help. They readily agreed. Bun, the young community treasurer who worked for an insurance company and was relatively well-educated, helped us to create the signs, and copied our English with impressive accuracy. At one point, however, he missed a detail—an "i"—and when we pointed this out, he refused to let my wife or me carry out the correction for him, but remedied the situation with an artistic flourish that made the omission of the letter appear to be deliberate—it was added at a higher level than the line of lettering, but with a floral flourish of ornament that made it point to the word as a whole. Not only was our friend insisting on his own autonomy of action—this was, after all, "his" community—but he successfully managed a symbolism associated with us, visually incorporating it into his world and making us his assistants in a process of projecting the community to the wider world. This brief action reproduces a pattern of co-optation that is more broadly displayed in the brown-and-white signs indicating historical details in Thai and English that mimic the official signage of the municipal authorities—and parodically celebrate local specialties such as fish maw soup, rather than the glorious histories of the monumental structures. Residents are adept at seizing the initiative both in moments of opportunity and over the long haul.

The second example also concerns the young treasurer. Along with most of the other residents, he had followed the procession through the community of the elegantly suited city council president Samart Malulim and his entourage. A Muslim, Samart was apparently more sympathetic than many other politicians to this marginalized community (which includes two Muslim-headed households). He was visibly startled to encounter an obvious foreigner who spoke even clumsy Thai, and wonderingly commented on this to his followers. He seemed to have no objections to my filming his progression through the community; I was interested in recording the event because this was the first time in a long while that someone of such importance had troubled to visit Pom Mahakan, and it stood in dramatic contrast to the municipal city clerk's ostentatious habit of ignoring the community and its residents. Samart seemed genuinely interested; he took his time, and as he pursued his stately course he seemed to attract an ever-growing tail of journalists who hung on his every word.

At the end of his site inspection the politician held a press conference. Flanked by his own entourage as well as by senior residents, he offered a sober assessment of the legal issues that would now have to be addressed. But then he unexpectedly suggested that the journalists should also ask the anthropologist for his views! As I nervously stumbled forward, taking out my visiting cards to present them with a formal *wai* to the journalists, I felt the video camera being gently removed from my hands. It was the young treasurer. The film he took shows two journalists looking at each other in some perplexity; how were they to speak with the foreigner? And then they relaxed as I presented my card and began a little speech in Thai, praising the community and arguing against the authorities' determination to evict it.

CHAPTER SIX

Note how the treasurer had managed the situation. Not only did he successfully take over the filming, but he ensured that I would have no escape from the politician's invitation. His knowing smile as he handed the camera back to me after my speech was sufficient to make it clear who was really running *this* show! But he was also clearly pleased that I had cheerfully accepted the impetus he had created. In this regard, his gentle management was all of a piece with the events that had originally lured me into my connection with the community. It was an assertion, polite but firm, of agency, while I remained in possession of a remarkably smooth videotape of my first-ever impromptu press conference in Thai.

Such experiences help to link the theoretical discussion of tempo with the themes of emplacement and reification. What I have called "monumental time" is the Ozymandias-like attempt to achieve immortality through the monumental celebration of particular periods—here, the reigns of the present dynasty—and especially their reproduction in architectural styles organized in neatly demarcated space.[26] The large historical claims gain force from the community's location near several temples that are intimately bound up with the history of the reigning dynasty. But against the looming presence of statues and temples, the eddies and agitations of social interaction link the everyday with the majesty of court history even as they sometimes contradict it. Small gestures conveying a sense of intimate mastery flow around and implicitly challenge the rigid temporality of official history; they syncopate its ponderous predictability, rarely challenging it but democratizing it by making it the backdrop of individuals' agency—and indeed the object of their energetic attempts to seize and deploy it—rather than only the imposing background of their daily attention. Official time is, simply and ineluctably, present, an inert and immovable past, pure context, against and within which a tiny, transient gesture can spark a vivid flash of everyday life.

Emplacement and Movement

State and municipal control of urban space often entails vast and brutal clearance projects.[27] Populations that offer an inconvenient rebuttal to the official sense of order are peremptorily expelled to the outer edges of cities or even further away, while the arrangement of "historic sites" on the ground reinforces the exclusion of those groups by turning the classification of space into a concrete, physical reality—often in the form of formalized empty spaces and minatory fencing and signage.[28] The phenomenon is not unique to Bangkok; people have been expelled from such sites as Ayutthaya, the pre-Rattanakosin capital of Siam.[29] The attempt to turn Pom Mahakan into an empty park mostly consisting of green lawn and a monumental balustrade, already fronted by official signs detailing the orthodox history of the site, similarly exemplifies this process.

In the case of Pom Mahakan, moreover, the point of departure was explained to me during a tense public meeting by a senior bureaucrat from the BMA's Department of Public Works, who claimed that during the reign of King Rama V the entire area had been a lawn. That does not appear to be true, since several of the houses are of older date; although in a photograph taken during the Fifth Reign there are no signs of habitation in the immediate vicinity of the citadel, it appears to show only the front area, where, except for one narrow band, the residents had never lived.[30] The evidence of the surviving old houses clearly belied the bureaucrat's generic claim about the whole area. His motives, however, cannot be separated from the ideological purpose of official intervention. Given the intention of dedicating the site to the queen, and especially given the attitudes of the Rattanakosin City Project committee, the justification for turning the site into a swathe of grass was bound to hark back to the architect of the crypto-colonial Siamese state.

The regulation of space produces a concomitant disciplining of time. Periodic or monumental time—the march of reigns, for example[31]— provides both a background and a contrast against which *tempo*, the materialization of social time, marks the presence of contingency, of agency, and of sometimes deliberately contrarian volition. Periodic time is itself social, but its reasons lie in bureaucratic logic rather than in the imperatives of daily living. Because it is social it can be challenged; but it has power and organization on its side, and its massive monumentality often discourages reflection on its ultimate impermanence.

The social rhythms of everyday life thus disrupt the pretensions of the state to a reified permanence. They are not always violent or disruptive; but when they are consensual, they challenge officialdom's exclusive claims to being the arbiter of order. Much as parliamentary decorum frames sometimes heated debate, local idioms of harmony not only frame and constrain disagreement but also challenge the state's monopoly of order.

Contentious Harmonies: The Conduct of Meetings

Pom Mahakan's communal meetings provided a dramatic illustration of this. Some little while before each such gathering, a few residents would roll out mats defining the space of debate, a space respectfully treated in accord with Thai mores through the rather ostentatious display of shoes removed and left along the edges of the mats. Younger people would sit on the mats, their legs decorously tucked under them or bent to one side; elders sat on the chairs and faux stone seats on one side, their shoes still on their feet. The relative height of these groups was significant in that elders occupied the physically and symbolically higher position. The young people, arrayed on the mats, nevertheless had more direct access to the discussion (and sometimes to the president's harsh, peremptory demands for answers). Their ability to participate in this way perhaps befitted the youths' relatively higher level of education, although one or two of the seniors would also raise from the back a voice too loud and too opinionated to leave room for doubt about its owner's standing. Once again, the arrangement of space, seemingly hierarchical, in fact embodied the ambiguous tangle of authority and equality.

The fanning of the older women, with its steadily increasing coordination, rhythmically cooled their faces as, like a visual *basso continuo*, it paced the sometimes heated but always well-scripted debates of the men and younger women. Its soothing regularity seemed to reproduce these women's deliberate passivity in letting the leaders take charge, providing a solid base on which the latter could build solidarity out of the sometimes painfully roiling arguments and anger of individual households with competing economic interests. In the segmentary logic of the community, moreover, it offered a compelling parallel with another, imperious demand for hierarchy: the royal portraits and flag ceaselessly served to remind the residents that their democratic aspirations would only succeed if they operated through the rhetoric of national unity and essence.

But there was no ambiguity about the tension, anger, and distress as well as the political toughness that won praise for the community as embodying the finest traits of Thai self-sufficiency and pride. A *basso continuo* provides the backdrop against which the syncopation and disruption of conventional temporalities stand out with demanding clarity. Thais "hear" that backdrop of companionable fanning mainly, I suspect, as a means of foregrounding the sharper eruptions of disagreement; but it also reminds them that the state does not have a monopoly on democracy—indeed, often does not do democracy very well at all.[32]

In the tension thus dramatized and made palpable in political performance within local communities at odds with state and municipal authorities, Thailand looks very different from most modern European states. There, political opposition is direct, aggressive, and cleft by party-political allegiances that often seem more pressing than loyalty to the nation. Not that similarities between Thai and European attitudes are lacking; the Thai desire for consensus and compromise under a crowned head recalls such formulations as the British locution "Her Majesty's loyal opposition." In Thailand both monarchy and democracy were largely configured, especially during the past century and a half, in accordance with European models; and Thai independence itself is, in an encompassing paradox, the product of this larger imperial structure, especially in the Victorian idiom that it so often seems to reproduce. In this context, Thailand displays both exaggerated emulation and creative reworking in its crypto-colonial relationship with the Western powers.[33] A community like Pom Mahakan, in order to survive, must adjust to this complex reality and tailor its politics accordingly. But its meetings are exercises in realism, and, in the next chapter, we will see how the leadership deals with disagreement and disruption while trying to encourage the fullest possible participation—in the process enacting a polity, one might add, from which national politicians have a great deal to learn.

SEVEN

The Polity in Miniature

The Thai state is the enthusiastic heir to a markedly positivistic understanding of society that permeates every aspect of state activity.[1] The state's officials seek to consolidate by legalistic means a particular vision of culture that is often not shared at the local level—a frozen and impossibly pure and timeless diorama, perhaps best represented by the National Museum in Bangkok, that merges the Sanskritic language of *watthanatham* with European-derived models of national culture. This can sometimes, as at Pom Mahakan, emerge as a clash over territorial control, enacted as a battle over definition; the rejection of the land-sharing plan on the grounds that a public park and living inhabitants were not compatible with each other is a striking example of the positivism of the official perspective, which has an active presence also in some areas of Thai academic life and social activism and appears everywhere—even in local communities—in an audit-culture obsession with carefully packaged "data" (*khaw mun*).[2]

"Data" versus "Knowledge"

The pervasive positivism of Thai intellectual life also serves to give intellectual respectability to NGO rhetoric about participation. The resulting language resounds in the echo chamber of Thai political discourse, some versions of the national constitution included.[3] A booklet for the campaign of one of the candidates for the governorship election in 2004, Wutipong Phriebjariyawat, contains a drawing of enthusiastic community members sitting cross-legged on the ground and heatedly debating a pile of documents marked *khaw mun* (data), while the accompanying text rehearses the increasingly familiar platitudes about the need for participation "in solving problems and collective political decision-making" and achieving "circumspection and transparency in administering the work of the BMA more than the order of 'knights on white horses' or 'Super-CEOs' that are being widely disseminated."[4] Such eminently recognizable attacks on the Thaksin government and its rhetoric of transparency and CEO-style management do not disguise an equally populist, and equally hierarchical, understanding of political action.

The focus on "data" is the clearest clue that Wutipong's program did not express a strictly egalitarian vision. In the drawing, the one person wearing glasses is also wagging a didactic finger at the others, while the only person raising a hand to speak appears to be wearing some kind of uniform and the sole figure wearing a street food vendor's conical hat is sitting in the background. On the back cover of the booklet, there is a drawing of "the politicians' side" and "the people's side"; the chief politician is enthroned and he and his lieutenant are beribboned with formal decorations, while the antlike "people" are climbing a ladder onto the balance in the hope of tipping it in their own favor. Their chances do not look very good.

Be that as it may, the rhetoric of data and participation—given legitimacy by the realization that it "has become virtually mandatory in international institutions today"[5]—in practice thinly masks, and thereby reinforces, distinctly authoritarian assumptions about governance. The public meetings that amount to little more than lectures to a passive audience illustrate this process, which is reinforced by the Thai sense of hierarchical decorum. In the sphere of urban planning, even well-intentioned calls for participation may all too easily morph into processes that result in higher rents and eventual eviction.[6] Significantly, this positivistic rhetoric also informs the attitude, already mentioned, that engagement in the political struggles of a community would predispose one against an objective assessment of its activities. In short, this rhetoric both enables top-down governance and discourages opposition to it.

That some residents actively opposed the idea of giving data to even apparently friendly outsiders suggests that they, at least, were not so easily seduced. But everyday conversation and the rhetoric of the leaders and their NGO supporters did often reproduce the data-talk of the dominant paradigm. And the term for "data" does not always mean anything more rigid than "information." One of the community's most effective supporters, the architect Chatri Prakitnonthakan, was an early advocate of showing "how far the community of Pom Mahakan had qualities (*khunkhah*) worth conserving so that this would be basic data for the general public in assessing on the issues and problems that have occurred."[7] This focus on quality, rather than numbers, became a clarion call, with the community leaders and outside supporters (including this writer) insisting that indeed this was a community that "had quality" (*mi khunkhah*). But sometimes, whether for the practical purposes of the planning exercises that Chatri and his team developed or simply as a way of dealing with a public educated in the positivistic rhetoric of market surveys and scientific reporting in the media, the residents themselves developed an agile capacity for data-speak.

"Local knowledge" has now similarly become a widely used concept. Journalists increasingly laud its significance, but perhaps betray its lingering crypto-colonial implications by praising foreigners—this writer included—for having promoted local knowledge at a time when the local bourgeoisie had not yet begun to appreciate it. While appearing to praise local knowledge as worthy of respect, such efforts all too often, as Akhil Gupta has noted in the Indian context, end up placing it in opposition to true science or scholarship. As so often happens with artisanal crafts, which are treated as picturesque rather than as artistic, placing local knowledge on the pedestal of tradition serves, even with the best of intentions, as condescension that effectively excludes the bearers of such knowledge from positions of authority. Binary oppositions of this kind, to which the informal-formal distinction also belongs, are never politically neutral.[8]

In criticizing this use of local knowledge as borrowed from authoritative forms of cultural expression, however, we must be careful to acknowledge that its more derivative aspects are a consequence not of some besetting lack of genuineness, but of the tactical uses to which "it" is put. Like local history, it takes forms that the state can recognize, because it would otherwise simply be rendered as extraneous or irrelevant, or dismissed as mere tradition and as evidence that local people are not yet ready for modernity, this to include political voting rights.[9] Such attitudes remain common among the Bangkok bourgeoisie; indeed, the Yellow Shirts' call for a predominantly unelected parliament was based on their view that the working classes, especially in the poverty-stricken Northeast (Isan), were not yet ready for electoral responsibility. The regime that came to power in 2014 has embraced similarly paternalistic attitudes.

Such condescension has a long history in Thailand, and is often invoked to show that working-class people are prey to unscrupulous patronage. Yet the evidence belies such claims and suggests what motivates them;

6   The "Pavilion of the Community's Local Knowledge"

Katherine Bowie was able to demonstrate that northern Thai peasants actually resisted such corrupting influences exercised on their comparatively well-ordered political life by people emanating from the very classes that accused them of ignorance and gullibility.[10] Local knowledge, which is based on experience, includes a full awareness of these processes of subordination, and treating it as a separate *kind* of knowledge only serves to disempower its bearers and protect the true patrons and manipulators.[11]

Thus, when Bun took over the painting of the "i" on the English-language sign, his action took back the initiative of expert outsiders (experts, that is, in nothing much more than their own language) and at the same time, in a flash of spontaneity, offered a beautiful illustration of bricolage in action.[12] But it was a kind of knowledge that represented the inner face of what the community, a scant four years later, was to present to the world as formal fact, its museum called the "Pavilion of the Community's Local Knowledge" (fig. 6) Many of the museum's exhibits were curiously opaque; they included, for example, religious objects that were of no obvious political import, as well as children's paintings that schematically reproduced the formal properties of the citadel and the adjoining city wall—obvious claims on a disputed home only if one knew that the competition for which the children had made the paintings had been one of the events held by the residents to publicize their cause. There were also several CDs I had made for the community containing records of some of their more momentous meetings and acts of resistance. A casual visitor would also not have easily deciphered these for their real significance to the community; technology colludes in masking the subversive possibilities it provides.

The officializing name of the museum expressed well the formal self-presentation of a community poised between complicity or resistance and prepared to move in either direction according to need. And the shingle that announced it and gave it the status of incontrovertible reality *as a category* was a fine example of formal Thai calligraphy, in graceful embossed gold lettering on a deep red background, hung in front of the stylized Thai house that serves as the community's museum archive.

Englobing Authority

The necessity of oscillating between the two extremes of political structure produced an adaptability that, at one level, is the official story of the Siamese response to the threat of colonial invasion. What is happening at Pom Mahakan replays the early years of the kingdom's adaptation to Western pressures, with similar oscillations between an allegedly feudal and hierarchical system of governance and the embrace of a Western-style polity claiming to provide egalitarian participation for all its members. The reification of local knowledge and Pom Mahakan's collective self-celebration as encompassing cultural diversity in a communal adherence to tradition both reproduce the centralization of moral authority in an internally variegated national culture; this is a refraction of what the encroaching colonial forces demanded of the Siamese state as the price of its conditional independence.[13]

Such comparisons may seem far-fetched; there are clearly differences between the grand history of the state and the local evolution of the Pom Mahakan community. The traditionalizing discourse of Pom Mahakan, moreover, appears superficially to reject rather than to submit to Western-style cultural prototypes. But it is clear that Pom Mahakan represents exactly the kind of challenge to the legitimacy of central authorities that we find in other societies where rebellion against a foreign oppressor has continued as subordination against a national authority, and the symbolic and stylistic inversions of official attitudes that we find in Pom Mahakan are a consequence of the claims to a specifically Thai modality of moral and cultural leadership at the official level. As they insistently reiterate the mantra that "we are Thai people," the residents of Pom Mahakan seek to wrest the moral initiative from the authorities by emphasizing the fact that their community does indeed—as the authorities complain—derive from multiple locations and regional cultures, but arguing that it is precisely this internal variety that makes them distinctively Thai. In this way they also implicitly challenge the legitimacy of the bureaucrats, whom they repeatedly portray as betraying fundamental principles of Thainess. The bureaucrats thus appear not only as hostile "invaders" but as foreign to Thai culture; and in this sense the residents bring the concentricity of the local community with the national polity into focus as a lien on the moral authority of the *moeang*—the original and intimate form of the Siamese polity.

They show great tactical acuity in advancing the "unity in diversity" argument, which plays official ideology back at officialdom and makes counterarguments difficult to justify. Officialdom is morally compromised and pragmatically baffled by the rhetoric. In a cultural context that also favors avoiding the direct confrontation in which the residents excel, and views public embarrassment—losing face—with particular distress, this rhetoric has for many years helped to shield the community from the threat of imminent dissolution.

In short, what I have just described is the underlying method whereby the residents "buy time." They are at once both rebellious and complaisant. Not for them the forms of resistance that reject the rhetoric and practices of the state. Rather, they cannily deploy the state's own symbolic resources against its bureaucratic operators. Under Thai law, for example, delaying a legally mandated exercise of eminent domain beyond a reasonable time limit—a conveniently vague restriction—can force the authorities, at least in theory, to restore the property to its owners or their legal heirs.[14] The residents have used those resources in ways that proactively claimed them for the local community and made it morally absurd for the authorities to charge the residents with disloyalty to the official values of the state. At a time of continuing internal political tension, this gives the community a considerable moral and practical edge.

Such tactics would perhaps not have worked so well had the municipal authorities not also exposed their own claims on moral leadership to question, at least in the residents' eyes. Threatening to destroy sacred trees and shrines, failing to show Buddhist loving-kindness and compassion, and ignoring the residents' loyalty to central national ideals have all become part of the litany of complaint against the bureaucracy. Indeed, one resident said, "They would have to destroy the shrines" as well as trees thought to contain benign deities (*thewadah*) and angels (*thaep*)—adding that the bureaucrats would think nothing of it, implying (but never saying outright) that this made the bureaucrats thoroughly un-Thai and that only bad Bangkokians would evict the angels from which the city drew its name. The residents, said my interlocutor, would try to rescue the shrines, as they had moved some of the shrines in the past when moving house, but the trees were too big to dig up and replant.

Portraying the authorities as defiling what Marc Askew has called "sacralized space" places the residents firmly on the moral high ground.[15] This strategy, in an ostensibly authoritarian political system, allows them to "englobe" the encompassing power of the state against its bureaucratic functionaries.[16] The residents also, however, view the bureaucrats as having failed modernity; by remaining entrapped in the older social order, they have forfeited the right to treat the residents as lesser citizens. In their hauteur and condescension toward the residents, the bureaucrats frequently appeared to be evoking the feudal hierarchy known as the *sakdina* system and relegating the residents to the level of servile commoners—an accusation that echoes the rhetoric of poor people's opposition to established power at least since the time of the Assembly of the Poor.[17] During one confrontation with a group of BMA officials, for example, Thawatchai's mother tackled a bespectacled senior official of the Department of Works head-on. When he asked her whether she knew the meaning of the rather formal word *phumitat* (landscape), she replied that she did. He responded with ill-disguised, ironic condescension, "What *does* it mean, then? *I* don't know!"

While such overbearing comportment is quite common in modern Thai political life, the residents could reject it, especially when (as here) it was directed to a respected elder of their community, as inconsistent with supposedly fundamental Thai ideals. Observers of Thai bureaucracy have long noted that its internal hierarchy is tempered by the respect due to such aspects as age and friendship and to the demands of reciprocity, but that what to an outsider might look like an interest in productivity-oriented human relations is better understood as a way of keeping the established routines running smoothly in place.[18] While such assessments may smack of orientalist prejudices, they also accord with the expectations of today's citizens who, with raised expectations of democracy and consumerist comfort, are more willing than perhaps used to be the case to hold the bureaucrats at least morally accountable for the system's failures. Yet it is also convenient to be able to use such images, through which they can turn the bureaucrats' condescension back against its perpetrators.

The Pom Makakan residents thus increasingly treated their interactions with the bureaucrats as expressions of the unfolding historical drama of struggle between feudal lords and humiliated commoners. They understood, it seems, that many bureaucrats lived in fear of the dire personal consequences of appearing to connive in illegal actions, but the collective image of feudal power was one that resonated with the larger public's perceptions. Indeed, all the actors in this social drama evoked familiar models.[19] Samak, for example, acted out the role of the warrior king at whose coming all commoners must tremble with fear, and his minions merely reproduced that arrogance.

Performance and Governance

Samak's successor, Apirak Kosayodhin, represented the opposite image: the compassionate leader who was accessible to his people and whose modest and attentive mien signified not so much a Western democratic ideal (although it certainly served that role as well[20]) as the Buddhist monk-monarch who considers it meritorious to serve the poor and treat them with gentle understanding. When Apirak first visited the community, he sat on a low seat so as not to tower over his elderly and largely female interlocutors and refused the microphone. Apirak, one resident was to remark some years later, "is a person who understands people"—a rare compliment for a politician from a working-class observer. Another resident commented, "He understands the role of the community better than anyone."

Performance has in fact been crucial to the self-governance and even the survival of Pom Mahakan.[21] Residents entertained very specific ideas about what constituted true Thainess; an opportunity like the filming of the historical drama allowed them, quite literally, to take on the lineaments of an ancestral culture, to wear it on their bodies, and to participate actively in "the regime of images."[22] In the day-to-day management of self-images, too, the personalities of those charged with specific responsibilities facilitated a seamless interchange of performance styles during the socially intense phases of communal meetings—of which, at times of crisis, there could be as many as three in a week. This capacity was all the more remarkable because the community was able to develop its own internal mode of self-governance, which required a high degree of consistency at the level of its formal structure—making nonsense, it is worth noting again, of the conventional distinction between formal and informal settlements.[23]

The self-governance of the community lies primarily in the hands of an elected "community committee." The declared functions of this entity are, according to a document prepared by the leadership, as follows:

1. They must reform the site and make it a place of decent habitation and not a site of degradation
2. To reduce and resolve on-site problems of vice and drugs so as to lighten the burden of the work done by state officials
3. To have the families in the community enjoy love, harmony, and excellence together
4. To arouse in the youth feelings of love for cleanliness and order
5. To build the disposition and consciousness of living together as a community
6. To expand each person's power to take collective responsibility in the livelihood of the community
7. To build the knowledge of saving in each person in the community ([one task] is to organize the community savings fund)
8. To maintain and preserve the customs, morality, and traditions of the community that we have investigated over several people's lifetimes so that it will be a [good] place for tourism
9. It must make every working office of the state bureaucracy admit that our community is an exemplary community and is correct in respect of the law
10. The community committee including [i.e., representing] all the people in the community is pleased to offer succor and is ready to act according to the law and order of the nation (*bahn moeang*) and to offer its cooperation

This description, which resounds with legalistic and moralistic orotundities of mostly Sanskrit derivation, demonstrates the community's chameleon-like ability to adopt, with every intimation of sincerity, the moral goals of the official state. It incorporates the language of the very similar documents that govern the committees of officially recognized communities,[24] but, in an interesting departure, omits the focus on inculcating respect for the king; on the other hand, it appears to protest more forcefully than the official document the importance of acting according to the law (rather than working with officialdom, which is not necessarily always the same thing). It also emphasizes such notable and already achieved dimensions of communal living as the suppression of drug use and the operation of the community savings fund.

There is more than a hint of segmentary thinking in the invocation of the "nation" as *bahn moeang* (the home-polity), a term that nicely blends the implications of home village or house with the more abstract notion of the moral community. At the same time, the assertions of fidelity to the law are the template for the leaders' repeated assurances that they wish to do nothing that actually breaks the order of the state, while the insistence on respect for law and order echoes not only the stated values of the (relatively friendly) police but also the language of municipal and national governance. The allusion to vice, far from being a careless handle on which hostile bureaucrats could seize, is an unambiguous reminder of the community's success in suppressing the use of drugs, while the sudden mention of tourism at the very end of the document suggests that the community leaders think this may be their strongest selling point. Be that as it may, there is nothing here that could reasonably incite the ire of the state, although the slight departures from the usual formula are interesting indications of the community's specific strategy and public standing.

Operating within this well-ordered structure, the community leaders understood the importance of managing their various roles. The president's role was both more ever present (Thawatchai often sat to one side, rather than at the back, when others were leading the action) and more ambiguous. In part, the ambiguity sprang from the way the governance document described his functions and role as being "to open meetings and control the meetings, [and] to take care of (*du lae*) the work of the committee that entrusts him to be ready to sign various documents." That description encapsulates a seemingly deliberate vagueness about the location of real power. The president represents the committee when he signs documents, but he must also exercise a measure of public control. In reality, while Thawatchai has been the dominant leader and most public face of the community throughout its long struggle, he has never abandoned his air of dejection at having to shoulder such a heavy burden. Notably allergic to even indirect hints that he was like a petty tyrant, he remarked with satisfaction of the way the leaders actually shared roles according to the needs and moods of each moment that, no matter what the formal governance document claims, "it's a case of each one to his own style"—in other words, momentary roles are set by character as much as by specific duties.

Maew, himself a member of the leadership group, noted that the members had all enjoyed long experience of working together, so that meetings shifted seamlessly from one leader to another as occasion and mood demanded; there was, apparently, no prior discussion of who would take which role. The considerable differences among these several personalities became a resource that the entire community shared; when crisis threatened, Thawatchai would take command and would sometimes hector his audience until they responded to his questions, but if tensions reached breaking point during the ensuing discussion, Tao—a man with a notable capacity for cracking jokes but also a talented debater (he played a notable cameo role from the floor at the Chulalongkorn University conference)— would take over, his whimsical expression a perfect foil for the quips he flung into the crowd. When organizational details had to be threshed out, Maew, an activist with extensive contacts with NGOs and communities

CHAPTER SEVEN

elsewhere in the country, would lead; at other times, and especially when financial matters or design details had to be discussed, Bun, the quiet young community treasurer, would assume the presiding role. Bun was often highly visible at communal events, but tended to be silent, writing with felt-tipped marker s on the portable sheet board in various colors to clarify the financial and organizational details of the moment, although on a few occasions his relatively high-pitched voice would be raised in exhortation of his fellow residents to follow the agreed procedures.

The alternation among leaders who have worked together for many years is a remarkably smooth operation. None of the shifts in leading discussions appear to be premeditated, and Maew confidently assured me that they were not orchestrated in advance; rather, a group of people who have worked together for so long under almost intolerable pressure has developed an instinctive grasp on its own dynamics and its relationship to the community as a whole. This leadership collective frequently elicits the admiration of outsiders who see it in action—a far cry from the situation only two decades earlier, when critical observers claimed that slum community leaders generally had a poor understanding of the roles to which they had been elected or appointed.[25]

Leadership and a Drunkard's Rage

Perhaps the clearest indication of the leaders' skills came with an incident—actually two, almost identical incidents—in which they had to deal with a disruptive fellow resident. A meeting had scarcely begun when a middle-aged man, morose from the start, began interrupting and expostulating, and eventually exploded with anger at the leaders. It was evident that he was very drunk. Incoherent with rage, he began to scream at the leadership and, as far as it was possible to tell from his rant, at Thawatchai in particular. While we may safely assume that the leaders were dismayed at such a potential threat to their collective unity, their response illustrated the flexibility with which the group of leaders always reacts to the collective mood. Bun swiftly moved over to where the drunk was by now shouting almost continuously. He put a soothing hand on the man's back and began, with slow, rhythmic movements, to massage him, all the while edging him toward the open space beyond where the community had convened its meeting. Eventually the man calmed down, although he was still muttering irritably to himself. Then, standing free, he glared around the gathering, shrugged his shoulders in a display of contempt for the entire proceedings, and shuffled off on his own two feet, unsupported but also unmarred by a serious loss of face.

Such reactions to unruly behavior are indicative of how hard the leaders must sometimes work to keep the community unified behind a drive to survive that is emotionally, psychologically, and economically draining. The daily toll in sheer exhaustion, frayed nerves, and economic hardship is relentless. Thawatchai, who once pointed out to me that looking after 308 people (the population at that high point) "isn't an easy matter," frequently claims he would rather cede his position as president to someone else; he is tired, he says, and he has increasing health problems. But his skills are not easily replaced, and so he stays on, aging and tiring visibly from year to year. Maew confided that he could not earn any money when community affairs kept him so busy; he lived off the tiny income his wife brought in as a laundrywoman, supplemented by occasional bribes from police officers who needed someone to impersonate a prisoner so that the prisoner himself, for a considerable kickback, could conduct his business affairs outside the jail.[26] Other residents complained that they were simply weary from the constant tension of everyday vigilance, and this did occasionally lead to some muttering against Thawatchai's authority—his relatively stentorian and decisive style acted as something of a lightning conductor for outbursts of anger that the unrelieved tension generated from time to time—and that of the leadership group in general.

Above all immediate and local considerations, however, was an ongoing commitment to act as good Thais—the key to the community's chances of gaining full legitimacy in the public's view. This meant not letting any other resident lose face; humiliation is a dangerous poison, and uncontrolled anger, in Thai interaction, usually humiliates both bearer and target. And so, while it is easy to see why the temptation to start drinking arises so easily (especially in a society where masculinity and the ability to drink heavily are closely linked), one can also see that the residents are faced with a dilemma when one of their number becomes abusive as a result of drinking: do they try to control his behavior and risk an internal fight, or do they let him disrupt their business and perhaps, in the process, confirm outsiders' older and negative stereotypes of slum communities?

By the time I encountered this particular disruption, the leaders had acquired valuable experience in dealing with a much more serious problem. Probably the community's most important achievement was its successful antidrug campaign, the success that it now used to try to persuade the police not to be party to any eviction attempt. Drug addiction is a serious issue throughout Thailand, and especially in Bangkok. During the Thaksin years, a vicious campaign of extrajudicial killings of suspected users and pushers attracted widespread international condemnation. At that time, five members of the Pom Mahakan community were formally appointed as community police (*tamruat chumchon*) by the official police bureaucracy; their specific task was to stamp out this particular scourge among their fellow residents. In the event they were notably successful, but they did not achieve their results by following the generally sanctioned pattern of violence. Instead, they approached the known drug users (they still claim that there were no vendors among the residents) and gave them a choice: cease using drugs immediately or be forced to leave the community. Two elderly men who were quietly running their lives down in a drug-induced stupor were allowed to live out their days at home; those days were few, and they never constituted an active threat to others. The remaining users all yielded to the pressures to desist; the leaders cleverly drafted family members, who were suffering as a result of their breadwinners' addiction and were also doubtless distraught at the idea of having to find new places to live, to exert that pressure by threatening to report any instance of drug use to the community police officers.

The results were swift and spectacular: today, there seem to be no regular users at all in the community. Because, as we have seen, one of the BMA's less pleasant tactics had been to put it about that Pom Mahakan was drug infested, this remarkable success had a double value: in addition to protecting the community's young people from the damage that drug addiction would bring to their lives, it allowed the leadership to rebut the officials' calumny, of which, indeed, nothing much has been heard since Apirak's election in 2004 and the subsequent and rapid departure of the city clerk who had been most assiduous in promoting the rumors. (The leaders complained bitterly at the time that she frequently passed the community on her way to taking the longtail boat at the Phahn Fah Lilaht pier but never took the trouble to visit; they had no doubt that it was this willful ignorance of the community that had allowed her to spread such lies.) It seems likely, too, that this reversal of the community's reputation had a direct impact on the attitude of the Crown Property Bureau, already perhaps alarmed at the idea that the empty park between a high stone wall and a canal offering a fast escape route might become an open invitation to addicts and pushers.

When I told Maew how impressed I had been with the efficient and yet compassionate management of the drunken man's behavior, he responded by saying that he hoped I would not write about the persistence of drunkenness in the community. Surely, I responded, my readers, their credulity already strained by the claim that Pom Mahakan was drug-free, would simply laugh out of court any attempt to deny that drunkenness still occurred in the community; it is a widespread problem throughout the country.[27] Far better, I said, that readers should understand how well the community managed its affairs; the leaders' quick-witted dexterity had prevented drunkenness from becoming more than an occasional aberration, and had prevented further hemorrhaging of communal solidarity. That, I pointed out, was an impressive achievement in itself, as was the care and concern shown for a fellow community member's self-respect. No one would believe that a poverty-stricken Bangkok community would be free of drunkenness; what mattered was how the community leadership dealt with it and how it exemplified an unusual capacity for self-management that was also evident in the relatively gentle way the community had addressed its drug problem. After some reflection, my interlocutor conceded that I was probably right.

The Consequences of Smallness

Despite the small physical size of the populated area, for the purposes of the everyday management of community affairs it is subdivided into five "zones," each with its appointed head. Each zone head is entrusted with day-to-day management of problems and the "direction of development" in the relevant group of homes, and is expected to represent constituents' interests in community discussions—a fact that creates a small internal hierarchy in that it effectively absolves other residents from the necessity of speaking up. The zone heads are also expected to take an active role in making sure that every individual participates in the various activities of the community; less surprisingly, they are also supposed to convey any issues that arise to the community committee. Finally, more vaguely but perhaps also more ominously, they are expected to serve, according to the governance document, as the "links between the community, allied networks, NGOs (*ongkahn isara*, literally 'free bodies'), departments of government, etc." In reality, their effective role seems to revolve principally around liaising with the president and other community leaders and sometimes livelier-than-average participation in community meetings. They also serve as eyes and ears on the mood of the community, both within its internal power structure and, occasionally, to not always benignly interested parties outside. On the whole, however, they are an important key to community cohesion, representing a "middle level" of local management and thus a useful device for anticipating problems before they can grow into a serious nuisance.

Leadership of the community is generally conceived in moral terms, as

CHAPTER SEVEN

a duty to be assumed for the collective good, and the leaders' frequent insistence on the centrality of Buddhist values also provides a rich source for their criticism of the authorities. In this, they even shared some rhetorical capital with their foes; Samak, whom I heard addressing a UNICEF event when he was still governor, was wont on such occasions to expatiate on the importance of "caring" (*du lae*, literally "watching over")—an attitude, however, that he clearly did not choose to exhibit toward the residents of Pom Mahakan, any more than he was prepared to recognize their goal of "caring for" (*du lae*) the place for which they professed such enduring love. Even when community and authorities were talking past each other, they often did so in a shared vocabulary of affect and attachment. At the level of the community's internal political dynamics, I suggest, this shared vocabulary is a pivotal component in the community's ability to represent itself—to itself as much as to outsiders—as a microcosm of the larger polity.

That identification represents a dynamic that one can observe in many poor communities in Thailand, and the leaders of Pom Mahakan were at pains to assure me that they were not unique in terms of their struggle or their values. The issue is not that the community is in some way typical of the country as a whole, but that it reflects and even exaggerates aspects of the national political culture that might be much harder to discern in a larger setting. Moreover, Pom Mahakan, although small, occupies a symbolically central space in the capital city, surrounded as it is by some of the best-known temples and other monuments in an area densely frequented by tourists—some of whom find their way into the inhabited spaces of the community, usually when trying to board a longtail boat on the canal or having slightly misdirected their way to the famous Temple of the Golden Mount.

Few of the visitors have heard of Pom Mahakan before discovering its shy presence among the trees and behind the wall; even fewer, however, then remain unimpressed by the evidence they find of a welcoming community, plastered with documentation about its history and its struggle, living quietly in one shadowy hollow of this loudly monumental landscape. They see then that the people of Pom Mahakan represent a different view of the past than that presented by the state and by the tourist industry. For without question Pom Mahakan is a conduit for much of the contestation over the past that is currently shaping the country's future. It is hardly, therefore, irrelevant to national concerns. The exact relationship between a somewhat eccentric and very small community and the very large nation-state to which it belongs is both complex and opaque. The critical analysis of that relationship may permit some revealing insights into the constitution of both entities.

The total space of Pom Mahakan, even if we add the area sequestered by the army in 2003, is certainly small—some five *rai* (eight thousand square meters) in all. One quite reasonable concern expressed by planners seeking to justify the proposed eviction was that as more children were born, the population would swell to unsustainable proportions. The population *has*—perhaps—grown very slightly. It is actually hard to be sure; an estimate of "the almost 300 *phi nawng* of the Pom Mahakan community" appears in a letter written in February 2003 to various city officials, including Samak,[28] and casual statements a decade later indicate roughly the same size, but the exact number in a floating and bureaucracy-shy population is necessarily difficult to determine. The evidence of these approximate numbers suggests a fairly stable situation. More noticeable by far than the continuing births is the considerable number of young people who have chosen to leave and develop their lives elsewhere. As one female leader remarked to me, there is a lot of work involved in maintaining the community, and young people are not always inclined to shoulder such a heavy responsibility. Those who stay must share the work as well as the worries and the economic hardship.

Above all, the residents must work out viable ways of coexisting within such compressed confines—not an easy task, especially as the conflict between Red Shirts and Yellow Shirts cuts straight through this community as well; the residents are proud that supporters of both groups have managed to coexist without rancor, a rare phenomenon that has stood them well when they were threatened with being overrun by street demonstrations since they had people who could talk to both sides. There was some precedent for this balancing act, in that apparently some of the politicians from Thaksin's Thai Rak Thai party had privately expressed some solidarity with the Pom Mahakan leaders even after it had become apparent that they were being supported by Apirak, a standard-bearer in the capital for the rival Democrat Party. In short, despite all the public evidence that many residents were Yellow Shirt and Democrat Party supporters, the lines were never clear and rarely led to confrontation beyond an occasional argument.

It is nevertheless revealing that meetings have decreased in frequency since the escalation of public confrontation in 2009. Avoidance is itself a way of asserting Thainess as a unifying principle that can, and often does, transcend incipient forms of political factionalism even as the community also reproduces those divisions internally. Emphasis now falls instead on preventing the larger factional disputes from destroying community solidarity. During the height of the rioting that led up to the 2014 coup, the Pom Mahakan leaders, in a remarkable departure from earlier habit, discouraged large groups of visitors. Although outside visitors had previously been welcome as they discouraged the official authorities from harassing the community, they now threatened to draw unwanted attention on the part of the demonstrators camped outside beside the sandbags arrayed in front of the Prajadhipok Museum. The delicate political ecology of the community was such that an invasion of its space by demonstrators of either side could undo what over two decades of official pressure have failed to destroy.

The residents must always ponder how to organize their lives within their very limited space. They are auto-ethnographers[29]; they analyze their own society and its physical setting, just as they also analyze the intentions of those they encounter in the course of their struggles with the political forces of the encompassing national polity. As one woman told me, "We study them too!" While they may deride the entrenched city bureaucracy as "dinosaurs," there is enough common cultural ground for them to recognize and play on shared assumptions and values. The effect is especially palpable in the uses to which the residents put terminology and symbolism that emanates from official sources, from academia, and from the sometimes quite specialized vocabulary of the NGOs. That rhetoric, as Henry Delcore has pointed out, often—as in Pom Mahakan—plays an important role in the ways in which local communities conceive and recast their histories to suit a model of Thai identity.[30] In 2003—the earliest point at which I could obtain documentation from the community, an indication in itself of a carefully orchestrated progression in self-education by the community leaders—the letters addressed to BMA officials were already replete with the language of participation, with appeals on behalf of children and elderly people, and concern over the psychological and physical health of the residents. The jargon of these letters also permeated the speeches made by community leaders at internal meetings and in talking to visitors.

The use of this language is strategic; it is also strikingly competent and often also seems entirely spontaneous and unforced. It is not uncommon, for example, for community leaders to play with terms such as society (*sangkhom*), culture (*watthanatham*), and quality (*khunkhah*), throwing the official ideology back in the faces of functionaries who are supposed to be sensitive to its implications for the treatment of all citizens. When the anthropologist Charles Keyes visited the community in my presence, he was struck by the extent to which residents used the language of the NGOs—with which he had been familiar for decades—to express their concerns.

They have a sophisticated grasp on the possibilities that the NGO rhetoric affords them. Their claim that officials "don't understand the word 'society,'" an effective riposte to those who dismissed the residents as uneducated thugs, symbolically inverted the moral relationship between bureaucrats and citizens. My use of the formal term for "cultural diversity" was quickly picked up by residents after I reported on a conversation in which I had told a BMA official that the internal diversity of the community was what especially aligned it with the Thai national ideology of cultural assimilation—a view that the official in question bluntly rejected since, for him, genuine communities would have to have a common point of origin and have a long-term entitlement to their land. (Apparently he was unaware that the older neighborhoods, or *yahn*, were "specialist, multi-functional, and internally diverse, incorporating functions relating to local communities as well as the city at large."[31]) The residents of Pom Mahakan quickly realized that what the bureaucrat had chosen to represent as the weakness of their claim was, in the context of the national ideology, a potential strength, instantly recognizable to almost the entire (and highly diverse) population of Bangkok.

One senior bureaucrat, however, admitted that the problem was circumstantial. Had Pom Mahakan been a Muslim or other minority community, like Ban Khrua, he ruefully conceded, they might have been more successful at establishing their rights to remain on site. Ban Khrua, a Muslim community of Khmer (Cham) origin that Rama I rewarded with a grant of land at its present site for volunteering to fight for the Siamese kingdom, and that thereafter absorbed Muslims taken as prisoners of war in subsequent conflicts, acquired economic significance for the Thai state when Jim Thompson, an American entrepreneur, developed its domestic silk production as a commercial enterprise. Although Thompson's mysterious disappearance in 1967 sent Ban Khrua's silk production into abrupt decline, the community has relatively successfully resisted attempts to relocate or disrupt it.[32] This was probably because Ban Khrua, a minority community devoted to a nationally significant, recognizable, and singular profession and holding royally sanctioned title to its physical location, satisfied the key criteria demanded by BMA officials.

Pom Mahakan could not make such claims based on ethnic singularity. The official's admission that ethnic distinctiveness would have made a stronger argument for the community's collective survival, moreover, seems inconsistent in a member of a bureaucracy that is committed to an assimilative understanding of national identity, and it seems unlikely that it would ever be adopted as an explicit policy. The residents of Pom Mahakan, by contrast, can claim to represent a more acceptably Thai perspective; their *moeang* is not a separate enclave, marked by irreducible difference, but the innermost circle in a concentric set. Moreover, the unceasing interchange between pondering their own predicament and analyzing the motives and actions of those who officially represent the nation-state further enhances the residents' sense of living in a microcosm of Thainess. Nothing that governs their daily actions is disconnected from their understanding of national identity, so that even—or perhaps especially—their acts of resistance serve as an instructively perverse demonstration of their fundamental loyalty to shared ideals and, indeed, as a demonstration of their determination to expose the unworthiness of those who hold unelected bureaucratic office. Even the hated BMA is respected as an institution and a recognizable form of orderly, structured organization (*rabop*); it is the individuals who staff it who earn opprobrium for their alleged betrayal of principles of compassion and tolerance—principles, in short, that are held to be deeply Thai and Buddhist. The frequent insistence on the residents' Thainess makes this identification explicit, and, with it, the rejection of the haughty attitudes of "people with power" (*phu mi amnaht*).

It is for this reason that I would argue that Pom Mahakan reflects, reproduces, and generates some of the key elements of Thai political life. It is perhaps more a mirror than a microcosm—a reflection of encompassing cultural value rather than a model of political relations. Whichever metaphor one prefers, the community directly experiences the larger dynamic in immediate form, as, for example, in the well-documented tensions between the police and the army; in 2013, there were real fears of a confrontation between a police force widely assumed to be loyal to the Thaksin family and an army that opposed its presence.[33] The very intense intimacy within which one learns how the various key paradoxes are acted out on a daily basis would not be accessible in larger, more impersonal settings, even though the latter may—and almost certainly do—exhibit, in more diffuse form, many of the characteristics described in this book for Pom Mahakan.

EIGHT

Building the Future of the Past

After the agreement with Apirak and Chatri stalled and Apirak left office, the residents attempted to build the first new houses, holding their breaths lest the new governor, Sukhumbhand, see their temerity as an excuse to attack. When nothing happened, they proceeded to construct several more houses, each time becoming a little more convinced that they would not be stopped (fig. 7).[1]

Building Forward

Along this trajectory from caution and fear to judicious daring, the people of Pom Mahakan have literally experimented with fitting their bodies to imagined living spaces, and have thus worked, in effect, on redesigning not only the architecture but the *habitus* of their own lives. Over time, they have, with an increasing intensity of focus and detail, reimagined and redesigned their space. On the one hand, they express a deep desire to achieve modern, reasonably comfortable living conditions within a traditionalizing architectural idiom. On the other, the available space for experimentation is extremely limited.

Moreover, they fear—not unreasonably—that any action on their part to replace their old houses will lead conclusively to eviction: at any moment at which an old house has been demolished, their right to use the land is at its lowest, since not even the moral argument of compassion for an existing

CHAPTER EIGHT

7   Houses old and new

home can then be invoked. Once a roof has been constructed on a house, it becomes legally more difficult to justify its destruction. For a long time, however, the residents hesitated to take the risk of provoking a massive intervention. In the end, however, it was to this refurbishment or replacement of existing houses that so many of their efforts have been directed, most notably through the community savings fund that eventually did lead some of them to dare to replace their dilapidated old houses with well-designed new constructions.

Even at a relatively early stage in its struggle, the community's embodied sense of belonging was being shaped in the very young. A painting competition led some of the children to depict a stylized representation of the citadel itself, while others drew houses and trees as they imagined their community in the future. Shortly after the tsunami of 26 December 2004, the community's Children's Day featured the recitation of poems that repeated Thawatchai's rhetoric about the importance of recognizing suffering no matter what the religion or the ethnicity of the group. Most significantly of all, children were encouraged to absorb the value of "participation," a favorite component of NGO-speak. One student's report emphasized the importance not only of involving the residents directly in the planning process but particularly of giving the young children a participatory role in design. Clearly a powerful effort was being directed toward inculcating into the next generation a systematic and deliberately orchestrated orientation to the constraints and contours of the community's space.

Living spaces habituate individuals to move in harmony with others similarly housed. An early (July 2003) attempt to take a census of existing building materials thus seemed to presage the reconstruction of both the existing physical stock and existing dispositions. This was partly—largely?—a question of economics; it is easier to reuse old wood, stone, plastic, and brick than to replace them. So this early initiative, aimed primarily at assessing and conserving resources already available, made the residents more aware of the materials they had at their disposal; it materialized their sense of place.

The most impressive and concerted move to engage the residents' bodies in rethinking the spatial dimensions of community life came in 2004, however, when a retired architect, a bespectacled former civil servant with experience of working on community projects, gave his services in much the same merit-making spirit as the lawyer who had defended the community's interests in the Central Administrative Court. This man, son of poor fisherfolk who had made a choice early in life to study and get out of a world for which he had no aptitude, nonetheless retained a powerful sense of the capacities as well as the problems of the poor; he was a good listener and a remarkably persuasive speaker, and it was clear that the residents trusted him to help them create better living conditions even when he appeared, as he sometimes did, to be demanding a sustained level of commitment. Operating before the arrival of the more comprehensive plan designed by Chatri and in some respects anticipating its intentions, he persuaded the residents to start discussing the kinds of houses they wanted to build, where they would build them, and how they would relate to their needs and their social relationships. There followed a series of meetings over a period of about three months (June–August 2004). During these meetings, the residents explored many facets and possibilities of the physical coexistence they were trying to imagine for their future life as a community.

In these and other collective endeavors, they were unquestionably guided by this architect and by other NGO experts, and they quickly absorbed the discourse of these educated supporters. The resulting jargon conveys a strong sense of conformity and expertise; its emphasis on history and culture masks the tension between its message of resistance and the ideology of the state. The image of regimented cohesion and complaisance that it creates can in fact be somewhat deceptive. It seems to follow the usual Thai convention whereby followers (*phu tahm*) do the behest of leaders (*phu nam*) even when they really disagree, a split that old Auntie

CHAPTER EIGHT

Mae insisted was why Thawatchai had no choice but to accept reelection time after time despite his insistence that he did not even like the concept of being a leader; for him, true participation, he claimed, necessitated debate and the realization that not all residents were equally adept at the same tasks. In short, he recognized that the allocation of political and administrative tasks should always reflect individual capacities and choices. The Pom Mahakan leaders have by now, in fact, generated some space for the arguing that may be necessary for a community under such constant and potentially debilitating pressure to adapt successfully to the political, social, and economic demands of urban life.[2]

Yet such freedom has limits born of the ethics in which it is embedded. While everyone recognizes that there are stresses and strains, these are assimilated to a discourse of national belonging and karmic outcomes and justifications. As one man expressed it, "Why is it that I dare to talk to Maew quite openly, and why is it that I don't respect Mu even though he is a more senior person? What this means is that've learned how to interact with reciprocity. We honor someone on condition that he honors us," adding, "That's the way of Thai tradition!" And he had more to say on this topic: "That's Thai tradition—to honor people who have experience. True, no? But the experience that each person brings is not the same as everyone else's. It's not the same!" And, he observed philosophically, "in the same person we find both the good and the bad," all of it—especially in a place where people have struggled together for so long—observable in everyday behavior and actions, and all of it indicative of an individual's karma: "If we people do something good, it can send us something good, right?"

In recognizing the differences among their followers, leaders also recognize that they will have to bring some of the latter into line; when they do not contribute to the collective work of keeping the community clean or resist paying their dues into the community savings fund, leaders must try to find a way to create effective pressure to conform. Leaders are thus proactive, and the appeal to karma is not fatalistic; rather, it is a socially proactive way of justifying further action—for example, by Thawatchai, who, incensed by the traitorous acts of the elder who had allegedly arranged with the BMA for one of the historic houses—at that point being used as a community museum—to be carted away, found in karmic retribution a justification for acting as the agent of that fate by helping to banish the offender to the margins of community politics.[3]

Leaders also, not surprisingly, while sometimes admired for the qualities that put them at the head of the community, are sometimes the objects of deep suspicion. But theirs is a karma that others—especially respected elders like Auntie Mae—also impose on them by refusing to consider replacing them at election time. This, too, has consequences. The exhaustion that has marked the leaders' faces and posture—Thawatchai suffers from rheumatoid arthritis, his hair is turning white, and the furrows on his brow match his weary stoop—also bears out the probable sincerity of their desire to escape a burden their fellow residents will not allow them to shed.

This dynamic reveals the local social basis of the oscillation between authoritarianism and egalitarianism. The leaders serve their people, who realize the karmic imperative by voting over and over for those they consider to be karmically destined for leadership. It is not that they readily accept dictatorship—they are quick to complain if they suspect that one of the leaders is exceeding the expected limits of power. But for much of the time they find complaisance to be an effective way of securing the leaders' services. Conversely, much as Thai police operate with two varieties of power—one is a harshly arbitrary stance that allows them to violate the rights of the hapless minor offenders they arrest while the other allows them, equally arbitrarily, to release these people soon afterward and sometimes even to help them on their way[4]—local leaders seem to see no contradiction in almost abusively hectoring their followers to fight for their rights. Here, too, we see how a segmentary view of social relations allows leaders and followers alike to encompass practices of relative freedom in a style of authoritarian hierarchy. The leaders fuse their command of official discourse and the language of control with a rejection of older, more arbitrary modalities of local power, perhaps recognizing that internal debate actually helps them push back at the increasing bureaucratic encroachment on their self-governance. Such is the cultural background to what would otherwise be the puzzling coexistence of two mutually opposed and incompatible political styles.[5]

As leaders harangue followers, in an apparently sincere attempt to get them to express differences of opinion, it sometimes sounds as though the verbal utterance of disagreement is at risk of becoming a convention and an end in itself. Yet discussion, especially when it concerns such real concerns as the type and location of future housing or decisions on how and when to fortify the community against a possible attack, is often lively and contentious, and decisions are not always predictable. Especially when the community had to decide whether to open up the barricades again after the 2003 siege, there was a great deal of open disagreement, although it is also true that the leaders' view—that it would be foolish and dangerous to continue illegally blocking access to the canal—did eventually prevail. Meetings are far from passive occasions. There are noticeably gendered differences in the forms of participation; women used to be more afraid than men of expressing their views openly. That situation has gradually evolved. Nit, a genial, middle-aged laundrywoman who leads her "zone," told me early on in my fieldwork that the women's attitude could be summarized thus: I don't want to do it—I don't dare speak!" She added, "They think for themselves, but they don't speak." She was, and to some extent still is, an exception to this pattern. Today, however, she is far from alone; women, especially those who are known to be active in promoting the community's day-to-day activities, often call out facetious remarks, while some of the men are not averse to challenging the explanations offered by the leaders. There are differences in style according to both gender and age, with younger women generally being more inclined to make lighthearted but pointed comments. Despite the rhetoric about the importance of making major decisions together, there is rarely any serious disagreement about who is ultimately in charge of executing those decisions or of directing the discussions that lead to them. But open discussion is encouraged; Thawatchai sometimes makes a point of keeping rather quiet, hoping to encourage others to talk instead, but keeping a watchful eye on the proceedings so that he can always intervene if the discussion flags. Over time, the strategy has clearly paid off.

Pom Mahakan may strike some observers, especially Thais who are used to seeing community affairs as more meek procedures, as anarchic or as riven with factional differences. The potential for both tendencies is always present, but—with the exception of the family of the one leader who quarreled with the others on the grounds of their perceived lack of respect for his seniority—what the residents have actually shown is a capacity for constructive debate, disagreement, and original reflection, as well as for the absorption of the conventions of virtually any discourse that might suit their goals. This capacity is a crucial element in the explanation of why a community widely believed to be both poor and ill educated has been among the most successful in standing up to official pressure—even to the point of becoming a leading force, albeit intermittently, in the wider resistance of Rattanakosin communities to the municipal administration's pressure tactics.

The pursuit of collective house design was an adaptive rather than an original strategy. As Thawatchai expressed it, "Everyone must think this through together . . . so that poor people can live [there]." Community, home, and body were brought into convergence through the construction of model houses (known as "dolls," *tukatah*) and the fitting of these to the ground plan of the inhabited space. First, people indicated approximate locations for their homes; then they were invited to consider, and criticize, model houses that had clearly been skillfully prepared. That each resident, or a representative of each household, was then encouraged to make such a model gave them all a direct identification with the individual designs, while the collective rearrangement of the residential arrangements inserted that sense of individual ownership firmly into a collectivity. This technique reflects the results of extended process of experimentation by NGOs involved with the government-supported *Bahn Mankhong* (secure housing) project.[6]

Turning these imaginary constructions into real homes was a more complex matter. Not only did it require determination, but the risks were considerable; if the authorities chose to disrupt a house construction before it was complete, they could legally raze the entire building to the ground and take over the land it occupied. So demolition and building began cautiously; one woman, whose home had been destroyed in the army's sole assault, fearfully asked, "Who will be the first to build?" The new buildings, however, are extremely robust. The foundations are reinforced concrete floor plates, on which a construction of hollow concrete blocks is reinforced by iron rods, making quick and discreet demolition virtually impossible.[7] Only the upper floors are of wood, to harmonize with the goal of creating a "community of wooden houses" that would recall Pom Mahakan's earlier appearance, and these are further protected by laws that specifically prohibit the destruction of houses that already have roofs over them. Moreover, the reconstruction, once finally initiated, also drew sustenance from what had hitherto been the sometimes divisive institution of the rotating credit system. Since that system allowed members of the community to engage in construction that would otherwise have been hopelessly beyond their individual financial means, it served a collective purpose, though the suspicion never quite dissipated that some people gained more advantages from it than others. Once the residents dared to begin demolition and rebuilding, the insidious fear that the money was disappearing into individual pockets began to dissipate.[8]

Despite their misgivings, most residents have regularly paid their dues over the several years during which the community savings fund has been in operation. Accounting is ostentatiously visible; it is conducted by a group of women who meticulously record every baht paid in, although the fact that they are led by the president's wife did occasion some grumbling in the past. The account books are on display throughout the entire process, as residents—sometimes a housewife, sometimes an older man— come up to the table, staffed by the president's wife and at least one of the other women, to pay in their weekly contribution and have it entered into the accounting books. Initially, perhaps, the grumbling may have been occasioned by the feeling that the fund was primarily directed at a utopian and unrealizable future. Now that a few new houses have begun to materialize, however, the benefit of the system is a great deal more apparent.

The fund and the collaborative efforts in house and community design are inseparable from each other. They represent comparable tensions between individual needs and collective goals, the former being largely subordinated to the latter. Quite clearly, the emphasis on democratic participation also encourages the pursuit of self-serving arguments; indeed, the less edifying example of some of the nearby middle-class communities (Golden Mount, Phraeng Phuthorn) suggests both the advantages and the drawbacks of a more selfish way of dealing with communal issues. In nearby Tha Phra Jan, too, as I was able to observe, a class of renter-shopkeepers became deeply dissatisfied with the BMA's attempts to gentrify the area, but, instead of uniting to resist the architect-led "participation" initiative of the BMA, they became progressively less interested and began to drift away.[9]

Economic improvement is often more divisive than unifying. The relative poverty of the Pom Mahakan community has sustained its cohesion. The example of some neighboring middle-class areas suggests, however, that success in its immediate goals could eventually undermine the current solidarity. Indeed, local observers frequently contrast Pom Mahakan with the wealthier communities, which have not managed to articulate collective policies and contingency plans—and perhaps feel that they do not need to do so. But Pom Mahakan has developed a more robust tradition of internal activism, so that it may also develop along an atypical trajectory even if it succeeds in its goals of achieving security of domicile and the greater wealth that such security would certainly also bring.

Practical Politics: Deferring Disaster

In a characteristic statement made in August 2007, Thawatchai declared, "The residents are trying to find a way of reaching a compromise with the BMA so that they would be able to preserve this [place] as a community of ancient wooden houses and organize the space as a living museum (*phiphitthaphan chiwit*) as the BMA's tenants; and the community would be caretakers of the place as a source of cultural and historical tourism—something that would be compatible with the approach to developing Rattanakosin Island as a tourist spot; but the [legal] interpretation of the [eminent domain] decree (*kritsadikah*) makes the residents fear that they could be evicted at any time."[10] Their fear was understandably enhanced by the fact, conveniently and perhaps deliberately omitted in this comment, that the legal document was specifically a royal decree (*prarahtkritsadikah*).

The attempt to reach a compromise was indeed rejected a couple of years later. The BMA began to prepare again for action. A news item in the daily *Matichon* for 3 June 2009 announced that the BMA had announced the imminent eviction of the Pom Mahakan community. It turned out that the BMA was even prepared to pay an additional 70,000 baht per head to each evictee.[11] But the residents were not to be bought. This was at a point when the Democrat Party led by Abhisit Vejjajiva was still in control of the central government, while the BMA was also under Democrat governor Sukhumbhand. The threat of eviction therefore explicitly posed a critical test for the government (and thus also to the party, with Abhisit facing the crisis that eventually led to the dissolution of his administration). That point did not escape concerned observers. The Mahidol University Research Center for Peace Building, for example, although housed in a university that is a royal foundation, clearly had no sympathy for the Yellow Shirts or the Abhisit government. Yet the center's website noted that Pom Mahakan was "different from the hundreds and thousands of communities violently evicted by the government because it is has deep historical roots," namely, Rama III's decision to give local bureaucrats as well as several temples title to the land. While such exceptionalism may seem invidious, and would certainly undermine any claim that Pom Mahakan was somehow typical of Thailand as a whole, it points up the growing value of history and heritage as forms of added value.

The center's statement tackles the "common good" rhetoric of the municipal administration, and specifically the proposed use of the park for the "ordinary people" (*prachahchon*), only to suggest, in a subsequent paragraph, that the "ordinary people" should be directly involved in any conservation project—exactly, once again, what the Pom Mahakan community was demanding. Indeed, the statement thundered, it was the responsibility of the state to ensure that ordinary people had a role to play in public policy as a matter of constitutional right.[12] Since Abhisit and Sukhumbhand belonged to the same party as Apirak, and since that party's commitment to social responsibility was increasingly under fire on the streets of Bangkok and throughout the country, this was a politically astute defense of the community's interests. At the top of the list of urgent demands came a renewed call for fixing the law that governed collaboration between the BMA and the communities under its authority, a law that was clearly at odds with the communities' constitutional rights. All along, it is clear, the major hurdle had been the legal inconsistencies that

CHAPTER EIGHT

both sides could exploit to "buy time"; but the longer that state of affairs continued, the more the community would suffer.

As soon as the news of the impending new eviction threat broke, it became clear that the community's support in other quarters was as strong as ever. An international hue and cry went up and the community's allies at home and abroad were mobilized. Following an urgent e-mail from Pthomrerk, I wrote an op-ed piece for the *Bangkok Post*[13] and sent a letter of appeal to the governor. Although it is known that Sukhumbhand received the letter, he did not respond. He was, however, reliably reported to have complained that I obviously had no idea how complicated the situation was. Such hand-wringing was widely recognized as his usual response to crisis. When his Five-Year Plan for the development of Bangkok was publicly criticized for its neglect of any serious attention to questions of historic conservation, for example, he responded in similar fashion—by doing nothing. In a sense, however, he did then act, by allowing a key adviser to start serious discussions with the critics; he was just in time to avoid a major embarrassment, as it transpired, because local activists had already asked the National Human Rights Commission to intervene.[14]

His inaction over both Pom Mahakan and the more general question of conservation in the Rattanakosin Island area was thus tactical; he apparently did not actively seek to silence community concerns, but he could reasonably claim not to have encouraged their public airing. This tactical passivity, as we might dub it, has attracted a fair amount of criticism even in a country among whose aristocracy, of which the governor is a high-ranking member, the avoidance of direct confrontation is an especially hallowed tradition. But as with the larger question of the Five-Year Plan, his inaction amounted to a form of action; it bought more time for the community. His failure to appear there, which for the residents presents a fundamental contrast with Apirak's active presence, seems to have been less a sign of hostility than it was a deliberate avoidance of stirring up new controversy.[15] At any rate, the threatened eviction, once again, was quietly shelved.

It would be easy to dismiss the governor's complaint that I did not understand the complexities as nothing more than yet another example of prevarication and excuse-making, but it does at least suggest that he was not simply bent on eviction at all costs. It seems at least possible that he was caught between members of his party who saw any betrayal of the original commitment as a potentially fatal blow to the party's image as a socially responsible force on the one side, and the legal maneuverings of entrenched bureaucrats on the other. He is also known to be personally disinclined to engage in any form of confrontation. So it seems likely that he simply hoped that this new headache would quietly go away. The residents and their friends, however, were no more willing than their foes to let that happen. At the time of writing, the Pom Mahakan community is still in place, guarded by ever-vigilant watchmen and united in its determination not to yield to the forces of bureaucracy and capital. And the most recent negotiations with the BMA suggest that once again the possibility of allowing at least part of the community to remain on the site is being given consideration—but the residents are not privy to the details, and the future is still uncertain.

Survival and Suspense

Why has Pom Mahakan succeeded in holding out for nearly two and a half decades? Certainly the "resilience" of the residents, and especially of their leaders, has been a major factor. So has their skill in "buying time." But the most telling factor, perhaps, has been their ability, navigators of intrigue with their bodies attuned to the sudden shifts and squalls of Thai politics, to pass the rudder from one to another as they tacked this way and that, refusing the rigidity that had forced other communities under the engulfing waves.

When the colonial powers sought total control of southeast Asia, it was only the Siamese kingdom, at least in terms of the official historiography, that bent with the winds. Whatever the historical veracity of this story, it has served as a model for local-level adaptations as well, notably the fitful and sometimes bloody introduction of ideals (if not always of practices) of democratic and egalitarian governance. These ideals have frequently struck observers, Thai as much as foreign, as best represented at the most local levels of self-help and mutual support across the entire nation. The emergence of the Assembly of the Poor in the 1990s, the Pom Mahakan residents' volunteer activity on behalf of the tsunami-stricken South, and the local response to the 2011 floods amply illustrate this capacity for collective resilience and flexible response to disaster and oppression. If some countries pride themselves today on being inherently and uncompromisingly democratic, Thailand often experiences the besetting paradox that democracy and dictatorship coexist in the same institutions and even in the same individuals.

Pom Mahakan's leaders have invested enormous effort in representing the community as a microcosm of this *moeang thai*, the segmentary Thai polity. At the same time, however, they have deliberately cultivated their community's concentricity with the encompassing bureaucratic nation-state. Despite their obvious sympathies for the Democratic Party and the monarchy, they have neither sought nor desired identity as a purely "yellow" community. Theirs is a rhetoric, reflected as far as possible in practice, of national rather than party-political allegiance. The president's insistence that I should speak with his enemies forms a part of this stance of unceasing political adjustability and inclusiveness, as does his pride in the community's accommodation of "red" and "yellow" followers alike and in the residents' acknowledgment that the price of collective survival—the one goal on which they, like their country as a whole, would not compromise—was acquiescence in the master-narrative of official Thai identity.

Residents know that monolithic political positions do not work in the Thai context; it is such positions that have repeatedly brought city and country to a standstill and provided the proximate self-justification offered by the architects of the 2014 military coup. If Pom Mahakan has survived for nearly a quarter of a century under siege, albeit with constant fear about the future, it has done exactly what the Thai polity claims to have done for a century and a half; and it has done it, differences of scale notwithstanding, in much the same way as the officially imagined nation-state, imitating its distinctive mixture of firmness and compromise on questions of territorial sovereignty, and openly but with devastating courtesy scorning the contempt of those with the power to destroy it.

Attention to the rules of courtesy, the mark of a civilized citizenry, buys time and respect, and discourages the powerful from attempting outright violence by removing the pretext of a civilizing mission. When the city police wanted to remove the protest signage in 2003, the residents showed themselves to be accommodating; but the change, they insisted, would be on the street side of the wall, where the police risked losing face if the placards and banners remained—the residents understood this perfectly. With a mixture of self-deprecating humor, a flurry of possibly ironic but unexceptionably polite *wai* gestures, and appeals to Thai models of decency, they succeeded in persuading the city police to leave the placards in place on the inside for a while. They have also lost many battles. Especially since the meeting at the BMA on 12 August 2004 that led to the army's destruction of the residents' garden in turn, they have experienced defeat on the ground and in the courts. But still they have remained in place.

If the state now dismantles the Pom Mahakan community altogether, the residents suggest, it will be destroying a model of itself and of its own conditional independence. Pom Mahakan also strikingly exemplifies the communal solidarity with which the entire country deals with unexpected disasters. Foreigners were astonished at the Thai response to the tsunami of 2004 and the flooding of 2011. After the tsunami, the people of Pom Mahakan held an auction of clothing to raise money for the suffering coastal South. Thawatchai, in order to ensure that they all understood the importance of this charitable act, treated them to an impassioned speech about the importance of seeing in the sufferings of others—Thai and non-Thai, Buddhist and Muslims—an experience with which they could identify through their own suffering.

The tsunami and the floods led Western newspapers, in particular, to express deep admiration for the self-sacrifice and resilience of desperately poor people facing ruin in the aftermath of both disasters. But the praise, well-deserved though it was, mostly missed the remarkable aspect of these responses. It was clear, as the extent of disaster became evident, that ordinary Thai people, without much help from governments in which they had little faith, were able invoke principles of solidarity and compassion—the very qualities that they feel bureaucrats lack—as an intrinsic part of their collective cultural inheritance. Some viewed the interventions of wealthier donors and NGOs with cynicism; and in some cases they may well have been right—the protestant Buddhism, as it were, that views prosperity as the sign of good karma being closely associated in their minds with religious and state officialdom and official values. But their efforts, and their own ability to maintain a remarkable good cheer in the face of calamity, were certainly no mark of fatalism. On the contrary, these were integral to the agency that became in itself a rallying point for acts expressing nationwide and even international solidarity. The post-tsunami auction and Children's Day recitations at Pom Mahakan revealed the ultimate paradox of the segmentary Thai *moeang*: even foreign victims of disaster were part of the community of suffering that defined collective being at both the local and the national levels.

Despite the sense of resilient survival, nagging questions remain. In particular, there is the close affiliation between the residents and elements of the Democrat Party, with its very clear identification with bourgeois culture and values. This is where the ground-up view from Pom Mahakan is especially revealing. While anthropological studies of urban development often emphasize that the reorganization of urban space entails social mobility on the part of those who are able to stay under conditions that are broadly—too broadly—classified as "gentrification,"[16] the Pom Mahakan settlement is not a massive reconstruction project. On the contrary, it is a tiny space, spectacularly so amid the vastness of Bangkok's sprawling reaches. But its proponents aim to recapture for a population of mixed modern origins a distinguished history of middle-class and royal identity closely identified with the older polity and its symbols. If this is gentrification, it is self-gentrification. If formalized by the city authorities, it could eventually exclude some residents, because their involvement would clearly require a cap on population increase. But the municipal authorities' goal through most of the past quarter-century has not been gentrification but outright removal.

In pursuit of a distinctive presence, the residents play on what superficially appear to be opposed modes of self-representation: as traditional villagers and as modern citizens alert to their participatory rights. In fact, there is no contradiction here. The bourgeois discourse of rural identity and Thainess is already driven by a capitalist economy creating new forms of modern desire—a desire that is thwarted, but that can to some extent be satisfied by emergent neoliberal idioms of do-it-yourself voluntarism. "Heritage is a symptom of the production of space in an era when capitalism, the state, and identity formation have become closely intertwined," Daniel Goh remarks of heritage development in other southeast Asian cities, and he goes on to note: "It is nothing less than the spirits of capitalism that the people are seeking to domesticate in their material lifeworld."[17] Whether the residents of Pom Mahakan domesticize these relatively new spirits by fetishizing their own old spirit shrines as monuments to the entire nation or by organizing their communal space as a model of the ancient Siamese polity, they ostensibly play the state's game because it is the dominant game in town. They, to be sure, play that game in their own way, with their own understanding of the polity, and in pursuit of their own goals. But only through demonstrative incorporation into the official project of the nation-state can they realize the immediate, material goal of staying in place and, perhaps through tourism, of eventually attaining the economic status to which they aspire.

In their entrenched, opposed projects for the site, the community and the authorities both hope to satisfy two aims: physical upgrading of the space and a lasting presence loyal to the throne. The difference between the two sides lies not in the goals themselves but in the way each side intends to reach them; it is also a highly revealing difference of scale. The authorities, heirs to a Western-derived, modernist planning tradition, redolent of the crypto-colonial restraints on Thai independence,[18] believe that a green lung and some elegant but conventional architectural ornaments will produce the same kind of museological spectacle that we can see, for example, in the Acropolis in Athens. There, a green belt separates the Sacred Rock from the modern city in a way that violates the ancient arrangements but ensures a respectful framing of what has become resacralized as a nationalist rather than a religious monument.[19] The Pom Mahakan community, by contrast, aims at a more involuted design, in which it would participate in an already-existing sacred space, enjoy the living standards of the middle class that was and is most closely associated with that particular form of royally sanctioned sacrality, and perform the role of a romantic enclave of traditionalism for the benefit of tourists bewildered by Bangkok's raucous modernity and seeking the true Thai experience. Its leaders talk of "home stays" and of constructing a small hotel. They are far from averse to profiting from the dominant economic ideology and from the comforts that tourism can bring. But their principal interest lies in staying on the site to which events have bound them ever more tightly.

If self-gentrification were all the residents aimed to achieve, it would be easy to dismiss their long history of resistance as an obdurate and perhaps cynical focus on profit and comfort. While we can never know the true motives of any individual, however, it is clear that many Thai observers have today come to accept that the residents have close affective bonds with the place itself, and that these bonds are the best guarantee that their self-appointed role as guarantors of the site's preservation and good order will always succeed where the municipal and state bureaucracies have failed. Moreover, the small size and tight focus of the community also make it a model that deserves consideration and perhaps also emulation.

There also remain serious questions about the participatory process of self-management, a process that may be leading the few who succeed in staying in places like Pom Mahakan along an ineluctable path of embourgeoisement. It has become clear that the participatory style has been very strongly supported by the NGOs, which, as predominantly middle-class organizations, were more frequently targeted by the aggressively populist Thaksin government than by any Democrat administration at either the state or the municipal level. The residents' participation, moreover, is often a palpably guided activity; without the strong leadership and the external resources of which it disposes, it is extremely doubtful that the residents could have remained together on the site for so long. Is the price of success, then, a feigning of passive adherence to the values of a social class to which few residents currently feel they belong and to a political party representing only one side of a currently tense political standoff?

Any answer to this question must be historicized through a central question: what were the alternatives? Initially, there was a widespread impression that the poor supported the Red Shirts and the Pheu Thai party associated with the two Shinawatra prime ministers, while the middle classes—especially in Bangkok—tended to support the Yellow Shirts and the Democrat Party.[20] It is now certain that the contrast cannot be so sharply drawn. By the time of the 2014 coup, the major factions were exhibiting considerable overlap in tactics as well as regional and class base. This is reflected in the situation at Pom Mahakan, where the leaders' strategy entailed subsuming the two ostensibly incompatible models in a stance we might best describe as *flexible morphing*. This was not so much an opportunistic response to the state of political crisis as a logical consequence of recognizing the two sides' commonalities while also following the segmentary *moeang* model of political identity.

It is a pragmatic stance. Under the lens of a curious public and increasingly friendly media, the residents could hardly afford to identify only with a movement viewed as hostile by much of the Bangkok establishment. To do so would risk alienating the ready-made source of support of their bourgeois patrons and neighbors, and all the more so because, as Hewison points out, "Yellow"-leaning Bangkok was now virtually "encircled" by "Red"-leaning suburbs and, increasingly, by a countryside leaning in the same direction.[21] In short, Pom Mahakan is under siege within a city that feels itself to be under siege in turn, reproducing the concentric circles of the segmentary system as politically contrasted bands of population. At the same time, the residents acknowledge, both in their rhetoric and in the pragmatic alliances that they enjoy, that in class terms they have more in common with the vast numbers of the poor who support the Red Shirts and the populist politicians. And they are acutely, even uncomfortably, aware that the narrative in which they are participating may change with the political winds, although no one is prepared to say in which direction—precisely the unpredictability that Hewison and other observers of the Thai political scene have noted. They are, I suspect, ready to adapt to any such eventuality.

Even were the overall political context less tense and volatile, the city stands to gain little by expelling the residents of Pom Mahakan, whereas it may well create far more serious social problems by so doing. The residents have already demonstrated their capacity for articulating self-management plans and explaining the viability of their ideas for land sharing to a skeptical city audience. Moreover, the diversity they represent—particularly because it is political as well as regional and cultural—makes them ideal arbiters of the future use of a space that forms part of so visibly contested a symbolic area at the heart of the kingdom. No doubt both the entrenched civil servants and certain politicians with their potentially precarious careers are reluctant to contemplate the possibility that any future-oriented vision at all could prove so evanescent; especially in an age of increased use of *lèse-majesté* accusations, it would be too dangerous for them even to broach such a possibility.[22] But they are also, for the most part, realistic social agents, as adaptable and as aware of future possibilities in their own way as the residents of Pom Mahakan are in theirs.

I have argued that the residents view themselves as a microcosm of the entire polity, relying on the logical structure of the *moeang* to make this claim. From an external perspective, as I have suggested, they are not so much a microcosm as a mirror, a mirror that reflects many of the tensions and brittle balances that plague Thai politics and governance today. To take just one example, the contrast between their fear of the military and their amiable accommodation with the police suggests a parallel with media reports on alleged conflicts between the two forces—and, at the same time, confounds expectations that a community that is predominantly hostile (or at least neutral) toward the Shinawatra political machine would find the army a greater source of comfort. As we have seen, moreover, the various official bodies with a direct interest in the site are internally divided as well as at odds with each other. These divisions emerge with some clarity as we follow the trajectory of the community's struggle and track the engagement of its actors, each of whom is pursuing an interest at once institutional and individual.

Pom Mahakan may not be, in any literal sense, a microcosm of the Thai polity, whether as *moeang* or as *prathaet*. But its ability to move between these two models, to play into the official cultural narrative while maintaining a distinctive identity of its own, and to ride out the precarious and shifting space among contending political forces all exemplify ways in which the country itself claims to have negotiated its past and its future. The forces the community faces are global, and are exemplified by the drive toward an increasingly ruthless spatial cleansing of the urban environment. That drive is framed in terms of nationalist cultural ideologies but is also, paradoxically, based on crassly universalizing models of urban beautification.

When Rama V imperiously smashed "the king's walk" through the mandala-based city plan, with its reproduction of the walled ground plan of Ayutthaya, he literally paved the way for the old order's replacement—though the new roadway was sanctioned by his own royal power—by a grid-like European city. The royal avenue framed the wall and the Mahakan citadel as proud but now isolated and imprisoned trophies held up in triumph by the conquering forces of modernization. The irruption of Rachadamnoen Avenue across the old city wall occurs at precisely the point at which Rama I had caused the Mahakan citadel to be constructed. Dwelling in the comforting historical embrace of citadel and wall, the Pom Mahakan community has strategically reversed that displacement, creating an urban village with all the civilizational claims of a true *moeang* and thereby rejecting the modernist logic of official planning. It is in its adoption of the old *moeang* order that we find the roots of its success in stopping the new developmentalist bureaucracy in its tracks.

After more than two decades of this historically inflected struggle, the staying power of the Pom Mahakan community increasingly looks like a success of sorts. But nothing is resolved and serious dangers still threaten. Not the least of these is posed by the risk of over-identification with the Democrat Party—a political entity that, while largely unsympathetic to the Assembly of the Poor, has extensive connections with the predominantly middle-class NGOs that so provoked the ire of Thaksin Shinawatra—or, contrastively, with the remnants of the Assembly of the Poor itself. That balancing act remains a tough challenge, one that the military coup of 2014 has not simplified. The law courts, too, present an intractable obstacle, given the sheer difficulty of persuading any government to open the Pandora's box of serious legal reform.

The residents are very aware of these risks, and for the moment prefer to lie low. But they also know that any attempt to move them without providing them with decent alternative housing will meet with an international outcry; it will make them highly visible—"tangible"—again. They and their supporters also know that the future of the past is at stake. If they are eventually forced to leave the site, a last, lingering trace of the old Siamese polity—the polity of the ghosts venerated in the community's shrines—will vanish, a barely perceptible wisp trailing the fast-fading echoes of memory into the greedy smog of modern Bangkok.

Notes

PREFACE

1. See his comments, supportive of the most recent scheme to save the community ("if the project can persuade us to do it this way, it will be a classic"), reported verbatim in Thanaphon 2007: 208–10. See also the similarly positive assessment offered by the project's architect, Chatri Prakitnonthakan (2007: 92).

CHAPTER ONE

1. For the 2010 census figures, see, conveniently, http://www.citypopulation.de/php/thailand-admin.php (last accessed 26 April 2015).
2. For a detailed account of all the citadels, see S. Plainoi 2001: 145–60. Thanaphon (2007: 34) specifically dates the construction of the citadels to 1783.
3. Dovey (2001: 269–71) offers a usefully detailed discussion of this transformation.
4. The problem of canal pollution is serious throughout the city; see Montira 2012: 196.
5. See the aerial view shown in the map insert at the beginning of this chapter. Pranee (2004: 113) speculates that passersby might easily miss the presence of a living community behind the old wall. Ploenpote (2003b) reports a community leader's comment that the foliage hides the community.
6. For a critical discussion, see Chatri 2012: 115–17; Napong forthcoming.
7. Sinkhronkrup 1995: 25.
8. The admission in a 2003 BMA document detailing a proposed park for the nearby Temple of the Golden Mount admits to a lack of competent experts; in the case of Pom Mahakan,

the administration clearly does not have at its disposal enough people to perform even simple maintenance. On domicide, see Shao 2013.
9. The continuing clashes between the Red and Yellow Shirts has been the subject of endless journalistic as well as academic investigation. There is no exact correlation between these groups and political parties, although the Red Shirts—often, if far too crudely, represented as dominated by rural people from the northeastern (Isan) region—have *tended* to side with the political faction originally represented by Thaksin's Thai Rak Thai party and its successors, the People's Power Party and Pheu Thai, and have been suspected by some of their detractors of harboring republican sentiments; the opposing Yellow Shirts, or People's Action for Democracy group, have been regarded, just as stereotypically, as Democrat Party supporters, have opposed the power of the Shinawatra family, and have called for a reduction in the elected proportion of parliamentary deputies.
10. See, notably, http://www.youtube.com/watch?v=4XmMD1IxIr4; www.youtube.com/watch?v=nSpBXpXWioc; http://www.youtube.com/watch?v=E4z6xjPnUpI
11. The book is Thanaphon 2007. I briefly discuss Apiwat's film elsewhere in these pages.
12. Bristol's creation of the Centre for Architecture and Human Rights (CAHR) in Bangkok and Vancouver was partly inspired by his encounter with Pom Mahakan. See especially Bristol 2009.
13. See especially Sudjit and Apiwat 2003: 12; they recognize that a central problem concerns the middle-class identity and outlook of most of the architects who are involved in major works in the city, and suggest that the training that research on Pom Mahakan provides can alter those outlooks in productive fashion—very much the goal that led Graeme Bristol to take his students there and eventually to found the Centre for Architecture and Human Rights.
14. Skiotis 2003, now available on YouTube courtesy of the Centre for Architecture and Human Rights (CAHR). CAHR is an NGO based in Victoria, B.C., and Bangkok, and directed by Graeme Bristol; the vision behind this organization was born of Bristol's work and experience at Pom Mahakan. https://www.youtube.com/watch?v=72hRsF8qe0s (last accessed 12 April 2015).
15. See also Jean Du Plessis 2005. Among Graeme Bristol's writings, see especially Bristol 2007, 2009.
16. See the discussion in Abhayuth 2009: 16–17. On the relationship between social movements and the status of urban heritage, see De Cesari and Herzfeld 2015.
17. Thaksin, a populist, soon found himself deeply at odds with both NGOs and academics. Among the latter, the anthropologist and former left-wing guerrilla Thirayuth Boonmee was perhaps the most colorfully outspoken and frequently drew Thaksin's sarcastic ire.
18. On the avoidance of direct confrontation, which nevertheless sometimes

masks a genuine dynamic of engagement, see Aulino's (2014: 421-22) vivid account.
19. Some authors (e.g., Hinton 1992) apparently regard such ritualism as in conflict with serious action. That view ignores the performative force of all ritual, secular and religious alike—a view, ironically, that was particularly developed in the Thai context (by Tambiah 1979). In fact, as I hope to show in this book, the reassurance that the repetition of familiar forms of interaction provides has also been an enabling factor for the development of more forceful forms of action.
20. Letters of "Friends of the Pom Mahakan Community" International Committee, the Pom Mahakan community leaders to the commission, and Michael Herzfeld to Birte Scholz of the COHRE Geneva office, all dated 12 May 2003.
21. See Herzfeld 1991 on Greece and 2009b on Italy.
22. See particularly Akin 1999; Apiwat 2013: 46-50; Askew 1994: 66-69; Askew 2002a: 139-69; Johnson 2009; Maier 2005; Ockey 2004: 124-50; Rittirong 2009; and Sopon 1992.
23. The term is widely used; it primarily implies congested living conditions. The community's old houses are so described in Sinkhronkrup 1995: 26, captions to figs. 5-6. But Pom Mahakan residents adamantly reject high-rise "solutions" that, while they could reduce congestion, would disrupt social relations and interfere with the livelihoods of the many street vendors among them.
24. Here I follow Missingham 2003: 8, 157-58; see also Aulino 2012: 77, 230; Delcore 2003: 67. Bantorn Ondam, a key figure in the articulation of the assembly with academic and other "established" interests (Missingham 2003: 207-8), was also generous with his advice to the Pom Mahakan leadership during the period of my initial field research there.
25. Baker (2000: 25) was not entirely wrong, at least at the rhetorical level, in asserting that "the Democrats stand for democratization, but with a heavy urban bias." Subsequent events, notably the assumption of power by the unelected Abhisit government of 2008-11, have suggested that even that limiting assessment has become too generous.
26. The demonstrators' shirt color evoked the king's birth on a Monday, the day symbolized by the color yellow.
27. See Harvey 1990a. Abhayuth (2009: 16) specifically notes that "free market capitalism" drives up prices far beyond the capacities of slum dwellers to maintain their presence. See also Porphant 2008: 182; Nut 2004: 1; Thanaphon 2007: 34.
28. Paritta 2002: 218, 237-38.
29. Thanaphon (2007: 34) claims that the entire attack on Pom Mahakan represents capitalist control over the state at national as well as local government levels. I am sympathetic to this argument, but his evidence is general and circumstantial; it is nevertheless certainly true, as he says, that the plans

developed by the authorities for the area as a whole were specifically aimed at tourist development, and there can be little doubt that the interests of royal display and commercial development conveniently converged. What is less clear is whether the authorities' determination to crush the resistance of Pom Mahakan in particular represented anything more focused than a desire to start the process with a show of strength against what seemed at first—and in economic terms certainly was—one of the weakest communities.

30. David C. Harvey (2001: 324) sagely rejects the idea "that heritage is *only* about the economic practices of exploitation."
31. On this last point, see BMA-ESCAP 2002: 26, where local administrative corruption is openly described as "a chronic problem that cannot be solved at all."
32. Sopranzetti 2012b; 2013: 208.
33. For illustrations of very similar antecedents, see the photographs and text in Suwit n.d. Thai middle-class activism is in this regard very different from what Zhang (2010: 165; see also Shao 2013) describes for China, where such activism seems to be directed mainly at protecting the recent gains of the emergent middle class. In Thailand, by contrast, although middle-class neighborhood activism also exists (as in the case of the self-gentrification of much of the Banglamphu district, also in the Rattanakosin area), it frequently makes common cause with the poor as well. Banglamphu activists, for example, were supportive of the Pom Mahakan case, although their practical involvement was perhaps limited by the time-consuming character of their own immediate concerns.
34. See especially Smart and Zerilli (2014: 226–28), who nevertheless find it useful to retain the concept of informality as "a different and ubiquitous way of doing things," albeit one that we find in "even the most formal institutions" (p. 228). State officials are often party to such a "community of complicity" (Steinmüller 2010). There is an exact parallel here with religious concerns with "folk" and "ecclesiastical" forms, as Stewart (1989) astutely notes. See also Milgram 2013: 73–74; Gandolfo 2013. On the inadequacy of the formal-informal distinction to describe the complexities of social justice in urban planning, see especially Roy 2009.
35. See Apiwat 2013: 54n8.
36. See Bourdieu 1977: 40. On the rules governing "illegal" activities, see, e.g., Herzfeld 1985: 20–26, 163–231; Konstantinov 1996.
37. This is what Austin (1975) called "performativity."
38. On disclaimers, see Bauman 1977: 21–22.
39. Jackson 2004. This reading of Jackson's analysis accords with Aulino's (2016) observations, in another Thai context, on the importance of seeing ritual action as performative regardless of the sentiments that animate it.
40. Note that I do not claim that the result of such performances is "conviction," which is an unreadable psychological inner state, but complaisance; see Herzfeld 2009c; Loizos 1975: 301n2. The process of norm distortion in performance is what I call "social poetics" (Herzfeld 2005: 21–26). On the

significance of performance in the politics of Thai consumerism, especially among aspiring rural-to-urban migrants, see Sopranzetti 2013: 89–103.
41. Displacement by railway expansion, and the fierce protests that it provoked, was not confined to Bangkok; see Elinoff 2013.
42. See especially Connors 2003.
43. See, notably, Day 2002; Harms 2011; Kirsch 1973; Leach 1956; and, on Thai political culture specifically, Connors 2003. Kirsch's (1973: 1–5) preference for religion over Leach's politics and power as an explanatory factor should remind us that to a very large extent religion and politics are inseparable in all these instances, a fact that perhaps explains how the ritualistic feel of much ostensibly political engagement led Hinton (1992) to view the conduct of meetings as divorced from practical reality. In the present study, by contrast, ritualistic-sounding rhetoric emerges as a strategic and tactical instrument of political engagement in the ongoing tension between authoritarian and egalitarian tendencies.
44. Siffin 1960: 262–63 (also partly quoted in Riggs 1966: 362). See also Herzfeld 2012.
45. See Missingham 2003, especially pp. 215–17.
46. In real conversations, however, especially among men, the closing of the conversation in a spirit of general agreement is marked by an acceleration of machine-gun-like bursts of *khrab! khrab! khrab!*; one analogy to this is the rhythmic fanning of women at meetings, described elsewhere in these pages.
47. This terminology actually has a relatively long history in Thai academic culture. Such writers as Luang Wichit Vadakan (Barmé 1993), influenced by European master narratives of history and culture, had introduced some of this language in the first half of the twentieth century. But its popularization, doubtless reinforced by the extremely high literacy rate Thailand enjoys, is a comparatively recent phenomenon, fueled, in part, by the neoliberal inflation of the value of "history."
48. The reciprocal pronoun *kan* means both "each other" and "together," and thus expresses an ideal, deeply embedded in everyday speech, of the inseparability of people's lives. This did not prevent the exhortations to "think together/help each other think" from sounding peremptory at times, exemplifying a sometimes acute tension—which we will visit repeatedly in this book—between egalitarian and authoritarian tendencies.
49. See Herzfeld 2010.
50. For trenchant critiques of this paradigm, see Ferguson 1990; Gupta 1998. The official ideology of "sufficiency economy," advanced by the present king and heavily endorsed by the ruling junta, expresses a rejection of "Western" consumerism but not of "development" as such.
51. See Thongchai 2000.
52. I also made the point that the objective-subjective distinction itself represented a preemptive philosophical position that did not necessarily advance understanding.

53. Also reported in the daily newspaper *Matichon*, 23 April 2003, p. 18. See Darlington 2013; Delcore 2004.
54. This seems less extortionate than what I have reported for local police in Rome (Herzfeld 2009a: 238–44), but it resonates with the rather mixed treatment of prostitutes by Bangkok police as reported by McCargo (n.d.). Police generally seem more interested in satisfying arrest quotas while maintaining an amiable relationship with the street than in actively pursuing the sources of crime.
55. See Sopranzetti 2012a, 2013.
56. There are obvious parallels with Geertz's (1973: 412–53) justly famous story of the Balinese cockfight. The main difference is that in this case neither the authorities nor their hired toughs actually appeared. That detail appeared to have little impact on the residents' appreciation of the commitment we had made to them simply by showing up.
57. Initially I could persuade no one to tell me which newspaper had been involved, and I was told that now that the relationship with that newspaper was cordial the community was reluctant to risk incurring its hostility anew. I have respected that anonymity intentionally here.
58. A *tuk-tuk* is a three-wheeler taxi named for its noisy two-stroke engine.
59. This bridge, in colloquial speech usually called simply the Phahn Fah bridge, marked the outermost geographical limit of the protests in 1973 that eventually brought down the military dictatorship of that time.
60. Thanaphon (2007: 66–67), in the context of explaining his theoretical orientation, while citing the distinction I make between social and monumental time in Crete (Herzfeld 1991), strangely shows no awareness of my active involvement in the Pom Mahakan case. Nevertheless, his book does at least reflect some interest in my approach to the relationship between social issues and conservation. His critique of the "high culture" pretensions of the Rattanakosin conservationists, moreover, although it does not substantially depart from a nationally based paradigm, at least offers a useful challenge to the official projection of true Thai culture as defined by royalty and power (Thanaphon 2007: 41–43, 191). Given the current tendency to conflate royalism and nationalism, a tendency instrumentally promoted by the military and social elite currently in power, it is important to disaggregate these two ideologies and to recall that Thai antimonarchism can take highly nationalistic forms.
61. *Ajahn* originally meant "religious teacher" and is a word of Sanskrit origin. *Thahn* is an honorific that can be used as a second-person pronoun (both singular and plural), as a referent, and as a prefix to a title (as here). The *wai* is derived from the Indian *namaste*.
62. Under King Prajadhipok a member of the "palace police" (*tamruat luang*, "gentlemen-at-arms" in the British tradition) was stationed in front of the Grand Palace and had the function of passing any citizen's petition to the king (Dhani 2012: 17).

63. For analyses of Thailand's partial cultural dependence on the European colonial powers in the nineteenth and twentieth centuries, see Harrison and Jackson 2009; Peleggi 2002a.
64. Charles Keyes and I were both praised in an English-language newspaper article (Sanitsuda 2002) for our endorsement of "local knowledge" as opposed to academic and bureaucratic epistemologies. But in fact I am more inclined to the critical view of this concept so elegantly analyzed by Gupta 1998. My discomfort with the concept is of a piece with my view of UNESCO's Cartesian separation of "intangible" from "tangible" heritage (see Herzfeld 2014). A well-meaning deputy city clerk is even reported (in Thanaphon 2007: 212) as speaking of the need to "come up with a plan with the local knowledge of ancient people," as if the age of community elders and the antiquity of monuments and tradition somehow belonged to the same temporality.
65. Zhu 2012; see also Schein (1999: 386) on the Miao, a minority group in China.
66. Here I allude to Scott's (1998) notion of legibility as the goal of state surveillance of social life.
67. I allude to Harvey's (1990b: 260–307) well-known concept of "time-space compression."
68. The community has remained remarkably stable in size; in 1995 it had about the same population, made up of ninety-eight families (Sinkhronkrup 1995: 25). This stability is partly due to the fact that when some residents opt to live elsewhere, they are often replaced by newcomers. Given official concerns that an expanding population would make living conditions intolerable, this demographic stability ought to have been reassuring.
69. See, very similarly, Askew 1994: 64, 2002a:140, the latter passage being in part an extension of arguments first strongly advanced by Akin (1999).
70. An excellent and broadly contextualized discussion is to be found in Van Esterik 2000: 109–18. For a brief biography of founder Lek Viriyaphant, see http://www.ancientcitygroup.net/ancientsiam/en/acontent/21.html (last accessed 18 April 2015). Thongchai's (1994) discussion of the role of cartography in the subordination of Siamese to Western interests is also highly germane to this phenomenon, as are Harvey's (1990a: 424) observations on the role of cartography in the reshaping of power and temporality with the rise of capitalism. The English name of the Ancient City is one possible translation of its Thai name, *Moeang Boran*, but the double meaning of *moeang*—as city and as segmentary moral community—suggests that the English translation addresses a Western audience in more restrictive terms than those understood by Thai visitors.

CHAPTER TWO

1. Tambiah 1976: 102–24; 1977; Thongchai 1994.
2. See the discussion of egalitarianism and authoritarianism in Herzfeld 2012,

especially pp. 148–52, and see above, chap. 2, section titled "Two Models of the Polity").

3. I am indebted to Professor Chayan Vaddhanaphuti for a most illuminating conversation (August 2014) in which he shared his knowledge of the northern Thai usages. On the historical process of the displacement of *moeang* by *prathaet*, see Anderson 1991: 173; Thongchai 1994: 48–49. For a relatively recent discussion of *civiltà*, see Herzfeld 2009a: 3–5, 182.

4. Empire, especially in the nineteenth century, was primarily a capitalist enterprise. See especially Harvey 1990a.

5. Segmentation is, minimally, a multilevel arrangement of nesting oppositions between opposing factions. In patrilineal systems—the most famous example is to be found in Evans-Pritchard's *The Nuer* (1940)—this can be represented as a hierarchy of levels, at each of which groups are opposed to each other in feuding relations while coalescing as solidary units at the next level up. While segmentary systems were originally viewed as radically different from bureaucratic states, it has become apparent that, at the very least, *cultural* segmentation can and does coexist with—and may even reinforce—highly centralized political and bureaucratic systems; see, e.g., Ben-Yehoyada 2014 and Herzfeld 1987: 152–85, for further discussion.

6. Taylor 2008: 33. The metaphor of *emboîtement* (emboxment) comes from Condominas (1990: 35–36), but Tambiah (1976) had much earlier recognized the pattern as one of segmentation—in other words, as a system of morally analogous (because conceptually concentric) entities. Thongchai (1994: 82) has a brief but useful discussion of the relation between the mandala and royal power.

7. Aulino (2014) calls this common framing the "social body," and shows how everyday polite comportment—of which I give numerous examples in this book—reproduces and reaffirms its moral implications.

8. There is some resemblance between the Thai term *moeang* and the Italian *paese*, which can mean both a country (without, however, implying any specific distinction between its segmentary and pyramidal realizations) and a village; "all the world is a *paese*," a common Italian expression, suggests the capacity to find something familiar in the places most distant from home, especially as urban districts often resemble Pom Mahakan conceptually in imagining themselves as rural communities. See Herzfeld 2009a: 17.

9. See Anderson 1991: 171–73; Thongchai 1994: 20–80.

10. An article in *Siam Rath* (13 September 2004) and distributed by CODI reported that of 394,065 residents registered as living in poverty, 259,458 claimed to have a housing problem. See also *Daily News* (Thai newspaper), 3 September 2003, pp. 3 and 19; Pravit 2003.

11. The sibling idiom is used to distinguish between students of different years in a school or university. Customers will address even visibly older waitstaff in a restaurant as *nawng* (younger sibling), thereby showing that the term is

both hierarchical and (relatively) friendly. For another usage, see Sopranzetti 2012a: 68. Pitch Pongsawat (personal communication, 2014) has pointed out that this terminology displaces another pair expressive of more unilaterally hierarchical relations between aristocratic observers and the community (*luk phi luk nawng*, older and younger children).

12. An example of the last usage is found in the introduction to Bangkok governor Apirak Kosayodhin's policy leaflet issued shortly after his election (Apirak 2004: 1), where in the very first sentence he writes of the *phi nawng chao Krungthaep* (literally, "the elder and younger siblings [who are] the people of Bangkok").

13. See Askew 1994: 120–21; O'Connor 1991: 65. O'Connor appropriately chooses the term "*moral* community," which is how Evans-Pritchard (1940) originally characterized the basic unit of the Nuer segmentary system. Such systems encourage the development of a tensile relationship between hierarchy and egalitarianism because they are inherently unstable, a situation that sedentarization and urbanization may exacerbate as often as they appear to suppress it (e.g., Meeker 1979). O'Connor's analysis also allows us to see that the heavy influx of pro-Thaksin villagers from the northeast of the country decisively changes the character of the urban-rural divide; the newly urbanized migrants from the poorest part of the country, their appetites whetted by the new consumerism and by their contact with the bright lights of the capital (Mills 1999; Sopranzetti 2013), will not be persuaded to retreat into passive acquiescence in their marginalization by the traditional (and traditionalizing) power brokers. There is thus a strong resonance between O'Connor's historical account and my own ethnographically based analysis. Scott's (2009) *longue durée* analysis of highland-lowland relations offers a possible explanation of the origins of the tension that we have thus identified, but such claims would have to be purely speculative in the context of today's rough-and-tumble Thai political scene, which more closely reproduces the features of a classic class conflict.

14. I am indebted to Chu Jianfang (Nanjing University) (personal communication by e-mail; quoted here, 23 June 2014) for all the information about the Dai Daikong (as he and other Chinese scholars call this group) contained in this and the preceding paragraphs. Confusingly, the Yunnanese Tai, like the Thai, are part of a larger language group that also has significant branches in Vietnam and elsewhere and includes Lao, of which the Isan dialect of Thai is sometimes described as a Thai variant. On Tai identity in the area, see especially Yos 2008. On the Western derivation of objects and styles deemed to represent *khwahm pen thai*, see, notably, Koompong 2009, especially p. 41: "For Thailand, several culturally significant structures supposed to express the characteristic of Thainess, like the passenger terminal at Suvarnabhumi [designed by an American architect for Bangkok's recently constructed international airport], are of contributions from foreigners and their cultures."

Koompong (2010: 51) also explicitly argues a more general link between Western-derived aesthetics and crypto-colonialism in Thailand. For my original formulation of crypto-colonialism, see Herzfeld 2002.
15. Aulino 2012: 88.
16. The closest parallel may be the role of the *shaykh* in Arab nomadic societies. See, e.g., Shryock 1997.
17. This word itself means "stage," and gives some indication of the highly formalized language and conduct of the proceedings. Missingham (2003: 39) translates the term as "platform," thereby showing how the literal "staging" of protest can also be extended to frame protest at a wider level—a perfect fit for a segmentary view of political activism.
18. This is standard NGO rhetoric; for a very similar example from up-country, see Suwit n.d.: 22, where we similarly hear that a self-developing community of *phi nawng khon jon* (the siblings [who are] the poor) can become an example for others. On the importance of ensuring that each community work cooperatively with the *phi nawng* of all other poor communities throughout the land, see Abhayuth 2009: 23.
19. Sopon 1992: 106.
20. See, e.g., Johnson 2009; Sopon 1992.
21. See also Chatrathip 1997: 47. By pointing to an inclusive ancestry, residents are also claiming depth in terms of what Evans-Pritchard (1940: 106–8) called "structural time."
22. See Aulino's (2014: 425–26) helpful discussion of the *wai* as it articulates the physical with the social body.
23. Examples include Taman Mini in Indonesia (Hitchock 2005) and Miniatürk in Turkey (Türeli 2010).
24. On the materialization of national identity in the production of recognizable categories of artifacts, see especially Penny Van Esterik's (2000) suggestively titled *Materializing Thailand*.
25. See Askew 1996. Unlike its European equivalents, in which property succession is deeply bound up with questions of personhood (Handler 1985), and unlike its Lao cognate with its recently acquired affective undercurrent (Berliner 2010), the Thai term is a legalism that has never really caught the imagination of either ordinary people or state officials. This may be the result of the fact that the Western models for the concept have been equipped, as David C. Harvey (2001: 321–325) remarks, with a surprisingly shallow history of their own; this has discouraged reflection on the cultural and historical specificity of the term and to some extent rendered it exportable only to those interested in perpetuating their own present-day power rather than in exploring a common but complex past. "History" (*prawatisaht*) is a much more appealing concept, with its obvious links to *prawat khwahm pen mah* ("background"), and has especially featured in the political struggle of communities that, like Pom Mahakan, can claim to be "historical." In that sense, the resonance is perhaps greatest with

the Italian designation of *centro storico* (historic center), used of places that resonate with official and local perceptions of the past alike (see Herzfeld 2009a).
26. See Van Esterik's (2000: 109) useful discussion of the key terms for culture, custom (or tradition), and heritage. On the risks attendant on the use of international heritage discourse ("heritagization"), see De Cesari 2012: 400.
27. See Denes 2015; see also Rhum 1996: 338, 343, for yet another variant of the battle over spirits local and national, helpfully framed in terms of official management of "tradition."
28. For fairly obvious reasons, Daniel's (1996: 13–45) discussion of the tension between history and heritage would work better in the context of understanding the civil war in Thailand's Deep South (*pak tai*), where an embattled, Muslim, and Jawi-speaking local majority (and national minority) has been in a troubled relationship with the Thai state for many years.
29. See Thongchai 2001 for a critical account of this effect in Thailand. In Europe, the association of far-right politics with heritage localism is well documented. See, e.g., Herzfeld 2009a: 194; Stewart 2010.
30. See Choay 2001; Herzfeld 1991, 2009a; Lamprakos n.d., 2014, 2015; Ottolini n.d.
31. Napong forthcoming.
32. Transcript (in English) of the BMA-ESCAP joint seminar on the "Rattanakosin Pilot Project," 28 June 2002; I have modified the punctuation slightly.
33. BMA-ESCAP 2002: 2.
34. Saowanee 2005; see also Thanaphon 2007: 303. The language adopted here comes directly from the 1997 "People Constitution," as the latter publication also makes clear.
35. In this respect, the conical form of the citadel reproduces the effect of the "Dome" (not, in fact, a dome at all) of Thammasat University, a building that became the symbol of the entire institution and, as such, was associated with resistance to the relocation of the greater part of the university to the suburban Rangsit campus.
36. See Barry 2013 and, within that volume and in part specifically on Pom Mahakan, the very balanced account by Ho and Pornpan (2013). These authors note (p. 77) the threat that intergenerational and residential mobility poses for cultural rights claims; one could also argue, however, that this mobility eases what would otherwise in time become an intolerable demographic explosion within the community's very restricted space, and indeed Ho and Pornpan are also quick to recognize that the Pom Mahakan goal of assuming site guardianship duties in exchange for the right to continue living there represents a feasible and appropriate option. Thanaphon (2007: 200), analyzing the 1997 national constitution, characteristically links cultural rights to "local knowledge," thereby reproducing the tactically appealing rhetoric of the community and many of its supporters; the risk of this rhetoric, however, which dresses community concerns in the terms of official

discourse, lies in placing local expertise on a pedestal that separates it from what those with power are willing to treat as "real" knowledge (see Gupta 1998; Herzfeld 2004). For a more general treatment from a legal standpoint, see Khemthong 2010, 2011.

37. E.g., Anon. 2003a; Ariya n.d.; Suchit 2003b, 2003c, 2004b; Suwit n.d.; Thanaphon 2007: 33.

38. Compare the Four Regions Slum Network's verbally playful slogan, "We are pioneers (*bukboek*), not squatters (*bukruk*)" (Abhayuth 2009: 11). The land-sharing plans put forward by the community's supporters, notably that created by Chatri Prakitnonthakarn and his team, did not ignore the dimension of public recreational space (see Bangkok Metropolitan Administration 2004: 5); the student team from the King Mongkut Institute of Technology led by Graeme Bristol had earlier argued, before the eviction notice was served, that the concept of "park" should be expanded to incorporate some housing. Significantly, Thanaphon (2007: 309), arguing that under the 1997 constitution there should be joint participation between national government and civil society, talks of the way the central government, through the Rattanakosin City Project Committee, was trespassing (*buklam*, a word cognate with *bukruk*) on the residents' right to participation in local governance; his terminology reproduces here and elsewhere the standardized rhetoric of the residents and the NGO activists.

39. See, variously, Bowie 1997; Reynolds 1987; Riggs 1966; Thongchai 1994. While these works are very different in orientation and ideological thrust, together they provide a portrait of a country where anger at official inaction, corruption, and even brutality is real and open. They have penetrated the "cultural intimacy" (Herzfeld 2005) of an official mechanism whose representatives would doubtless prefer that they had not succeeded.

40. The act of raising one's hands in the *wai* gesture explicitly calibrates height to the degree of respect: the higher the *wai*, the greater the acknowledgment of the other's superiority—although this can also be done, in contexts where people are prepared to understand the reversal, as ironic. When royal personages visit a building or pass along a lower road, all visible human presences are removed from higher placements. Once, when I was heading to the airport, all traffic was stopped by police as the crown prince was expected to pass underneath the fast highway and it was not known at exactly what time he would do so.

41. See Karin 2005 for an example.

42. On the earlier modality, see Tambiah 1976. Here one can see a potential explanation for the apparent paradox of the military overthrow of a king (Rama VII Prajadhipok) as the prelude to the military's own refurbishment of the monarchy in the person of the present king. Critics of the laws of *lèse-majesté* have similarly argued that if such a law is to prevail, it should only be invoked by the palace—a clever (and demonstrably effective) means of avoiding the charge by those who would prefer to see the law abolished

altogether, and a potential trap for any royal personage who dared to bring charges (Streckfuss 2011). The physical celebration of the coup against Rama VII, a militaristic presence athwart Rachadamnoen Avenue, is, significantly, called the Democracy Monument; it is thus incorporated into a street that celebrates the prosperity and progress of the monarchy. Respect for an institution (*rabop*) can in some situations be enhanced by attacks on those who embody its powers; in a segmentary view of the political universe, this does not lead to the abolition of the institution, but it can lead to a temporary waning of its legitimacy. An obvious resemblance to the *gumsa-gumlao* oscillations described by Leach (1956) is indicative of a wider regional pattern of political relations.
43. Bangkok is officially a *maha-nakhawn*, a "great city," as its full name indicates.
44. The event was organized by activist Chaiwat Thirapantu; see his autobiographical note and account of that event at http://www.collectivewisdom initiative.org/files_people/Thirapantu_Chaiwat.htm (last accessed 18 April 2015). As often happens with NGO activities in Thailand, some muttered about the possible motives for setting up Big Bang, though it is difficult to see how the organizer could have profited beyond ensuring greater visibility for his movement.
45. See Ho and Pornpan 2013: 66 and 79n2; for a comparative discussion of this kind of "spatial cleansing," see Herzfeld 2006.
46. Perhaps the extreme case is the Brazilian capital, Brasília, where "sectors" are concentrations of narrowly defined functions; for example, most hotels are grouped in two such sectors. For a history of the planning logic involved and an account of some of its consequences, see Holston 1989. Again, such disaggregation of functions can sometimes, as in Bangkok, take the relatively violent form of spatial cleansing.
47. For the language cited here, see especially Abhayuth 2009: 13. Chaiwat explains there that the event was intended to provide a forum to pressure the candidates for election into considering the real issues that Bangkok faced. Others were skeptical of his intentions, wondering how he might profit personally from such an intervention, although it is hard to see what he gained from it beyond greater visibility for his movement. On the term *moeang nah-yu* (livable city), see the title of Suwit n.d. On spatial cleansing, see Herzfeld 2006.
48. In English, the term "polity" is derived from Greek *polis*, "city-state," and shares this root with "politics." While such etymological links can be deceptive, this particular assemblage does at least remind us that the conceptual separation of the urban from the political represents a relatively recent and European-derived development. Political corruption is often described as "eating the *moeang*" (*kin moeang*).
49. Askew 2008: 16; Askew's analysis of the ways in which the Democrat Party in the southern part of Thailand was able to manage cultural images offers instructive parallels with the strategies of the community leadership as

NOTES TO PAGES 62-70

described here. On the collective nature of face, see Aulino 2014: 426-31. On the term *chaobahn* applied to urban dwellers, see also Askew 1994: 64; cf. Delcore 2003: 66. The term *jaobahn*, which can sound very similar to non-Thai ears, means "householders," and appears in contexts concerned with legal ownership.
50. Missingham (2003: 166) describes this device in detail.
51. On the association of ghosts with modernity, see Johnson 2014; Klima 2002; Morris 2000.
52. The word *thi* (with a falling tone) means "place"; the collocation *thi din* is thus compounded of two nouns to mean "landed property, lot."

CHAPTER THREE

1. See *Sawatdi Krugthaep*, 12 August 2004, pp. 1, 6-7.
2. Suchit 2004b. Suchit's article appeared after Governor Apirak announced that he would head a commission to protect the interests of people living in the historic areas of the city; Suchit, unconsciously echoing my own comment to the governor (see below, chap. 5, in the section titled "A Change of Guard, a Change of Heart") that the entrenched civil service bureaucracy would resist reform, worried that these particular bureaucrats were not willing to make concessions to ordinary people but would continue to press for mass evictions. His (and my) fears proved to be well founded, as his subsequent embarrassment and resignation, discussed below, demonstrated.
3. Sinkhronkrup 1995: front matter; see also p. 51.
4. Nattika 2014: 8. Dovey (2001: 272) nevertheless points out that Rachadamnoen Avenue retained enough of the original symbolic orientation to suggest an expansion rather than a rejection of the traditional association of the monarchy with ritual power.
5. On the impact of beautification on the poor of Seoul and especially on its acceleration of the pace of eviction in that city, see Davis 2011: 588.
6. Smith (1979; see also 2006) was specifically inveighing against gentrification. The Pom Mahakan case is of a rather different ilk, although similar commercial and class interests are at stake there.
7. Sinkhronkrup 1995: 1; see Jackson 2004.
8. Van Esterik (2000: 100-107) argues for a very similar assessment; see also the discussion of crypto-colonialism in Herzfeld 2002 and 2013a.
9. See the discussion in Rüland and Bhansoon 1996: 59-61.
10. On this, see Rittirong 2009: 18, 27-28.
11. Harms 2011: 173-74; 2013: 355.
12. See Tambiah 1976: 102-24; 1977) for a detailed analysis of the larger tendency in southeast Asia to pattern cities on the logic of the mandala, the Buddhist figuration of the universe. While Bangkok's modern development has certainly also been influenced by Buddhist conceptions of space, these have become more diffuse and also more varied amid the phantasmagoria

of Bangkok's modernist architecture (see Taylor 2008: 34). On Westernizing planning models, see especially Askew 2002b.
13. Crypto-colonial states were also generally forced to adopt clearly defined borders, a centralized bureaucracy, and the trappings of a reified national culture as the price of their claim to independence (Herzfeld 2002). The listing of such countries—which include Greece, Iran, and Nepal—should be interpreted as a heuristic device rather than as a definitive category, but the Thai case is so close to the ideal type that the term can be usefully employed here as a concise reminder of the country's political status and its cultural consequences.
14. Of the two national names, Siam and Thailand, "Siam" is less focused on the ethnic primacy of Thai speakers, but it has implications of vassalage that are also irksome to some. See also Thongchai 1994: 18–19 for a discussion of the shifting semantics of both terms.
15. In Greece communism was similarly represented as alien to Greek values; the U.S. House Un-American Activities Committee is another obvious example of this rhetorical move.
16. E.g., Karin 2005. Thanaphon (2007: 163–64) suggests that the cumulative combination of the Phibul and Sarit dictatorships produced a policy emphasis on both nativist culture and commercial development, with the result that the approach to historic conservation that emerged focused on monuments (which could be developed as tourist attractions) but ignored the communities associated with them.
17. See Herzfeld 2002, 2009d; see also Thongchai 2001. On the impact of crypto-colonialism on architecture, and especially on that of Rattanakosin Island, see Woranuch 2002; for a slightly different view, but one that suggests a complementary rather than an alternative vision (resistance rather than colonial mimicry), see Dovey 2001: 271–72.
18. For extremely perceptive analyses of this process, see Handler 1985, 1988.
19. Koompong (2009) perceptively shows how the Suvarnabhumi international passenger terminal was dragged into debates about whether a patently foreign design could be accepted as an expression of Thainess. Subsequent revisions of the plan and visual additions (such as freestanding representations of Thai mythology) represent the more literal-minded nationalists' doubts. The shops, significantly, represent a virtual monopoly of airport sales by the suggestively named and well-connected King Power company.
20. Choay 2001: 12; for a complementary and southeast Asia-specific perspective, see Byrne 2007, 2009, 2013.
21. Karin 2005. The stifling impact of top-down conservation is not confined to state systems, but their effects are sometimes reinforced by international bodies' endorsement of state policies (see, e.g., De Cesari 2010).
22. Pthomrerk Kedudhat, conversation during the period of my main fieldwork; see also the detailed account of the committee's activities in Bangkok in Askew 2002a: 284–95, and the briefer summary in Karin 2005.

23. Nut 2004: 34.
24. Janssen 2011; Yongtanit (2012: 115–16) outlines the bureau's most recent policy in this area.
25. Hamilton (2004), for example, writing of the seaside resort of Hua Hin, eloquently describes the massive destruction of elegant old houses and workers' dwellings to make way for hotels and other tourist services—a process in which the old aristocratic owners are sometimes complicit, and which is accompanied by sometimes wrenching personal adjustments to the presence of large numbers of culturally insensitive visitors.
26. As Rüland and Bhansoon (1996: 59) observe in the context of Bangkok slum policies, protracted confrontations are expensive for the landowners. Only when there is no rental profit to be made from the land, as in the case of Pom Mahakan, can the landowner afford to sit out a long period of uncertainty.
27. Tiamsoon and Akagawa (2012: 159).
28. On the CPB's current approach, see Yongtanit 2012.
29. Delcore 2003: 64. The proliferation of billboards and hoardings with royal portraits, a phenomenon that reaches an apogee of sorts at the recently constructed Suvarnabhumi Bangkok airport, beautifully exemplifies the fusion of royal symbolism with modern consumerist advertising techniques. The Thai concern with images (on which see Jackson 2004) represents another cultural feature well adapted to feeding off the most recent technologies of dissemination. For an extremely useful account of Rachadamnoen Avenue, including a discussion of its multiple layers of political significance, see Koompong 2012; see also Dovey 2001: 269–80.
30. This double significance is illustrated by Peleggi's (2002a: 114–29) discussion of the implications of Rama V's dramatic inaugural "progress" (i.e., procession) along the avenue (see also Nattika 2014: 7); in the terms of this book, the idea of "progress," a residue of Victorian-era survivalism, is materialized in the shift from the meaning of *moeang* as one moral community among others concentric to it to the centralized urban space of a national capital. Dovey (2001: 270–71) suggests the translation of the name Rachadamnoen a as "royal route," a rendition that nicely conveys this combination of modernity and procession as dramatized in the king's predilection for using motor cars in the ceremonial events staged along the avenue. For the models that apparently inspired the avenue's construction, see also Thanaphon 2007: 149.
31. See Thanaphon's (2007: 150) suggestion to this effect.
32. On the history of the Democracy Monument and Rachadamnoen Avenue, see Dovey 2001; Wong 2006: 65. On Mussolini's remodeling of Rome, see Herzfeld 2009a: 124; Insolera 2001. Another example—which, like the cases of Bangkok and Rome, reflects but does not truly realize the never-implemented city master plan devised by modernist planners—is that of Bogotá, Colombia, where the equivalent avenue, the Carrera Décima, was

envisaged as providing a highway that would simultaneously remove the roots of urban degradation; see Pérez 2010.
33. See Missingham 2003: 153–58, especially fig. 10 on p. 153. Missingham, however, points out (169) that the Democrat Party, which has increasingly been perceived as the sole source of national-level political support for Pom Mahakan, was completely unsympathetic to the major goals of the Assembly and, when it came to power in late 1997, rejected the agreement previously reached between the Assembly and the Chavalit government; at the same time, the first Thaksin government that came to power at the beginning of 2001 was also unsympathetic and paternalistic in its responses (213). We should beware of simplistic associations of protest style with political alignment; rather, style is a component of protest strategy.
34. See also the important discussion in Chatri 2012: 133–34, from which I have taken the suggestively translated quotation from the master plan.
35. Koompong (2012: 27) provides some valuable detail on this aspect of the monument's history. See also Koompong 2012: 33 for a realistic view of the military's relationship with the monarchy.
36. See the sympathetic account in Prudhisan 2012: 108.
37. Prajadhipok was not convinced that the Thai people were prepared for democracy or culturally predisposed to manage it well, but he also apparently felt that refusing them the right to exercise it could lead to greater difficulties internationally. These views held by the king with regard to his role and to the importance of the monarch's character in establishing royal legitimacy are discussed at some length, in the context of Prajadhipok's response to the coup and to the other difficulties of his reign, in Prudhisan 2012.
38. Dhani 2012: 17. This is doubtless a somewhat idealized portrayal. It is also interesting that Prince Dhani cites Malinowski (14–15) to justify the maintenance of such august traditions as monarchy as the basis for cultural survival (the reference, perhaps through a significant slip, appears not as *Magic, Science, and Religion*, the original title, but as *Magic, Science and Reality*!).
39. Quoted in Missingham 2003: 158.
40. See Aulino 2012: 77; Missingham 2003: 8; for a contrasting view, note Thanaphon's (2007: 102) utopian focus on altruism as the appropriate attitude of civil society (*prachah sangkhom*). Indeed, Thanaphon seems to reflect typically well-meaning (and, to be fair, perhaps partly practical) middle-class and NGO attitudes as well when he suggests that community residents "have to be pushed and pressured" into a participatory attitude toward culture and especially toward its historical and archaeological dimensions (Thanaphon 2007: 44–45).
41. The model of rural purity, which also reflects a version of royalist ideology, seems to have entered popular Thai usage during a period of fascination with European fascism (see Barmé 1993; and cf. Mosse 1988) that itself represents a deep-seated European fascination with the rural as a source of genuine,

"natural" culture (Williams 1975). Taylor (2008: 14–16) offers a brief but incisive discussion of the ideological significance of the pursuit of rurality in the heart of Bangkok.
42. Suchit 2003c.
43. See Williams 1975. On the concept of "living heritage "and its vicissitudes in Cambodia, see Miura 2010: 106–14.
44. Chatri 2003: 132.
45. Here too I am grateful to Chayan Vatthanaputri for information that allowed me, with his approval, to make this connection explicit. There is also a direct analogy here with the Italian notion of *civiltà*, conceived as the urban-based cultivatedness that distinguishes Italians from others and endows them with a distinction that places loyalty and moral solidarity above mere legalism (see also Herzfeld 2009a: 3–5, 182).
46. Suchit 2003a; see also Suchit 2003b, 2004a. Pranee Glamsam (2004: 114) also notes the strong similarity between the fortresses and walls of Ayutthaya and this part of Rattanakosin Island, while Nattika (2014: 4) notes that the entire area, encompassing the old palace and the Royal Ground (now Sanam Luang), was reconstructed as a resurrection of the old Siamese capital in the new location; Thanaphon (2007: 37, 130, 134) suggests that the life of the community and understanding of the space were similarly imitative of those of the corresponding part of the old capital—a useful argument against those who want to "restore" the space without regard to its social history—while also noting (2007: 127) diachronic continuity with the Ayutthaya period inasmuch as there were already agricultural temples on the site at that time. This engages two very different perspectives on history in the process of claiming to be original (*dang doem*) inhabitants, a claim the same author (2007: 200) uses to argue for the community's right to conserve its own local culture while also participating in the care of cultural monuments of national significance.
47. The range of commentaries on this concept is by now vast. For helpfully nuanced and grounded perspectives, see Delcore 2003; Elinoff 2013, 2014.
48. For a comparable Chinese case, see Non 2013.
49. See Vallard 2013: 128–33.
50. For a useful, extended discussion of the original formulations of gentrification by Glass (1964) and Smith (1979), see Lees, Slater, and Wyly 2008.
51. The town is Rethemnos (Rethimno), Crete; see Herzfeld 1991. One mark of the embourgeoisement of the town's residents is that our old landlords, specialty bakers who were living a modest and fairly "traditional" existence when I did my fieldwork there in 1983–84, had two decades later become habituated to overseas tourism themselves; one trip took them to Thailand. See also Herzfeld 2015.
52. Elinoff (2014: 100–103) makes a very similar observation for the poor in a northern Thai town, Khon Kaen. For a useful discussion of the relationship between development ideologies and idioms of Thainess, see Delcore 2003.
53. Wutipong n.d. [2004]. This booklet is also discussed in the section titled

"'Data' versus 'Knowledge'" in chap. 7. The subtitle might be better translated as "Weaving People Power," but since the complaint of the poor is that those in office wield power (*amnaht*) the poor do not possess, such a translation could also be misleading.

54. The Four Regions Slum Network is "a movement of poor people in the city (*moeang*) that propels issues of housing rights, quality of life development for slum dwellers, and strives for social justice, engages in a process of building a balance of power in negotiation with the state through proceeding with work that is conducted freely and without concealing the interference of power or any kind of special interest" (Abhayuth 2009: 8). Impressively, the network includes more than a hundred communities in its membership.
55. Abhayuth 2009: 17; see also 19–20 for a discussion of the importance of building up the popular base (*thahn muan chon*) as a strategic necessity. The Marxist language is not coincidental, and reflects the educated origins of much of the NGO rhetoric. At the same time, the focus on "raising the level of thought and the consciousness of the slum dwellers" suggests a degree of condescension that, as is perhaps consistent with what I have noted here about the play of egalitarianism and authoritarianism, does not strike poor Bangkok residents as particularly incongruous.
56. See the cover photograph in Missingham 2003.
57. See Zhang 2010: 150–56 for a rich account of "nail households" in Kunming.
58. The metaphor of "refraction" is taken directly from Evans-Pritchard's (1956) study of the religion of the Nuer in what is now South Sudan. In that study, it signals the filtering of perceptions of divinity through the perceived divisions of the natural and, especially, social worlds, the Nuer being the *locus classicus* for the ethnographic analysis of political segmentation.
59. See Sopranzetti 2012a.
60. This was the Chalerm Thai Theatre. See Koompong 2012: 27; Askew (2002a: 289) uses a different designation but clearly intends the same theater.
61. Variably detailed sources for this necessarily abbreviated historical account include Ariya n.d.; Bristol 2009; Pacharin 2003; Suchit 2003a; and Thanaphon 2007 (especially pp. 178–83, 282–85, 289–93, although this work often bypasses key dynamics connecting the highlighted events); and a brief lead article that appeared in *Khao Sod*, 24 April 2003, p. 2. The lead article, highly sympathetic to the Pom Mahakan inhabitants' desire to remain on the site, described the community as *dang doem* ("original, aboriginal"), an appellation that occludes the demographic changes that have taken place with the departure of most of the families installed in the earlier historical phases but emphasizes instead the preservation of an older way of life and of the old buildings. See also the comparison of old Bangkok, including Pom Mahakan, with such Western cities as London, Rome, Venice, and Oxford by the journalist and political critic Pravit Rojanapruck (2003).
62. Davis 2011; see also Shao 2013. It is also true that in Bangkok, with an arguably weaker central administration than Seoul, such international events

triggered the temporary concealment of slums more often than mass evictions. See Klima 2002: 40.
63. *Khao Sod*, 1 September 2003, has a picture of the community president proudly showing the residents' handiwork in a part of the garden that was already almost complete.
64. See especially Johnson 2009: 178–79.
65. On the segmentation of divine grace and its associated images in the Catholic and Orthodox Christian words, see, respectively, Christian 1989; Herzfeld 2005: 88.

CHAPTER FOUR

1. On the embodiment of hierarchy in the *wai*, see Aulino 2014; on foreigners' absorption of the stance, see Herzfeld 2009d.
2. Sopranzetti 2012a: 167–68.
3. See Ploenpote 2002.
4. In Thai, *kahn damnoenkahn "patthanah khong rath*," reported in *Khao Sod*, 31 August 2003, p. 3; the author of this op-ed piece accordingly called for a "revision of the development plan." For an example of ironic local critique in northern Thailand, see Johnson 2014: 29.
5. Wheeler 1954: 15.
6. This was reported, e.g., in *Thai Rath*, 12 January 2004, p. 12.
7. For a valuable discussion of the relationship between law and temporality, see Greenhouse 1996. In the spirit of her argument, I suggest that the Western derivation of so much of Thai law (see Loos 2006) overlays different temporal understandings and capacities, which may surface, as here, as disruptive instantiations of the *moeang*-based polity in action.
8. See documents of Mahidol University's Research Center for Peace Building; the specific source at http://www.peace.mahidol.ac.th/th/index.php?option=com_content&task=view&id=498&Itemid=155, accessed 25 September 2011, is no longer accessible.
9. For a critique of the notion of "common good" (*bene comune*) in Italy, see Cellamare 2008.
10. Some of the key concepts used here feature in Anon. 2010. This document shows the importance and persistence of a terminology that is closely linked to the desire for "urban renewal" and "beautification."
11. Thanaphon (2007: 31–32) notes that the urgency was based on the governor's desire to proceed with work that had been sanctioned by a royal edict—but that edict had been promulgated in 1992!
12. See, e.g., *Thai Rath*, 23 April 2003, p. 11.
13. I use the term "ecumene" here in its original sense of "inhabited universe," which captures the convergence of the local with the larger polity and religious community. On the ritual activity, see *Khao Sod*, 23 April 2003, pp. 1, 11–13; on p. 6 of the same newspaper appears a brief notice of the proposed

eviction, while the same page also hosted an article lamenting the community's predicament by Suchit Wongthes (Suchit 2003b). *Khao Sod* ("Fresh News") was one of the newspapers that often supported the community in its struggle.
14. See Khemthong n.d.: Abstract.
15. Ibid.: 12.
16. See Abhayuth 2009: 13–16 for a useful discussion of the history of official reluctance to welcome a type of scheme that would have allowed slum dwellers to develop their economic and living conditions in the places where they had already coalesced as communities.
17. See also, e.g., Elinoff 2014: 101 and 105n9. On Khlong Thoey, see especially Maier 2005. In Italy, retrospective acceptance of previously illegal construction is done on a more ad hoc—but legally enforceable—basis, and represents the authorities' recognition that massive clearance would create greater social problems than some degree of compromise; see Herzfeld 2009a.
18. Tiamsoon and Akagawa 2012: 156.
19. On the term *chumchon*, see especially Reynolds 2009 on the evidence for its recent coinage and its adoption by state bureaucrats as a convenient source of identity building during the Cold War. On its yoking to notions of culture, see Parnwell 2005. Barmé (1993) offers a useful history of the arrival and development of the term *watthanatham* in Thai political discourse. For an example of the view that *chumchon* are populations that can feed themselves, partly by relying on nature, see Chatrathip 1997: 47. On the emergence of "community culture" and its links to the discourse of Thainess, see Delcore 2003: 66; on legal issues concerning community status and cultural rights, see Khemthong 2010, 2011. For a more general comment on the difficulty of defining community, see Bortolotto 2012: 269; Kutma 2012: 27, 31; Noyes 1995.
20. This is a joint publication of the BMA, the Thailand Cultural Environment Project, and DANIDA (Danish International Development Association)—an undated publication that does not show much in the way of vernacular architecture (but see p. 53) and virtually nothing of the cultural and social life of the area in the present day. *Chumchon* appears in this context as an abstraction rather than as a social entity, rather like the old-style archaeological sense of "culture." The Danish firm Jul and Frost issued a document outlining its plan for the Rattanakosin area; totally subordinated in practice to the expectations of the Rattanakosin Committee, its authors wrote grandiosely (and no doubt with the best of intentions) about the importance of local participation and democracy (to be achieved through "dialogue meetings") but said virtually nothing beyond generic bromides about how local interest was to be rendered genuinely independent; the emphasis on "invited special groups" as representing "the public" is suggestive of the overall attitude (Jul and Frost 2002: 4). The engagement of a Danish firm with little or no obvious understanding of local political and social dynamics illustrates with par-

ticular clarity the extent to which the authorities conceived of Thai culture in Western terms.
21. See, for example, the description of how slum communities emerged in this way in the Khlong Thoey harbor area, in Abhayuth 2009: 9–11.
22. On Northern Thai usage, see Anan 2001: 118–19. See also chap. 2 above, in the section titled "Strategies for Claiming the Past."
23. See Herzfeld 2009a: 78–84.
24. I have kept the Thai word here to show how the tautology that is characteristic of bureaucratic thinking creeps into the most well-intentioned critical responses to it.
25. I was present at this meeting, and spoke; so did Pthomrerk Kedudhat. Another academic observer who appeared several times at such events privately expressed concern that her presence could be considered a violation of her contractual obligation to stay out of politics.
26. Sudjit and Apiwat 2003: 7.
27. On the "network monarchy" and the similarity of its techniques to those of the party considered most inimical to its interests (the then-regnant Thai Rak Thai party of former prime minister Thaksin Shinawatra), see McCargo 2005. On the role of motorcycle-taxi drivers in enabling such networks at the ground level, see Sopranzetti 2012a, 2012b. On the more conventional sense of networking as a performance-based means of building relations of patronage with local communities, see Askew 2008. These works together do not show that Thais have a monopoly on political networking, but more modestly that behind the facade of national unity they are highly adept at creating networks that serve partisan political goals intended to capture the management of that unity for particular groups. It is surely not coincidental that the usual term for "demo" is *mawp*, derived from the English term "mobilization." The term has dynamic implications that are not as apparent in the one-shot image of the "demonstration." On Pom Mahakan's participation in various forms of networking, see also the useful summary in Supreeya 2009: 2–7.
28. See especially Missingham 2003.
29. The other members of this group were Marc Askew (University of Victoria), Graeme Bristol (King Mongkut Institute of Technology), Charles Keyes (University of Washington), Pthomrerk Kedudhat (Thammasat University), Shigeharu Tanabe (National Ethnological Museum, Osaka), and myself. It is never easy to assess the impact of such arrangements, but it certainly did not hurt the community to have a committee of senior scholars expressing their solidarity with its members.
30. I was able to obtain a copy of a document in which the residents had laid out these demands. The impending destruction was reported on the day it was supposed to begin, in *Daily News* [Thai], 16 January 2004, p. 34; the reporter noted that the BMA had not waited for the result of the final appeal to the Supreme Administrative Court. But resistance on the part of the residents

delayed the final action for another four days. See also *Thai Post* [Thai], 14 January 2004; and *Khom Chad Loek*, 21 January 2004, p. 7.
31. In this sense, the *phu nahm* are somewhat like the *shaykhs* of the Arab world (see, e.g., Shryock 1997). Although they are credited with charisma and are viewed as natural leaders, however, in contrast to the strongly patrilineal Arab groups they primarily depend for their powers on the insistence (not always received with conviction) that they speak for the community, and for the larger world of the poor, rather than as representatives of specific groups of kin or for reasons of self-interest or self-aggrandizement.
32. *Khom Khad Loek*, 21 January 2004, p. 7. Her position would not have fallen exclusively on unsympathetic ears; decisions regarding the Rattanakosin Island project, once made, were often understood by educated observers as irrevocable.
33. There are suspicions that the relocation of Thammasat to the suburb of Rangsit, although obviously motivated in part by simple demographic pressures, also serves the interests of those who want to see a famously politicized university removed from the symbolic center of the capital, with its royal and conservative associations.
34. For a slightly different reading of this term, albeit one that similarly allowed establishment praise for communal solidarity to coexist with the stirrings of active resistance, see Elinoff 2014: 100.
35. See Bristol 2007: 5–6 for a lively account of that first encounter, which certainly served to shock his middle-class students into a better understanding of the plight of the urban poor. The full report can be read at https://drive.google.com/file/d/0B136cP_HAhb3NjJVZEZNV1NRV1U/view?usp=sharing (last accessed 19 January 2015). On the history of CODI, see Somsook 2004.
36. See *Thai Rath*, 11 June 2003, p. 12.
37. See *Sayahm Rath*, 12 June 2003, p. 10.
38. See *Krungthaep Thurakit*, 14 June 2003, p. 11; *Matichon*, 14 June 2003, p. 11. This was the event that particularly prompted one prominent resident to confide that he feared the army far more than the police.
39. *Krungthaep Thurakit*, 21 August 2003, p. 15. Most of the information in this paragraph appears in that news report; see also Ploenpote 2003b, 2003c. See also the description of the residents' assumption of an air of unconcern, as well as comments from several of the community's academic supporters (including this writer), before the verdict in Chai chana lang Pom Mahakan, *Krungthaep Thurakit*, 29 August 2003, Jud Prakahi section, pp. 1–2.
40. The discussion appears in a document circulated by the network and dated 4 October 2004; the edict in question is decree no. 44 of the Revolutionary Council, issued in 1959.
41. See Kesinee and Napanisa 2003; *Krungthaep Thurakit*, 30 August 2003, p. 11.
42. See *Krungthaep Thurakit*, 1 September 2003, p. 15. See also Klima 2002: 40–42, for an earlier campaign of the same kind. Governor Samak's heartless comparison of the homeless with stray dogs prompted angry protests from resi-

dents in the area (including some representation from Pom Mahakan), supported by the Four Regions Slum Network; Samak's eviction and demolition policy made no sense to people attacked for having thereby been rendered homeless. One of their placards read, "We are people, we are not dogs!" (see especially *Khom Chad Loek*, 7 October 2003; see also *Bangkok Post*, 17 September 2003). And any comparison of humans with dogs is considered a major insult among Thais (see Tambiah 1969: 435, 450). The BMA also prohibited garland sellers and other street vendors from plying their trade during the distinguished guests' visit to Bangkok, presumably on the argument that this was not a seemly activity for a modern country.

43. *Khao Sod*, 31 August 2003, p. 3.

CHAPTER FIVE

1. *Khao Sod*, 31 August 2003, p. 1.
2. See especially *Khao Sod*, 26 August 2003, p. 13, in which I am (correctly) quoted as saying that I thought that a major problem lay in the municipal authorities' refusal to discuss the situation directly with the residents or to understand their plight in the residents' own terms. Pthomrerk is cited as criticizing the authorities' understanding of the term "conserve" (*anurak*) (see below, section titled "An Unexpected Visit"), while the architect M.R. Chanwut Worawan is quoted with a blunt attack on the BMA plan for its intended destruction of the old wooden houses and most of the trees on the site.
3. See *Khao Sod*, 30 August 2003, pp. 1 and 11. The final judgment allowed the BMA to demolish all the houses within a period not to exceed seventy-five days from 24 August, and allowed "injured parties"—including those who had not yet received compensation under the eminent domain expropriation—to appeal the decision to the Supreme Administrative Court within thirty days. See also *Daily News* (Thai-language newspaper), 1 September 2003, p. 28.
4. On the internal dynamics, see Ampa and Anchalee 2004.
5. See *Bangkok Post*, 6 July 2004, p. 1.
6. See *Bangkok Post*, 3 July 2004, p. 3.
7. See Onnucha 2004.
8. San Dusit poll, reported in *Bangkok Post*, 12 July 2004, p. 6. While such polls are based on a rather small sample (512 respondents interviewed over a six-day period), they are at least an indicator of what might motivate people's choices in an election. For reportage on the Khlong Thoey residents' bitter complaints about being neglected by all the candidates, see *Khao Sod*, 13 July 2004, pp. 29–30. Khlong Thoey is where "Father Joe" Maier for years conducted heroic rescue work under conditions that make Pom Mahakan seem a minor problem (see Maier 2005). While Maier wished me luck in my efforts with Pom Mahakan, he understandably made it clear that he was utterly

preoccupied with the terrible problems of drug addiction, grinding poverty, and appalling living quarters in Khlong Thoey. The reportage suggests some division among the residents as to whether they wanted attention drawn to their difficulties; one said that their problems were merely the usual ones of flood damage and garbage disposal. But Maier's work, in particular, reveals a devastatingly extreme situation for the poorest residents.

9. The number of communities is debatable and may depend on symbolic as well as political factors; Governor Apirak, in his reply, mentioned 23 such communities, whereas a later estimate put the number at 21 (https://th-th.facebook.com/pages/*chumchonPomMahakan*/157651854267254?sk=info, last accessed 18 April 2015; the italicized segment of the URL must be typed in Thai characters).

10. Thanaphon (2007: 203–4) accurately (according to my own recording) provides the entire question and answer in their original Thai.

11. This has been a recurrent theme in Bangkok planners' rhetoric, often not realized in practice and subject to all manner of temporizing. See, e.g., Niti 2010: 9–10.

12. He announced as one key goal "to enhance the BMA bureaucrats' readiness to serve the people with willingness and devotion"; another was to "develop the institutions and personnel of the BMA" (Apirak 2004: 4)—goals that cynical residents, unfairly in some cases, would not have deemed possible.

13. Apirak 2004: 11. For a critical view of this concept, see Pravit 2004.

14. *The Nation*, 5 September 2004; letter quoted in Karin 2005.

15. See, e.g., Gray 2014; Napong forthcoming; Non 2013. This is not to say that "participation" is unproblematic either (see especially Arnstein 1969); as Lavalle, Acharya, and Houtzager (2005: 961) remark, moreover, "participatory institutions are fundamentally political products, the rules of which are negotiated by political actors with different capacities."

16. Quoted in Ploenpote 2003a.

17. See "Mahakan Fort: Apirak Snubs Locals Trying to Save Homes," *The Nation*, 25 March 2005.

18. An excerpt from the letter, including these quotations, appears in AGFE 2007: 24 and Tiamsoon and Akagawa 2012: 155. The entire letter, addressed to then COHRE executive director Scott Leckie at the organization's Geneva address, appears as Annex 2 in AGFE 2007: 94. Leckie, who had been resident in Bangkok, was personally familiar with and actively engaged in the Pom Mahakan community's struggle.

19. While that respectful stance appears to have frayed during the recent confrontations between Red Shirts and Yellow Shirts, the community has always refrained from disrespectful or violent acts in its own demonstrations.

20. The concept of "common good" is a political football. It is highly ambiguous and therefore easily deployed against weaker groups on the grounds that they represent a minority interest (see especially Cellamare 2008). That is what happened to Pom Mahakan.

NOTES TO PAGES 136–149

21. Quoted in Chai chana lang Pom Mahakan, *Krungthaep Thurakit*, 29 August 2003, Jud Prakahi section, p. 2. See also Ploenpote 2003b. She had not supported the residents in their refusal to leave the site during the Bhichit governorship (Thanaphon 2007: 263), but the residents had meanwhile more fully demonstrated their capacity for self-management and, in addition, a governor supported by the opposing political party was now in power.
22. See Bangkok Metropolitan Administration 2004: 2. The report retains the English term "land sharing" for what was in fact becoming a more widely discussed strategy in Thailand.
23. AGFE 2005: 13.
24. On the "right to the city," see Lefebvre 1968. The phrase now has global currency.
25. Democrat Party Governor Apirak Kosayodhin enunciated a budget based on the sufficiency economy (see, e.g., http://www.manager.co.th/Qol/ViewNews.aspx?NewsID=9500000151103, 20 December 2007; last accessed 7 September 2014), and this was later cited as the basis of his support for the Pom Mahakan residents' land-sharing plan (see Thanaphon 2007: 213).
26. See http://www.prachatai.com/english/node/1541 (last accessed 20 March 2014).
27. See Chatri 2003.
28. See especially Kutma 2012: 22–23; she emphasizes "curatorial concerns," and we might note that this term is similarly derived from Latin *curare*, "to care for [something]." On care in Thai culture, see Aulino n.d.
29. Reported in *Khao Sod*, 26 August 2003, p. 13.
30. Bangkok Metropolitan Administration 2004: 1–4.
31. Ibid., pp. 6–7.
32. Ibid., p. 8.
33. See, e.g., Mills 1999; Sopranzetti 2013; on Pom Mahakan specifically, Thanaphon 2007: 166–67.
34. Viphaphan 2007: 73. The author of this master's thesis was also working as my assistant. The term *du lae*, which appears several times in this book and is often translated as "taking care," is less imbued with affective intensity and implies a relatively matter-of-fact attitude (see also Aulino n.d.).

CHAPTER SIX

1. Hage (2009) offers an important contribution to the phenomenology of waiting.
2. Bourdieu 1977: 6–7.
3. See Herzfeld 2009b on the notion of being *accommodanti* as the product of nearly two millennia of Vatican control over the Romans' everyday lives; here, too, energetic protest is coupled with an almost cynical acceptance of the necessity of responding *tactically* (de Certeau 1984: 52–60) to oppressive power.

4. The Roman expression, *lassa stá*, corresponds to the Thai *chang man thoe*. Neither expression will translate easily into English, but the general meaning—"let it go"—is to express a stance (rather than an attitude?) of passivity in the face of a problem that can only end with the humiliation of anyone foolish enough to pursue it. Romans explain this as an adaptive strategy for dealing with the oppressions of the papal past, whereas Thais tend to attribute it to national character and perhaps religious attitude. The effect in the two cases is nevertheless very similar.
5. This is a revealing example of what Bourdieu (1977: 6–7) calls *tempo*. Mastery over time means a capacity to disrupt one's opponents' plotting and planning.
6. Peleggi 2002a. See also the very useful discussion of the dynamics that contribute to this linkage between bourgeois and elite culture in Paritta 2002: 221. The term *riap roi* gained considerable currency during the Sarit and Phibul dictatorships, a source of negative associations today; see Thak 2007, and cf. Jackson 2003.
7. See, e.g., Chai chana lang Pom Mahakan, *Krungthaep Thurakit*, 29 August 2003, Jud Prakahi section, p. 1.
8. At least one journalist (Aek 2003) saw Pom Mahakan's capacity for resilience as a model that other communities might wish to emulate.
9. Shao 2013: 68.
10. See, e.g., Herzfeld 2004: 28–29, 117–20, for an example of the double play of boredom in artisans' workshops.
11. The numbers are those of the kings of the present dynasty, each of whom carries the name Rama. In many cases it would appear that the residents' attributions of date were, from the perspective of what Berardino Palumbo (2003: 305) ironizes as "philological correctness," much more accurate than the choices as to whether they should call their houses "Venetian" or "Turkish" made by the people of the Old Town of Rethemnos (see Herzfeld 1991).
12. See the comment in AGFE 2005: 13; Du Plessis 2005: 130.
13. See also the role of the savings fund in relation to other aspects of governance as laid out in the community's current charter (chap. 7, section titled "Performance and Governance," item 7 of the document).
14. The rules of participation explicitly state that members must have an occupation and an income.
15. See Askew 2004: 108.
16. Letter from Ms. Khanachai Praphaiphum of Gimmick Direction to the Pom Mahakan Community Committee, 19 June 2003.
17. The historical association of *likae* with the site was first signaled by Suchit Wongthes in an article in *Khao Sod* titled "The first place where *likae* was performed in Siam is on the edge of the Pom Mahakan wall" (Suchit 2003d).
18. See the excellent summary in Karin 2005; see also Askew 1996, 2002a, 2002b.
19. Punning, perhaps because of Thai's tonal complexity, is more popular with

NOTES TO PAGES 159–161

speakers of Thai than of English. Thanaphon (2007: 34) makes a slightly different distinction, saying that the community is "in front of the wall" for "those who dare" but that officialdom, in regarding it as a squatter settlement, has placed it instead "behind the wall." I did not hear the first term during my fieldwork, which suggests that for city officials and residents the inside/outside contrast is more salient; historically, the community has always been outside the city circumvallation.

20. The residents broadcast their own verbal protests rather than, most of the time, commercially available music, although they use the latter for celebratory events such as New Year's Eve. On the complex interaction among sound, morality, politics, and economic ideology, see Tausig 2014.
21. Taxis often have a notice asking passengers to close the door "softly" (*bao*)—a term that perhaps is better conveyed by the French *doucement*, with its similar implications of good behavior and consideration for others.
22. http://www.geographical.co.uk/Magazine/Weavers_Oct07.html, accessed 7 April 2012, but no longer accessible.
23. Relative height conveys status differences in architecture as well as gesture; when a royal personage enters a hotel, for example, ordinary people on upper floors may not be visible from the ground level, and no one may drive along an overpass under which a member of the royal family is imminently expected to pass. Glassman (2011) suggests that embodied habits of deference (especially in relation to the institutions of monarchy) are showing signs of collapse, but Aulino (2012), in a critique that confirms my own impressions, suggests that despite ongoing class upheavals the bodily habitus may not be undergoing radical change, and she points to the persistence of royalist sentiment, with its hierarchical implications, among members of poor communities resembling Pom Mahakan in some respects. My own experience of the social imperatives that produce gestural conformity suggests that resisting these would require powerful acts of self-aware political will (see Herzfeld 2009c). Such conformity reinforces what Jackson (2004) calls "the regime of images," but, precisely because the outward forms are so standardized, it also allows considerable play to nuance and interpretation.
24. The similarity of the soundscapes surrounding the respective gatherings of the Red Shirt and Yellow Shirt factions is suggestive in this context; the latter group, arguing (in the spirit of Phibun's erstwhile "democracy" and now in that of the current junta's "Thai-style democracy") that only a system that allowed the palace and the military 70 percent of the seats in parliament could guarantee true democracy because the electorate was not yet mature enough to choose wisely, was nominally defending the same ideal as the more radically egalitarian Red Shirts, and using the same language and noise level to do so.
25. This is usually not followed by the polite particle *khrab*, a detail that suggests (with an ambiguity that reinforces everything else discussed here) both the informality of friendship (close friends rarely use these particles when chat-

ting informally) and, conversely, the abruptness appropriate to those who are tough enough to wield power.
26. On social and monumental time, see Herzfeld 1991.
27. For a brief but trenchant summary of this process, see Abhayuth 2009: 105–6.
28. This is what I mean by "spatial cleansing," a term I derive from "ethnic cleansing" (Herzfeld 2006; cf. Thanaphon's [2007: 69] use of "spatial purification," similarly derived in part from the writings of Mary Douglas [especially 1966]), and Appadurai's (2000) "urban cleansing." See also Abu El-Haj 2001.
29. Kajornjob (1999) describes the way resentment at being displaced has created alternative histories of the Ayutthaya site.
30. The photograph appears in S. Plainoi 2001: 153. This is the area that has already been turned into a lawn.
31. All the Thai kings of the Chakri dynasty carry the name of Rama; the present king is thus Rama IX. Thais speak of reigns (*rachakahn*) by number, so the present reign is the ninth.
32. In the confrontation between Yellow Shirts and Red Shirts, the rhetoric used by both factions alike plays on the alleged failures of the political establishment and the consequent importance of returning power to "the people" (*prachahchon*).
33. On Western influence on the law, see Loos 2006; on its impact on architecture and especially on the paraphernalia of monarchy, see Peleggi 2002a and 2002b.

CHAPTER SEVEN

1. See Rabinow (1989) for insights into the relationship between Cartesian logic and colonialism. The religious modernization and rationalization initiated by Rama IV Mongkut and its conflation with bureaucratic practice under his successor Rama V Chulalongkorn (see Loos 2010: 86–87) arguably set the stage for the conviction on the part of some Thai interlocutors that positivistic thinking is "Buddhist," a view that also encourages the dismissal of cultural elements other than state-recognized Thai Buddhism as irrational. The rejection of spirit cults follows this logic.
2. It also exemplified what Wilson and Mitchell (2003) call "documentary fetishism."
3. The constitutional right to participation infuses the rhetoric of social activism. Thanaphon (2007: 104–6), for example, offers a brief overview of the constitutional provisions for participatory administration as a basis for community activism at Pom Mahakan.
4. See Wutipong n.d. [2004]: 8–9. On "transparency" as a device for achieving its opposite in the Thaksin administration, see Morris 2004. "Participation" (*kahnmisuanruam*) is now sometimes upheld as the true key to "good gover-

nance" (*kahnpokkhrawng baep tham-aphibahn*) (e.g., Bangkok Metropolitan Administration 2004: 5).
5. Graezer Bideau 2012: 305.
6. On this, see Ghertner 2011. Arnstein's (1969: 218) discussion of participation as a form of manipulation is also highly germane. As I have noted above, some former residents of refurbished Crown Property Bureau real estate have already left because of rent increases that they feel the new policy has generated. This situation raises serious questions about the real intentions underlying what has been presented as a proactively benign approach to gentrification.
7. Chatri 2003: 132. See also Chatri 2007 for a discussion of the public benefit that would have accrued as a result of his proposal.
8. See, for example, Sanitsuda 2002, and the helpful discussion by James Taylor (2008: 14). Thongchai (2001) is critical of the model of "local history." Gupta (1998: 172–79), in a trenchant critique of the separation of knowledge into the two categories of "local" and "scientific," argues that *all* knowledge is necessarily hybrid. This is a classic illustration of how such condescension that animates the bourgeois and academic recognition of "knowledge" can turn the pedestal into a constraining tethering post (Herzfeld 2004: 31, 34).
9. In this regard I seek to go beyond Jean Jackson's (1995) compelling call to consider whether constructivist criticisms of local identity formations might not expose small communities to greater risk of attack on the grounds that such formations were invented—as if those of the state were not. While I agree with her caution and the ethical concerns that animate it, I would argue here that local actors actually show up the constructed nature of the *state's* rendition of identity and history and engage with it in ways that stem from a real sense of social cohesion. When Bangkok municipal officials denied the Pom Mahakan residents' right to call themselves a community on the grounds of their mixed origins, for example, they were implicitly undermining the official understanding of Thailand as a country that as a whole also had historically fused multiple origins, whereas the residents could demonstrate that they had *actively achieved* social and cultural unity while also demonstrating loyalty to the monarchical state and its ideals.
10. See especially Bowie 2008: 498–504.
11. I am not arguing that local people never pursue dishonest political goals; that would be nonsense. But the denial of the commonalities they share with the elite, including forms of knowledge, only reinforces the *political* inequality that marginalizes them by excluding them from the sources of power.
12. And this, not so much in the Lévi-Straussian sense as in that of the "muddling through" of which Scott (1998), de Certeau (1984), and Reed-Danahay (1996) have all written. It is a canny and serendipitous adaptation to the needs of the moment that represents, not an act of resistance, but an assertion of creativity—a very different proposition.

NOTES TO PAGES 172–175

13. This process, which typifies crypto-colonialism as it occurred in Siam/Thailand (Herzfeld 2002, 2009d, 2013a), is related to the reification of culture analyzed by Handler (1985, 1988) in the context of Quebec nationalism.
14. The phrase "weapons of the weak" comes from the title of Scott's (1985) justly famous study of resistance tactics. On the legal restriction of eminent domain, see Thanaphon 2007: 186.
15. See Askew 2004: 109–10; see also Taylor 2008: 21–22.
16. On "englobing," see especially Ardener 1975: 25.
17. In fact, references to the *sakdina* system represent a radical oversimplification of history; common allegations of a continuity in attitudes between the old aristocracy and present-day bureaucrats are not, as Johnson (2009: 24) points out, historically accurate; they do, however, exemplify the way the poor appeal to national history to justify their sense of grievance—complaints about the treatment of the poor as *phrai* (commoners) similarly reflect this historical metaphorization of modern state-citizen relationships. See Reynolds's (1987: 150–55) fascinating historical account of the term's vicissitudes. Riggs (1966: 245–46) and Siffin (1966: 18) both briefly describe the transformation of a landholding designation into bureaucratic rank (although Johnson [2009: 25] would prefer not to dignify modern Thai administration with the label of bureaucracy at all). Van Esterik (2000: 100), with an anthropologist's bottom-up perspective, sees continuity in much the same terms as do poor Thais—as a continuity of attitude rather than of the specific perquisites of rank.
18. Siffin 1966: 222–23.
19. On social drama, see Turner 1974.
20. When he was forced out of office by a scandal initiated in large measure by Samak, who had meanwhile become prime minister, he announced his prompt resignation as an intentional act, to be contrasted with the way others had clung to power, claiming that he wanted to set a good example to the largely corrupt world of Thai politics.
21. In this respect the residents were taking a leaf out of the book of the political group—the Democrat Party—that most seemed to favor their cause; see Askew 2008. But to some extent all political parties everywhere depend on performance to deliver both ideology and electoral commitment.
22. P. Jackson 2004. To see such reliance on images as a sign of insincerity—not, to be sure, a necessary corollary of Jackson's argument—is to read Thai self-stereotypes too literally, however, and I join Askew (2008) in finding performativity a useful concept in explaining *how* these images are worked by purposeful actors.
23. That distinction, while it has permitted some excellent research and interesting activism on behalf of communities regarded as "informal" (see, e.g., Huchzermayer and Karam 2006), perpetuates the misconception that only a state or similar authority has the right to recognize and implement formality in matters of law and regulation.

NOTES TO PAGES 176–191

24. See the translated example in Johnson 2009: 61.
25. E.g., Sopon 1992: 103. See also Johnson 2009 for a nuanced account of the variability of leadership skills in Bangkok slums.
26. Such arrangements are, apparently, far from rare. Internet discussions of police bribery are very numerous, especially by foreigners who have been fingered for bribes to avoid traffic penalties. Chuwit Kamolvisit, whose political activities are mentioned in these pages, caused considerable scandal by making a very public declaration about the bribes he claimed to have given police officers.
27. See, for example, Maier's (2005: 26) searing description of drunkenness and its consequences in a particularly rough part of Khlong Toey.
28. The letters sent to the various officials were identical in their main content, but the version sent to the governor was typed whereas all the others, including one destined for the city clerk who had been one of the most implacable foes of the community, were hand-lettered in a painstakingly elaborate handwritten script.
29. On auto-ethnography, see Reed-Danahay 1997.
30. Delcore 2003: 62–63.
31. Askew 2002b: 231–33.
32. The threats have nevertheless not ceased; most recently plans to build an expressway would have cut Ban Khrua off from the rest of the city and were vigorously opposed by the residents. Their special status has nevertheless aided them considerably in such conflicts.
33. This is clearly a simplification of the reality; the army and the police were both also known to be internally divided. Nonetheless, Thaksin Shinawatra long continued to use his police rank, and there were rumors of an impending clash between the two forces as a result of the provocations of Suthep's "shut down Bangkok" movement in January 2014—the movement that immediately preceded the coup and perhaps was what some thought had successfully aimed to trigger it.

CHAPTER EIGHT

1. This is the tactic that Johnson (2009: 159–60) sees as ignoring the authorities when it is more convenient to do so. The risk always remains that the authorities will react sharply, but here the residents calculated—rightly, as it turned out—that the governor was notoriously reluctant to engage in confrontation.
2. See Scandurra 2003, discussed in Herzfeld 2009b: 77.
3. Attributions of fatalism usually reflect the global inequalities through which those with power vicariously represent weaker groups' inability to act.
4. McCargo n.d. The terminological distinction noted by McCargo between *pradet* (harshly arbitrary power) and *prakhun* (power compassionately wielded) seems to fit the inclusive model of a rigid national bureaucracy

that sometimes conceals relatively gentle forms of collusion and complicity articulated in a segmentary arrangement of social relations.
5. See, for an insightful analysis of analogous cases, Johnson 2009: 131, 160–61.
6. Some of the initial difficulties and the means used to address them are discussed by Rittirong (2009: 14–16). On the presence of Bahn Mankhong experts at Pom Mahakan, see Thanaphon 2007: 191. CODI's model for this kind of participatory planning is laid out in Anon. 2003c: 21–24. The Bahn Mankhong initiative began in earnest and with government support and a considerable budget at about the same time that I was beginning my fieldwork at Pom Mahakan; see Anon. 2003b: 3.
7. I am indebted to Non Arkaraprasertkul for the technical information in this description.
8. It was in any case infinitely preferable to falling into the hands of loan sharks. A serious concern at the time was that the civil authorities, in their enthusiasm for new commercial ventures, were not doing enough to help the poor by creating a means of furnishing loans at reasonable interest rates. See, e.g., Vitit 2004.
9. My informal observations are borne out by the much more thorough study conducted by Nut (2004: 81), who interviewed many of the Tha Phra Jan residents in question.
10. http://www.peoplepress.in.th/archives/autopagev3/show_page.php?group_id=1&auto_id=19&topic_id=1394&topic_no=31&page=1&gaction=on, accessed 25 September 2011 but no longer available.
11. Reported on 14 September 2010 in *Thannews*; accessible at http://www.skyscrapercity.com/showthread.php?p=66870051, last accessed 17 April 2015. The baht has fluctuated historically at a rate of between about 25 and 40 to the U.S. dollar.
12. See Phoemsak 2009.
13. Herzfeld 2013b, copies of which were immediately posted up at strategic points in Pom Mahakan. I was away from Thailand at the time.
14. Recall that the Human Rights Commission had also played an important role in protecting the people of Pom Mahakan.
15. It has also been suggested to me that, as a landowner with considerable interests in the area, the governor might have felt conflicted about attempts to freeze construction in the name of conservation. Although a trust owned by some of the governor's kin owns significant portions of the neighboring area, however, the evidence shows that he was not directly involved (see http://www.matichon.co.th/news_detail.php?newsid=1312550898, last accessed 12 January 2015).
16. See Pérez 2014; Zhang 2010.
17. Goh 2014: 98–99. On capitalist desires among Thailand's socially and geographically mobile rural poor as they seek work and prosperity in the city, see the incisive analysis by Sopranzetti (2013: 91–115).
18. See, e.g., Non and Rabitaille 2009.

19. Askew (2002a: 231) describes this process for Bangkok. See Yalouri (2001) on the resacralization of the Acropolis of Athens.
20. Hewison (2013: 190–95).
21. Ibid.: 193–94.
22. The specter of such accusations looms large over the domestic political scene; see especially Streckfuss 2011. In some respects, this use of civil suits that transform into criminal prosecutions resembles the witchcraft trials of seventeenth-century New England; parallels between witchcraft accusations and political attacks have long been noted in the anthropological literature (e.g., Douglas 1970).

References

Abhayuth Chantrabha. 2009. *Kreuakhai salam 4 pakh: tuaton lae prasopkahn kahnkhleunwai.* Bangkok: Four Slums Network.
Abu El-Haj, Nadia. 2001. *Facts on the Ground: Archaeological Practice and Territorial Self Fashioning in Israeli Society.* Chicago: University of Chicago Press.
Aek Phomyao. 2003. Phiphithaphan Chumchon Pom Mahahkahn. *Daily Liberty,* 15 October, p. 8.
AGFE. 2005. *Forced Evictions: Towards Solutions?* Nairobi: Advisory Group on Forced Evictions [UN-Habitat].
———. 2007. *Second Report: Forced Evictions: Towards Solutions?* Nairobi: Advisory Group on Forced Evictions [UN-Habitat].
Akin Rabibhadana. 1999. *Chumchon Ae-Ad: Ongkhwahmru kap khwwampenjing.* Bangkok: Office of the Department for Research Support.
Ampa Santimatanedol and Anchalee Kongrut. 2004. "Krasae Decides Not to Run." *Bangkok Post,* 13 July, p. 3.
Anan Ganjanapan. 2001. *Miti chumchon: Witthikhid thongthin wah duay sitthi amnaht lae kahn jadkahn saphyakawn.* Bangkok: Research Support Fund Office, Chulalongkorn University.
Anderson, Benedict. 1991. *Imagined Communities: Reflections on the Origins and Spread of Nationalism.* Rev. ed. London: Verso.
Anon. 2003a. "Pom Mahahkahn" (editorial). *Khao Sod,* 24 April, p. 2.
———. 2003b. *"Bahn Mankhong": Poea sahng khwahm man khong nai kahn yu ahsai hai khon jon nai chumchon ae ad.* Bangkok: CODI.
———. 2003c. *Bahn Mankhong utradit.* Bangkok: CODI.
———. 2010. *Khrongkahn prap prung phumitat saphahwaetlom lae panhah sangkhom nai phoenthi Sanam Luang lae parimonton.* Bangkok: Bangkok Metropolitan Administration.
Apirak Kosayodhin. 2004. *Pathinyah wisyathat yutthasaht nayawbai.* Bangkok: Bangkok Metropolitan Administration.

REFERENCES

Apiwat Ratanawaraha. 2013. "Thailand: Bangkok." Pp. 40–55 in *Asian and Pacific Cities: Development Patterns*, edited by Ian Shirley and Carol Neill. Abingdon: Routledge.

Ardener, Edwin. 1975. "The Problem Revisited." Pp. 19–27 in *Perceiving Women*, edited by Shirley Ardener. London: J. M. Dent.

Ariya Aruninta. n.d. "Controversies in Public Land Management Decision-Makings: Case Study of Land Utilization in Bangkok, Thailand." http://www.land.arch.chula.ac.th/data/file_20090921165036.pdf (last accessed 3 September 2015).

Appadurai, Arjun. 2000. "Spectral Housing and Urban Cleansing: Notes on Millennial Mumbai." *Public Culture* 12:627–51.

Arnstein, Sherry R. 1969. "A Ladder of Citizen Participation." *Journal of the American Institute of Planners* 35:216–24.

Askew, Marc. 1994. *Interpreting Bangkok: The Urban Question in Thai Studies*. Bangkok: Chulalongkorn University Press.

———. 1996. "The Rise of Moradok and the Decline of the Yarn: Heritage and Cultural Construction in Urban Thailand." *Sojourn* 11:183–210.

———. 2002a. *Bangkok: Place, Practice, and Representation*. New York: Routledge.

———. 2002b. "The Challenge of Co-Existence: The Meaning of Urban Heritage in Contemporary Bangkok." Pp. 229–44 in *The Disappearing 'Asian' City*, edited by William S. Logan. New York: Oxford University Press.

———. 2004. "Bangkok: Transformation of the Thai City." Pp. 85–115 in *Cultural Identity and Urban Change in Southeast Asia: Interpretative Essays*, edited by Marc Askew and William S. Logan. Geelong: Deakin University Press.

———. 2008. *Performing Political Identity: The Democrat Party in Southern Thailand*. Chiang Mai: Silkworm Books.

Aulino, Felicity. 2012. "Senses and Sensibilities: The Practice of Care in Everyday Life in Northern Thailand." PhD diss., Harvard University, Department of Anthropology.

———. 2014. "Perceiving the Social Body: A Phenomenological Perspective on Ethical Practice in Buddhist Thailand." *Journal of Religious Ethics* 42:415–41.

———. 2016. "The Ordinary and the Profound: Rituals of Care in Northern Thailand." *American Ethnologist* 42.

Austin, J. L. 1975 [1962]. *How to Do Things with Words*. 2nd ed. Edited by J. O. Urmson and Marina Sbisà. Cambridge, MA: MIT Press.

Baker, Chris, 2000. "Thailand's Assembly of the Poor: Background, Drama, Reaction." *South East Asia Research* 8:5–29.

Barmé, Scot. 1993. *Luang Wichit Wathakan and the Creation of a Thai Identity*. Singapore: Institute of Southeast Asian Studies.

Barry, Coeli, ed. 2013. *Rights to Culture: Heritage, Language, and Community in Thailand*. Chiang Mai: Silkworm Books.

Bauman, Richard. 1977. *Verbal Art as Performance*. Rowley, MA: Newbury House.

Ben-Yehoyada, Naor. 2014. "Transnational Political Economy: A Central Mediterranean Example." *Comparative Studies in Society and History* 56:870–901.

REFERENCES

Berliner, David. 2010. "Perdre l'esprit du lieu. Les politiques de l'UNESCO à Luang Prabang (RDP Lao)." *Transmettre, Terrain* 55:80–105.

Bangkok Metropolitan Administration. 2004. *Krongkahn wijai jat tham phaen mae bot phoea anurak lae patthanah chumchon ban mai boran "Pom Mahahkahn."* Report presented to the Office of Social Development, BMA. Bangkok: Bangkok Metropolitan Administration.

BMA-ESCAP. 2002. BMA-ESCAP Seminar on Rattanakosin Pilot Project, 28 June 2002. Bangkok, unpublished document.

Bortolotto, Chiara. 2012. The French Inventory of Intangible Cultural Heritage. Pp. 265–82 in *Heritage Regimes and the State*, edited by Regina F. Bendix, Aditya Eggert, and Arnika Peselmann. Göttingen: Universitätsverlag Göttingen.

Bourdieu, Pierre. 1977. *Outline of a Theory of Practice*. Translated by Richard Nice. Cambridge: Cambridge University Press.

Bowie, Katherine. 1997. *Rituals of National Loyalty: An Anthropology of the State and the Village Scout Movement in Thailand*. New York: Columbia University Press.

———. 2008. "Vote Buying and Village Outrage in an Election in Northern Thailand: Recent Legal Reforms in Historical Context." *Journal of Asian Studies* 67:469–511.

Bristol, Graeme. 2007. "Strategies for Survival: Security of Tenure in Bangkok." Case study prepared for Enhancing Urban Safety and Security: Global Report on Human Settlements 2007. Available from http://www.unhabitat.org/grhs/2007.

———. 2009. "Rendered Invisible: Urban Planning, Cultural Heritage, and Human Rights." Pp. 117–34 in *Cultural Diversity, Heritage, and Human Rights*, edited by William Logan, Máiréad Nic Craith, and Michele Langfield. London: Routledge.

Byrne, Denis. 2007. *Surface Collections: Archaeological Travels in Southeast Asia*. Lanham, MD: Altamira Press.

———. 2009. "Archaeology and the Fortress of Rationality." Pp. 68–88 in *Cosmopolitan Archaeologies*, edited by Lynn Meskell. Durham, NC: Duke University Press.

———. 2013. "Love and Loss in the 1960s." *International Journal of Heritage Studies* 19:596–609.

Cellamare, Carlo. 2008. *Fare città: Pratiche urbane e storie di luoghi*. Milano: Elèuthera.

Chatrathip Nathsupha. 1997. *Prawatisaht Watthanatham Chumchon lae Chon Chat Thai*. Bangkok: Chulalongkorn University Press.

Chatri Prakitnonthakan. 2003. "Pom Mahahkahn: Anurak roe Thamlai Prawatisaht?" *Silapawatthanatham* (February): 124–35.

———. 2007. "Phoenthi Pom Mahahkahn: Jak panha roeang kananurak su wikoet panha tangkanmoeang." With English translation. *Asa* [Journal of the Association of Siamese Architects], February–March issue, pp. 81–92.

———. 2012. "Rattanakosin Charter: The Thai Cultural Charter for Conservation." *Journal of the Siam Society* 100:123–48.

REFERENCES

Choay, Françoise. 2001. *The Invention of the Historic Monument.* Translated by Lauren M. O'Connell. Cambridge: Cambridge University Press.

Christian, William A., Jr. 1989. *Person and God in a Spanish Valley.* Rev. ed. Princeton, NJ: Princeton University Press.

Condominas, Georges. 1990. *From Lawa to Mon, from Saa' to Thai: Historical and Anthropological Aspects of Southeast Asian Social Spaces.* Translated by Maria Magannon. Canberra: Australian National University, Department of Anthropology.

Connors, Michael Kelly. 2003. *Democracy and National Identity in Thailand.* New York: RoutledgeCurzon.

Daniel, E. Valentine. 1996. *Charred Lullabies: Chapters in an Anthropography of Violence.* Princeton, NJ: Princeton University Press.

Darlington, Susan M. 2013. *The Ordination of a Tree: The Thai Buddhist Environmental Movement.* Albany: State University of New York Press.

Davis, Lisa Kim. 2011. "International Events and Mass Evictions: A Longer View." *International Journal of Urban and Regional Research* 35:582-99.

Day, Tony. 2002. *Fluid Iron: State Formation in Southeast Asia.* Honolulu: University of Hawaii Press.

de Certeau, Michel. 1984. *The Practice of Everyday Life.* Berkeley: University of California Press.

De Cesari, Chiara. 2010. "World Heritage and Mosaic Universalism: A View from Palestine." *Journal of Social Archaeology* 10:299-324.

———. 2012. "Thinking through Heritage Regimes." Pp. 399-413 in *Heritage Regimes and the State,* edited by Regina F. Bendix, Aditya Eggert, and Arnika Peselmann. Göttingen. Studies in Cultural Property, vol. 6. Göttingen: Universitätsverlag Göttingen.

———, and Michael Herzfeld. 2015. Urban Heritage and Social Movements. Pp. 171-95 in *Global Heritage: A Reader,* edited by Lynn Meskell. New York: Wiley-Blackwell.

Delcore, Henry D. 2003. "Nongovernmental Organizations and the Work of Memory in Northern Thailand." *American Ethnologist* 30:61-84.

———. 2004. "Symbolic Politics or Generification? The Ambivalent Implications of Tree Ordinations in the Thai Environmental Movement." *Journal of Political Ecology* 11:1-30.

Denes, Alexandra. 2015. "Folklorizing Northern Khmer Identity in Thailand: Intangible Cultural Heritage and the Production of 'Good Culture.'" *Sojourn* 30:1-34.

Dhani, Prince, Nivat. 2012. "The Old Siamese Conception of the Monarchy." Pp. 24-32 in *Monarchy and Constitutional Rule in Democratizing Thailand,* edited by Suchit Bunbongkarn and Prudhisan Jumbala. Bangkok: Institute of Thai Studies, Chulalongkorn University. Originally published in *Journal of the Siam Society* 36 (1947): 91-106.

Douglas, Mary. 1966. *Purity and Danger: An Analysis of Concepts of Pollution and Taboo.* London: Routledge & Kegan Paul.

———, ed. 1970. *Witchcraft Confessions and Accusations*. London: Tavistock.
Dovey, Kim. 2001. "Memory, Democracy and Urban Space: Bangkok's 'Path to Democracy.'" *Journal of Urban Design* 6:265–82.
Du Plessis, Jean. 2005. "The Growing Problem of Forced Evictions and the Crucial Importance of Community-Based, Locally Appropriate Alternatives." *Environment and Urbanization* 17:123–34.
Elinoff, Eli. 2013. "Smouldering Aspirations: Burning Buildings and the Politics of Belonging in Contemporary Isan." *South East Asia Research* 20:381–97.
———. 2014. "Sufficient Citizens: Moderation and the Politics of Sustainable Development in Thailand." *PoLAR: Political and Legal Anthropology Review* 37:89–108.
Evans-Pritchard, E. E. 1940. *The Nuer: A Description of the Modes of Livelihood and Political Institutions of a Nilotic People*. Oxford: Clarendon.
———. 1956. *Nuer Religion*. Oxford: Clarendon.
Ferguson, James. 1990. *The Anti-Politics Machine: Development, Depoliticization, and Bureaucratic Power in Lesotho*. Cambridge: Cambridge University Press.
Gandolfo, Daniella. 2013. "Formless: A Day at Lima's Office of Formalization." *Cultural Anthropology* 28:1–35.
Geertz, Clifford. 1973. *The Interpretation of Cultures*. New York: Basic Books.
Ghertner, D. Asher. 2011. "Gentrifying the State, Gentrifying Participation: Elite Governance Programs in Delhi." *International Journal of Urban and Regional Research* 35:504–32.
Glass, Ruth. 1964. *London: Aspects of Change*. London: MacGibbon & Kee.
Glassman, Jim. 2011. Cracking Hegemony in Thailand: Gramsci, Bourdieu and the Dialectics of Rebellion. *Journal of Contemporary Asia* 41 (1): 25–46.
Goh, Daniel P. S. 2014. "Between History and Heritage: Post-Colonialism, Globalization, and the Remaking of Malacca, Penang, and Singapore." *TRaNS: Trans-Regional and -National Studies of Southeast Asia* 2:79–101.
Graezer Bideau, Florence. 2012. "Identifying 'Living Tradition' in Switzerland: Re-enacting Federalism through the UNESCO Convention for the Safeguarding of Intangible Cultural Heritage." Pp. 303–25 in *Heritage Regimes and the State*, edited by Regina F. Bendix, Aditya Eggert, and Arnika Peselmann. Göttingen: Universitätsverlag Göttingen.
Gray, Denis D. 2014. "Bulldozing the Past in Name of Progress." *Shanghai Daily*, 30 August, p. 12.
Greenhouse, Carol J. 1996. *A Moment's Notice: Time Politics across Cultures*. Ithaca, NY: Cornell University Press.
Gupta, Akhil. 1998. *Postcolonial Developments: Agriculture in the Making of Modern India*. Durham, NC: Duke University Press.
Hage, Ghassan. 2009. "Waiting Out the Crisis: On Stuckedness and Governmentality." Pp. 97–106 in *Waiting*, edited by Ghassan Hage. Melbourne: Melbourne University Press.
Hamilton, Annette. 2004. "Dizzy Development in Hua Hin: The Effects of Tourism on a Thai Seaside Town." Pp. 149–65 in *Cultural Identity and Urban Change*

in *Southeast Asia: Interpretative Essays*, edited by Marc Askew and William S. Logan. Geelong: Deakin University Press.

Handler, Richard. 1985. "On Having a Culture: Nationalism and the Preservation of Quebec's *Patrimoine*." Pp. 192–217 in *Objects and Others. History of Anthropology*, vol. 3, edited by George Stocking. Madison: University of Wisconsin Press.

———. 1988. *Nationalism and the Politics of Culture in Quebec*. Madison: University of Wisconsin Press.

Harms, Erik. 2011. *Saigon's Edge: On the Margins of Ho Chi Minh City*. Minneapolis: University of Minnesota Press.

———. 2013. "Eviction Time in the New Saigon: Temporalities of Displacement in the Rubble of Development." *Cultural Anthropology* 28:344–68.

Harrison, Rachel, and Peter Jackson. 2009. *The Ambiguous Allure of the West: Traces of the Colonial in Thailand*. Hong Kong: Hong Kong University Press; Honolulu: University of Hawaii Press.

Harvey, David. 1990a. "Between Space and Time: Reflections on the Geographical Imagination." *Annals of the Association of American Geographers* 80: 418–34.

———. 1990b. *The Condition of Postmodernity: An Enquiry into the Origins of Cultural Change*. Cambridge, MA: Blackwell.

Harvey, David C. 2001. "Heritage Pasts and Heritage Presents: Temporality, Meaning and the Scope of Heritage Studies." *International Journal of Heritage Studies* 7:319–38.

Herzfeld, Michael. 1985. *The Poetics of Manhood: Contest and Identity in a Cretan Mountain Village*. Princeton, NJ: Princeton University Press.

———. 1987. *Anthropology through the Looking-Glass: Critical Ethnography in the Margins of Europe*. Cambridge: Cambridge University Press.

———. 1991. *A Place in History: Social and Monumental Time in a Cretan Town*. Princeton, NJ: Princeton University Press.

———. 2002. "The Absent Presence: Discourses of Crypto-Colonialism." *South Atlantic Quarterly* 101:899–926.

———. 2004. *The Body Impolitic: Artisans and Artifice in the Global Hierarchy of Value*. Chicago: University of Chicago Press.

———. 2005. *Cultural Intimacy: Social Poetics in the Nation-State*. 2nd ed. New York: Routledge.

———. 2006. "Spatial Cleansing: Monumental Vacuity and the Idea of the West." *Journal of Material Culture* 11:127–49.

———. 2009a. *Evicted from Eternity: The Restructuring of Modern Rome*. Chicago: University of Chicago Press.

———. 2009b. "Convictions, Paradoxes, and the Etymologies of Social Life: Embodied Rhetorics of Earnest Belief." Pp. 182–206 in *Culture and Rhetoric*, edited by Ivo Strecker and Stephen Tyler. Oxford: Berghahn.

———. 2009c. "The Cultural Politics of Gesture: Reflections on the Embodiment of Ethnographic Practice." *Ethnography* 10:131–52.

———. 2009d. "The Conceptual Allure of the West: Dilemmas and Ambiguities of Crypto-Colonialism in Thailand." Pp. 173–86 in *The Ambiguous Allure of the West: Traces of the Colonial in Thailand*, edited by Rachel Harrison and Peter Jackson. Hong Kong: Hong Kong University Press; Honolulu: University of Hawai'i Press.

———. 2010. "Engagement, Gentrification, and the Neoliberal Hijacking of History." *Current Anthropology* 51, supplement 2: S259-67.

———. 2012. "Paradoxes of Order in Thai Community Politics." Pp. 146–57 and 276–77 in *Radical Egalitarianism: Local Realities, Global Relations*, edited by Felicity Aulino, Miriam Goheen, and Stanley J. Tambiah. New York: Fordham University Press.

———. 2013a. "The Crypto-Colonial Dilemmas of Rattanakosin Island." *Journal of the Siam Society* 100:209–23.

———. 2013b. "Pom Mahakan Eviction Would Be a Calamitous Loss." *Bangkok Post*, 27 September, p. 11.

———. 2014. "Intangible Delicacies: Production and Embarrassment in International Settings." *Ethnologies* 36:41–57.

———. 2015. "Heritage and the Right to the City: When Securing the Past Creates Insecurity in the Present." *Heritage and Society* 8:3–23.

Hewison, Kevin. 2013. "Weber, Marx, and Contemporary Thailand." *TRaNS: Trans-Regional and -National Studies of Southeast Asia* 1:177–98.

Hinton, Peter. 1992. "Meetings as Ritual: Thai Officials, Western Consultants and Development Planning in Northern Thailand." Pp. 105–24 in *Patterns and Illusions: Thai Patterns of Thought*, edited by Gehan Wijewewardene and E.C. Chapman. Singapore: Institute of Southeast Asian Studies.

Hitchcock, Michael. 2005. "'We Will Know Our Nation Better': Taman Mini and Nation Building in Indonesia." *Civilisations: Revue internationale d'anthropologie et de sciences humaines* 52:45–56.

Ho, K. C., and Pornpan Chinnapong. 2013. "Conserving Bangkok's Premier Heritage District: Ambitious Plans and Ambiguous Rights." Pp. 59–83 in *Rights to Culture: Heritage, Language, and Community in Thailand*, edited by Coeli Barry. Chiang Mai: Silkworm Books.

Holston, James. 1989. *The Modernist City: An Anthropological Critique of Brasilia*. Chicago: University of Chicago Press.

Huchzermayer, Marie, and Aly Karam. 2006. *Informal Settlements: A Perpetual Challenge?* Cape Town: UCT Press.

Insolera, Italo. 2001. *Roma Fascista nelle Fotografie dell'Istituto Luce*. Rome: Riuniti and Istituto Luce.

Jackson, Jean E.1995. "Culture, Genuine and Spurious: The Politics of Indianness in the Vaupés, Colombia." *American Ethnologist* 22:3–27.

Jackson, Peter. 2003. "Performative Genders, Perverse Desires: A Bio-History of Thailand's Same-Sex and Transgender Cultures." *Intersections: Gender, History, and Culture in the Asian Context* 9. http://intersections.anu.edu.au/issue9/jackson.html.

———. 2004. "The Thai Regime of Images." *Sojourn: Social Issues in Southeast Asia* 19 (2): 1–39.

Janssen, Peter. 2011. "Showing Love to Shophouses: UNESCO Awards Effort to Preserve Bangkok's Historic Straits-Style Structures," *The Nation* [Bangkok], 22 September, available at http://www.nationmultimedia.com/2011/09/22/life/Showing-love-to-shophouses-30165851.html (last accessed 27 April 2015).

Johnson, Alan R. 2009. *Leadership in a Slum: A Bangkok Case Study*. Eugene: Wipf and Stock.

Johnson, Andrew Alan. 2014. *Ghosts of the New City: Spirits, Urbanity, and the Ruins of Progress in Chiang Mai*. Honolulu: University of Hawaii Press.

Jul, Helle, and Flemming Frost. 2002. *Bangkok: Proposal for a Dialogue-Based Conservation and Development Strategy for the Central Area of the Phranakhon District*. Christianshavn: Jul & Frost.

Kajornjob Kusumawali. 1999. "Kahn jadkahn 'Phoenthi prawatisaht' jahk koroni soeksah boriwaen Wihahn Phramongkhonphaphit." Master's thesis (anthropology), Thammasat University.

Karin Klinkajorn. 2005. "Creativity and the Settings of Monuments and Sites in Thailand: Conflicts and Resolution." In 15th ICOMOS General Assembly and International Symposium: Monuments and Sites in Their Setting—Conserving Cultural Heritage in Changing Townscapes and Landscapes, 17–21 October, Xi'an, China. http://openarchive.icomos.org/328/ (last accessed 30 March 2014).

Kesinee Tangkhieo and Napanisa Kaewmorakot. 2003. "Mahakarn Fort Group Loses Case." *The Nation*, 30 August, p. 2A.

Khemthong Tongsakulrungruang. n.d. "Community Land Deed: Leveling the Playing Field." Paper presented at Eighth Asian Law Institute Conference, Kyushu, Japan (2011). Cited by permission.

———. 2010. "Chumchon, Chumchon Thong Thin, lae Chumchon Thong Thin Dang Doem" (part 1). *Warasahn Nitisaht* 39:799–821.

———. 2011. "Chumchon, Chumchon Thong Thin, lae Chumchon Thong Thin Dang Doem" (part 2). *Warasahn Nitisaht* 40:153–78.

Kirsch, A. Thomas. 1973. *Feasting and Social Oscillation: A Working Paper on Religion and Society in Upland Southeast Asia*. Ithaca, NY: Cornell University Southeast Asia Program Publications.

Klima, Alan. 2002. *The Funeral Casino: Meditation, Massacre, and Exchange with the Dead in Thailand*. Princeton, NJ: Princeton University Press.

Konstantinov, Yulian. 1996. "Patterns of Reinterpretation: Trader-Tourism in the Balkans (Bulgaria) as a Picaresque Metaphorical Enactment of Post-Totalitarianism." *American Ethnologist* 23:762–82.

Koompong Noobanjong. 2009. "The Passenger Terminal at Suvarnabhumi International Airport and Thai Identity in the Midst of Globalization Era." *Journal of Architectural Research and Studies* 6 (3): 25–43.

———. 2010. "The Aesthetic of Power: A Critical Study on the Politics of Representations at Wat Benchama Bophit and Wat Phra Sri Mahathat, Bangkhen." *Journal of Architectural Research and Studies* 7 (2): 43–63.

———. 2012. "The Rachadamnoen Avenue: Contesting Urban Meanings and Political Memories." *Journal of Architectural Research and Studies* 9 (2): 15–37.

Kutma, Kristin. 2012. "Between Arbitration and Engineering: Concepts and Contingencies in the Shaping of Heritage Regimes." Pp. 21–36 in *Heritage Regimes and the State*, edited by Regina F. Bendix, Aditya Eggert, and Arnika Peselmann. Göttingen: Universitätsverlag Göttingen.

Lamprakos, Michelle. n.d. "Old Heritage, New Heritage: Building in Sana'a, Yemen." *Viewpoints*, special issue: *Architecture and Urbanism in the Middle East*, pp. 33–36. Accessible at http://www.mei.edu/content/architecture-and-urbanism-middle-east (last accessed 27 April 2015).

———. 2014. The Idea of the Historic City. *Change Over Time* 4 (1): 8–38.

———. 2015. *Building a World Heritage City: Sana'a, Yemen*. Burlington: Ashgate.

Lavalle, Adrián, Arnab Acharya, and Peter P. Houtzager. 2005. "Beyond Comparative Anecdotalism: Lessons on Civil Society and Participation from São Paulo, Brazil." *World Development* 33:951–64.

Leach, E.R. 1956. *Political Systems of Highland Burma: A Study of Kachin Social Structure*. London: Athlone Press.

Lees, Loretta, Tom Slater, and Elvin K. Wyly. 2008. *Gentrification*. New York: Routledge.

Lefebvre, Henri. 1968. *Le droit à la ville*. 2nd ed. Paris: Editions Anthropos.

Loizos, Peter. 1975. *The Greek Gift: Politics in a Cypriot Village*. Oxford: Basil Blackwell.

Loos, Tamara. 2006. *Subject Siam: Family, Law, and Colonial Modernity in Thailand*. Ithaca, NY: Cornell University Press.

———. 2010. "Competitive Colonialisms: Siam and the Malay Muslim South." Pp. 75–91 in *The Ambiguous Allure of the West: Traces of the Colonial in Thailand*, edited by Rachel Harrison and Peter Jackson. Hong Kong: Hong Kong University Press; Honolulu: University of Hawaii Press.

Maier, Father Joe. 2005. *Welcome to the Bangkok Slaughterhouse: The Battle for Human Dignity in Bangkok's Bleakest Slums*. Hong Kong: Periplus.

McCargo, Duncan. 2005. "Network Monarchy and Legitimacy Crises in Thailand." *Pacific Review* 18:499–519.

———. n.d. "Policing Bangkok: Detective Raids in the Thai Capital." Unpublished paper, cited by permission.

Meeker, Michael E. 1979. *Literature and Violence in North Arabia*. Cambridge: Cambridge University Press.

Meier, Father Joe. 2005. *Welcome to the Bangkok Slaughterhouse: The Battle for Human Dignity in Bangkok's Bleakest Slums*. Singapore: Periplus.

Milgram, B. Lynn. 2013. "Taking the Street into the Market: The Politics of Space and Work in Baguio City, Philippines." Pp. 71–92 in *Street Economies in the Urban Global South*, edited by Karen Tranberg Hansen, Walter E. Little, and B. Lynn Milgram. Santa Fe: SAR Press.

REFERENCES

Mills, Mary Beth. 1999. *Thai Women in the Global Labor Force.* New Brunswick, NJ: Rutgers University Press.

Missingham, Bruce D. 2003. *The Assembly of the Poor in Thailand: From Local Struggles to National Protest Movement.* Chiang Mai: Silkworm Books.

Miura, Keiko. 2010. "World Heritage Sites in Southeast Asia: Angkor and Beyond." Pp. 103–29 in *Heritage Tourism in Southeast Asia,* edited by Michael Hitchcock, Victor T. King, and Michael Parnwell. Copenhagen: NIAS Press.

Montira Horayangura Unakul. 2012. Reconnecting Bangkok's Heritage Landscape. *Journal of the Siam Society* 100:183–208.

Morris, Rosalind C. 2000. *In the Place of Origins: Modernity and Its Mediums in Northern Thailand.* Durham, NC: Duke University Press.

———. 2004. Intimacy and Corruption in Thailand's Age of Transparency. Pp. 225–43 in *Off Stage/On Display: Intimacy and Ethnography in the Age of Public Culture,* edited by Andrew Shryock. Stanford: Stanford University Press.

Mosse, George L. 1988. *Nationalism and Sexuality: Middle-Class Morality and Sexual Norms in Modern Europe.* Madison: University of Wisconsin Press.

Napong Rugkhapan. Forthcoming. "Mapping the Historic City: Mapmaking, Preservation Zoning, and Violence." *Environment and Planning D: Society and Space.* DOI: 10.1177/0263775815604916.

Nattika Navapan. 2014. "Absolute Monarchy and the Development of Bangkok's Urban Spaces." *Planning Perspectives* 29:1–24.

Niti Kasikoson. 2010. "Hahp Rae Phaeng Loi: Tha Phra Jan." *Chulasahn Thai Kadi Soeksah* 17 (2): 3–14.

Non Arkaraprasertkul. 2013. "Traditionalism as a Way of Life: The Sense of Home in a Shanghai Alleyway." *Harvard Asia Quarterly* 15 (3/4): 15–25.

Non Arkaraprasertkul and Reilly Paul Rabitaille. 2009. "Differences, Originality and Assimilation: Building Nine at Panabhandhu School." *Thresholds* 35: 8–15.

Noyes, Dorothy. 1995. "Group." *Journal of American Folklore* 108:449–78.

Nut Nonthasuti. 2004. "The Role and Relations of Stakeholders Involving the Changes in the Inner City District of Bangkok: The Case Study of Thaprachan-Thachang-Napralan." M.Sc. thesis, Mahidol University, Bangkok.

O'Brien, Kevin J. 1996. "Rightful Resistance." *World Politics* 49:31–55.

Ockey, James. 2004. *Making Democracy: Leadership, Class, Gender and Political Participation in Thailand.* Honolulu: University of Hawaii Press.

O'Connor, Richard. 1991. "Place, Power, and Discourse in the Thai Image of Bangkok." *Journal of the Siam Society* 78 (2): 61–73.

Onnucha Hutasingh. 2004. "Chuwit Out to Get the Gay Vote." *Bangkok Post,* 6 July, p. 2.

Ottolini, Cesare. n.d. "Strategie popolari per difendere la residenza nei centri storici delle città." Pp. 4–32 in *Strategie popolari nei Centri Storici,* vol. 2: *Europa,* edited by Anon. Padova: Habitat International Coalition.

Pacharin Jorajad. 2003. "Phakhniphon: Roeang kahn soeksah lae kahnphatthanah chumchon Pom Mahahkahn khwaeng Boroniwet khaet Phranakhawn Krungthaepmahakankhawn." Class essay. Bangkok: Srinakharinwirot University.

Palumbo, Berardino. 2003. *L'UNESCO e il Campanile: Antropologia, Politica e Beni Culturali in Sicilia orientale*. Roma: Meltemi.

Paritta Chalermpow Koanantakool. 2002. "Thai Middle-Class Practice and Consumption of Traditional Dance: 'Thai-ness' and High Art." Pp. 217–41in *Local Cultures and the "New Asia*,*"* edited by C.J.W.-L. Wee. Singapore: Institute of Southeast Asian Studies.

Parnwell, Michael J. G. 2005. "The Power to Change: Rebuilding Sustainable Livelihoods in North-East Thailand." *Journal of Transdisciplinary Environmental Studies* 4:1–21. http://www.journal-tes.dk/vol_4_no_2/NO4_MI_1.PDF.

Peleggi, Maurizio. 2002a. *Lords of Things: The Fashioning of the Siamese Monarchy's Modern Image*. Honolulu: University of Hawaii Press.

———. 2002b. *The Politics of Ruins and the Business of Nostalgia*. Bangkok: White Lotus.

Pérez, Federico. 2010. Laboratorios de reconstrucción urbana: Hacia una antropología de la política urbana en Colombia. *Antípoda* 10:51–84.

———. 2014. "Urbanism as Warfare: Planning, Property, and Displacement in Bogotá." PhD diss., Harvard University, Department of Anthropology.

Phoemsak Makaraphirom. 2009. "Koroni Pom Mahahkahn bot tod sawp newthang samanchan rataban Abhisit." http://www.peace.mahidol.ac.th/th/index.php?option=com_content&task=view&id=498&Itemid=155 (13 June, last accessed 23 March 2014).

Ploenpote Atthakor. 2002. "Residents of Fort Mahakarn in Bid for City to Review Eviction. *Bangkok Post*," 18 September, p. 4.

———. 2003a. "Canal-side Community Sets the Tone for Others to Follow." *Bangkok Post*, 17 June, p. 8.

———. 2003b. "Residents Vow Not to Move Out Whatever the Court May Decide." *Bangkok Post*, 27 August, p. 4.

———. 2003c. "Fort Residents Under Heavy Siege." *Bangkok Post*, 29 August, p. 10.

Porphant Ouyyanont. 2008. "The Crown Property Bureau in Thailand and the Crisis of 1997." *Journal of Contemporary Asia* 38:166–89.

Pranee Glumsom. 2004. "Chumchon Pom Mahahkahn: 'Adit' thi kamlang rai anakot." *Warasahn Moeang Borahn/Muang Boran Journal* 31:112ff. Also available at http://www.muangboranjournal.com/modules.php?name=Sections&op=viewarticle&artid=51; English summary at http://www.muangboranjournal.com/modules.php?name=Sections&op=printpage&artid=56 (both last accessed 18 April 2015).

Pravit Rojanapruck. 2003. "Nayawbai salai chumchon (kao)." *Krungthaep Thurakit*, 22 August, p. 10.

———. 2004. "Thainess Is a Limited Definition." *The Nation*, 9 July, p. 10A.

Prudhisan Jumbala. 2012. "Prajadhipok: The King at the Transition to Constitutional Monarchy in Siam." Pp. 106–202 in *Monarchy and Constitutional Rule in Democratizing Thailand*, edited by Suchit Bunbongkarn and Prudhisan Jumbala. Bangkok: Institute of Thai Studies, Chulalongkorn University.

Rabinow, Paul. 1989. *French Modern: Norms and Forms of the Social Environment*. Cambridge, MA: MIT Press.

Reed-Danahay, Deborah. 1996. *Education and Identity in Rural France: The Politics of Schooling*. Cambridge: Cambridge University Press.

———, ed. 1997. *Auto/Ethnography: Rewriting the Self and the Social*. Oxford: Berg.

Reynolds, Craig J. 1987. *Thai Radical Discourse: The Real Face of Feudalism Today*. Ithaca, NY: Southeast Asia Program, Cornell University.

———. 2009. "*Chumchon*/Community in Thailand." Pp. 286–305 in *Words in Motion: Toward a Global Lexicon*, 'edited by Carol Gluck and Anna Lowenhaupt Tsing. Durham, NC: Duke University Press.

Rhum, Michael R. 1996. "'Modernity' and 'Tradition' in 'Thailand.'" *Modern Asian Studies* 30:325–55.

Riggs, Fred. W. 1966. *Thailand: The Modernization of a Bureaucratic Polity*. Honolulu: East-West Center Press.

Rittirong Chutapruttikorn. 2009. Squatter Life in Transition: an Evaluation of Participatory Housing Design. *FORUM Ejournal* 9:13–30. Available at http://research.ncl.ac.uk/forum/volume9.html (last accessed 12 April 2015).

Roy, Ananya. 2009. "Why India Cannot Plan Its Cities: Informality, Insurgence, and the Idiom of Urbanization." *Planning Theory* 8:76–87.

Rüland, Jürgen, and M. L. Bhansoon Ladavalya. 1996. "Managing Metropolitan Bangkok: Power Contest or Public Service. Pp. 30–70 in *The Dynamics of Metropolitan Management in Southeast Asia*, edited by Jürgen Rüland. Singapore: Institute of Southeast Asian Studies.

S. Plainoi. 2001. *Lau roeang Bangkok*. Bangkok: Saitharn Publication House.

Sanitsuda Ekachai. 2002. "If Only We Can Respect the Poor." *Bangkok Post*, 19 September.

Saowanee Woranuch. 2005. "KawTawMaw nun Chumchon Pom Makakan pen laeng kahn rian ru." *Sawatdi Krungthaep*, 22 December, p. 35.

Scandurra, Enzo. 2003. *Città morenti e città viventi*. Rome: Meltemi.

Schein, Louisa. 1999. Performing Modernity. *Cultural Anthropology* 14:361–95.

Scott, James C. 1985. *Weapons of the Weak: Everyday Forms of Peasant Resistance*. New Haven, CT: Yale University Press.

———. 1998. *Seeing Like a State: How Certain Schemes to Improve the Human Condition Have Failed*. New Haven, CT: Yale University Press.

———. 2009. *The Art of Not Being Governed: An Anarchist History of Upland Southeast Asia*. New Haven, CT: Yale University Press.

Shao, Qin. 2013. *Shanghai Gone: Domicide and Defiance in a Chinese Megacity*. Lanham, MD: Rowman and Littlefield.

Shryock, Andrew. 1997. *Nationalism and the Genealogical Imagination: Oral History and Textual Authority in Tribal Jordan*. Berkeley: University of California Press.

Siffin, William J. 1960. "The Civil Service System of the Kingdom of Thailand." *International Review of Administrative Sciences* 26:225–68.

———. 1966. *The Thai Bureaucracy: Institutional Change and Development*. Honolulu: East-West Center Press.

Sinkhronkrup (Borisat). 1995. *Phaen Patibatkahn anurak lae patthanah Krung Rattanakosin boriwaen Pom Mahahkahn naew kampaeng moeang lae boriwaen doi rawp*. Bangkok: Ministry of Science, Technology, and the Environment.

Sirisak Wanliphodom. 2003. Moeang prawatisaht Krungthaep kap Pom Mahahkahn lae Songkrahm "Khid Mai-Tham Mua." *Silapawatthanatham* (February): 116–23.

Skiotis, Fionn. 2003. *Pom Mahakan: People of the Fort*. Film. Geneva: Centre on Housing Rights and Evictions.

Smart, Alan, and Filippo Zerilli. 2004. Extralegality. Pp. 222–38 in Donald M. Nonini, *A Companion to Urban Anthropology*. New York: John Wiley.

Smith, Neil. 1979. "Toward a Theory of Gentrification A Back to the City Movement by Capital, Not People." *Journal of the American Planning Association* 45: 538–48.

———. 2006. "Gentrification Generalized: From Local Anomaly to Urban 'Regeneration' as Global Urban Strategy." Pp. 191–208 in *Frontiers of Capital: Ethnographic Reflections on the New Economy*, edited by Melissa S. Fisher and Greg Downey. Durham: Duke University Press.

Somsook Boonyabancha. 2004. "A Decade of Change: From the Urban Community Development Office to the Community Organizations Development Institute in Thailand." Pp. 25–53 in *Empowering Squatter Citizen: Local Government, Civil Society and Urban Poverty Reduction*, edited by Diana Mitlin and David Satterthwaite. London: Earthscan.

Sopon Pornchokchai. 1992. *Bangkok Slums: Review and Recommendations*. Bangkok: School of Urban Community Research and Actions, Agency for Real Estate Affairs.

Sopranzetti, Claudio. 2012a. *Red Journeys: Inside the Thai Red-Shirt Movement*. Chiangmai: Silkworm Press.

———. 2012b. "Burning Red Desires: Isan Migrants and the Politics of Desire in Contemporary Thailand." *South East Asia Research* 20:361–79.

———. 2013. "The Owners of the Map: Motorcycle Taxi Drivers, Mobility, and Politics in Bangkok." PhD diss., Harvard University, Department of Anthropology.

Steinmüller, Hans. 2010. "Communities of Complicity: Notes on State Formation and Local Sociality in Rural China." *American Ethnologist* 37:539–49.

Stewart, Charles. 1989. "Hegemony or Rationality? The Position of the Supernatural in Modern Greece." *Journal of Modern Greek Studies* 7:77–104.

———. 2010. "Immanent or Eminent Domain? The Contest over Thessaloniki's Rotonda." Pp. 179–200 in *Archaeology in Situ: Sites, Archaeology, and Communities in Greece*, edited by Anna Stroulia and Susan Buck Sutton. Lanham, MD: Lexington Books/Rowman & Littlefield, 2010.

REFERENCES

Streckfuss, David. 2011. *Truth on Trial in Thailand: Defamation, Treason and Lèse-majesté*. London: Routledge.

Suchit Wongthes. 2003a. "Chumchon Pom Mahahkahn chahn kampaeng moeang Krungthaep." *Matichon Sapdah*, 1 May, p. 68.

———. 2003b. "Chahn kampaeng Phranakhawn chumchon kao kae mi chiwit Krungthaep." *Khao Sod* 23 April, p. 6.

———. 2003c. "Krungthaep mai chai 'Ko Rattanakosin' tae pen "Moeang Rattanakosin." *Khao Sod*, 26 May, p. 6.

———. 2003d. "Wik likae haeng raek nai Sayahm yu rim kampaeng 'Pom Mahakahn.'" *Khao Sod*, 27 May, p. 6.

———. 2004a. "Phrahn pah khah khon *Brand name* rathabahn nah ngoen." *Khao Sod*, 25 June, p. 6.

———. 2004b. "Krungthaep thi thae tawng mi khon, mai chai tae phi sahng thewadah." *Khao Sod* 27 December, p. 6.

Sudjit Sananwai and Apiwat Saengpattasima. 2003. "Botbat sathahbanik kap pawakahn rai thi yu ahsai an mankhom khong sangkhom thai." *Proceedings, Silpakorn Architectural Discourse, 3rd Symposium*. Bangkok: Faculty of Architecture, Silpakorn University. [Paginated separately by item.]

Supreeya Wungpatcharapon. 2009. "The Roles of Informal Community Networks in Public Participation: The Case of Thailand." http://linesofflight.files.wordpress.com/2008/03/the-roles-of-informal-community-networks-in-public-participation-the-case-of-thailand.pdf (last accessed 25 March 2014).

Suwit Khonpaen. n.d. *Lilah khon jon: Phalang khap khloen chumchon lae moeang nahyu*. Bangkok: privately published with support from four NGOs.

Tambiah, Stanley J. 1969. "Animals Are Good to Think and Good to Prohibit." *Ethnology* 8:423–59.

———. 1976. *World Conqueror, World Renouncer: A Study of Buddhism and Polity in Thailand Against a Historical Background*. Cambridge: Cambridge University Press.

———. 1977. The Galactic Polity: The Structure of Traditional Kingdoms in Southeast Asia. *Annals of the New York Academy of Sciences* 293:69–97.

———. 1979. A Performative Approach to Ritual. *Proceedings of the British Academy* 65:113–69.

Tausig, Benjamin. 2014. "Neoliberalism's Moral Overtones: Music, Money, and Morality at Thailand's Red Shirt Protests." *Culture, Theory and Critique* 55: 257–71.

Taylor, James. 2008. *Buddhism and Postmodern Imaginings in Thailand: The Religiosity of Urban Space*. Farnham: Ashworth.

Thak Chaloemtiarana. 2007. *Thailand: The Politics of Despotic Paternalism*. Rev. ed. Ithaca, NY: Cornell University Southeast Asia Publications.

Thanaphon Watthanakun. 2007. *Kahnmoeang roeang phoen thi: pholawat thang sangkhom khawng chumchon. Koroni soeksah: Chumchon Pom Mahakahn* (Politics of Place: Social Dynamics of a Community. Case Study: The Pom Mahakan Community). 14 October. Bangkok: Scholarly Institutional Foundation.

Thongchai Winichakul. 1994. *Siam Mapped: A History of the Geo-body of a Nation*. Honolulu: University of Hawaii Press.

———. 2000. "The Quest for '*Siwilai*': A Geographical Discourse of Civilizational Thinking in the Late-Nineteenth-Century and Early-Twentieth-Century Siam." *Journal of Asian Studies* 59:528–49.

———. 2001. Prawatisaht thai baep rachahchahtniyom: jahk yuk anahnikhom amphrang su rachahchahtniyom mai roe latthi sadet phaw khon kradumphi thai nai pachuban. *Silapawathanatham* 23 (1).

Tiamsoon Sirisrisak and Natsuko Akagawa. 2012. "Cultural Rights and Conservation of Old Bangkok." *Journal of the Siam Society* 100:149–66.

Türeli, İpek. 2010. "Modeling Citizenship in Turkey's Miniature Park." Pp. 105–25 in *Orienting Istanbul: Cutural Capital of Europe?*, edited by Deniz Göktürk, Levent Soysal, and İpek Türeli. London: Routledge.

Turner, V. W. 1974. *Dramas, Fields, and Metaphors: Symbolic Action in Human Society*. Ithaca, NY: Cornell University Press.

Vallard, Annabel. 2013. *Des humains et des matériaux: Ethnographie d'une filière textile artisanale au Laos*. Paris: Pétra.

Van Esterik, Penny. 2000. *Materializing Thailand*. Oxford: Berg.

Viphaphan Siripakchai. 2007. "Roeanglao jahk chumchon thi thuk lairoea haeng noeng." Master's thesis, Thammasat University.

Vitit Muntharbhorn. 2004. "Reflections on Economic and Social Rights in Thailand Inc." *Bangkok Post*, 3 July, p. 8.

Wheeler, R.E.M. 1954. *Archaeology from the Earth*. Oxford: Clarendon.

Williams, Raymond. 1975. *The Country and the City*. St. Albans: Paladin.

Wilson, Richard Ashby, and Jon P. Mitchell. 2003. Introduction. Pp. 1–15 in *Human Rights in Global Perspective: Anthropological Studies of Rights, Claims and Entitlements*, edited by Richard Ashby Wilson and Jon P. Mitchell. London: Routledge.

Wong, Ka F. 2006. *Visions of a Nation: Public Monuments in Twentieth-Century Thailand*. Bangkok: White Lotus.

Woranuch Charungratanapong. 2002. Phaen mae bot poea kahn anurak lae phathanah krung Rattanakosin. In *Phu ying kap khwahmru*. Bangkok: Khrongkahn satri lae yaowachon soeksah Mahahwithayalai Thahmasaht.

Wutipong Phriepjariyawat. n.d. [2004]. *Yutthasaht KhawThawMaw Sahn Phalang Prachahchon*. Campaign booklet.

Yalouri, Eleana. 2001. *The Acropolis: Global Fame, Local Claim*. Oxford: Berg.

Yongtanit Pimonsathean. 2012. "The Crown Property Bureau and Heritage Conservation." *Journal of the Siam Society* 100:103–22.

Yos Santasombat. 2008. *Lak Chang: A Reconstruction of Tai Identity in Daikong*. 2nd ed. Canberra: Australian National University Press.

Zhang, Li. 2010. *In Search of Paradise: Middle-Class Living in a Chinese Metropolis*. Ithaca, NY: Cornell University Press.

Zhu, Yujie. 2012. "Performing Heritage: Rethinking Authenticity in Tourism." *Annals of Tourism Research* 39:1495–513.

Index

Abhisit Vejjajiva, 6, 7, 132, 195, 207n25
academics, role of, 8, 9, 12, 28, 29, 35, 36, 95, 115, 125, 136, 168, 227n39; attacked by Thaksin, 7, 206n17
Acropolis (Athens), 200, 238n19
activism, activists, 15, 19, 25, 28, 35, 52, 59, 77, 95, 99–100, 102, 107, 108, 110, 121, 126, 136, 168, 178, 194, 196, 208n33, 233n3, 235n23. *See also* NGOs
aesthetics, 69–70, 72, 85, 143, 151
age (of individuals), 174, 192
agency, 28, 36, 40, 93, 152, 162–64, 165, 171, 199, 203
Akin Rabibhadana, 32, 115
alcohol. *See* drunkenness
almsgiving, 161
amplification, 58, 160, 161
amulets, 36, 69, 138
Anan Ganjanapan, 108–9
ancestors. *See* spirits and spirit shrines
"ancient" as designation, 31, 64, 91, 153, 155, 156, 157; as official designation, 87, 139, 156–57
Ancient City (theme park), 42, 44, 54, 90, 211n70
anger, expression of, 58
Apirak Kosayodhin, 7, 60, 121, 126, 127–29, 132–33, 134, 135–42, 145, 147, 150, 151, 152, 159–60, 174, 180, 183, 187, 195, 213n12, 218n2, 229n12, 230n25, 235n20

Apiwat Ratanawaraha, xi
Apiwat Waengwatthaseema, 9, 112, 113, 117, 158
Appadurai, Arjun, 233n28
Aranya Siriporn, xi
Arc de Triomphe. *See* Democracy Monument
archaeology and archaeologists, 68, 73, 94, 95–96, 147, 156, 221n40
architects and architecture, 9, 11, 13, 40, 68, 69, 72, 109, 141, 164, 187, 189, 194, 206n12, 213–14n14, 232n23; vernacular, 73, 97, 141, 155, 225–26n20. *See also* Centre for Architecture and Human Rights
Ardener, Edwin W., 235n16
army, 12, 66, 67, 87, 93, 93–95, 96, 115, 153, 186, 198, 203, 227n38, 236n33
Arnstein, Sherry R., 234n6
art, 68
Asian Commission for Human Rights (ACHR), 10
Asia-Pacific Economic Cooperation (APEC) forum, 67, 87, 123, 125
Askew, Marc, 61–62, 174, 217–18n49, 226n27, 226n29, 235n22
Assembly of the Poor, 19, 29, 62, 77, 81, 85–86, 115, 174, 197, 204, 221n33
astringent, production of, 38, 105–6
Athens, Greece, 200, 238n19
attrition, war of, 31, 117, 120, 147, 148

255

INDEX

auction, to raise money for tsunami victims, 199
Aulino, Felicity, xi, 49, 206–7n18, 212n7
Austin, J. L., 208n37
authenticity, 40, 41
authoritarianism, 7, 15, 24, 27, 44, 52, 77, 116–17, 162, 166, 169, 173, 191, 209n43, 209n48, 211–12n2, 223n55
auto-ethnography, 184, 236n29
Ayutthaya, 81, 83, 165, 203, 222n46, 233n29

bahn (home, community), 109
Bahn Mankhong (Secure Housing) project, 134, 193, 237n6
bahn moeang, 61, 176, 211n70
Banasophit Mekvichai, 136, 230n21
Bangkok: Big Bang, 60, 217n44, 217n47; Master Plan (2004), 73, 143; population, 1; "shut down" movement, 48, 66–67, 236n33; Thai name of, 67
Bangkok Metropolitan Administration (BMA, city hall), x, 10, 11, 90, 101, 226–27n30; alleged corruption at, 129; attitudes of, 70; attitudes toward Pom Mahakan, 34–35, 61, 87, 144, 146; building as protest site, 131; correspondence with, 150; Department of Public Works of, 100, 111–12, 113, 115, 151, 165; destruction of old market by, 67; divisions within, 70; embarrassment of, 16; entrenched practices at, 7–8, gentrification by, 194; hides unseemly ongoing negotiations with, 197; legal position of, 103; problems, 227–28n42; protest at, 133–34; publication, joint, of, 225–26n20; recognition of community by, 16; reform of, 129, 169, 229n12; refusal to compromise, 52, 75, 99, 101, 195, 228n2; relations with police, 33, 179–80; respect for, as institution, 186; scripted meetings of, 14; structures of, 93; symbol of, 59; sympathizers within, 12, 75; and traffic problems, 57; vote counting at, 129; zones of, 135, 147, 180–81, 179–80, 192. *See also* elections
Bangkok Post (English-language newspaper), 10, 196
Banglamphu, 99, 208n33
Ban Khrua, 161, 185, 236n32
Bantorn Ondam, 207n24
barricades, 17, 32, 118, 191
beauty and beautification, urban, 68, 69, 74, 91, 92, 99, 113, 120, 123, 128, 130, 203, 224n10
Behide the Wall (documentary), 112, 158
Ben-Yehoyada, Naor, xi
Bhichit Rattakul, 127, 134, 136, 230n21
Bhumibol Adulyadej (king), 16; portraits of, 26, 63, 77, 84, 134, 166, 207n26, 209n50
Bickner, Robert J., xi
binary oppositions. *See* formal-informal; polarization and polarity
bird cages, 38, 39
Bogotá, Colombia, 220–21n32
boredom, 152, 231n10
borough (*khet*) structure, 92
Bourdieu, Pierre, 25, 148, 231n5
Bowie, Katherine, 171
Brasília, 217n46
Brent, T. David, xi
bribery, 33, 179, 236n26
bricolage, 171
Bristol, Graeme, x, xi, 9, 112, 121, 206nn12–13, 216n38, 226n29, 227n35
Buddhism, 6, 11, 22, 31, 46, 59, 80, 81, 99, 118, 152, 173, 174, 186, 199; ascetics in, 38, 54; associated with positivism, 233n1; attitude to those outside, 86; identity and, 82; impact on the city of, 218–19n9; purism in, 55, 156, 199; symbolism of, 78. *See also* permanence
budget, 103, 136; based on sufficiency economy, 230n25
building materials, census and reuse of, 189
bureaucracy, 3, 20, 25, 26, 42, 45, 53, 66, 67, 86, 93, 95, 111–13, 196; centralized, 55, 219n13; collusion with, 236–37n4; criticized, 83, 174, 183; cultural, 71; developmentalist, 204; as excuse, 67; expert knowledge of, 11; failures of, 5; and fear, 8, 23, 92, 108; and feudalism, 66, 111, 152; governance of, 6; hierarchy of, 14; and history, 64; implicit recognition of rights to utilities, 5; intransigent, 8; international, 16; logic of, 88, 110, 111, 165; modernist, 9, 46; opposed to and combined with segmentation, 212n5; oscillation within, 27; paralyzed, 89; powers of, 85; reform of, 129, 218n2, 229n12; relocation by, 61; respect for royalty of, 86, 111; rigid, 236–37n4; royal, 37, 53, 86, 134; and sacrilege, 59; special interests and, 67–68; strategies of, 31; as tautologous, 226n24; temporalities of, 151;

as un-Thai, 152, 174, 199; Western-oriented philosophy of, 24, 46, 61. *See also* Bangkok Metropolitan Administration

Cambodia, 222n43
canals, 2, 73, 130. *See also* Ong Ang Canal
capitalism, 20, 21, 45, 197, 200, 207n27, 207–8n29, 212n4, 237n17
care (*du lae*): affective dimensions of, 142, 146, 182, 230n28, 230n34; as category of political relationship, 36, 41, 177, 182
Carrera Décima (Bogotá, Colombia), 220–21n32
Catholicism, 152, 224n65
Cellamare, Carlo, 229n20
Centre for Architecture and Human Rights (CAHR), x, 206nn12–13
Centre on Housing Rights and Evictions (COHRE), x, 9, 10, 15, 16, 133, 207n20, 229n18
Chaiwat Thirapantu, 217n44, 217n47
Chakri Dynasty, 1, 4, 26, 78, 231n11, 233n31; reigns of as measure of historical time, 64, 153, 164, 165, 233n31
Chalerm Thai Theatre, 223n60
Chalerm Yubamrung, 127
Cham (ethnic-religious group), 83, 185
Chamlong Srimuang, 5
Champs-Élysées. *See* Rachadamnoen Avenue
Chanwut Worawan, 228n2
chaobahn (term for residents), 11, 61
Chao Phraya River, 60, 81–82
Chart Pattana (political party), 126
Chatri Prakitnonthakarn, 141–47, 169–70, 187, 189, 205n1, 216n38
Chavalit Yongchaiyudh, 221n33
Chayan Vaddhanaphuti, 212n3, 222n45
children's art, 40, 171, 188
Children's Day (*wan dek*), 4, 39, 105, 188, 199
China, 40, 86, 152, 208n33, 211n65, 222n48, 223n55. *See also* Shanghai; Yunnan
Chinese in Bangkok, 53, 56. *See also* Yaowarat
Choay, Françoise, 72
Christianity. *See* Catholicism; images; Orthodoxy
Chu Jianfang, xi, 213n14
Chulalongkorn (Rama V), 76, 79, 86–87, 142, 155, 165, 203, 220n30, 233n1
Chulalongkorn University, 35, 125, 134, 136, 177
chumchon. *See* community

Chuwit Kamolvisit, 127, 236n26
cities, capital, 72, 75, 83, 182, 220n30
city, right to the, 140, 230n24
city pillar, 61, 75, 76
civico and *civile*, 110
civilization: as goal, 30, 130, 198, 203; as Italian *civiltà*, 45, 212n3, 222n43; represented by city, 45, 59
civil society, 221n40
class, 2, 19–20, 21, 24, 35, 39, 47, 48, 69, 77, 84, 85, 109–10, 143, 170–71, 175, 194, 199, 201, 202, 204, 208n33, 221n40, 227n35
cockfighting, 38, 138
Cold War, 71, 106, 225n19
collusion, 33, 236–37n4
Colombia, 220–21n32
colonialism, 18, 19, 20, 30, 37, 45, 80, 149, 172, 197, 211n63, 233n1; mimicry in, 219n17. *See also* crypto-colonialism
Commission on Cultural, Economic, and Social Rights (United Nations, Geneva), 15–16, 207n20
commoners. *See phrai*
common good, 58, 134, 182, 195, 224n9, 229n20
communism, 71, 219n15
community: among communities, 114, 199; definition of, 104–5, 107, 108, 134; historic, 22, 56, 127, 130, 131, 134; solidarity of, 107, 109–10, 117, 147, 175–76; terminology (Thai) of, 108–10, 225n19
Community Organizations Development Institute (CODI), 10, 121, 212n10, 227n35, 237n6
community shrine, 4, 53
compassion, 59, 81, 86, 92, 111, 118, 152, 173, 174, 187, 199
compensation, 22, 98, 107, 119, 122, 135, 195
concentricity, 18–19, 41, 42–43, 47, 50, 61, 90, 173, 197, 202, 220n30
conflict avoidance, 27, 74, 95, 142, 183, 196, 206–7n18
Confucian values, 152
conservation, historic, 4, 12, 18, 22, 31, 56, 62–63, 72–73, 74, 94, 118, 128, 130, 142, 146, 153, 155, 156–57, 210n60, 219n16; brutality of, 164; compared across cities, 223n61; and compared with care and curatorship, 230n28; Sukhumbhand's alleged neglect of, 196; terminology of, cognate with term for "love," 142, 228n2

257

INDEX

constitutional rights, 195, 233n3
constitutions, Thai, 101, 144; People Constitution, 19, 101, 215n34, 215–16n36, 216n38
consumerism, 20, 24, 84, 174, 208–9n40, 209n50, 220n29; anti-consumerism, 152
contingency, 165
cookies, 39
cooperation, 91, 102, 109
corruption, 21, 33, 45, 81, 86, 129, 171, 217n48. *See also* bribery
cosmology, 23, 46, 59, 61, 66, 96, 100, 151
countryside, romantic view of, 11, 31, 81–82, 108, 200, 221–22n1
coups: in 1932, 216–17n42; in 2006, 52; in 2014, 7, 24, 48, 79, 170, 184, 198, 202, 236n33
courtesy. *See* politeness
courts: Administrative, 46, 100, 101, 103, 122, 125, 126, 131, 145, 189, 226–27n30, 228n3; Constitutional, 6, 7
crafts, 38, 54, 58, 170
Crete, 210n60, 222n51, 231n11
crime, 40. *See also* drugs; prostitution
Crown Property Bureau (Thailand), x, 12, 74–75, 112, 180, 220n28, 234n6
crypto-colonialism, 49, 70–71, 72, 75, 82, 85, 109, 143, 145, 156, 165, 167, 170, 172, 218n8, 219n13, 219n17, 235n13
Cultural Heritage Atlas of Rattanakosin (*Phaenthi Chumchon Krung Rattanakosin*), 107
cultural resource management, 153
cultural rights, 57, 105, 215–16n36, 225n19
culture: archaeological understanding of, 225–26n20; attitudes to, 144; community, 225n19; in governance, 19; national, 72, 168, 172, 182; official discourse of, 30, 54, 106, 108, 184–85, 215n26; as property, 72; as resource, 18
"current" (*krasae*, public interest), 125

Dai Daikong (Dehong Thai), xi, 213n14
dance, 31
Daniel, E. Valentine, 55
Danish International Development Association (DANIDA), 225–26n20
data, 30, 169, 170, 222–23n53
Davis, Lisa Kim, 87
death, 96
Delcore, Henry, 75, 184
democracy and democrats, 5, 7, 15–16, 17, 24, 27, 66, 71, 78, 85, 159, 161, 162, 166, 174, 197, 225–26n20, 232n24; Prajadhipok's views on, 221n37; "Thai-style," 232n24; Western models of, 167, 174. *See also* Democrat Party; egalitarianism; populism
Democracy Monument, 76, 78, 216–17n42, 220–21n32
Democrat Party, 5, 6, 7, 19, 20, 24, 121, 131–32, 136–37, 145, 149, 183, 195, 198, 199, 201, 204, 206n9, 207n25, 217–18n49, 221n33, 235n21
demolition, 18, 96, 98, 122, 123, 153, 154, 187, 193, 228n3
demonstrations. *See* protests
Denes, Alexandra, 55
dependency, risk of, 81
development: developmentism, 85, 88, 152, 204, 222n52; national, 120; as paradigm, 30, 94, 209n50; plan, 224n4; self-development, 30, 85; urban, 59, 128, 130, 134, 138, 140, 142
Dharia, Namita, xi
dictatorships (Thailand), 4–5, 7, 24, 122–23, 197, 209n50, 210n59. *See also* coup
dignity (as constitutional term), 102
disagreement, access to, 50, 52
disclaimers, 25
diversity: cultural and ethnic, 4, 50, 55, 173, 185, 202; economic, 50. *See also* ethnic minorities
divide-and-conquer tactics, 116
documentary fetishism, 233n2
documentation, 97, 100, 101, 122, 135–36, 182
dogs, as insulting metaphor for homeless people, 227–28n42
domicide, 5
Don Muang Airport, 5
Douglas, Mary, 233n28
Dovey, Kim, 205n3, 218n4, 220n30
drivers: motorcycle taxi, 34, 136, 226n27; taxi and *tuk-tuk*, 35
drugs, 33, 34, 58, 63, 67, 140, 161, 176, 177, 179–80; Thaksin's campaign against, 180
drunkenness, 178, 179, 180–81

Economic and Social Commission for Asia and the Pacific (ESCAP, United Nations, Bangkok), 10, 57, 215n32
education, 11

258

egalitarianism, 44, 48, 52, 77, 79, 166, 169, 172, 191, 197, 209n43, 209n48, 211–12n2, 213n13, 223n55. See also democracy; oscillation
elections: electioneering at Pom Mahakan, 137; gubernatorial, 60, 29–30, 48, 85, 126, 128–29, 135, 168
electricity, 108, 123
Elinoff, Eli, 222n52, 227n34
embodiment, 37, 156, 166, 175, 188, 189, 224n1. See also gesture; *wai*
eminent domain, 22, 87, 98, 99, 102, 103, 122, 144, 173, 194, 228n3, 235n14
energy. See power
engaged anthropology, 30, 36
English language, use of, 162, 163
englobing, 172, 173, 235n16
environment, environmentalism, 3, 11, 12, 31, 116
ethnic minorities, 45, 56, 71, 81; historical antecedents of, 83; threat of constructivism toward, 234n9
ethnography, as method, 40, 41
Evans-Pritchard, E. E., 45, 212n5, 213n13, 214n21, 223n58
eviction: announcement of, 224–25n13; causes of, 29, 87, 169; constitutional objections to, 101; deferred, 136, 150; economics of, 21; of entire community, 5, 100, 195; ethics and politics of, 2, 21, 22, 58; justification of, 182; of market, 67; mass, 218n2; notices of, 31, 100; patterns of, compared, 18–19, 152, 218n5; resistance to, techniques of, 28, 33, 58; seeking alternatives to, 9, 16; successful resistance to, 70, 141; timing of, 100, 111, 121, 150, 194; unpredictable consequences of, 113; as violence, 131, 150
experts, 237n6; attitudes toward, 11; opinions of, 31, 101
expropriation. See eminent domain

face, loss of, 61–62, 92, 179, 198
factionalism: in armed forces and police, 12, 71; in bureaucracy, 70, 111; in community, 17, 24, 39, 49, 52, 107, 118, 132, 146, 183–84, 190, 192; in Crown Property Bureau, 12, 74; endemic, 66, 149, 183
fanning, 64, 166, 209n46
fascism, 151, 221–22n1
fatalism, 96, 149, 152, 162, 190, 199, 236n3

femininity, 69
feudalism, 172; survivals of in bureaucracy, 66, 111, 152, 173, 174
films and filming, 9, 118, 133, 155–56, 163, 175
Fine Arts Department, 73, 83, 87, 94, 95
fireworks, 4, 88, 157
fish maw soup, 39, 104–5
flexible morphing, 202
food: banned from streets by BMA, 227–28n42; hawkers and producers, 17, 39, 49, 63, 98, 104–5, 128, 169; politics and promotion of, 105
formal-informal binary, 24–25, 175, 208n34, 235n23
formality (etiquette), 36, 123–24
Four Regions Slum Network, 10, 11, 85, 101–2, 104, 112, 122–23, 216n38, 223n54, 227–28n42
France, 45; as enemy and model, 1. See also Paris
friendship, 36, 174

garbage collection, 108
gender, 13–14, 191–92
gentrification, 18, 60, 69, 75, 84, 199; self-gentrification, 84–85, 194, 199–200, 201, 208n33, 218n6, 222n50, 234n6
gesture, 36, 64, 93, 157, 164, 232n23. See also embodiment; *wai*
Ghassan, Hage, 230n1
Goh, Daniel, 200
Golden Mount, Temple of, 2, 3, 4, 32–33, 57, 60, 80, 182, 205n8; community of, 147, 194
gold extraction, 38, 87
governance, 46, 52, 175–76; cultural, 19; good, 233–34n4
government edicts, status of, 102, 144
governors (BMA), 4–5, 6–8, 60, 133. See also Apirak Kosayodhin; Chamlong Srimuang; Samak Sundaravej; Sukhumbhand Paribatra
Grand Palace (Bangkok), 26, 74, 75, 210n62
Greece, 18, 19, 71, 73, 84–85, 156, 200, 210n60, 219n13, 219n15
Greenhourse, Carol J., 224n7
gumsa-gumlao, 216–17n42
Gupta, Akhil, 91, 170, 234n8

habitus, 187. See also Bourdieu; embodiment
Hamilton, Annette, 220n25

259

INDEX

Handler, Richard, 235n13
Harms, Erik, xi, 70
Harvard University, 28
Harvey, David, 45, 53
Harvey, David C., 208n30
Haussmann, George-Eugène, 76
height and status, 2, 59, 119, 161, 166, 174, 216n40, 232n23
heritage: and capitalism, 200; contrasted with history, 55; cultural, atlas of, 107; international language of, 41; politics of, 8, 18, 21, 68; signage associated with, 105, 157; tangible and intangible, 41, 211n64; Thai concept of, 54, 214–15n25, 215n26; uses of, 195
Herzfeld, Cornelia Mayer, x, 32–33, 91
Hewison, Kevin, 202
hierarchy, 8, 14, 37, 38, 44, 48, 54, 77, 79, 92, 161, 162, 166, 169, 172, 173, 174, 191, 212–13n11, 213n1, 224n1. *See also* authoritarianism
history (and historiography): contrasted with heritage, 55, 214–15n25; local, 55, 83, 170, 234n8; neoliberal inflation of, 209n47; official, 38, 64, 68, 83, 197; pushed to appreciate, 221n40; terms for, 215n26; uses of, 2, 4, 18, 22, 28, 29, 37, 54, 56, 57, 62, 108, 128, 144, 189, 195; variable meanings of, 55
Ho, K. C., 215–16n36
Ho Chi Minh City, 70
homeless people, 60, 102, 123, 227–28n42
honorifics, 37
hospitality, 13–14
houses, 17–18; historic, 75; imagined and modeled, 189, 192–93; new, 187–88; wooden, 3, 4, 31, 32, 34, 40, 63, 91, 139, 141, 193, 194, 228n2
housing, 47, 139, 191, 204, 212n10; Bank, 122; rights, 3, 133, 223n54
Hua Hin, 220n25
human rights, 85, 100. *See also* Asian Commission for Human Rights; cultural rights; housing; National Human Rights Commission of Thailand

images: Christian, 89; Thai regime of, 25, 69–70, 71, 175, 220n29, 232n23, 235n22
India, 170
indirect and inexplicit reactions, as tactic, 150
international relations, 19

Internet, 14
interviewing, problems of, 30–31
intimacy, 23, 31, 36, 135; cultural, 216n39; of state, 68
"invasion": as metaphor for bureaucrats' actions, 173; as metaphor for squatting, 135
Iran, 71, 156, 219n13
irony, 21, 22, 23, 41, 66, 80, 96, 161, 174, 198, 216n40, 224n4
irredentism, 44
Isaacs, Bronwyn, xi
Isan (northeastern region of Thailand), 23, 62, 84, 170, 206n9, 213n14
Israel, 73
Italy, 18, 45, 110, 212n8, 214–15n25, 222n43, 225n17. *See also* Rome

Jackson, Jean E., 234n9
Jackson, Peter, 25, 70, 232n23, 235n22
Jessadabodindra (Rama III), 86, 195
Johnson, Irving Chan, ix–x
journalism, journalists, 20, 94, 118, 138, 163, 170
Jul and Frost (firm), 225–26n20

Kajornjob Kusumawali, 233n29
Kalaya Sophonpanich, 136–37
Karin Klinkajorn, 130
karma (*kam*), 152, 190–91, 199
Keyes, Charles, 184–85, 211n64, 226n29
Khanachai Praphaiphum, 231n16
Khao Sod (newspaper), 224–25n13
khemkhaeng (as term to describe residents). *See* resilience
Khemthong Tongsakulrungruang, 102
Khlong Thoey, 104, 127, 225n17, 226n21, 228–29n8, 236n27
Khmer culture in Thailand, 55, 83, 185
Khon Kaen, 222n52
kickboxing, Thai, 38, 39
king: idealized roles of, 49, 174; respect for, 175
King Mongkut's Institute of Technology, 9, 121, 216n38
King Power shops, 219n19
kinship: extension and model of, 45, 49, 53, 54, 62; strategic limitations of, 56; term, honorific use of, 37
knowledge, local, as category, 40, 58, 106, 130, 170–73, 211n64, 215–16n36, 234n8
Kovarik, Chiara, xi
Kunming, 223n57

Kutma, Kristin, 230n28

land: expropriation by 1928 act, 26, 101; expropriation by 1987 act, 101; landscape, 127, 128, 174; ownership of, 64–65, 90, 97, 122, 145; possible ownership by governor, 237n15; reform, 47; sharing, 103, 104, 119, 121, 139, 141, 168, 202, 216n38, 230n22, 230n25; speculation in, 21; titles, 18, 86, 97, 107; values, 12, 75. *See also* eminent domain; space
Lao: ethnic group, 83; language, 213n14
Laos, 84
law, laws: attitudes toward, 17, 175–76, 191; breaking, 119, 176–77; constitutional, 99, 101; of eminent domain, 22, 120, 122; inconsistencies of, 67, 102, 123, 144, 195–96; intransigence of, 152; obedience, to, 175–76; official uses of, 58, 120, 131; need to amend, 102, 104, 108, 195, 204; special, 22; and temporality, 97, 122, 224n7. *See also* government edicts; lawyers; legalism; *lèse-majesté*
lawyers, 13, 103, 112, 113, 122, 189
leaders and leadership: in Arab world, compared, 227n31; attacks on, 120, 178–79, 180; changes in official, 68; compared with party-political, 217–18n49; election of, 5, 24, 146, 160, 161, 175, 177, 190; encouraging debate, 17, 50; and followers, 15, 63, 117, 161, 189–90, 191; levels of, 181; organization of, 16, 146, 181; roles and personalities of, 159, 175, 176–77, 190–91; skills and tactics of, 8, 14–15, 18, 23–24, 27, 62, 63, 84, 103, 146, 159, 160–61, 178–79, 180–81, 201, 236n25; support for, 16, 23–24, 63, 107; use of language by, 184–85, 189
Leckie, Scott, x, 229n18
legalism, 9, 17, 30, 46, 58, 64, 97, 100, 101, 104, 105, 107–8, 150, 168, 175, 222n43
legibility, 41, 211n66
legitimacy, royal, 78, 79, 221n37
Lek Viriyaphant, 211n70. *See also* Ancient City
lèse-majesté, 46, 77, 115–16, 202, 216–17n42; trials for, compared with witchcraft trials, 238n22
likae, 134, 156, 231n17
liquor, 13–14
"livable city," 59–61; conditions, 141–42
loan sharks, 153, 237n8

London, 223n61
lottery, state, and sellers, 71, 76, 78
loudspeakers, 159. *See also* amplification; sound and sonar dynamics
Luang Wichit Vadakan, 209n47

Mahidol University Research Center for Peace Building, 195, 224n8
Maier, Father Joe, 228–29n8, 236n27
Malinowski, Bronislaw, 221n38
mandala, as basis of old city plan, 46, 61, 75, 77, 78, 83, 203, 212n6, 218–19n9
Mankekar, Purnima, 91
Marxism, 223n55
masculinity, 69, 179
massage, 38, 39; used to calm drunk, 178
Matichon (newspaper), 195
McCargo, Duncan, xi, 226n27, 236–37n4
McDonald's, 21
meetings: argument at, 15;, 191 between community and officials, 112–14, 115–18, 165, 198; community, 14–15, 165–67, 191; content of, 49; disturbance at, 178; election, 126–27; family problems discussed at, 49; formality and procedure of, 14, 165, 175–76; imagined by DANIDA, 225–26n20; recorded, 172; roles of leaders at, 177, 191; royalist tone of, 49; scripted, 14; stated purpose of, 50; women's presence at, 209n46
merit-making, 100, 174; *pro bono* work as, 13, 103, 189
metonymy, 42, 48, 53–54, 62, 84, 156
Miao (ethnic group), 211n65
microphone, use of, 138, 139, 159–60, 174
military. *See* army
military rule. *See* dictatorships (Thailand)
Missingham, Bruce, 214n17, 221n33
modernism, modernity, and modernization: architecture, 218–19n12; bureaucratic, 3, 46, 89, 173; and citizenship, 200; and comfortable living conditions, 187; and desires, 200; and its antithesis, 166; monasticism and, 59; monumentality and, 56, 71–72; nation-state as, 19, 70, 89, 156; origins, 199; in planning, 9, 46, 56, 60, 69, 88, 130, 142, 200, 203–4; and political relations, 162, 170; religious, 233n1; royal symbiosis with 75; as stage in political evolution, 170, 200; Western model of, 30, 55, 69, 70

261

moeang, 173, 186, 197, 199, 202, 203–4, 212n3, 212n8, 217n48, 220n3, 223n54; adaptability of, 59; *bahnmoeang*, 61–62; as city, 44, 46, 61, 113, 142, 143; as community, 142; as country, 45; as expressed architecturally, 75–76, 80–81; and leadership in, 117; meaning of, 44–45; moral cartography of, 46; northern Thai concept of, 55; opposed to *prathaet*, 44–45, 61–63, 70–71, 114; as polity and moral community, 61, 113; segmentary, 47, 50, 53, 88, 114, 117, 151; and transcendence of, 83–84, 93; Yunnanese Tai equivalent of, 48–49
Mon (ethnic group), 83
monarchism and monarchy: absolute, end of, 4; bourgeois culture of, 151; in Cold War, 77; as component of Thai state, 66; constitutional status of, 67, 78; images of, 77; institution of, 80; loyalty to, 11, 26, 80, 234n9; narratives inspired by, 19; refracted, 86; relations with military, 79; Western models of, 167. *See also* Bhumibol; Chakri Dynasty; Chulalongkorn; *lèse-majesté*; Mongkut; Phutthaloetla Naphalai; Phutthayotfa Chulalok; Prajadhipok
Mongkut (Rama IV), 88, 156, 233n1
monks, 13, 31, 100, 161, 174
monuments and monumentality, 56, 58, 61, 67, 70, 72, 73, 182, 222n46; to the 14 October events, 78. *See also* time
moral community, 20, 45, 48, 61, 82, 83, 176, 213n13. *See also moeang*
museum: community, 4, 40, 54, 72, 153, 171; in and about Bangkok, 82–83; living, 81–82, 88, 101, 194, 222n43; older model of, 84. *See also* National Museum
Muslims, 38, 161, 163, 185, 199, 215n28
Mussolini, Benito, 76, 220–21n32

nail households (China), 86, 223n57
Napong Rugkhapan, 56
Nathanon Thavisin, 120, 129
Nation (English-language newspaper), 10
"Nation, Religion, King" (slogan), 72
National Human Rights Commission of Thailand, 9, 10, 100, 103, 196, 237n14. *See also* human rights
nationalism, 19, 26, 42, 46, 56, 71, 77, 129, 200, 203, 210n60, 219n19; of Parliament building, criticized, 141; in Quebec, 235n13
National Museum (Bangkok), 54, 72, 168

National Research Council of Thailand, x
nation-state: and divergence from, 77; European model of, 5, 20, 24, 45, 75, 167; Greek, 19; Thai, 1–2, 9, 18, 19, 20, 44, 55, 68, 70–71, 78, 182, 200. *See also prathaet*
nature: harmony with, 84; as ironic metaphor, 66; romanticized, 82
neighborhoods (*yahn*), 185
neoliberalism, 200, 209n47
Nepal, 71, 219n13
networks and networking, 22, 29, 37, 112, 114, 115, 119, 226n27; network monarchy, 226n27. *See also* Four Regions Slum Network
newspapers, 10, 35
NGOs: activists and activities of, 9, 10, 28, 29, 108, 216n38; alleged exploitation of, 119; attacked, 7, 206n17; culture, 81, 114; engagement of, 189; event organized by, 60; goals, questioned, 199, 217n44; goals of, 47, 107, 201; hegemonic aspects of, 81; housing and, 193; jargon and rhetoric of, 18, 85, 127, 128, 130, 159, 168, 169, 185, 188, 201, 214n1, 216n38; local connections of, 118, 177, 181; Marxist origins of, 223n55; middle-class attitudes and background of, 21, 204, 221n40; rural origins of, 11
nicknames, 49
Non Arkaraprasertkul, x, xi, 237n7
noodles, 39
Norasingha, 118–19
northern Thailand, culture and language of, 45, 55, 82, 212n3, 222n52, 226n22
Nowwanij Siriphatiriwut, ix
Nuer, 213n13, 223n58
Nut Nonthasuti, 74, 237n9

objectivism, 30
O'Brien, Kevin, 4
O'Connor, Richard, 213n13
Ombudsman's Office, 79
Ong Ang canal, 2, 64
order, 59, 64, 67, 128, 165, 175, 176–77, 231n6; orderliness, 151; rules of, 15
"original place," origins, 64–65, 98, 107, 119, 123, 135, 145, 146, 156, 222n46, 223n61, 234n9
Orthodoxy (Christian), 224n65
oscillation, political, 27, 37, 44, 172, 191; in bureaucracy, 27. *See also* authoritarianism; democracy; egalitarianism

OTOP economic production ideology, 67, 105–6
Oxford, 223n61

Pahk Khlong Talahd, 67
Palumbo, Berardino, 231n11
Pandit Chanrochanakit, xi
Paris, 76
Paritta Chalermpow Koanantakool, xi, 20
participation, 17, 127, 130, 159, 167, 168, 169, 184–85, 188, 190, 194, 200, 201, 225–26n20, 233n3, 233–34n4; as problematic concept, 229n15, 234n6; residents', in conferences, 35
passivity, strategies of, 231n4
Paveena Hongsakul, 126, 129
pavilion of the community's local knowledge. *See* museum
Peleggi, Maurizio, 151, 220n30
People's Action for Democracy. *See* Yellow Shirts
People's Power Party, 7, 206n9
performance, performativity, 14–15, 16, 25, 29, 166, 175, 208n37, 208n39, 208–9n40, 235nn21–22
permanence, absence of in Buddhist cosmology, 23, 59
Pérez, Federico, xi
Petburi, 38
Phahn Fah Lilaht Bridge, 3, 35, 96, 180, 210n59
Pheua Thai (political party), 7, 24, 201, 206n9
Phibul Songkhram, 72, 76, 219n16, 231n6, 232n24
philological correctness, 231n11
Phim, Uncle (masseur), 39–40, 96
phi nawng, 24, 35, 45, 47, 48, 49, 50, 54, 61, 117, 128, 135, 146, 161, 183, 212–13n11, 213n12, 214n18
photography: display, 64; as historical evidence, 60, 165; king's interest in, 78
Phraeng Phuthorn, 147, 162, 194
phrai (commoners), 93, 173, 174, 235n17
Phutthaloetla Naphalai (Rama II), 87
Phutthayotfa Chulalok (Rama I), 1, 4, 56, 203
Pitch, Pongsawat, xi, 212–13n11
planning, city, and planners, 9, 21, 68, 69, 70, 73, 76, 130, 142, 169, 183, 200, 204, 217n46, 218–19n9, 220–21n32, 229n11
poetry: children's, 188; traditional epic, 118–19
polarization and polarity, 23, 24, 52, 170
police, 12, 33, 58, 66, 67, 176, 179, 186, 198, 203, 210n54, 227n38, 236n26, 236n33; community, 105, 179–80; divergent operational modes of, 191; palace, 37, 93, 210n62
politeness (*marayaat*): in dealings with officialdom, 27, 198; removal of shoes at meetings, 166. *See also* gesture; language; speech; *wai*
politicians' reception at Pom Mahakan, 136–37
politics (Thai), 6–7, 20, 24, 48, 66, 77; attitudes toward, 29; power and, 85. *See also* Democrat Party; People's Power Party; Pheu Thai; Thai Rak Thai
polities, Thai: opposed models of, 9, 18, 20, 24, 44, 90, 199, 204, 211–12n2; pulsating galactic, 44, 53, 151. See also *moeang*; *prathaet*
Pom Mahakan (community and place): alarm system at, 31, 32; citadel of, 1, 31, 32, 57, 76, 77, 118, 153, 172, 188, 203; committee structure of, 5, 16, 175; community status of, 1, 19; conferences about, 35; confrontation with BMA, 91–94, 160; crafts at, 38; defense of, 32–33, 41, 191; drug issues in, 33, 34, 175, 176–77, 179–80; as family, 49, 54, 108, 109; fears and expectations of, 74–75; films about, 9, 10; first encountered, 25–26, 27–30; "friends of," 115, 207n20; historic status contested, 56; history of, 37; legitimacy of, 5, 22, 26, 40, 41, 42, 56, 80, 84, 88, 104–5, 110, 111, 135, 179; as "lesson," 57; as microcosm and model, 20, 38, 42, 47, 50, 53, 54, 90, 156, 158, 159, 186, 197, 200, 203; Minburi, proposed relocation to, 98; and modernity, 70; as moral community, 82; Muslims in, 38, 66; opposition to BMA, 5, 18, 81, 87; order and cleanliness in, 64; organization of, 147; as park, 21, 22, 67, 87, 97, 99, 101, 103, 115–16, 121, 122, 134, 135, 140, 145, 165, 195; people of, x, 9, 11; political orientation of, 20, 24; population of, 23, 24, 42, 97, 104, 111, 183, 211n68, 215–16n36; pressures on, 31; prostitution alleged at, 34; public relations of, 90–91, 125; relations with army and police, 33–34, 38, 87, 93–95, 122, 203; religion at, 24; respect for institutions at, 80, 86, 133, 186; royalism of, 26, 49, 50, 52, 79, 80, 86, 88, 108, 198, 200; as section of larger plan, 68; unity and dissension in, 109, 111, 115; visibility of, 8, 10, 151. *See also* factionalism; leadership; oscillation

263

INDEX

Pom Phra Sumaen, 27, 60, 83, 105–6
population figures, 1, 4
populism, 6, 7, 132, 169, 202, 206n17
Pornpan Chinnapong, 215–16n36
positivism, 30, 168, 169, 170; Cartesian, 233n1. *See also* legalism
postmodern condition, 42
poverty and poor people, 9–10, 47, 50, 69, 85–86, 102, 103, 107, 130, 140, 147, 152, 159, 180, 181, 189, 194, 199, 202, 212n10, 214n18, 218n5, 222n52, 222–23n53, 223n54, 227n31, 227n35, 228–29n8, 237n17. *See also* Assembly of the Poor
power, 22, 66, 119; administrative, 67; age and, 119; balancing, 223n54; burdens of, 161, 177, 191; centralized, 71; contrasted with popular, 85–86; exclusion from, 234n11; games, 52; and height, 59; impermanence of, 55; and intransigence, 152; location of, 176; mandala and, 212n6; "people with," 12, 186; resistance to, 4, 26; returning to the people, 233n32; Thai terminology of, 85, 222–23n53; varieties of, 236–37n4
Prajadhipok (Rama VII), 4, 26, 71, 78–79, 210n62; Museum, x, 26, 78, 79, 88, 183, 216–17n42, 221n37
Pranee Glamsam, 222n46
prathaet (nation-state model), 44, 45, 55, 59, 62, 63, 70, 75, 76, 81, 114, 120, 203, 212n3
Pravit Rojanapruck, 223n61, 229n13
Prawanrangsri community, 57
precedent, fear of, 108
Priyawat Kuanpol, ix
protests, 6, 7, 19, 21, 22, 27–29, 58, 75, 77, 80, 114, 120, 133–34, 149, 198; as mobilization, 226n27; strategy of, 221n33
protocol, 37; royal and religious, 15
Prudhisan Jumbala, xi–xii, 221n37
Pthomrerk Ketudhat, x, 112, 113, 136, 142, 143, 147, 196, 226n25, 226n29, 228n2
punning, 231–32n19

quality, 170, 185
questionnaires, 143–44

Rabinow, Paul, 233n1
Rachadamnoen Avenue, 1, 26, 57, 60, 69, 71, 75–78, 86, 88, 203, 216–17n42, 220n29, 220n30, 220–21n32; as "Champs-Élysées of Asia," 76; contested politics of, 78, 218n4
Rachanatdaram Temple, 86–87
radio, community, 29
railway expansion (Bangkok), 26
Rama, god, symbol of BMA, 59
Rama I. *See* Phutthayotfa Chulalok
Rama II. *See* Phutthaloetla Naphalai
Rama III. *See* Jessadabodindra
Rama IV. *See* Mongkut
Rama V. *See* Chulalongkorn
Rama VI. *See* Vajiravudh
Rama VII. *See* Prajadhipok
Rama IX. *See* Bhumibol Adulyadej
Rangsit, 227n33
Rattanakosin City and Island, 26, 34, 73, 75, 81, 83, 104, 107, 113, 120, 128, 130, 225–26n20; project, ix, 4, 56, 68, 70, 71, 87, 97, 103, 111, 141, 150, 156, 192, 194, 196, 219n17, 222n46, 227n32; project committee, 6, 73–74, 143, 144, 165, 216n38, 225–26n20
Rattanakosin era, 71
reciprocity, 30, 31, 48, 49, 115, 174
record-keeping, 149–50
Red Shirts, 7, 20, 23, 24, 47, 48, 52, 58, 77, 93, 132, 136, 183, 198, 201, 202, 206n9, 229n19, 232n24, 233n32
refraction, 43, 86, 151, 156, 223n58
Regulation on Community Land Deeds, 102
reification, 40–41, 52–53, 54–55, 172; cultural, 72, 219n13, 235n13; official, obscured by repetition, 110; self-reification, 145. *See also* local knowledge
reigns. *See* Chakri dynasty; time
rent, rental arrangements, 75, 97, 100, 115, 169, 194, 220n26
renunciation, 59
resilience, 35, 121, 145, 152, 159, 197, 199, 231n8
resistance, 18, 26, 27, 120, 121, 141, 172, 173, 189, 207–8n29, 219n17; "rightful," 4
Rethemnos (Rethimno), 222n51, 231n11
rhetoric, 18, 20, 29, 47, 56, 57, 58, 59, 61, 62, 64, 65, 71, 90, 98, 99, 108, 117, 120, 134, 166, 168, 169, 170, 172, 173, 184–85, 188, 192, 202, 209n43, 214n18, 216n38, 223n55, 229n11, 233n32
Rhum, Michael, 55
rhythm, 96, 148, 151, 157, 158

264

riap roi. See order
ritual, 13, 31, 39, 62, 118, 120, 153, 208n39; music for, 87. *See also* meetings
romanticism, middle-class, 11, 31, 81–82, 84, 107
Rome, 18, 76, 149, 152, 210n54, 220n3, 223n61, 230n3, 231n4
royal decree, 194–95
royalism and royalty: avoidance of placing in lower space, 232n23; symbolism of, 20, 21, 74, 75, 77, 78, 210n60, 220n29. *See also* monarchism and monarchy

sacredness, sacrality, 3, 60, 88, 238n19; of space, 173, 201; violation of (sacrilege), 22, 54, 59, 62
Saigon. *See* Ho Chi Minh City
Saipin Suputtamongkol, ix, xi
sakdina, 173, 235n17. *See also* feudalism
Samak Sundaravej, 5–6, 7, 87–88, 100, 103, 104, 112, 113, 121, 123, 126, 128, 129, 141, 149–50, 174, 181, 183, 227–28n42, 235n20
Samart Malulim, 137, 150, 163
Sanam Luang, 75, 78, 222n46
Sarit Thanarat, 71, 72, 219n16, 231n6
savings fund, community, 13, 109, 117, 153, 154, 175, 177, 188, 190, 193–94, 231nn13–14
scale, 22, 41, 54, 61, 62–63, 68, 198, 200
Scholz, Birte, 207n20
script, Thai, 172
segmentation (political and social), 45, 46, 47, 49, 50, 53, 55, 58, 59, 62, 71, 78, 80–81, 88, 89, 93, 109, 114, 117, 151, 166, 176, 191, 197, 199, 202, 211n70, 212n5, 212n6, 213n13, 216–17n42, 223n58, 236–37n4. *See also* Evans-Pritchard, E. E.; *moeang*
Seoul, 218n5, 223–24n62
Shanghai, 152
Shao Qin, 4
shophouses, 12, 74
shrines. *See* community shrine; spirits and spirit shrines
Siam (conceptualized in contrast to Thailand), 44, 45, 61, 70, 71, 72, 82, 84, 149, 165, 172, 197, 200, 204, 219n14, 222n46, 231n17
Siam Society, x, 14
siblinghood, fictive. *See phi nawng*
signage: at Ancient City park, 44; creating, 162–63; heritage, 105, 157, 163, 164; official, 165; parodic, 105, 157; protest, 91–92, 108, 198
silk: Lao, 84; production, 185; Thai, 69
Silpakorn University, 139, 141, 142, 144
sincerity, 25
Sirikit, Queen, 21, 87, 88, 120, 122, 165; portraits of, 26, 77, 133, 166
Skiotis, Fionn, x, 9, 10
Skytrain (Bangkok), 127
slums, 19, 42, 50, 52, 60, 61, 63, 69, 70, 102, 104, 107, 115, 123, 127, 139, 179, 207n27, 220n26, 223n54, 223n55, 223–24n62, 225n16, 226n21, 236n25. *See also* Four Slums Regional Network
Smart, Alan, 208n34
smiles, interpretation of, 21, 58
Smith, Neil, 69
social poetics, 208–9n40
social science (Thailand), 30
society, as concept, 53, 68, 134, 185
Somchai Wongsawat, 5
Somsook Boonyabancha, 103, 121, 131, 133
Sopranzetti, Claudio, x, xi, 21, 133, 136, 226n27
sound and sonar dynamics, 159–60, 162, 232nn20–21, 232n24
southeast Asia, 197, 200; characteristics of, 5, 27, 61, 218–19n9
South Korea, 218n5
South Sudan, 223n58
sovereignty, 53–54, 90, 198
space: concentrated, 63, 148, 183; model of, 54; organization of, 18, 22, 35–36, 189; restructuring of, 45, 164, 187, 192; sacralized, 173. *See also* time
spatial cleansing, 60–61, 164, 203, 216–17n45, 217n47, 233n28
speech: polite, 29, 38, 54, 62, 95, 112, 116, 160, 161; soft, 40, 158, 159–60
spirits and spirit shrines, 3, 50, 51, 53, 62, 67, 82; attached to commercial interests, 53; attacked, 65, 88, 173; as collective ancestry of Thais, 89, 100, 200; defense of, 55; design of, 72; rejection of veneration of, 55, 233n1; responsibility for, 64
squatters and squatting, 36, 56, 57, 97, 99, 108, 122, 123, 135, 155, 216n38
Sri Lanka, 55
state, powers of, 24–25

INDEX

Steedly, Mary, ix, xi
Stewart, Charles, 208n34
strategies: necessity of, 223n55; officializing, 25, 56; of passivity, 230n3; of protest, 221n33
students, 11; involvement of, 9–10, 12, 142, 144, 146, 188; as revolutionaries, 5, 11
stupa, 80, 83; form of, 78
Suchit Wongthes, 67, 81, 83, 218n2, 224–25n13, 231n17
sufficiency economy, 84, 141, 152, 209n50, 230n25
Sukhumbhand Paribatra, 7, 79, 147, 149, 187, 195, 196
Surin province, 55
survey techniques, market, 170; polls, 228–29n8
Suthaep Thaugsuban, 48, 236n33
Suvarnabhumi Airport, 6, 72, 213–14n14, 219n19, 220n29

tactics, 236n1; importance of, 230n3
Tai language family, xi, 48, 213n14. *See also* Thai language
Tambiah, Stanley J., x–xi, 44–45, 83, 151, 212n6, 218–19n9
Tanabe, Shigeharu, 226n29
tangibility, 41, 110, 204, 211n64
tattoos, 69
Taylor, James, 46
television, 8, 29
temples, 53, 57, 60, 67, 86, 161, 164, 182, 222n46. *See also* Golden Mount; Rachanatdaram Temple
tempo, 96, 148, 154, 164, 165, 231n5
temporality. *See* time
terra-cotta production, 38, 54
Thai Community Foundation, 10, 105, 121
Thai language, ix, x, xi, xii, 28, 38, 164; central, 55; northern, 45; politeness formulae in, 29, 37, 54, 61, 62, 86, 135, 158, 160, 232–33n25; tonality of, 160, 231–32n19. *See also* speech; Tai language family; transliteration
Thainess, stereotype and essence of (*khwam pen thai*), 18, 21, 26–27, 40, 42, 48, 54, 55, 58, 69, 71, 72, 80, 81, 83, 86, 90, 105, 130, 145, 156, 166, 173, 175, 183, 186, 200, 213–14n14, 219n19, 222n52, 225n19
Thai Rak Thai (political party), 7, 126, 132, 145, 183, 206n9, 226n27

Thaksin Shinawatra, 5–6, 11, 24, 52, 66, 67, 77, 100, 114, 123, 126, 132, 145, 169, 179, 183, 186, 201, 204, 206n9, 206n17, 213n13, 221n33, 226n27, 236n33
Thammasat University, 5, 11, 16, 35, 76–77, 121, 133, 134, 144, 215n35, 227n33; election meeting at, 126–27; student uprisings at, 5, 6, 78–79
Thanaphon Watthanakun, 8, 205n2, 207–8n29, 210n60, 216n38, 219n16, 221n40, 222n46, 224n11, 229n10, 231–32n19, 233n28, 233n3
Tha Phra Jan, 11, 194, 237n9
Tha Tian, 12
Thawatchai Woramahakhun (community president), 8, 12–13, 17, 29, 36, 37, 41, 47, 49, 50, 52, 92–93, 107, 108, 123, 127, 130, 133, 136, 137, 138, 145–46, 158–59, 161, 166, 177, 178–79, 188, 190, 191, 192, 194
Thiele, Brett, 16
Thirayut Boonmee, 206n17
Thompson, Jim, 185
Thonburi, 81
Thongchai Winichakul, 234n8
time and temporality: buying and using, 23, 92, 100, 149, 151, 172–73, 196, 197, 229n11; calendric, 97; conversion, 56, 64; and death, 96; and expansion, 42; as experiential domain, 38, 148, 151; and law, 224n7; mastering, 153; monumental, 164, 165, 233n26; multiple, 166; as resource, 52; restructured, 45; social, 152, 233n26; structural, 214n21; time-space compression, 211n67; understanding of, 4. *See also* rhythm; space; tempo
tourism and tourists, 13, 21, 33, 34, 57, 68–69, 73, 74, 82, 83, 125, 135, 144, 150, 175, 176, 182, 194, 200, 201, 207–8n29, 219n16, 220n25, 222n51
tradition, 31, 54, 55, 56, 84, 170, 172, 175, 190, 215n26; traditionism, traditionalizing, 187, 201
traffic problems (Bangkok), 127
tranquility, 23, 92, 158
transliteration, xii
transparency, 233–34n4
trees, 2–3, 54, 91, 228n2; ordination of, 3, 31, 62; sacred, 82, 88, 173
tsunami (26 December 2004), 188, 197, 199
turn taking, 160
typicality, 42, 68, 181–82, 195

266

UNESCO, 211n64
UN-Habitat, 10, 140
UNICEF, 182
United Kingdom, 45
United Nations: building, in Bangkok, 10. See *also* Commission on Cultural, Economic, and Social Rights; ESCAP; UN-Habitat
upkeep, responsibility for, 140
urbanity, 45

Vaidya, Anand, xi
Vajiravudh (Rama VI), 72, 76
Van Esterik, Penny, 235n17
Venice, 223n61
Vietnam, 70, 213n14
Viphaphan Siripakchai, ix
voluntarism, 200
voting rights, 170

wai (gesture), 36–37, 54, 93, 135, 138, 161, 163, 198, 210n61, 214n22, 216n40, 224n1
waiting, 152, 154, 230n1. *See also* time
wall, city, 9, 27, 56, 64, 86, 157–58, 171, 203; in relation of community to city, 231–32n19; removal of citadels from, 76

water supply, 108, 123
way of life, 29, 40, 57, 58, 73, 82, 83, 107, 128
Western cultural, legal, political, and urban models, 72, 73, 83, 111, 143, 151, 172, 203, 218–19n9, 221–22n1, 224n7, 225–26n20, 233n33. *See also* crypto-colonialism; nation-state
women: intimidated, 147; rights of, 126; roles of, 17, 33, 34, 49, 135, 161, 166, 191–92, 209n46; and Thainess, 69
Wutipong Phriebjariyawat, 85, 168–69

Yaowarat (Bangkok Chinatown), 38
Yellow Shirts, 6, 7, 20, 24, 48, 52, 58, 66–67, 80, 170, 183, 195, 198, 201, 202, 206n9, 207n26, 229n19, 232n24, 233n32
Yingluck Shinawatra, 7, 48, 66, 80, 126, 127, 201
Yongyuth Prachasilchai, x
YouTube, 8
Yunnan, xi, 48, 49

Zambotti, Giovanni, xi
Zerilli, Filippo, 208n34
Zhang Li, xi
Zhu Yujie, 40

Lightning Source UK Ltd.
Milton Keynes UK
UKHW021815180719
346411UK00008B/738/P